Fire in the Mind
The 1970s computer decade

Darrel VanDyke, PhD

ISBN-13: 978-1533426604

ISBN-10: 1533426600

Contact the author at DARRELVAN@GMAIL.COM

Pictured on the cover is James Murez, holder of the U.S. patent granted for the first portable computer. See G. M. Research for an interesting story about a very creative individual.

Dedication

I feel very lucky to have worked with and made friends with outstanding people during my 40-year career in the computer industry. One person, Dave Mickle, stands out because of his intelligence, wit, and humor—he was just damn fun to work with and he taught me a lot about software. I miss him both as a co-worker and friend.

Acknowledgements

My thanks beyond words to my editor, Carolyn Moore, who kept challenging me to tweak here and there for the betterment of the final result. (I'm sure she is cringing now at how I butchered even that sentence!)

I would like to offer a special thank you to the many people, companies, and museums that granted me permission to use their material. Specifically, I would like to thank the following individuals for their contributions and edits:

Bryan Blackburn

Sergei Frolov

John Grimaldi

James Murez

Chris Pickles

Contents

Chapter 1
Setting the stage

"How comes it that human beings, whose contacts with the world are brief and personal and limited, are nevertheless able to know as much as they do know?" (Chomsky, Knowledge of Language, 1986).

Granted, Noam Chomsky was attempting to define life in terms of language broken down into performance and competence, but he beautifully sums up the human quest to learn. From the creation of the first fire-making tools, estimated at around 125,000 years ago, until today where we can crash atoms together and watch the beautiful and intriguing results, think of the strides that humans have taken in technology. While some might argue that some technology is misplaced (e.g., creating the atomic bomb and "social media" products), for the most part, technology has made most lives easier. But how did earlier technology set the stage for what we use on a daily basis today?

With the exception of only a few groups, people in the world now write and/or speak in some language. It wasn't until around 3500 B.C.E. that Mesopotamia really put some thought to this and figured out a system by which others could share information through writing in a way others could understand. But numbers were an odd business because showing a value of, say, "1,000" (or even "15") was difficult. Pause and think about this for a moment—let's say you come up with some form of counting from 1 to 9. Then what? What if someone gives you 10 of something? Certainly we think nothing of this, but was it that simple to figure out? Not really. Along came the Babylonians in 1800 B.C.E. who reasoned that there must be some way to simplify the representation of larger and larger numbers—and they figured out that by using a certain mark for "10" that could be very handy instead of carving out ten marks on a clay tablet.

Centuries rolled by with ideas abounding, but frustrations had to temper the enthusiasm when it was discovered that, in many cases, some sort of power source was needed to make an idea come to life. From Leonardo da Vinci's drawings, we know that he envisioned a flying rotor device (probably as a stage prop), but imagine how he pondered about supplying power to it at 30 feet (or even one foot) off the ground. He had to calculate something, didn't he? Surely, he didn't just guess, "If I make something spin it will rise, but how fast do I have to spin it?" There were other inventions that came about that changed the world, and somewhere in there, a pencil and paper were used to work out some mathematical computation. And the byproduct of this is there was a probably a written document or drawn picture that could be referenced. In its most basic form, this is what a computer does today.

Mathematicians were busy folks. They wanted to show that everything around us (including the universe) could be broken down into formulas, but to do those calculations sometimes took many reiterative steps (and with all human activities involving numbers, errors could occur). Technology and ideas started to merge (thanks to electricity being harnessed safely), and it was during this timeframe that the inventors really started to shine. More on Alan Turing, Bill Gates, and Steve Wozniak later in this book, but imagine if these technology wizards had been born, say, 500 years earlier? No matter their greatness of thought, something was needed to help jump-start their ideas into practicality – they simply didn't know about electricity yet. Conversely, now imagine a world in which

Leonardo da Vinci had a computer. As the old adage goes, timing is everything, and so it was with creative technologists of the 1970s. A convergence of technology and ideas was about to happen to change the world.

This book's original goal was to document the wonderful and amazing creations that came about in one decade. But as I stood back and marveled at these inventions, I became fascinated by the people behind them – not just the technology itself. These were not people who started the day with a ho-hum attitude, but rather people who said, "How can I change the world?" Or, "How can I disrupt the world and get them to think about approach X instead of approach Y?" These creative people were about to be presented with something they had never seen before – the microprocessor – the "power" needed to make their ideas come to life. From these ideas, companies started to form. Some of these companies (both people and their ideas), alas are now just a passing memory or footnote in history.

In my research, a one-word mention of a computer in some obscure journal would take me on a quest to find out more about that computer and/or person/company. Sometimes my research would lead to me uncovering quite a bit of history on the company, but at other times all I could glean was a rough idea of what the product did and where the company was located. All of these companies employed at least one (if not many) very inventive engineers who were only limited by their imagination of what they wanted a computer to do.

How does your laptop work when you turn it on? How does a car start when you turn on the key or push a button? When you swipe your finger across your smartphone display, how does that make your screen scroll up or down? It took some very bright engineers and creative people to get us to where we are today.

To give you an analogy of what was about to happen in the 1970s, imagine the world before 1886. Everyone in the world could only go from point A to point B by walking, riding a horse, riding in a buggy, using a locomotive, or sailing. That was it. And then a creative soul by the name of Carl Benz created a small motor called the internal combustion engine. But how to use it? And why was there a need for something like this when you had a horse?

The engine that Benz had created needed something to power it and keep it running (input), and some sort of spinning pin to make it useful (output). He took a buggy and figured out a way to position his engine so that it could make the wheels move. But how do you stop it? Do you say, "whoa"? How do you steer something without a set of reins? What about a constant supply of gasoline to keep it moving? All of these issues were solved.

Figure 1—1886 Benz Car

And then guess what happened? Others saw this internal combustion engine, and their wheels started turning (literally). Improvements were made in every aspect to this first car, and today we have cars that zip along at 200 mph, provide music, cruise control, and other wonderful features. Benz's little engine was the microprocessor of the 1880s; it changed the world.

The 1970s spurred innovation so quickly that it will take a long time for the world to see anything like it again. The 1970s could aptly be called the "Computer Revolution." I hope this book provides an awareness not only of the technology leaps that occurred in a span of only ten years, but also the people behind them.

Chapter 2
The Evolution of Computers

The *Shorter Oxford English Dictionary* (6th edition, 2007) defines a computer as dating back to the mid-17th century, and refers to it as "A person who makes calculations; specifically, a person employed for this in an observatory, etc." That certainly is an odd definition to us today. In the 1600s, though, the distance to stars was what they were trying to compute, not whether or not someone had their password set properly in Facebook!

The "FreeDictionary.com" (retrieved January 1, 2015) defines a computer as "A device, usually electronic, that processes data according to a set of instructions. The digital computer stores data in discrete units and performs arithmetical and logical operations at very high speed. The analog computer has no memory and is slower than the digital computer but has a continuous rather than a discrete input." Now that's more like it. This latter definition is more in line with what we think of today as a computer. I think we can agree that a computer is something that is powered by electricity or battery, computes and/or stores data, and what is computed usually gets observed. So, back to the basic question: What is a computer? Is it your laptop? Your mobile phone?

An abacus is a computer. The abacus, though, does one thing only—it deals with numbers and can sum the numbers you provide to it. Was Charles Babbage's Difference Engine of 1822 a computer? After all, it could add two numbers together and arrive an answer (although it was limited in scale). Was it Ada Byron's Analytical Engine a few years later that could be programmed by supplying cards with holes in them? And don't ignore Joseph-Marie Jacquard's programmable weaving looms in the early 1800s, or Blaise Pascal and Gottfried Leibniz who in the 1800s built machines to help with arithmetic calculations. Certainly, all of these machines were created from ideas that no one had before, but they still had a single purpose—to make a machine do something for us in a repeatable manner. Ah, if they had only had electricity, transistors, and a central processing unit known as a microprocessor! People continually want to do more, but sometimes they must wait until something else is invented—and so it was with these aforementioned machines.

Today, we think of a computer as being very sophisticated—something that is powered by electricity or battery. You turn it on, and applications (or simply "apps") come to life and provide the world at your fingertips. They can sense an eye movement easily and realize a sleepy driver is drifting out of their lane. And some computers today can even arrive at an answer by figuring out something on its own given only the rudimentary starting point—something that both Babbage and Byron said could not happen. I believe that we are in the fourth generation of computers, but this obviously means there was a first through third generation. So, before the journey into where computer technology is today, let me set the stage of what was going on before 1970.

In the (electrical) beginning

Using the definition that a computer is powered by something (other than a pedal or manual crank), the 1920s saw one of the earliest examples of a computer with Germany's Enigma Machine. The following picture shows one of the few existing Enigma Machines still in existence.

Figure 2—Enigma Machine

This computer's function was for the enciphering and deciphering of secret messages (at least that was the norm until brilliant Polish mathematicians got their hands on one and figured out how it worked years ahead of the British, by the way). The Enigma was powered by electricity, and with a few turns of some dials (also known as decryption keys), an operator could type in a coded message and out came a translated text version that was hopefully readable.[1] The Enigma Machine was very simple in design, with rotors, shafts, plug-boards, and some electric circuitry. When its power was turned off, it was a metal and wooden paper weight. The only thing it remembered when it started again was "what are my wheels and shafts set to?" It's just like your car — it doesn't recall where it has been, but when you start driving, it goes where the wheels are pointed. Basically, the Enigma had two functions to perform: 1) encrypt an outgoing message, and 2) decrypt an incoming one. Hardly a

---

[1] A decryption key is important to know because if the operator put in the wrong value, then the output would be unreadable—this occurred a lot when procedures were not followed closely by the operators. Today, decryption and encryption of messages occur a million times a second as messages flow around the world—they just don't have operators turning wheels; rather, they have computer programs doing this for us.

computer by today's definition, but it was an amazing machine for the 1920s (and for the next twenty years for its work for the German military). It was a unique computer in that it didn't computer numbers, rather it worked with non-numerical characters – like the ones in this sentence.

Then, the world of computers became more exciting. In the 1930s, the Massachusetts Institute of Technology (MIT), outside of Boston, Massachusetts, and Bell Labs were the "Silicon Valley" of the time. Much has been written about Alan Turing and his work on a machine to decipher the Enigma's messages, but it would be a mistake to give Dr. Turing all of the credit for this idea. To appreciate where the idea of how a computing machine could be built, one has to start with George Boole (1815-1864).

Boole had an incredibly simple way of approaching a problem—either something worked, or it didn't. In 1937, Claude E. Shannon, a student attending MIT and working at Bell Labs, dug out Boole's books and wondered if a computing device could be made to arrive at answer just by having it go through a series of "is it true or not true" instructions. His thesis, "A Symbolic Analysis of Relay and Switching Circuits," explained how Boole's "true/false" logic could be applied to machines. His key idea was that electrical relay switches could be set to an "on" or "off" state, and thereby through a series of "if this is 'on' then go here" instructions, an answer to a mathematical problem could finally be solved. Shannon fundamentally altered peoples' thinking about what was possible; unfortunately, he is but a footnote in computing history. Others, though, understood Shannon's idea, and the world of true computing machines was about to be born. For instance, later in 1937 Howard Aiken (whether he read Shannon's paper is lost to history, but the timing is suspect) suggested to his Harvard department head and to a small company called IBM that a modern "Babbage engine" could be built to do mathematic calculations faster. IBM must have used this idea to a large extent, because by 1941, in Endicott, New York, they were working on a large calculating computer they were calling the Mark I. (In 1944, the Mark I was completed; it consisted of mechanical relays, and was approximately eighty feet long.[2])

If you have never heard of Shannon, you probably haven't heard of Victor Shestakov at Moscow State University in Russia. Three years before Shannon published his work, Shestakov had the idea to use Boole's approach to design a machine that took its direction from "on/off" states. Unfortunately for Shestakov, the Russian government would not allow his work to be published until 1941. Remember these names — both Shannon and Shestakov had a tremendous impact on the design of what we know of as a computer today, and neither are given the credit due to them.

There were other men of note — Alonzo Church, George Stibitz, Konrad Zuse, John Vincent Atanasoff, Clifford Berry, John Mauchly, Proper Eckert, and Howard Aiken were what I would call the founding members of the original computer hobbyist club. They thrived on building machines (mostly based on Shannon's thesis) that could take the drudgery from computing large and complex arithmetic calculations, and come up with consistent results. For instance, John Atanasoff wanted a calculating machine to store information; his idea led him to coin the name "memory" that would become associated with a computer's ability to store and remember information. (In 1942 Atanasoff applied for a patent for his computer with memory, but somehow the filing was done improperly and the idea to patent his idea was dropped.) John Mauchly was doing a lot of mathematic calculations that were repetitive in nature, and it irritated him to the point that he built his own "personal" computer to do these functions. Presper Eckert worked with Mauchly to design

---

[2]Today's inexpensive $2 calculator that fits in the palm of a hand outperforms this large computer by thousands of times in speed and offers many more functions.

and build the ENIAC[3] computer in 1944 to help the United States' military. Ideas sprang to life in a basement in Iowa, as well as in English labs, MIT, German labs, and Bell Labs, and it was only through word-of-mouth, lectures, and long trips to one another's facilities that these people (including Turing) were able to see and touch these "computing machines." Turing reminds me of Steve Jobs after visiting the Xerox lab in the mid-1970s; both borrowed heavily from what they saw, and both capitalized on this knowledge. In Turing's case, he took ideas based on existing machines he had seen back to England, and in his 1936 paper, "On Computable Numbers," he described what he thought it was now possible for a computer to do. Volunteering to help the WWII war effort in the United Kingdom, Turing (with funding from the UK government) set out to develop a machine to break the Enigma Machine's encrypting. Located about forty miles north of London in the small town of Bletchley, Turing and a group of like-minded scientists and mathematicians went to work. The result was a machine that was far from what we think of as a computer today — it could not do math at a blazing speed, nor could it simultaneously perform other functions. But Turing could plug in an algorithm (not just a simple 1 + 1), and an answer would be presented. After focusing on breaking Germany's Enigma code (which he and his team did), he saw potential in a more generalized computer to solve more answers. Turing then introduced to the computing world the idea of a more "universal" machine.

Turing had the idea that if a machine could do arithmetic calculations, then maybe it could do even more — more of what, he wasn't quite sure of in a practical business sense, but he knew (rather hoped) that someone could figure it out. It is similar to the man who invented Velcro — he wasn't quite sure how it could be used, but he hoped the world would figure out a way — and it did. Turing's idea

---

[3] ENIAC – Electronic Numerical Integrator and Computer

for this universal machine was this: instead of hard-wiring a machine to do one task, could a program be fed in instructions somehow when the machine was turned on? "Yes, of course it could," he reasoned. So, with a slight modification to that theme, today's computers work exactly in that manner. Computers were about to take another leap in practicality with a push from not only Turing, but also from the other men mentioned above and the Polish mathematicians (who all deserve as much or even more credit than Turing for their "computer" ideas — but Turing got the movie made about him).

The first electromechanical computers

Sometimes living at home after high school can have its advantages. As Steve Jobs and Steve Wozniak would later start Apple in Jobs' parents' garage, in 1938 a young, brilliant German by the name of Konrad Zuse needed a place to work — so he took over his parents' living room. Konrad had no outside funding — only his genius mind — to come up with his idea of a computer he would call the Z1. This machine was mechanical in nature (imagine the noise as relays clicked and clacked as they opened and closed instead of the quiet circuity we never hear in our laptops or cell phones), but it had a feature that was truly remarkable for that time — it could be programmed to do certain tasks repetitively. WWII was in full swing, so one can only surmise that Zuse's creation caught the eye of the German military as improvements (namely electromechanical relays) were added to the Z1 to make it faster. His upgraded, faster calculating machine was called the Z2. To show the complexity of Zuse's creation (and imagine your laptop superimposed over the top of this), the following is a picture of Mr. Zuse in later years with the Z1 (actually a replica, as the original Z1 was lost over time; this can be seen at the Berlin Museum of Transport and Technology).

Figure 3—Konrad Zuse and the Z1 (replica)

In 1941, Zuse superseded the Z2 with the Z3. This computer was built with 2,000 relays/vacuum tubes (and lots of wiring), and relied upon a clock (this is important, and I'll explain more about this later) to regulate when current could flow to some component. To some, the Z3 is considered the world's first electromechanical programmable, digital computer. Data and programs were read in via holes punched on a type of semi-rigid film. (This punching of holes spawned a need for yet more machines to be able to punch the same size of hole in special positions, which then spawned the need for machines to verify that the holes were indeed punched correctly— thus, an entire hole-punching industry was born that would last another thirty-five years.) Before the Zuse machine, data was entered into a computing machine with a wheel that physically represented a number. Zuse apparently thought long and hard on this and decided that there had to be a better way. The numbers he wanted to compute where quite large in value, and would be hard to represent by an ever-increasing number of wheels and shafts to turn the wheels. Thanks to Konrad's thinking, the world was about to take a huge leap forward.

Welcome to Zuse's use of the binary system, which was truly an inspiration of genius. Zuse wanted any number to be represented by a combination of a "1" or "0." For instance, the number 8 could be represented as "0001000" and the number 9 could be represented as "0001001." Computers today still rely upon this simple yet elegant and compressed way of representing any value (or characters like those in this sentence) to a computer — all within a string of "1's" or "0's." With slight modifications over the years, computers everywhere know exactly what these rows of zeros and ones mean — even those cute emoticons that are sent racing around the world in emails and text messages are represented by zeros and ones inside of a computer. (See the section on "Zuse" later in this book for more about his company.)

Today, the mechanical computer shown in Figure 3 fit neatly on one small silicon chip, allowing electrons flowing from point A to point B to become a "switch," or a gate to be left opened or closed. (Remember Boole and Shannon? This was a machine that implemented simple "on/off," "true/false" states about which they had written.) Vacuum tubes were being used in radios, and some engineer had the brilliant idea of using these tubes to do the switching of those noisy gates and opened and closed. When this was done, the speed at which a calculation was completed doubled. The next generation of computers was ready.

Time to revisit the Enigma Machine used by Germany during World War II. The British had some brilliant mathematicians working on all kinds of formulas and models to try and break the Enigma Machine's encryption algorithms, but it was a matter of trial and error to arrive at the correct answer to break the Enigma's secret[4]. Enter a programmable computer called Colossus. Based upon the Zuse design of a programmable computer, Colossus was built specifically for entering ideas (through mathematical formulas) and seeing the result. This was a thousand times faster than someone turning wheels on an Enigma Machine hitting a button, pulling a lever, and seeing if the result made sense instead of spitting out gibberish like "xoyoyss 8nnopb," which was what the British were coming up with daily. The British had their Colossus (code named Mark I, or MK I) ready on January 18, 1944, and on February 5, 1944, they attacked their first message for decoding. This was yet another huge step forward in the development of the modern computer.

Nine MK II Colossus machines were eventually built (the original MK I was converted to an MK II, making ten machines in total). The Colossus MK I contained 1,500 thermionic valves (tubes). The MK II had 2,400 valves, and was five times faster and simpler to operate than MK 1 (and thus the speed of the decoding process was increased greatly).

The U.S. military was trying to catch on to what computers could do, as they desperately needed something to compute ballistics trajectory calculations. (Apparently, firing a rocket over long distances and only guessing where it might land was not making friends with people on the receiving end.) Enter the Electronic Numerical Integrator and Computer, or ENIAC; this was the first <u>electronic, programmable</u> computer built in the U.S.

---

[4] As mentioned earlier, the Poles had brilliant scientists who insisted they had broken Enigma's code. They took their solution to the British, but with either pride or ignorance, the British didn't want any help and insisted their scientists and mathematicians were smarter, so they ignored the Polish solution, and thus WWII took way too long to end because of this British arrogance.

The second generation of computers

Although the ENIAC was similar to the Colossus, it could interpret clock ticks[5] faster (and therefore execute instructions faster) and had more ways of inputting data and dispensing an answer — plus it was found that it could work on non-ballistics problems, such as determining how many people with incomes over $10,000 didn't pay any taxes last year. Like the Colossus, a "program" on the ENIAC was defined by where cables could be plugged into it. (Imagine today having to disassemble your desktop PC and reroute the wires depending upon whether you wanted to run Microsoft Excel or Microsoft Word!) Yes, depending upon what they wanted to "program," physical rerouting of wires had to be done. A program literally could be hundreds of multi-colored wires plugged into myriad specialized holes. If one wanted to change the program so that it would do something else, out would come the wire pullers (arguably the world's first "programmers") to alter where the wires went. Still, it worked — it could be programmed differently to solve different types of problems.

The ENIAC was unique in many ways and helped prod other companies into the world of making and designing computers. The ENIAC consisted of thirty units which could, theoretically, operate autonomously. Ten of these units were dedicated to working on number problems, and when done they could store a value in a register (a term for a location inside the computer for temporarily storing a value). As these smart programmers (wire movers) started to learn more about this computer, more sophisticated wiring allowed for "loops" and conditional branching based upon the results of a calculation. While

---

[5] Think of a secondhand on a clock; every time it moves it triggers a computer instruction to be executed. However, there was no clock per se inside the computer, but rather an electrical signal triggered by something (it could even be something that vibrated on a regular basis)—and these triggers would then cause the computer to execute an instruction.

these seem trivial to any programmer today, he or she should realize that no one had ever done this before — and to make this leap in programming was truly a giant step forward in making a computer do more. The ENIAC could do a whopping 5,000 instructions per second (which was a thousand times faster than any other machine before it — and approximately a million times slower than today's computers). It evolved to have specialized "pre-wired" boards to multiply, divide, and do square root calculations. One of its drawbacks (not to mention its massive electrical current usage, which generated a large amount of heat, and took up a fair amount of floor space) was that it couldn't remember much. In fact, its memory was limited to about 80 bytes.[6] To give one a perspective on its size, the machine weighed 30 tons, used 200 kilowatts of electric power, and contained over 18,000 vacuum tubes, 1,500 relays, and hundreds of thousands of resistors, capacitors, and inductors. By comparison, today's five-pound laptop draws about 65 watts and can outperform an ENIAC in all ways.

---

[6] A computer byte consists of 8 bits, where each bit is either a "1" or "0." A computer "word" consists of two bytes. A typical disk drive on a PC today can easily store 500 mega (million) bytes of data.

*Figure 4—The ENIAC computer (with permission from
Penn State University)*

As mentioned above, moving wires to change the
program was a hard way to program — and made it prone
to mistakes. Why not figure out a way to "store" a
program inside the computer itself? Enter Alan Turing
once again, who laid the theoretical basis for the stored-
program computer in his 1936 paper. In 1945, Mr. Turing
joined the National Physical Laboratory and began
developing a way to store a set of instructions (a
"program") on the computer so that wires would not have
to be re-plugged every time someone wanted to alter the
instruction path. Think of it this way: today, when you
want to run Microsoft Word, you select an icon and
somehow this program gets executed. There are lots of
steps to actually make this happen, but suffice it to say
that a lot of sophisticated programming in what is called
the operating system causes this to occur. The concept,
though, is important — a program is stored on a disk or in
memory inside the laptop. No one had ever stored a
program before (although it could be argued that
prewired boards were a form of storing a program), but
Turing was suggesting that it would make life so much
simpler if a program could be stored somehow inside the

computer. Again, think back to a time where no one had done this before—and now someone was proposing this radical new idea. And now today we have smartphones with "apps," which are actually stored programs—and we take this all for granted because, well, to most "it just works that way—didn't computers always behave like this?" No, they did not.

The result of Turing's and others' work was the Manchester Small-Scale Experimental Machine (SSEM), nicknamed "Baby." This machine, by most definitions, was the world's first computer to store a program for re-use. Although the computer was considered small and primitive by the standards of its time, it was the first working machine to contain almost all of the elements essential to a modern electronic computer. As soon as the SSEM had demonstrated the feasibility of its design, a project was initiated at the University of Manchester to develop it into a more usable computer; the output from this effort was the Manchester Mark 1. From an academic environment (which was to play an important role in future computer-related work in general), the Mark 1 morphed into the world's first commercially available general-purpose computer, named the Ferranti Mark 1.

Introducing the transistor

Vacuum tubes mostly used for amplifying power in these early machines; The vacuum tubes were big, which meant big holes in which to plug them into, which in turn meant a big cabinet to hold them. They generated a lot of heat, and were prone to failure after a relatively short life. In 1947 (on December 23 to be exact), a small device called the bipolar transistor (that many would claim one of the greatest technology inventions) was invented by Drs. William Shockley, Walter Brattain, and John Bardeen in Bell Labs in Murray Hill, New Jersey. Soon thereafter vacuum tubes were replaced by these smaller devices. Transistorized computers could now contain tens of thousands of binary logic circuits in a relatively compact space. The ball was rolling and an evolution in smaller and faster transistors was allowing smaller and faster computers. The latest model used a faster clock ticking at 125 kHz[7] to execute instructions.

Computers, though, were behemoths compared to today's computers, but newer technology was now making them at least more manageable in size. From the bowels of university labs, where computers worked on numbers, came people who saw the potential of using a computer for real business work. IBM was growing and testing the business waters with its new computers, but in England, several companies were leading the world in how to adapt a computer in a business environment.

Figure 5—The LEO 1 (with permission from Peter Byford)

The Leo 1 (created by Leo Computers Ltd.) was verified and certified by the Guinness Book of World Records as being the first <u>business</u> computer (in 1951) put to use in the world. Around this time, English Electric Ltd. (who went on to produce the Leo II and Leo III), Ferranti Ltd., and Elliott Brothers Ltd. were all making giant strides to get a programmable computer into the business market. England was on to something—and it didn't take long for the rest of the world to take notice and catch up.

---

[7]A "k" anything in "computerese" means a 1,000. A clock ticking at 125 kHz means that the clock was running along at approximately 125,000 ticks per second. At the time of this writing, it is common to have a clock ticking in the 200 gHz range (where "g" means a billion, meaning that a clock currently ticks along at approximately 200,000,000,000 beats per second—where each beat represents a computer's CPU capable of executing an instruction).

Integrated circuits replace transistors

The next great advance in computing power came with the advent of "a body of semiconductor material...wherein all the components of the electronic circuit are completely integrated." Jack Kilby was a bright engineer working at an electronics firm called Texas Instruments), and thus described the integrated circuit (IC)) in his patent request in 1959. Instead of electrons having to flow down a wire from point A to point B (transistor to transistor), an IC board consisting of hundreds or thousands of electrons could be corralled and thereby reduce wiring and heat — thus increasing speed. Kilby's ICs were made out of germanium (not to be confused with the flower, geranium, which probably could not conduct electric circuits very well). However, legal problems began for Kilby and TI since someone else (William Shockley) had already been granted a patent for this idea in 1956.

It would be easy to digress into the world of the legal wrangling and the subsequent questionable Nobel Prize awarded to Kilby (in this author's opinion). Suffice it to say, though, that the names of William Shockley, Julius Lilienfeldt, and Robert Noyce all contributed to this phase of making a better computer with their contributions of miniaturizing and better-quality electronic circuits.[8]

In 1962, the Strategic Air Command of the U.S. Air Force ordered 2,000 microchips from Texas Instruments. These

---

[8]Jean Hoerni of Fairchild Industries had an idea for a microchip (transistor). So did a company called RCA. So did Noyce. So did Shockley. So did Kilby, although he had Texas Instrument's lawyers. Fairchild actually applied for the first patent for a microchip, but Texas Instruments followed quickly with their claim. The U.S. Patent Office actually issued two patents for this technology, but since Kilby's application was the last one they saw, he ended up being awarded the patent. The world or both men would have been and for their respective companies if the patent office hadn't made a giant mistake.

microchips were used as part of the guidance control systems for missiles.[9]

The computer was getting faster, programmable, it could redo calculations with accuracy, it had storage where it could remember past work, and it could output and answer onto a something – a printer, for instance. Up until now, IBM and fellow giants in the computer industry were fairly comfortable defining what they called a computer. But now that scientists, mathematicians, and engineers were starting to agree on what a computer could do, and they were seeing the power of an IC, and they liked the idea of a pre-programmed set of instructions always being executed (think "booting" up your computer today when you turn it on), the idea of developing something smaller for the masses started to gel. Refinements and ideas were soon to come, but there was a "first" here that is important. It is an undisputed fact that the first commercial "chip" with ICs on a small slice of silicon was the Intel 4004, which was sold in 1971 (with a little help from the Japanese company Busicom; more on Busicom later). Today, (along with a few others) rests its whole existence on this same basic idea of compressing more and more components into smaller and smaller spaces, and the chip's use has spawned the development of many kinds of computers we use today in all aspects of our lives.

A few basics

I have included a Glossary at the end to help define computer terms in case your eyes glaze over from too much computerese. But, before I get into describing these amazing creations listed herein, it is important for the reader to understand five basic definitions:

---

[9] Smaller electronics on a missile meant less fuel to propel it (making the missile smaller), and it also meant that potentially heavier payloads (i.e., explosives) could be put on board.

Hardware - It is the only physical part of a computer anyone can touch. It is disk drive, a circuit board, the cabinet it all fits in, wires, cables, etc. Think of hardware as, well, something hard that one can feel. Electrical and design engineers typically fill positions for hardware engineers. It holds software and firmware.

Software - This is a computer program that tells the computer what to do; it is what makes up an operating system (O/S) that executes instructions, which tells other programs (other software) like Microsoft Word to delete a document that you meant to save but hit the wrong key instead. Typically, computer programmers write software (and some write it very badly).

Firmware - Any attachment to a computer (e.g., a printer) needs to be sent commands, and usually that device responds with either data and/or a "yes/no" acknowledgement of the command. It is possible to embed this protocol of exchanging messages with a device within the operating system, but what if the printer model changes or one wanted to modify the messages sent to and from the device? It would become very arduous to modify the operating system every time a device was added or modified so that the CPU could communicate with it. Therefore, specialized hardware containing specialized instructions for communicating to the device was developed simply out of practicality; these specialized instructions are called "firmware." Firmware was actually software once because they were instructions written by a programmer; it's just that now this software resides inside a silicon chip—and the average programmer cannot (or rather, should not) alter it.

Microprocessor bits - Konrad Zuse saved computer people a lot of work by coming up with the idea that any character can represented by a string of unique "zeros" and "ones". For instance, the number one could be represented by 00000001, a two was 00000010, a three was 00000011, etc. So, when a computer was told to add some bits together, it simply arrived at a string of bits to show the result. The largest number that can be represented in 8 bits is 256 (including the value zero). Programmers soon realized that they needed to do some programming magic to work with larger numbers – and they figured it out.

The original microprocessor could process numbers in only increments of 8 bits – ergo the name of an 8-bit microprocessor. Microprocessor manufacturers (e.g., Motorola, IBM, Intel, etc.) understood the programming problem of only having 8 bits of data to use, so the next generation of the microprocessor was developed out of need. It was called 16-bit microprocessor. The largest value that can be represented in 16 bits of zeros and ones is 65,512. Great for a while—until someone said, "Hey, I bet we can speed this up if we could develop a 32-bit computer!" And they did, and then that was followed by a 64-bit version, and I would venture to guess that sometime soon we'll have 128- and 256-bit computers. Basically, what you are seeing is the doubling of capacity and speed as microprocessors evolved—and being able to compute really large numbers quickly. In summary (and just to be clear about the concept of a "computer"), it doesn't know or care what a "1" is, or what "John Smith" is, or what an emoticon on a screen is. To a computer, it's simply a series of bits that are values of "zeros" or "ones".

Central Processing Unit (CPU) – The CPU is the brains of any computer; however, a CPU is not a computer, and vice versa. Rather, a CPU is what tells the the computer what to do and in what order. It schedules programs to be executed and in what order. In other words, it keeps track of things going on inside a computer. A computer actually consists of a CPU(s), memory, and other components.

Today's CPUs are capable of running thousands of programs at what seems to be the same time, but in reality, there is a constant juggling of who gets to run. Scenarios like this go on literally millions of times per second in today's computers. Here is what to remember: a CPU is but a small (but important) part of a computer. The computer consists of a CPU (or maybe more, depending upon the computer design), various memory components, firmware of all descriptions, and other interfaces. People sometimes use the terms CPU and computer synonymously, but they are wrong to do so.

Onward

There are countless books written on the inner workings of a computer, but this book's purpose is to not delve any deeper into that subject matter. Rather, this book's focus is on how companies in the 1970s figured out a way to make to take a little invention called the microprocessor and make it do unheard of things. Things that were at first fun "toys", but would quickly morph into wonderful business inventions.

The previous paragraphs described the monumental and important steps taken to make a computer better and faster. Who was the first to build a computer? It depends upon one's definition of a computer. It would take a hundred more pages to give more examples—and when done someone (or many) would take umbrage by saying, "But you forgot Betty's Calculating Gadget from 1541!" Okay, you got me—yes, Betty's machine was amazing.

Before I continue on to other subjects and companies, I want to discuss the lowly calculator. There were several computer companies that had their start making manual calculators—after all, aren't computers about adding numbers? Well, sort of, but computers can do so much more—especially when it comes to processing data like names, addresses, credit card transactions, letting you know you didn't pay your taxes, etc. Calculators were indeed very important in the miniaturization of the computer technology, but there is no comparison between a Texas Instruments or Hewlett-Packard programmable handheld calculator and a computer with a keyboard, monitor, storage devices, and networking capability.

Calculator-only companies (e.g., Bowmar, Sinclair, and a Soviet Union entry (which I could only find a passing reference, but could find no name to go with it) and probably other small makers were not included in this book, since their overall contribution to the world of computers was (in this author's opinion) of minor significance. (Apologies to those thousands of college students who relied upon their Hewlett-Packard programmable calculator to get them through their engineering classes.)

Today, computer users hit the power button, type in a command, use a touchpad to position a cursor, swipe a fingerprint over a reader, click on an icon, etc. But someone had to be the first to figure this all out—and in the 1970s, people did exactly that—and more. And what was most amazing (as I hope the reader will see) was that most did it for the adventure of figuring it out and sharing that idea to the world. Of course, if a reasonable return on investment (e.g., money) was to be made, that made it even better; to many in the early 1970s it was not just about money – it was fun.

Computers begin to catch on

Before, during, and after the '70s, universities were not only spawning people playing with computers in their own labs, but were also planting seeds for the military and (eventually) business people to see the potential market for smaller than traditional mainframe computers. The military, through its demand for specialized computers to do certain tasks (radar, nuclear modeling, and moon landings to name a few) also was a driving force for new ideas in the commercial sector.

Businesses were late bloomers when it came to using computers. Business automation up to and including halfway through the 1950s had relegated computers to accounting (really a giant calculator) types of functions and some rudimentary process-control work. Spurred on by United Kingdom companies mentioned earlier, the computer industry needed a shove to get into the commercial marketplace. U.S. manufacturers, as well as companies in Japan, were taking notice; in those respective countries, businesses would now be offered with a variety of business computers. Then, in the late '50s, the business world slowed down as it caught its collective breath and tried to figure out how to make use of this technology. And how to price it so businesses could profitably use it.

To explain how the military (and science) drove technology, in 1962, the U.S. Strategic Air Command ordered 2,000 microchips for missile control systems. When the U.S. Mercury and Apollo space programs came about, the demand for guidance systems that could fit within very confined spaces drove computer innovation and invention onward to levels few had dreamed of in terms of software programming and hardware miniaturization.

Languages and operating systems

A computer language is a way to write instructions for a CPU to interpret. For instance, a COBOL language instruction of "ADD 1 to DATA-ITEM-X" would be interpreted as a set of LOAD instructions that only the CPU itself could understand.

A reasonable person might think that once a computer language was written, this would then be the standard going forward. Alas, this was (and is) not the case, as it seems that few could agree on what a good programming language should look like. Therefore, languages such as COBOL, BASIC, RPG, RPG II, FORTRAN, FORTRAN IV, ALGOL, SNOBOL, PASCAL, Java, C, C++, Query, TAL, TAL II, ADA, Datapoint Business Language, SFER, Cogar Language Base, ComEnt Data Entry System, PL/1, PLN, MUMPS, pogo, SCELBAL, ALGEM, Forth, and several others have come and gone over the years. All of these aforementioned languages had their good points; some of these were designed as necessity (some would only work on a proprietary computer system), and some were developed because the compiler writer(s) thought they could improve on other languages written. Whatever the case (as you will see as you read about the following companies), ideas spurred on other ideas — and each iteration of a language hopefully made programming easier. Some of these languages survive today, and some are as extinct as the early computers for which they were written.

An operating system (O/S) is the true brains of a computer. From the ENIAC to today's latest iOS and Android cell phones, all of these computers had/have an operating system at their core — and most were different from other computer makers (although most borrowed heavily from others to make their computer behave slightly different — and hopefully better). Apple computers and computers that run Microsoft all run a version of an O/S that is meant to make the most efficient use of the firmware and components on that particular machine.

Big, established computer companies

Pre-1970

Before the 1970s, there were quite a few giants in the computer industry already making their mark. Using the analogy before the first car, these companies were the big trains or ships. If you wanted to go fast or move stuff, you had to use these companies — you had no other choice. Here is fairly comprehensive list of these large computer companies before 1970.

- Amdahl
- Burroughs
- Control Data
- English Electric
- Ferranti
- Hitachi
- Honeywell
- IBM
- LEO
- Mitsubishi
- NCR
- Sperry
- Univac

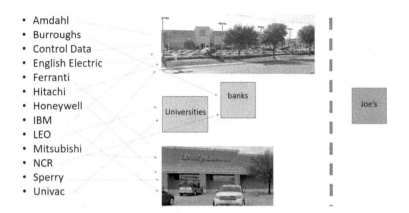

Figure 6—Large computer companies pre-1970

The arrows in Figure 6 show the penetration of these companies into the business world. If you were a bank, a university, or large company, you might be lucky enough to actually own your company. If you were a medium-sized company, say, with an annual revenue of less than $1,000,000, you could rent processing time from one of those big computer companies, but more than likely you could not afford to have your own computer system – they were expensive. And if you were the owner of Joe's Auto Parts store, you handled all of your accounting needs on pieces of paper and a manual calculator; having your own computer or access to one was out of the question – you simply did not have the revenues to buy this luxury.

Computers were mysterious to many because the programmers and computer maintenance people usually sat in rooms behind locked doors to hold in the heat and noise (not from the people, but from the computers) — and they wore white shirts and suits and ties. There was a mystique about everyone involved with computers.

Nine large (in terms of revenue) U.S. computer companies had a foothold in the computer industry in the 1970s: IBM, Honeywell, NCR Corporation, Control Data Corporation, General Electric, Digital Equipment Corporation, RCA, Burroughs, and UNIVAC. Japan had

Mitsubishi, Fujitsu, and Hitachi, and England had Ferranti, English Computers, and Elliott. France and Germany also had companies vying for the business computer market.

It had not taken IBM long to react to the competition, and with what can only be described as superior marketing, IBM leapt ahead of all competitors. In fact, IBM led all of these companies in revenue; IBM's share of the U.S. market at the time was so much larger than all of the others that it and seven of these U.S. companies (excluding DEC) were often referred to as "IBM and the Seven Dwarfs." By 1972, when GE and RCA were no longer in the mainframe business, the remaining five companies became known as the "BUNCH" (an acronym based on the initials of Burroughs, UNIVAC, NCR, Control Data, and Honeywell.) As business school graduates know, most large companies move slowly for almost anything—and it was the same with IBM and the BUNCH. They had no idea what was about to smack them right in their revenues.

The importance of IBM's presence in the computer market must be addressed. You may have heard the phrase, "the 800-pound gorilla in the room" when describing an overbearing presence of something…well, IBM was that gorilla and more. IBM's marketing in the 1950s set the stage for its tremendous growth across the world. Not resting on its laurels, IBM put much of its revenue dollars back into research and development. The outcome of this was yet more powerful hardware systems and very sophisticated operating systems and applications (for the 1960s, 1970s, and even today). IBM had a sales force second to none, and it was very creative in closing deals and locking customers into its technology. For instance, if IBM stored data in a certain manner on its disks and taught expensive programmers how to access it, why would a company want to go to the cost of figuring out how to move the data to another kind of system and then retraining the programmers? The answer is that companies didn't change—they were "locked in" to IBM. Because of IBM's large installed base, it was setting the standards by which companies were going to have to abide if they wanted to get access and store/retrieve data with an IBM system.

IBM's products (especially its terminals) were expensive primarily because it had so little competition. IBM had developed its own protocol[10] to talk to its terminals; this protocol was (and is today) known as 3270. With the 1970s, though, came small companies that saw a market they could quickly crack by developing less expensive terminals with more functionality, and which acted like an IBM terminal if it adhered to the 3270 protocol.

IBM knew that communication lines were expensive for businesses to rent time on from phone companies, so it developed a small system that could act as a sort of buffer to gather up data entered remotely and then batch it all at one time to a host IBM system. Of course, the company developed its own protocol for working with these remote, clustered terminals; the protocol was, and is today, known as 2780or 3780.

By design, IBM had set some very important protocols to allow terminals to communicate with the IBM host systems. These protocols were well documented, and thus open to the world to examine. However, IBM (being a large company) was failing to see competition, and thus it opened the door for many companies to bring their IBM compatible products to the market. Unfortunately for many of these smaller companies, they were now competing with other smaller companies for a dwindling piece of the market. This is why many small companies came and went out of business quickly—they simply could not capture enough market share to sustain their operating costs.

---

[10] Think of two people meeting on the street. One says, "hi", and the says something in return. That in a nutshell is what a computer protocol is.

When small startup companies wanted to play in the computer world, IBM's presence could not be overstated as the 1970s rolled around. Some companies, though, ignored IBM and simply wanted to play in the computer market with their own ideas. A fire was about to be lit.

Moving on

Now you are armed with some basic information about computers, including some of its history. Be sure to check out the Glossary for terms that are unfamiliar to you — especially the more technical terms you'll see in the following sections. All in all, here is what you need to remember: your laptop is a computer, your smartphone is a computer, and your post-1975 car probably has at least one computer in it, but more than likely 30 of them, and it all started with very creative people doing things that had never been done before.

One last thing before we jump into the 1970s. It is important to understand the late 1960s. Change was in the air for everything — the "establishment" of white shirts, black suits, and wing-tip shoes was being challenged. Music with lyrics of flowers, love, and peace was catching on to hundreds of thousands of young people. The Vietnam War was more intense than ever with pictures of dead young soldiers starting to haunt the American psyche. LSD and marijuana were making the rounds. President Nixon was lying about how the war was going and was hell-bent to do everything he could to get re-elected, no matter if it meant employing people who would eventually be convicted of felony crimes against the United States.

On July 20, 1969, the United States safely landed two men on the moon and brought them back to Earth. And don't forget August 15, 1969, on a small farm in upstate New York, where an event called Woodstock took place.

Additionally, an economic recession was in process, and this affected companies' spending. If a business was about to spend $1,000 for something, it had better return more than that in cost savings and/or provide an increase in revenue. Salespeople who were selling big computers were struggling.

The late 1960s was a periof of unrest in the United States and young people were challenging the status quo. Those big computer companies were about to learn a lesson about how small companies and young college kids would shake up their world and the world in general.

Chapter 3
Computing in the 1970s

In 1970, all one could do with a computer was to basically use punched cards to input data. Data that was stored on the computer system was limited to only a few million bytes (known in computer jargon as megabytes) of data.

But by 1971, Intel began production of its 4004 microprocessor chip, and once this announcement hit the press, it seemed that companies and hobbyists couldn't wait to get their hands on one. This chip came along at the right time — it fit in beautifully to allowing control to be taken away from the large "IBM" like mainframes. It would be a mistake to gloss over the hobbyists, as they were a key part of getting the world to recognize the capabilities of what a "personal" computer could look like by using a microprocessor. (For more information, do some research into one such club called the Homebrew Computer Club, of which Steve Wozniak was a member.[11] Although this particular club was in the Menlo Park, California, area, there were individuals spread across the U.S., France, and Canada who also were discovering on their own what they could build by using a microprocessor.) The microprocessor was the interstellar dust needed to start molding smaller computers that would change our universe; small startup companies were

---

[11] Steve Wozniak said in an interview that his attendance on March 5, 1975, was one of the most important nights in his life. Ideas were freely exchanged, and people could show and brag about anything related to a computer they were working on.

being formed by business people and computer engineers who saw an opportunity to build something better. Four factors were driving this: 1) military requirements (a missile out of control is not a good thing), 2) competition between the U.S. and the Soviet Union for outer-space superiority and bragging rights, 3) money to be made in the commercial business sector (no one imagined a "personal computer," but that would soon change), and 4) business people and engineers were growing weary of punched cards and IBM (and its peers).

IBM, and others of their ilk, hid a huge problem in plain sight. The issue that would come to haunt them later was the way they stored data and communicated to the devices connected to them – it was all proprietary. Even the cables that connected devices to computers were made specifically for only those companies. What this meant was that if a company wanted to move data from, say, Sperry to any other computer, it took an inordinate amount of work. And forget it if you wanted to connect an IBM printer to anything other than IBM. While this proprietary nature of things sold a lot of devices for a computer company, a business found itself being locked in more and more to that computer maker. Another thing proprietary to these big computers was that they had developed proprietary programming languages, which meant that a company could not move a programmer from IBM to Ferranti without retraining.

Up until the 1970s, computer manufacturers had developed their own customized processors within their own engineering labs — and kept these processors proprietary to their own systems. Similar to the guy in the movie *Field of Dreams* building a baseball field in the hinterlands of Iowa and exclaiming, "If I build it, they will come," Intel had a similar idea. Intel's idea was to mass-produce fairly inexpensive generic computer processors and let the market figure out what to do with them. It was a gamble, but Intel had been listening to the grumbling of businesses. As Intel produced the 4004 as its first microprocessor, it started to get requests primarily from universities for even faster and more condensed specialized computer chips (as they were soon to be called) to hold memory. Other microprocessor makers such as Zilog, Motorola, and Fujitsu) responded to this never-before-seen market for a demand in computer chips, and their reply was to develop and release a series of commercially viable microprocessors.

Key microprocessor 1970s dates included the following:

- 1970 – First RAM chip by Intel
- 1971 – Intel 4004
- 1971 – Intel 8008
- 1974 – Intel 8080
- 1975 – MOS Technology 6502
- 1976 – Zilog Z80
- 1977 – Motorola 6809
- 1977 – Motorola 6802
- 1978 – Intel 8086
- 1978 – Fujitsu MB8843
- 1979 – Motorola 6800
- 1979 – Intel 8088
- 1979 – Motorola 68000
- 1979 – Zilog Z8001 / Z8002

Microprocessors got faster because of being able to count "clock ticks" faster and therefore execute instructions faster. A standardized rating to count these clock ticks made its way onto the scene. This rating was (and is today) called MIPS, which is an acronym for millions of instructions per second. Think of a second-hand on a clock—every time it moves, a second in time has passed. Now think about counting to a million during that second. Then think of the processor being able to detect each of these tiny ticks and execute some instruction at the end of that. The higher the MIPS number, the faster the processor can do instructions, such as write to a database, move pixels around a screen, etc. Not to be happy with just making faster processors, the chip designers then started playing around with how instructions got loaded into the processor. Computer scientists were getting really smart on how to squeeze more instructions to be executed in a tiny bit of time.

What Intel essentially did was to make it possible for people with ideas to open up markts that did battle with IBM and the other mainframe makers. These new microprocessors opened up a new world of computer design, and terms that soon became part of the computer vernacular were midrange, minicomputer, and personal computer (PC). Basically, everyone agreed that a midrange or minicomputer (both terms interchangeable) would not mean a mainframe; they would be smaller, cost less, and be able to stand alone for processing data (meaning it wasn't necessary to be connected to a mainframe to have its data processed). A PC, on the other hand, would be smaller still, and had the following characteristics:

- Small, stand-alone
- General purpose
- Advanced microelectronics technology (microprocessor)
- Operated by a single individual, interactively
- No requisite computer training (I think they are still working on this!)
- Affordable by an individual or small group

Creativity comes into focus

Creative minds didn't necessarily know where their ideas might end up, but rather the fact that getting their idea out for others to consider was, in itself, a major contribution. Carl Benz, Albert Einstein, Guglielmo Marconi, Galileo Galilei, and many others worked for years to come up with their ideas, and then they laid them out for the world to ponder, improve upon, and change the world. The same phenomenon was about to happen with computer technology. The stars were aligning for smart and creative people living in the right place at the right time to figure out what computers could do.

Microprocessor-based computers cut the cord literally to the mainframes in many ways. Computer rooms would change from areas of mystique where programmers wore suits and ties, to places where people had fun — and wore sandals if they wanted. People would invite their friends over and compare notes on what they just had their microprocessor do. Getting a little icon going across a black-and-white screen while being shot at by other icons launched from a keyboard keystroke was a big deal — and even though many thought of these microprocessors as a toy (albeit an expensive toy), a few were starting to grasp the power of these little microprocessors and, thus, how businesses might be able to use them.

Recall Mr. Benz and his internal combustion engine? He knew how to put it into a buggy, but he would be the first to admit that steering, stopping, and the mechanics of keeping the engine running needed improvements. But he had lit the fuse. When the commercial microprocessor came into the world, the creative minds of whiz kids now had something new to play with.

Start-ups and their role

Small startup companies of the 1970s wanted to succeed just as much as any other company. One of their strengths was that they weren't putting a $500M company on the line. These small companies had ideas, some venture capital, or loans from friends, and some new toys in the form of small microprocessors to play with. To paraphrase the line from Shakespeare's play, *The Merry Wives of Windsor*, the world was about to be their oyster.

Startup companies are typically very nimble in everything they want to do—and it was thus with the start-ups discussed in this book. Being big at something is fine in some aspects, but reacting to the inexpensive microprocessor generation was not one of them. The big computer companies simply didn't know how to deal with this new tidal wave of ideas, nor (if truth be told) did they want to spend the time and money to learn about it. They were making millions of dollars on their big, expensive computers, so why alter that course to chase a market that was not defined?

An example of a big company missing an opportunity is well documented in books about Apple Computers. Steve Wozniak took his idea for a "PC" to his company, HP— and it turned him down. His idea simply did not fit in their business plan. Another example is when the president of DEC asked (paraphrased), "Why would anyone want a personal computer?" Why indeed? Small companies like Apple Computers, Sycor, Datapoint, Four Phase, and many others were asking that very same question—and, not surprisingly, got "We do" as an answer from businesses. IBM's business was in the early stages of being nibbled on.

In Malcolm Gladwell's book, *Outliers*, he provides some excellent examples of people such as Steve Jobs, Bill Gates, Robert Noyce, William Shockley, Alan Turing, and others who not only were born at the right time, but also took advantage of the ideas and technology starting to make itself known to the world. And the world was, indeed, about to change, thanks to not only these folks, but also to lesser-known hundreds of others who were at the right age and had the inquisitive minds to start to understand the capabilities of the microprocessor.

Research Notes

For non-computer people or novice users: Since there is a good deal of technical terminology included in the book (which you might expect in a book about computer companies), a Glossary is included toward the end of this book. If you are scratching your head about "core memory," you'll find a definition for it.

Also, to make reading easier, with the exception of a few places where a whole name is needed, I have used abbreviations for the following:

- Digital Equipment Corporation = DEC
- Hewlett-Packard Company = HP
- International Business Machines = IBM
- United Kingdom = UK
- United States = U.S.

Also note that while I tried to include every 1970s company involved in computing, I have undoubtedly missed some—it was an innovative era and companies were popping up everywhere. Please feel free to contact me (the author) with the names of companies you believe should be included in this book and I will research them for future editions.

To learn more, visit the many computer museums scattered around the globe. If you cannot get there physically, visit some of them online (several museums would not grant permission to use their images) via the following links:

Historical computers of Japan:
http://museum.ipsj.or.jp/en/computer/main/0029.html

Retro museum's launching page to other computers:
http://hub.computersninternet.org/hub/retrocomputing?w=1768;rh=http%3a%2f%2fwebspace%2ewebring%2ecom%2fpeople%2fcs%2fspeeda%2fncr605%2findex%2ehtml;rd=1

The core memory forum:
http://www.thecorememory.com/forum/index.php?topic=50.0

Germany digital museum: **http://www.museum-digital.de/**

Germany DB museum: **https://www.dbmuseum.de/museum_de/home**

LEO computer society: **http://www.leo-computers.org.uk/**

British early computers: **http://www.ourcomputerheritage.org/**

Mountain View, California: **http://www.computerhistory.org/**

Germany History museum: **http://www.hnf.de/en/museum.html**

Soviet museum: **http://www.computer-museum.ru/english/index.php**

The '70s Companies

To make it easier to read about these companies or search for a particular company, they are arranged alphabetically (with one exception noted below), rather than in some chronological date order, for two reasons:

1) If you want to look up a specific company, you should be able to quickly find it.
2) In the 1970s, a lot of things were happening in the computer industry almost simultaneously — not just in the U.S., but also in other countries such as Germany, France, and Japan. So, to say "company A did so and so first" could be wrong, since so many ideas were coming out so fast.

The exception to the alphabetical listing is the Soviet Union. This country contributed to the development of computers in their own way, but none were commercially viable like the products of the other companies in this book were attempting to be. For example, how many have heard of the MESA, BESA, or MIR computers? Probably very few, outside of the computer scientists inside the Soviet Union. These computers weren't from a company, but rather from a government — the Soviet Union. Therefore, I have grouped all computers from the Soviet Union under that heading.

This book is primarily about the microprocessor and what people did with them. But there are companies that were indirectly or directly "influenced" by the microprocessor, and they also are included.

Now, on to the companies!

Adage, Inc.

This Boston, Massachusetts, company was formed in 1957 by James Stockwell. Originally, it produced a graphics terminal system to compete with the IBM 2250 terminal. In 1967, Adage released the Adage Graphics Terminal (AGT) system. The key word in that sentence is "graphic." All input and display was accomplished with characters, as those in this sentence. Adage developed a way to essentially make the display characters so tiny that it looked like an image—a picture if you will. Their product provided not only an image but also the manipulation of it through a keyboard or light-pen. It sold for a whopping $50,000. While this might sound high (and today we think nothing of seeing 3-D images and being able to turn and twist them with a push of a mouse button), this was wonderful technology and engineering for the time.

In 1968, Adage merged with Computer Displays, Inc., which had introduced its own graphic terminal, and was selling for much less than Adage's. Using Computer Display's technology, and the integration of the Intel microprocessor, the AGT system came down to $10,000 in 1972.

The display part (the AGT-30) had a calligraphic display for the main console, and was driven by a hybrid analog/digital 3-D matrix multiplier. You think your mouse is fun to use? Their text editor had a very creative button box (foot pedals) to provide data searching. It used a 30-bit machine instruction, with 15 bits of operation "op" code and 15 bits for addressing space. The graphics display used 15 bits for each of the X, Y, Z coordinates. It supported a FORTRAN compiler.

Their machine was incorporating new products that were being brought about by the microprocessor world. It offered two 7-track tape drives, a card reader, teletype printer, a communications port for transmissions from

1,200 baud to over 40,800 baud, and magnetic disk storage of 3.1MB to 12.5MB. Its memory core was 8K, and could be upgraded to more core at 32K.

In 1977 a whiz kid and his business partner from the Silicon Valley came out with a nicely bundled Apple computer that offered graphics—something that Mr. Stockwell had figured out two decades earlier without the assistance of a microprocessor.

Addmaster Corporation

The minicomputer[12] market spawned a need for companies to develop peripherals to attach to those types of small systems. Peripherals such as magnetic tape storage, disk drives, printers, and communication devices were important to most minicomputers.

Companies making wonderful peripheral devices sprang up, but then the issue arose about what to do if something was not quite communicating between a peripheral and the minicomputer. What was causing the problem?

Addmaster came up with a solution. It developed the Model 55 Computer/Instrumentation Peripheral product. This product had connectors that allowed it to connect to a peripheral and the host minicomputer. Now, instead of either side (peripheral makers or mainframe computer makers) pointing fingers at the other and saying "It's not my problem, it's yours!" this device would allow a debugging person to see the actual bits flowing to and fro. It had a small roll of paper that would print out (twelve columns wide) what was being sent to/from a peripheral. It was very portable, as it was about the size of a large calculator.

---

[12] Computer magazines and newspapers weren't quite sure what to call these "smaller" computers. While to call them a "small computer" certainly was accurate, someone coined the term "minicomputer," and it stuck.

This book, for the most part, discusses companies coming to grips with the microprocessor, but I wanted to show this company to illustrate the markets being created by the microprocessor.

Amdahl Corporation

Amdahl, although a major competitor with Hitachi and other large computers, is included because of its business presence and how it tried to adapt to the new competition from the minicomputer market. Growing up in rural South Dakota and going to a one-room school, Dr. Gene Amdahl accomplished much in his career. Jumping ahead after his university days, U.S. Navy service, and much experience in the electrical engineering world, Amdahl eventually would be put in charge of developing IBM's successful 360 mainframe series, and was a co-designer of its 32-bit processor architecture and 24-bit memory addressing. (Both provided extra speed to the processing of data.) Some people who work for others decide to take a big step and leave the nest to start their own company. This is what Amdahl did when he left IBM, and in 1970 founded the Amdahl Corporation, located in Sunnyvale, California.

Amdahl recognized this phenomenon of what the world was calling the "IBM standard," and he wanted to market a computer to compete head-on with IBM in features and functionality that was lower in price in order to gain market share. In 1975, Amdahl launched its first product, the Amdahl 470/6. This computer competed directly against IBM's high-end machines – the System/370 family.

The 470 family had memory chips mounted in a 6 x 7 array on multi-layer cards; these were then mounted in vertical columns. Each card had eight connectors that attached the micro-coaxial cables, which connected to the other system components. Amdahl designers came up with a concept called a "backplane" into which circuit boards could be easily inserted and removed. This idea was borrowed when the microprocessor guys and gals started to design minicomputer, PCs, and laptops.

Amdahl decided to invent something different, and this was done by cabling directly from system components to other system components — thereby, Amdahl claimed, causing a positive effect on overall speed. (This was true, but by using this design, he automatically limited the scalability of his computer.) Each column of memory cards had three large fans to cool the immense heat-generated machine (which had a negative impact affecting the marketability of the machine).

IBM announced a modification to its 370 architecture, and Amdahl responded by dropping the 470/6 and announcing a newer version called the 470V/6. The first two 470V/6 machines were delivered to the National Aeronautics and Space Administration (NASA) (serial number 00001) and the University of Michigan (serial number 00002). Throughout the remaining '70s and into the '90s, Amdahl and IBM competed aggressively against one another.

Figure 7—Amdahl 470V6

Amdahl had early financial success with assistance from the U.S. Department of Justice, which sided with Amdahl in a lawsuit the company filed against IBM. IBM was bundling its hardware and software together as essentially one product, and therefore refused to let Amdahl's customers license the IBM software separately. The ruling was a critical one to the computer industry as a whole; what it said was that a vendor, such as IBM, had to offer licenses for its software (at a reasonable cost) that were unbundled from its hardware.[13]

Gene Amdahl left his company in 1980, but more enhancements occurred with more Amdahl products through the early 1990s. While he was there, Amdahl never wandered into other computer areas like PCs; rather, Amdahl remained focused on competing head-on with IBM's mainframe systems. After he left, however, the new president, Tom O'Rourke, developed and marketed IBM-compatible peripherals, storage products, and smaller computers (but never as small as PCs). Fujitsu became a major shareholder in the Amdahl Corporation, and quietly took over what was left of the company. In 1997, Amdahl ceased to exist as a corporation, but its products lived on with Fujitsu.

American Regitel

American Regitel was founded in 1968 in Palo Alto, California, with manufacturing moving about eight miles away to San Carlos, California, within two years. Most department stores and groceries had stand-alone cash register types of machines, which accumulated sales all day long. In the evening (or at the end of a shift), paper print-outs were done at the machines, and then a manual balancing of the money/receipts was done in the accounting department. It was a time-consuming job. Larger companies, such as IBM, NCR, Olivetti, and Burroughs, were developing point-of-sale (POS) machines

---

[13] This lawsuit by Amdahl against IBM still reverberates throughout the computer industry. It dramatically altered how computer makers sell their products then and today.

that not only acted as a cash register, but also could accumulate sales data and transmit this data to a collection point. As with many companies in the 1970s trying to find a niche, American Regitel saw a potential market in the POS terminal business. Its marketing strategy was to offer a better machine than IBM and others, and offer it at a better price.

The device itself was nicely packaged with a "calculator" keypad, printer, and cash drawer. It measured approximately 9 in. x 20 in. x 5 in. Additionally, in 1972 the company filed for a patent (and was granted) the rights to market what it called a helical printing wheel. While this might not seem like a big deal today, every alpha and numerical character took up a fixed position with fixed spacing between each character. This new invention allowed half-character spacing at times, thus enabling just a bit more printing on a spool of receipt paper.

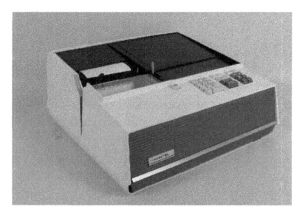

Figure 8—American Regitel point-of-sale (POS) machine

In 1970, Motorola acquired American Regitel because it thought this would give it an entry into the computer market, and it could use its own Motorola processor and memory chips in these devices. Eventually, Motorola found the POS market was not what it wanted to be in, and sold the rights to the software and hardware. Although this machine had nice features and was priced much less than a similar IBM product, American Regitel was one of many small companies that found IBM sales force too fierce and formidable.

Anderson Jacobson

Starting up in the 1970s, this Sunnyvale, California, company sold a line of computer terminals and data communication equipment. It produced the AJ Selectric Model 841 (an IBM typewriter with a communications adapter), the AJ 330 (a Teletype look-alike with a paper reader/punch built-in), the AJ 630 (a terminal with a roll of paper for output), the ADAC 1200 (acoustic coupler capable of connecting up to 1,200 baud), the ADAC 242 (a slower acoustic coupler than the ADAC 1200), the DCM 242 (modem), and later the AJ 830 (printer/terminal).

The AJ 830 product could print 30 characters per second (with an option to increase this to forty-five characters per second); it used the new "daisy wheel" print-head technology. It came with a full keyboard with numeric keypad, and a communication port that could have an acoustic coupler connected to it. It stood on its own stand, and looked like a wide typewriter in many aspects. An interesting feature was that the printer could support a rudimentary form of plotting.

Figure 9—Anderson Jacobson AJ330

All in all, the company made inexpensive terminals that many people liked. The price of terminals with a CRT was coming down, though, and Anderson Jacobson couldn't compete any longer in the market with its older ways of entering and printing data.

Ann Arbor Terminals

In the mid- to late 1970s, this Ann Arbor, Michigan, company set out to make a great terminal — and it did by integrating Intel's microprocessors to do programmable color character displays. Unfortunately for the company, that's all it did. It created a sleek-looking cabinet and keyboard combination, and sold it either as an "off-the-shelf" model, or it would custom build keyboards and protocols for those wanting something special, including custom cabinetry, if desired. All of its terminals could display graphics as well as characters.

Figure 10—Ann Arbor terminal

Initially, its idea of a rugged, custom terminal was a success, but by 1979, it saw its sales dwindling away. Since it had no other product ideas to fall back on, the company soon thereafter went out of business.

Apple Incorporated

Most people have heard of Sony—a large, international company (its legal name is Sony Corporation). Perhaps a few can link the Sony name to Akio Morita—its president for decades and considered the creative force behind all of those wonderful early Sony products. Actually, though, that would be a wrong characterization of Mr. Morita. True, he was president of the company, but it turns out one who was equally important to Sony's early success was Masaru Ibuka. Mr. Ibuka was an engineer who loved to tinker with electronics, sound, and generally anything that touched his creative spirit. By fate, Morita's and Ibuka's paths crossed during WWII, and after that conflict, their paths would cross again and their friendship blossomed. Starting in 1946, Sony, with Morita focusing on the business and Ibuka having fun creating products, would rise to lead the world in music, recording, and television products.

Thirty-one years later and 5,000 miles away, two men who also had a symbiotic relationship—Steve Jobs and Steve Wozniak[14]—would go on to form Apple. It would be a disservice for me to write pages and pages about these men as so much has already been written about them; therefore, to delve deeper into these personalities, please seek out one or more of those many excellent books.

It is important, though, to briefly talk about both Steves and how they drove Apple to greatness. Both of these young men lived in the San Jose, California, area—close to Stanford University (which had departments that were dedicated to computer science), and to HP and other "Silicon Valley" companies. Just as important for spurring on education through formal classroom work, though, were the many "computer clubs" that met weekly to "ooh" and "aah" over the latest magazine article someone had found in an electronics magazine. Jobs sort of knew

---

[14] Jobs was born in 1955, Wozniak in 1950, and Markkula in 1942.

what computers could do and what he wanted them to do—he just wasn't sure how to get there. Enter Wozniak, who worked full time at HP—and was the guy who could visualize and build the computer Jobs wanted. Together—along with several other talented engineers—they built a very successful company.

Steve Wozniak was a hacker's hacker. He loved to tinker with computer components, both hardware and software. HP was lucky to have him as an employee, as they needed smart engineers like him whom they could tell "Go figure this out," and Wozniak could. Unfortunately for HP, Wozniak's inquisitive mind drifted to things more challenging than making a bunch of characters capable of being input to a minicomputer.

As mentioned earlier, the area in which Wozniak and Jobs lived was an ever-exploding hotbed of ideas for anything to do with computers. Jobs and Wozniak would go to local computer club meetings, and Wozniak (like his other computer compatriots in the room) freely shared ideas they were having on building anything electronic. To Wozniak, it was all about fun and creativity—to hell with making a profit; if he could sell a board he made for his cost, he was a happy man. To Jobs, though, it was about business.

A little bit about Mr. Jobs. He was all about "doing things his way"; this included everything from dress code (sandals and t-shirts were his norm) to food (he was a vegetarian at one time) to religion. He enjoyed computers though, and his first job at Atari as a programmer turned him on even more. At that time, Atari was making a fortune with a game called "Pong," and Atari was looking to develop other games. Somewhere in the back of Jobs' mind, he was thinking, 'I could start a company and do this. After all, what is complicated about developing two paddles that hit a slow, moving ball across the screen?'

After crossing paths with Wozniak with the Homebrew Computer Club folks, Jobs got him to help Wozniak to design a new product for Atari (which is interesting if one things about it; Jobs was employed by them and Wozniak was working at HP). Wozniak did the work, and their relationship started to gel (even though the details remain murky to this day as to whether Jobs actually pocketed some bonus money without sharing it with Wozniak). They were starting to click in a way—Jobs with the business ideas, and Wozniak the guy who made it happen from a technology perspective.

By 1975, the microprocessor had been out for five years. Companies were springing up with new ideas on how to use them, and Wozniak's company, HP, was making a lot of money using them in their minicomputer market they had carved out. On March 5, 1975, Wozniak was attending a meeting of the Homebrew Computer Club when he had a eureka moment. Wozniak later stated, "This was one of the most important nights in my life." HP, Tandem Computers, and other minicomputer makes were selling systems, but what is a minicomputer anyway? It is a microprocessor that has a bunch of work-stations connected by wires, and it can store data. A lightbulb went on for Wozniak when he considered that instead of designing how to remotely enter keystrokes to a computer some distance away, maybe he could attach a keyboard directly to a microprocessor. Essentially shortening the wire from 200 feet to to two inches. Why not? Wozniak kept tinkering, and Jobs kept watching him and bugging him to package what he had so they could be sold.

With what could only be described as the ultimate in salesmanship, Jobs convinced a local electronics business, The Byte Shop, to buy fifty of Wozniak's "computers" at $500 each. Never mind that Jobs had nothing to sell other than "I know we can build this for you." With Wozniak's help and Jobs now focusing on how it all should look to fit inside a case, the first twelve computers were delivered and the Apple I was born. The owner of the store, Paul Terrell, was unimpressed because the box had no keyboard, no monitor, no power supply, no programming language, no way to store data, and didn't even have a case to hold it all. But he was impressed because he saw potential in the design of the circuit cards—and it did actually function as a rudimentary computer. The Apple I consisted of what was in the blue box below - everything else a user had to buy separately. But, if you plugged everything in correctly, it was your own personal computer system.

Figure 11—Apple I, sold on eBay for $365,000
December 12, 2014

Terrell figured he could unload them to local computer geeks, so he took delivery and then added the other components himself. This shows just how much pent-up demand there was for something—anything—that had a microprocessor in it and some memory, and that computer geeks were hungry to start playing with them.

Word spread locally about Jobs and Wozniak, and in July 1976, *Interface* magazine wrote an article about how Jobs (director of marketing) and Wozniak (head of creative and innovative talent) were "a well-disciplined, financially sound group that is opening new vistas in computer hardware, software, and service to their clientele." To say this description was an over-statement would embarrass the English dictionary. The reality was that Jobs was working out of his dad's garage and Wozniak was using his dining room table to assemble parts. Jobs' sister was inserting chips in a board, so technically, three people were loosely associated with the building and marketing of Apple products—but it was far from being a computer manufacturing company. Still, press was press—now the pressure was on Jobs to come up with something that was truly marketable.

While Jobs was the marketing guy, Wozniak was thought of as the guy to make the hardware work, but they needed an operating system to make it all work and sellable. Enter a bright software engineer named John Draper with whom Apple contracted, and gave him the responsibility of writing the operating system for the Apple I. Apple ended up selling about 500 Apple I computers. Jobs and Wozniak knew that even the hobbyists might have trouble understanding how to use it; therefore, specific instructions were needed for the user; here are the instructions from the Apple I *Operations Manual*:

> *Owners need to install a keyboard, display, and power source. Then to make sure all is working properly, type in the following instructions:*
>
> > *FIRST: Hit the RESET button to enter the system monitor. A backslash should be displayed, and the cursor should drop to the next line.*
> >
> > *SECOND:*
> > *Type-):A9b0bAAb20bEFbFFbE8b8Ab4Cb2b0 (RET)*
> >
> > *() is zero, NOT an alpha 'O'; b means blank or spaced; and (RET) hit the "return" key on the keyboard*
> >
> > *THIRD: Type-0.A (RET)*
> >
> > *(This should print out, on the display, the program you have just entered.)*

FOURTH: Type- R (RET)

(R means run the program.)

Once run, the program will spit out a stream of characters, showing that the keyboard, monitor, and computer are talking to each other. To stop the program, you needed to hit "reset." (Can you imagine having to do all this when you turn on your laptop?)

Jobs did many good things for Apple in his life, but what could arguably be his best deed was to leave Wozniak alone and give him the freedom to play — and play he did (and hopefully not write any more "operator manuals"). Wozniak liked to play games on the Atari system, so he figured out a way to add one of his favorite cartridges, "Breakout," to work in a similar fashion as his latest computer. In doing so, he figured out how to make the computer generate color, so he could use a regular color TV as a monitor. Today, no one even considers a computer without the colorful graphics we take for granted, but few had dared to go down this road with a microprocessor — it just took too much work, and memory. To turn a pixel (a small bit on a TV screen) red in multiple places was first hard to program, and it was harder yet to make things move when other things were going on — like a ball bouncing. Then, Wozniak figured out how to add sound, make the graphics better, add input devices that acted as paddles, and even built the BASIC language into his system. This meant that someone could take this machine, hook it up to a TV, and start programming it to do custom things. If it had been up to Wozniak, he probably would have exchanged this box with his friends for cases of cream soda. Jobs, though, thankfully kept his marketing hat on, so as Wozniak kept tinkering, Jobs was thinking, "How can we sell this?"

Computer chips were getting denser and faster, and Wozniak was on top of this thanks to his regular meetings with his geeky guys and gals. What this new technology meant was that now fewer boards were needed to make things run. Wozniak envisioned this new machine to be great for people to tinker with and come up with their own ideas on how to use it; Wozniak wanted extra card slots to accomplish this.

Jobs needed money for his ideas, and he approached another engineer by the name of Ron Wayne to invest. All three—Jobs, Wozniak, and Wayne—signed a formal legal document that gave them equal ownership, and Apple was born. Within a short time, Wayne (who had lost money before by starting small businesses) lost his nerve and approached Jobs and Wozniak about him (Wayne) dropping out the partnership agreement. Reluctantly, Jobs and Wozniak agreed, and Wayne went on to work at Atari and other computer-related businesses during his career—none approaching the financial reward Apple would have provided him. Interviewed a few years ago, Wayne said he had no regrets, as he said (paraphrased): "It just wasn't right for me."

Whether one calls Jobs' vision genius or some other descriptive word, he fought to make this machine simple to use and to give the users fewer options. (This mentality would carry over many years later in the design of the iPod, iPhone, and other "i" products—the simpler the better.) In other words, Jobs wanted to lead the users in how to use this computer. Stories have been told in other books regarding the life and times of Jobs and Wozniak in the early days—heated discussions ensued about how to package this new computer, and in the end, Wozniak won that round. Where the Apple I was for geeks and hobbyists, this new computer (yet to be named) was for people who wanted a computer to do actual work (playing games like "Breakout" fell under the category of work to Wozniak).

Here is an example of Jobs' influence. As the next generation of the Apple computer was being designed, Jobs was obsessed with not making the machine boxy and "metal"-looking—he wanted the new machine to stand out from the crowd. Computers at this time were using a power supply that generated a lot of heat, and therefore a fan was needed for cooling. Jobs insisted that no fan be used, and this created angst among the small engineering staff now working for Apple. The outcome was a power supply that actually wasn't on all of the time, but yet switched on/off literally thousands of times per second. The result was that the power supply itself was never not hot enough to require a fan.

In the spring of 1976, Wozniak (who could easily lay claim to being one of the most ethical people of that time — and I'm sure carries over even today), approached HP with his plan for a personal computer be added to HP's arsenal of minicomputers. Wozniak felt obligated because after his normal shift at HP, he would start work (on HP property) on his and Jobs' idea for a personal computer. Wozniak did his spiel to his management, and HP didn't think the idea would sell — they turned down the idea. Wozniak was now free to work on his machine with no feeling of conflict of interest — and work he did. In August 1976, both Jobs and Wozniak flew to Atlantic City to attend a computer show. They tried to sell a few Apple I's, but with mediocre success. However, they had in their hotel room a new, packaged computer to be named the Apple II that they were ready to foist upon the world — they were just waiting for the right moment. After walking around the floor of the convention center and examining the other computers on the market, Jobs and Wozniak concluded that their new computer was better than anything they had seen. They kept their computer secret, and Jobs started on his quest to find financing to put the Apple II into real production.

Figure 12—Apple II®

Back to Jobs parent's garage located at 2006 Crist Drive, Los Altos,[15] the two went. Wozniak went about fine-tuning the internals of the Apple II <u>and</u> still worked full-time at HP. Jobs was trying to find investors. Jobs ended up irritating Atari because of his barefoot (literally) approach to business, and other investors obviously were not overly impressed because money was not flowing in as Jobs had hoped. He did, however, secure a meeting with a small computer maker called Commodore. Jobs offered to seel Apple to them. He was willing to sign over all rights to Apple's products for $100,000, with the added stipulation that he and Wozniak would be hired for $36,000 a year in salaries. As can only be described now as a "close call" (by Jobs), and a "what were we thinking?" (by Commodore), the deal fell through as Commodore thought it could conquer the small computer market by making its own.

Jobs finally secured capital, and Armas Clifford "Mike" Markkula (the investor, and first CEO of Apple) predicted that Apple would make the Fortune 500 list of America's

---

[15] Go ahead and look it up; it is still there—the first assembly station/workshop for Apple.

biggest companies within only a few years. He also predicted that the Apple II was "the start of an industry"—and how right he was. In January 1977, Apple Computer Company was born with Jobs, Wozniak, and Markkula owning equal shares.

When many think of Apple, the names of Jobs and Wozniak come to mind. But, both of these guys were struggling for a focus for their Apple II.[16] They knew they had created a nice machine, but what to do with it? It could play a few games, but were people willing to shell out $1,000 to play Pong when they could drop a quarter in an Atari machine and have the same fun. How could they market it? And if orders actually started coming in, how could they ramp up production? Markkula, who had a successful career leading companies, knew how to secure capital for funding. Markkula, with Jobs and Wozniak's blessing, led Apple through a successful IPO and helped make millions of dollars in revenues for Apple. He also steered them to start developing applications that made the Apple II a true business computer, instead of simply a computer that could play games.

Keep in mind what was happening with "microcomputers" in general. MITS, Atari, and others had small computers in the market, and while the Apple II was nicely packaged, it still had lots of competition for the hearts and minds of hobbyists and small businesses. In 1977, one of first West Coast computer fairs was held, and Apple worked at a fast pace to get its latest computer ready. Jobs rented space at the front of the entrance, ordered a huge sign showing the now famous colorful apple with a bite taken out of it,[17] and had three computers on hand. According to the ticket sales tally,

---

[16] Wozniak had decided to use the Motorola 6502 microprocessor instead of Intel's model because the Motorola was cheaper. If Intel perhaps could have negotiated a better price for their microprocessor with Wozniak and Jobs, imagine for a moment how Intel's and Motorola's fortunes could have been altered.

[17] The bite taken out of the apple in Apple's logo was actually a computer reference to a computer byte, meaning one word—which described Apple perfectly.

13,000 people were there—everyone having to pass by the Apple booth. At the end of the fair, Apple had taken 300 orders for its computer—each selling for $1,298 (which was about $300 more than a fully assembled IMS Associates' (IMSAI) entry in the microcomputer marketplace). The first four months of 1977 showed little in sales, but by the end of September, Apple had sales of $774,000—with an eventual profit of $42,000 for the fiscal year ending in December.

As nicely packaged as the Apple II was, truth be told it was simply a smaller, faster version of other computers already on the market that played games and could be programmed—but it lacked something to really make it attractive for a business. Small disk drives[18] were just coming into the market, and Markkula suggested to Wozniak to figure out a way to attach one of these to their computers. After some tinkering, in the spring of 1978, a removable, external disk for storage was available for the Apple II. What this meant was that software (application programs) could be more easily sold, shared, and used on the Apple II. Apple's sales increased to $7.9 million by the fall of 1978. Companies such as Microsoft were learning that software could be just as important as hardware in driving computer sales.

When the Apple II was introduced in 1977, the total net worth of Apple (the company) was estimated at $5,309, with 2,500 sales of the Apple II. In 1981, sales of the Apple II totaled 210,000. Through Markkula, more investors were recruited by Apple, and more "private" shares would be sold to these new owners. In 1979, Jobs and Markkula sold a million dollars' worth of their shares, but at this point, Jobs had enough shares left that he was

---

[18] Small is a relative term; for instance, Burroughs sold a magnetic disk that was approximately three feet in diameter. In the world of Apple and similar sized computers, a smaller type of magnetic (writable and erasable) storage was needed. The latter disks became known as "floppy" disks because they were physically bendable. The first one was over 8 inches in diameter, then the next generation led to 5.25 inches, and eventually a smaller version was even introduced.

shown as being worth $10 million. Jobs, being the prudent businessman, could have sunk his own money back into the company, but instead kept seeking out others to invest theirs. One of those companies was the Xerox Corporation.

When many people hear the name Xerox, they may automatically think of copiers. In reality, though, Xerox was (and still is today) a very innovative company that was then trying to make sense of how to use microprocessors in its product line (or create new products in the process). In another twist of fate, Xerox had (and still has) a research lab in Palo Alto, California, (known as PARC by the people who work there — an acronym for Palo Alto Research Center). PARC just happened to be close to Jobs' office in Cupertino. Keep in mind that up until now most computer screens had black screens with either white, amber, or green characters. To play a game, a user would put a floppy disk in a drive, then type in something like: >RUN GAME, D1, then press the Return key. Although a tracker ball had been designed and used for some small systems, it was big and cumbersome — and definitely did not in any way resemble the beloved mouse that we use today. There was no concept of having something small that would allow pointing and clicking on a symbol on the screen — or at least that was known outside of PARC.

Jobs had visited PARC once or maybe twice, and he was aware that the PARC folks had some exciting technology — and Jobs wanted to see it. Apple was creating a reputation as a creative computer packaging company, and with Jobs' typical brashness he told Xerox that he would allow them to invest $1M in his company if Xerox would show him all they had developed. Xerox agreed, and when Jobs visited PARC, Xerox showed him that it had linked dozens of its Alto computers together in a private network. Xerox engineers had developed an application where they could send mail messages to one another, and had come up with a small rolling box next to their computers called a "mouse," which enabled a user to position the cursor anywhere on a screen. Additionally, Xerox's engineers created a concept called "folders" to hold categories of information, and had the idea of creating directories (or folders) in which to group documents on a disk. As the story goes (from people who recalled the demo to Jobs), Jobs got very animated while seeing all of these gadgets and said, "You're sitting on a gold mine!" Timing is everything in life, and this is an example of how being a small, nimble company like Apple, rather than a large, entrenched company like Xerox, made it easier to get someone's attention about a possible new product line like small computers. Small and nimble was about to kick the large company's butt.

A few still accuse Jobs of stealing Xerox's ideas. Jobs used this quote to describe Apple's actions in the early days when he and Wozniak were trying to figure out the best ideas for technology: "Good artists copy, great artists steal." (I have read this quote a dozen times, and I still don't know if Jobs was putting Wozniak down or admitting to theft, or some other esoteric reference — I'll let you be the judge.) Jobs went on to describe the leaders of Xerox as "toner heads" who just cared about selling copiers. (Actually, he was 100 percent correct in his assessment; more details on this in the section about Xerox.) Jobs described their inaction of getting into the small-computer market as "grabbing defeat from the greatest victory of the computer industry." (Think of the world today if Xerox was the standard for personal computers and Apple was out of business; this could have happened very easily.) Apple ran with the concept of creating symbols (later known as icons) on a screen and had their own idea and version of a mouse.

Wozniak kept working on improvements to the Apple II, and more software was being written to make it very useful in many aspects of business and personal use. Officially, a product called the Apple III was underway, but another product (with a low cost with minimum features) also was being worked on. This latter product was to be called Lisa.[19]

Before wrapping up Apple in the 1970s, it is important to understand the power of software to sell a product. The Apple I was, by all definitions, a hobbyist's computer. The Apple II was thought of by many at first as simply a continuation of the Apple I—just packaged better (and yes, it had better components). Then, a piece of software that allowed numbers to put into "spreadsheet" came on the market; it was called VisiCalc and was programmed for the Apple II by a software company called Personal Software, All of a sudden CFOs and other financial people (accountants for example) realized the capabilities at their fingertips. To use the vernacular of today, VisiCalc was a "killer app";[20] in fact, it could easily be called the first "killer app." This application, plus other business applications (e.g., tracking inventory, police data capture, etc.), helped Apple II's sales skyrocket once word spread through the business world that this little box sitting on a desk could actually do business work and not just play games. It also helped sales with creative marketing such as Apple's Apple Education Foundation in 1979 (where free Apple II products were donated to schools, and in return, hundreds if not thousands of students were quickly exposed to this new product).

As a side note, Xerox tried to beat the Lisa and Macintosh to the market by selling its Xerox Star system commercially. Xerox's problem was in marketing, as it priced its system at $16,595. While this does sound high, Xerox actually ended up selling 30,000 of them—which shows how much companies were willing to pay to

---

[19] You can read about Jobs' private life in the many books written about him; suffice it to say that Lisa did not stand for "Local Integrated Systems Architecture" as some at Apple wanted the world to believe, but rather it was named after Jobs' daughter.

[20] The term "killer app" is short for "killer application," and all it means is that the application is going to be bought by thousands and maybe only runs on a specific platform. In other words, it makes a killing in money for the company owning the "killer app." (Plus, it helps drive sales for the hardware.)

increase productivity through a "personal computer." As good as the Xerox Star was, both the Lisa and Macintosh sold for about $15,000 less—and Apple sold a lot of them at this price.

As the 1970s turned into the 1980s, the Apple III and Lisa were about to come to the market. The Apple III was a disaster in terms of workmanship[21] and sales. Lisa, though, was a culmination of pre-built icons, a mouse, folders, applications, nice cabinetry, and reasonable pricing. Apple would continue with innovations (e.g., Macintosh in 1984), along with Jobs' marketing ideas, Wozniak's inventiveness, and some software genius from a guy who got little recognition, Jeff Rafkin. Wozniak would eventually leave Apple, never to return; he now helps fund computer interest groups for school kids, and in general sits back and enjoys the fruits of his labor. Jobs also "retired," but was asked at a later point to come back to help instill some of the creative spark that seemed to be missing at Apple. Jobs did return, created new products (e.g., iPod, iPhones, iPad, to name a few), and suffered significant health issues.

Apple went public on December 12, 1980. Markkula eventually stepped down after successfully leading Apple to the world market, and Jobs took over leadership. The reins were eventually passed one last time from Jobs to a new leader, and Apple continues today to excel in new ideas and products. Wozniak is hopefully still enjoying life and his money. In 2011 Jobs died from pancreatic cancer.

---

[21] Jobs insisted on designing the case that the Apple III fit in, but it was too small, so circuit cards were modified badly to make them fit. So cramped were the chips on the board that every now and then the chips on the cards would pop loose, but by merely physically dropping the machine from a short height, the chips would usually be reset.

Applied Digital Data Systems, Inc.

Around 1978, this company decided to jump in on the kit phase and offer its Envoy-600 and Envoy-640 products. Basically, what this Hauppauge, New York, did was assemble parts, package them, include instructions, and ship them to a buyer.

What made its products unique was that it included a small monitor with either of two video boards (which affected the price). The company had a good idea, except that the lower-cost Envory-600 was $3,500 (512-character display), and the Envoy-640 was $3,700 (1,024-character display). This was very pricey—even if it did include a monitor (which, by the way, was only about 7 inches across). Other features touted in its ad was the ruggedness, acoustic coupler modem, and high-quality parts that were included. Assembled it weighed thirty pounds and fit into a 6 in. x 22 in. x 17 in. enclosure.

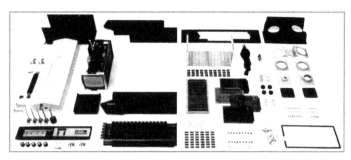

Figure 13—Applied Digital Data Systems Envoy model

Complete computers (e.g., Tandy, Apple, IMSAI, etc.) were coming on the market at a cost of at least 70 percent less than Applied Digital's models, so it is not hard to understand why the company couldn't compete in the burgeoning "PC" market.

ASK Group

As people started playing with small clustered minicomputers (e.g., Tandem Computers, HP, and DEC), customers had to develop their own applications to make the computer useful. As was seen with Apple, if the spreadsheet software had not come along Apple would have struggled to find and audience to buy its products. Applications (or in today's parlance, "killer app") were needed to make the computer more useful. If a company developed their own application, it was very custom to that one company. In other words, that application (or tools to develop that application) weren't easily re-used for other application development. IBM had solved this problem a decade earlier by developing a software tool called Customer Information Control System (known throughout the computer world as simply CICS). IBM told their customers that CICS made application development easier. It did accomplish that, but, of course, it only ran on IBM computers. IBM had developed a gold mine for almost unlimited revenues. Once an IBM customer had developed an application using CICS, the customer was more than likely going to be a customer for life because of the money and training a company would spend on CICS applications.[22]

HP, and other clustered minicomputer makers needed easy-to-use software to set their system apart from IBM. Enter Sandra Kurtzig, who had originally sold time-sharing systems (where a central computer was shared by many), but she saw the writing on the wall—time-sharing was being replaced by companies that wanted their own computer(s). In 1972, ASK Group was formed by Kurtzig, and soon thereafter had a product called MANMAN.

ASK struggled in its early days, as the idea was truly ahead of the software curve. Her potential customers

---

[22] In the year this book was written, IBM still has thousands of CICS licenses in use around the world and have customers locked into IBM systems even after sixty years!

didn't grasp what she was offering — which was software that would run their company (specifically manufacturing companies) better.

MANMAN did accounting, inventory control, and other manufacturing data collections. At first, she was a one-woman business, but she knew she was on to something with her idea and needed enhancements to it — and marketing to sell the idea to manufacturing companies. HP had developed their HP 3000 minicomputer, of which they were very proud. A lesson they were about to learn was that it was one thing to develop a super-duper calculator and have people figure how to use it, and another thing to have to try and sell a $100,000 computer to a company that had few skills at writing applications for it. This is where Kurtzig shined. She got it, and now she had to convince HP to give her a chance (and a computer).

ASK (with Kurtzig leading a small development team) ported their time-sharing/central computer MANMAN software to HP. Now HP could say to a customer, "We have the perfect software to help you to (fill in the blank)." ASK made a lot of money for HP in terms of computer sales, and ASK made a lot of money licensing its software to many HP customers. ASK sales soared from barely a profit in 1973, to over $8M by 1980. Sales continued upward for several more years.

A little bit about ASK itself. Almost all of its employees were Stanford University graduates. ASK reached its zenith in the late 1970s and early 1980s, but its core product needed enhancements to deal with more "real-time" data gathering and querying. ASK bought a company called Baan, named their new software MANMAN/X, and tried to compete with companies that had started to stake a claim to the manufacturing software space. ASK needed a savior that could put some money into the company for software enhancements and marketing. Computer Associates bought ASK in 1994, and the troubles now were exacerbated by several factors.

(One factor was Computer Associates' reputation of being difficult to work with, and another was the fact that many ASK employees didn't like the new company's management style—so many ASK employees quit.) In 1996 Computer Associates formed a company called MK Group (MK meaning Manufacturing Knowledge), and told this group they now were responsible for MANMAN/X. This new company renamed MANMAN/X to MK software.

Still determined to stay in the software business, Sandy Kurtzig, in 2012, went on to form a company called Kenandy, a cloud-based supply-chain software business based in Redwood City, California.

Atari Incorporated

Atari (the private company) was started in 1972 by Nolan Bushnell. Atari, Inc. was in business from 1979 – 1984, and Atari Corp. was in business from 1984 – 1992. Would Apple have happened without the successful teaming of Jobs and Wozniak? Or Sony had its success without Morita and Ibuka? It's doubtful. And so it was with Atari as Al Alcorn was brought on for his technical expertise in working with microprocessors. Al Alcorn had a brilliant mind for dealing with electronics, and packaging them for people to use. Originally starting as a one-game idea of "Pong"[23] at Atari's Grass Valley Research Center (originally known as a company called Cyan) in Grass Valley, California, the company soon moved about a hundred miles to the southwest to Campbell, California. Campbell was part of the many towns that started to make up what is known as the "Silicon Valley" area. By the way,

---

[23] Bushnell, the business man, thought that the Pong machine needed some instructions on it in order to make it more "user friendly." Alcorn, the technician, thought this was a crazy idea, as how complicated was it to drop a coin in a slot? But, with sarcasm in mind, he ended up putting the following instructions on the machine: "Deposit quarter, Ball will serve automatically, Avoid missing ball for high score."

the original Pong did not have a microprocessor; instead, with some very inventive wiring and electronic board design, Alcorn and a guy named Ted Dabney had a ball and paddles moving about a screen. Steve Mayer and Larry Emmons at the "research center" had an idea: make the game microprocessor-based and more flexible by allowing it to play different games based upon a "cartridge." When Alcorn came on board, he saw the potential to make Pong faster and easier to use with a microprocessor—and in 1974, it happened. Their creation was called STELLA, and in five years they sold over 12 million game consoles and cartridges.[24] Alcorn's, and Atari's, fire had been lit.

When many people think of Atari, they think, "Oh yeah, it made arcade games and "playstations"[25] for home and bars. Yes, it did do that initially, but what occurred for Atari was a natural evolution into personal computers. (As a side note, Atari had a side business of repairing pinball machines.) After all, its games had a microprocessor at the core, and since strides were being made to attach things to a microprocessor and people could write programs for it, why not enter the small-computer market? Steve Jobs was once an Atari employee, and he took note of what a microprocessor could do. This was a prime example of a fire being lit, as Jobs would take the ideas he was collecting and turn them into a successful company.

Moving from the bar/pub/bowling alley market to the home market was key for Atari to increase sales. While designing the Atari 2600 (also known as the Atari VCS, where VCS meant video computer system) in 1976, the engineering team felt that the 2600 would have about a

[24] Jerry Lawson at Fairchild had developed a similar concept in a home game system; he called it Channel F. Fairchild.

[25] The term playstation didn't come around until the marketing group of Microsoft and Song started using that term. Like many things from the 1970s, Atari had a small gaming console that was called, well, a gaming console; it had cartridges you could interchange, and you viewed the games on the TV—much like today's playstations.

three-year lifespan before becoming obsolete. Sears, the department store, ordered 75,000 Pong games, so Atari knew it was on to something. It started to work on other designs for a new console that it hoped would be ready by around 1979. The newer design would be faster than the 2600, have better graphics, and would include much better sound hardware. Work on the chips for the new system continued throughout 1978 and focused on much-improved video hardware known as the Alphanumeric Television Interface Controller (Texas InstrumentsC) and the Color Television Interface Adaptor (Texas InstrumentsA).

Figure 14—Atari 2600

Although its gaming systems had a good reputation for reliability and graphics and gave Atari a good revenue stream, the life of Atari computers was tumultuous for the company. Overall, its computer business lasted from 1979 until 1992. The Atari 8-bit computer line was, by revenue dollars, a commercial success — selling approximately two million units during its major production run between late 1979 and mid-1985. Atari chose to use a microprocessor called the Motorola 6502, which ran at 1.79 MHz (about twice the speed of similar designs). Atari tried something unique, though. The technology wasn't quite there for it to offload a lot of work to other firmware devices, but it knew that having two CPUs was probably better than one. What the company did was very creative in that it developed the first home computers designed with custom co-microprocessor chips. (Intel finally caught on to this idea by developing the multi-core microprocessors decades later.) Having two microprocessors in one system is an important concept to understand. Up until now, when a program wanted to display a character or have a spaceship float across the screen, this interrupted the CPU; in other words, other things that could possibly go on inside of a CPU had to wait. Not great, but it was fairly easy to program. Atari's new architecture now offloaded this video and sound work to a microprocessor outside of the main processor, thereby speeding up the capabilities of the main microprocessor so it could do other things. Welcome to the world's first true gaming platform that could display 3-D images and have little men and guns actually look like little men and guns. Their program, "Star Raiders," could be considered a leading and ground-breaking innovation.

The original Atari 400 and 800 models were released with a series of peripheral devices that could be plugged[26] into Atari's unique serial input/output (SIO) bus architecture. Over the following decade, several versions of the same basic design were released, including its XL and XE series. The Atari 400 (meaning it had 4K of RAM) and Atari 800 (8K of RAM) were first sold in January 1979. However, by the time the marketing name was assigned and the actual manufacturing had begun, prices of RAM had started to fall—so both models were sold with 8K of RAM. As memory prices continued to fall, Atari eventually supplied RAM of 48K to its models. Both computers had four joystick ports, but only a few of its games used all four joysticks where four simultaneous users could play.

These systems used the same basic logical design, but to help lower production costs, the packaging was slightly different. The early machines were expensive to build, but

---

[26] Atari could easily plug in peripheral devices (e.g. keyboard, printer, monitor, etc.) more than any other computer maker. Atari didn't know it at the time, but the term "plug-n-play" would later become a standard in how peripherals plugged into a personal computer—Atari just didn't know how to market this really neat feature.

quite dependable. Its later models (like the XE) were less expensive than its original models – and slightly slower. The XL and XE found a market, though, in Eastern Europe, as small computers of any kind or quality were hard to come by.

Atari's management identified two markets for the new fledgling computers: 1) a low-end version known as Candy, and 2) a higher-end machine known as Colleen. The primary difference between the two models was marketing; Atari marketed Colleen as a business computer, and Candy as a game machine. Colleen would include user-accessible expansion slots for RAM and ROM, two 8K cartridge slots, two types of connectors for a monitor output, and a full keyboard; Candy used a plastic membrane keyboard (cheaper to manufacture), internal slots for memory, and only one form for video output.

At the time, the Federal Communication Commission (FCC) was becoming involved with interference being caused at times by computers being hooked up to TVs (acting as display monitors). Signal leakage protection in the TV frequency range was extremely high. Since the Atari machines had TV circuitry inside them, they (and all makers now of microprocessor contained systems) were subject to this rule and needed to be heavily shielded. To solve the possible electrical interference issues, both machines were built around very strong cast aluminum shields.

Because of this extra shielding, the side benefit was that the computer itself was extremely sturdy – but it had the disadvantage of added manufacturing expense and complexity. An FCC standard was set that made it hard for any computer to have any sizable holes in the case (they didn't want those pesky interference signals to interfere with *I Love Lucy* re-runs). What this meant to Atari and others was that it eliminated expansion slots or cards that communicated with the outside world via its own connectors. So, Atari designed its computer serial bus (basically a bundle of wires) that allowed multiple, plug-n-play devices to connect to the computer through a single, shielded connector. The only internal slots were reserved for ROM and RAM modules.

An overarching goal for the new computer systems was user-friendliness. The Atari computers were designed to reduce fumbling with any hardware (including upgrades). The system did not require the user to enter commands to boot the system if a new device was added. Fifteen years later, a similar concept called a universal service bus (USB) would become ubiquitous in the PC market—our collective hats off to Atari for figuring this out so many years ago.

Atari had originally intended to port Microsoft's BASIC programming language to its computer. However, the Motorola 6502 version from Microsoft needed 12K of memory, and all of Atari's internal attempts to reduce it to 8K failed. Atari eventually gave up and hired the consulting firm Shepardson Microsystems, which ended up writing its own version of BASIC from scratch; Atari marketed this as Atari BASIC.[27] Shepardson Microsystems also wrote a disk operating system for Atari.

The Atari computer started early in the 1970s as a simple gaming machine, but it left its mark with new innovations in the about-to-explode PC market. Atari came out with other products in the 1980s, but it had some bad and confusing press (mainly rumors on pricing) that was to lead to its eventual ruin. To compound its problems, it also got involved in what could be called a full-blown price war with Commodore International (which was in its own price war with Texas Instruments)—Texas Instruments actually announced a model to sell for $99. Atari could not pay the high wages in the U.S. and

---

[27] Up until this time, the mainframe programming languages such as FORTRAN and COBOL were standardized. If a COBOL verb performed in a certain manner on one machine, then it should perform the same on another machine. BASIC didn't have this standard set as yet, so regular BASIC and Atari BASIC performed differently. This language difference was to rear its ugly head time and again not only in BASIC, but also in other subsequent languages developed over the years.

compete with pricing, so starting a trend that continues today, it moved production of the new machines to Asia.

Unexpected production and quality delays occurred, and the timing couldn't have been worse for Atari. Although Atari's newest models had excellent competitive pricing and nice features, it could not get enough units shipped in time to compete with Commodore for the critical 1983 Christmas rush. Atari was soon losing millions of dollars a day. Its current owners, Warner Communications (which bought Atari in 1976, but allowed it to function almost as a separate company with littler interference from the parent company) became disillusioned with Atari's sales forecasts, and decided to sell off the Atari division.

Eventually, all Atari computer models (some with leading architecture designs) were stopped. Their CEO, James Morgan, insisted that Atari was to return to its gaming roots if it had a chance to survive at all. On January 1, 1992, Atari Corp. officially dropped all remaining support of its business/personal computers.

Atron Corporation

Atron is one of those companies for which I found references for its computer, but could find very little about the company itself other than it was located in St. Paul, Minnesota. The company developed a minicomputer called the Atron 501 Datamanager, which was introduced in 1969, and lived on into the 1970s.

The Atron 501 was originally primarily developed and marketed for remote job-entry applications. What this meant is that users could simulate an IBM workstation using IBM's CICS, which was IBM's terminal control software programming tool), or simply batch data to be sent en masse (thereby saving money by not buying expensive IBM products.) At least this was the theory. Mohawk Data Sciences ended up owning the Atron 501, which was used as the basis of its MDS 2400 minicomputer and sold during the 1970s.

Figure 15—Atron 501

The Atron 501's developers were very creative in many aspects — one being in the way the machine was programmed. For example, what could be simpler to write and understand than a sentence such as "MOVE LEFT AND ELIMINATE LEADING ZEROS"? But developing a custom programming language is a double-edged sword. While the language might be full of wonderful features and easy to use, if only a handful of users adapt it, then the language is doomed to die off just as some obscure spoken languages die off. This meant that if the Atron 501 didn't sell, no one would care how good its programming language was.

The system itself had 4K of <u>core</u> memory (expandable up to 32K), and offered a two-microsecond CPU execution cycle. It supported one to four input/output channels with up to sixteen devices per channel. It could be bought with a choice of two off-line printers (280 or 1250 lines per minute), a card reader (capable of reading up to 400 cards per minute), a card punch (capable of punching up to 160 columns per second), a paper-tape reader, a 2.48MB disk storage unit, and 7- and 9-track half-inch magnetic tape drives. A console could be attached via an optional asynchronous terminal port. Overall, the system was a sophisticated key-punch station, albeit the data entry could be cleaner than a simple IBM terminal because of the programming capabilities of the system. The readouts were in large digital form for easy reading and verification. The basic system supported synchronous communications at up to a whopping 9600 baud, and sold for $7,475.

Basic/Four

In 1971, Basic/Four (also known as Basic 4 or Basic Four) was one of the first independent entries into the small business-computer system arena, and was a subsidiary of Management Assistance, Inc. (MAI). The computers primarily were marketed to handle inventory control and general accounting. To read more about Basic/Four, please refer to the MAI company information later in this book.

Bell & Howell

Founded in 1907 in Wheeling, Illinois, Donald Joseph Bell and Albert Summers Howell set out to build machinery to project motion pictures. Eventually, their exploits led them to almost everything involved with movies and cameras.

In the mid-1970s, Bell & Howell came out with a microprocessor-based system called the 3800 COM.[28]

---

[28] COM stood for Computer Output Microfilm.

Figure 16—Bell & Howell 3800 COM

The 3800 COM's main purpose was to create microfilm. It had a 16-bit processor, 28K RAM, two floppy disk drives, keyboard, printer, and displays (one for command control and one for viewing microfilm).

Bell & Howell is headquartered in Durham, North Carolina, and still uses a postal address in Wheeling out of respect to its founders.

Bendix Computer Division

Bendix Aviation Corporation started the Bendix Computer Division in the mid-1950s to perform scientific calculations. It had one terminal connected to its own custom computer. By the time the 1970s rolled around, it had expanded its thought of building scientific computers to develop what it called the Bendix Datagrid Digitizer. The digitizer had its own central custom computer residing in a cabinet, a noisy and clunky Teletype keyboard/printer, and what I would call an "optical mouse."

The way this optical mouse worked was that one could move it over a large schematic (say an integrated circuit) that could be several feet square. With a click of a button, all of that data would be captured and stored on its computer — a very creative design. Unfortunately, the company's marketing budget must have been limited; as what could be considered one of the worst marketing phrases ever, here is a quote from its ad: "The Bendix Datagrid Digitizer. It doesn't look like it works. But it does." Bendix was located in Southfield, Michigan.

Bit Incorporated

In a 1970 ad, this Natick, Massachusetts, company advertised its BIT 483 system. Maybe it was something in the surrounding Massachusetts water, or maybe some companies just weren't creative, but its system looked very similar to a DEC PDP system. (The only thing strikingly different on the front panel was that the PDP had toggle switches, and the BIT 483 had pushbuttons.)

Figure 17—Bit 483 (Why did they look so glum?)

The company advertised a one-microsecond CPU cycle speed, a system expandable to 32K RAM, direct memory access from data channels, priority interrupts, and binary and decimal arithmetic. Its market aim was to sell this system to other computer vendors who could slap their name on it and resell it as their own. Although the system had nice features, it never caught on.

Budapesti Rádiótechnikai Gyár

In 1979 (or possibly late 1978), this Hungarian company imported the ABC 80 gaming system (made by Dataindustrier AB). While the ABC 80 held up fine for most users in the rest of the world, this company replaced the plastic shell with a metal shell before reselling the units. When reading about the Soviet Union's requirements for strong computer systems later in this book, the metal casing starts to make sense.

Figure 18—ABC 80 (made by Dataindustrier)

Bunker-Ramo

Bunker-Ramo was founded by George M. Bunker and Simon Ramo in 1964, and was located originally in Trumbull, Connecticut. Originally setting out to design and manufacture electronics for the military, Bunker-Ramo did come out with a computer called the BR-133, but it had very limited sales and, therefore, production was stopped.

Core acquisitions came along (notably in the field of electrical connectors), and in 1970, Bunker-Ramo decided to try and compete in the then-hot terminal "IBM compatible but smarter" market. The Bunker-Ramo 2206 Data Display Station was announced at about the same time as the Bunker-Ramo 2212 Data Display Station.

The 2206 consisted of a keyboard with programmable function keys, numeric keypad, and a 10-inch monitor — all packaged together. It had a built-in modem and RS-232C connector for attaching/connecting to a host system. It had no built-in storage for holding keyed data.

Figure 19—Bunker-Ramo 2206 and 2212 (hands optional)

The 2212 was a strange-looking little device. It was self-contained like the 2206, except that the screen as about 3.5 inches square, and it had a numeric keypad, programmable function keys, while the typewriter keyboard was a bunch of characters laid out in seven rows by four columns. Apparently, the company expected this device to be primarily a calculator type of machine — or the person designing it just couldn't shake the calculator image.

In February 1971, this company brought to the market the very first National Association of Securities Dealers' Automated Quotations (NASDAQ) system. Also, in the early and mid-1970s, it developed and marketed custom banking peripheral equipment. Allied Corporation (aka AlliedSignal) bought Bunker-Ramo in 1981.

Burroughs

The Burroughs Corporation had a long history starting in 1886, with the introduction of the first commercial adding machine by William Burroughs. Everything about this machine was mechanical in nature (no electricity to drive any part of it), and because it did what it was supposed to do and was built tough, it quickly became a de facto standard internationally (and in the U.S.) as the adding machine to use for banks and larger retailers.

Jumping seven decades ahead of business success, in 1956 the company had a major shift in its product line, which now included typewriters in addition to adding electricity, of course, to its cash register machines. Burroughs (now based outside of Detroit, Michigan) bought ElectroData Corporation (which was headquartered in Pasadena, California.) ElectroData had built a large computer called the Datatron 205, and was working on a model yet to be named. Burroughs put some of its brightest engineers to work on understanding what a big computer could do, as Burroughs was watching IBM's rise to power — and Burroughs wanted in on it. Soon a new product emerged with a "B" in front of it. This "B" would become synonymous in many years to mean only one thing — that it was a Burroughs computer.[29]

Burroughs wanted to be seen as a major computer competitor to IBM. Like IBM, Burroughs tried to supply a complete line of products for its customers, including Burroughs-designed printers, disk drives, tape drives, computer printing paper, and even typewriter ribbons.

Burroughs developed three highly innovative architectures, but one stands out as exceptional (at least to this author). When a computer program was loaded (read from some source) into a computer's memory, the first thing the O/S did was to try and find room for it in

---

[29] Burroughs did have a "D" class of models; these were the same as the "B" models except designated for "defense" (military) use only.

memory. Programmers were always aware of this limitation of memory size, so the earlier programs not only were small in function but also limited in the number of instructions the programmer could make it do. The first programmers had to fit all of their instructions (programs) into only 4K (that's 4,096 bytes) of memory. If a program didn't fit, the O/S simply froze or gave an error message—both of which meant that it gave up running the program. Other computer companies were struggling with this memory problem, and Burroughs was one of the first innovator to solve this problem by developing and using what is today called "virtual memory." What this means literally is that no matter what the size of a programmer's program, the O/S will figure out a way to make room for it—the programmer need not worry about the size of his/her program.[30] Virtually, a programmer had as much space as was needed to run any program.

Banking was becoming global, or at least very big geographically within a country. Data communications between branches and the head office was a new requirement. Burroughs, because of its breadth of products such as check sorting and mainframe computers, became synonymous with the banking industry—and it capitalized on this in a huge way. Similar in concept to Triumph-Adler's small banking systems having success in Europe, Burroughs developed a small departmental system called the L-series; it used punch paper tape as input, and it came in various models with different storage sizes (starting with only a few megabytes) and memory sizes (from 4K to 32K magnetic core). They sold

---

[30] Virtual memory then, and today, is done by allocating disk space as needed. For instance, let's say a program 1MB in size wants to run in a computer with only 512K of memory. The O/S will load pieces of the program into whatever memory space it can find, work on those instructions, and as it needs other instructions loaded, goes to the disk and fetches more. That's just the instructions—the data a program is working on sometimes also has to be "swapped" to disk because there is no memory available. Yes, going out to disk and reading instructions is slower than having all instructions loaded into memory, but it freed programmers from worrying about memory space, and because of this, programs became much more enriched with more features and functions. Microsoft, say "thank you" to Burroughs.

from around $5,000 to no more than around $20,000, to do a range of functions in a bank branch including data communications with the bank's HQ, and as an accounting system for small businesses. For instance, if a company was doing payroll by hand, a small L-series would computerize that function. These systems were very successful and had little competition until the mini-computers came into the market. While the L-series was meant for the smaller applications, Burroughs also sold the B-series systems, such as the B700, B80, B800, etc., which they marketed as a "super mini" class of system designed to compete with mini-computers taking over a large share of the market from IBM.

The following picture shows a proud bunch of engineers (along with their pocket protectors) ready to tackle the world with their new mini-computer. The picture was taken (I believe) in the Burroughs facility located in Cumbernauld, Scotland.

Figure 20—Burroughs B80
(Courtesy of Chris Pickles and Ted Trakas; Ted is on the far right)

Another major innovation of Burroughs was the concept of having multiple CPUs acting as one computer system, with each CPU sharing the overall workload yet communicating to share data. Showing off this design was the D825, which was one of the first (if not the first) true multiprocessor computer ever developed. Multiprocessing systems would become the norm starting with the mini-computers in the early 1970s and continuing on to the present. The company also was heavily involved in the medium systems and mainframe sectors with its B1700 to B7700 and beyond. At its peak, Burroughs was the No. 2 computer company in the world.

After seeing years in decline in revenue growth from competition, Burroughs merged with Sperry Corporation (which also was seeing a similar decline in market share) in 1986. Their new, combined company was called Unisys, and to say that the computer industry was unimpressed would be an understatement. Both companies brought to the table competing operating systems, mainframe platforms, software products, and management styles that created havoc within the new company. By finally untangling competing products internally (but with a significant loss of its customer base), Unisys survived and still offers computer services and a line of small computers.

Busicom (aka Nippon Calculating Machine Corporation)

Was Busicom, a Japanese company, the true inventor of the commercial microprocessor instead of Intel? Some would definitely see it this way. At the very least, this company had significant input into microprocessor technology. This company bought the rights to the first microprocessor, the Intel 4004, which it created in partnership with Intel in 1970. Originally, Busicom made mechanical calculators, but quickly moved into the world of electronic calculators as technology changed around it.

Busicom did not envision itself as competing with the likes of IBM, Fujitsu, Hitachi, and others, yet it did have a significant impact on computing devices. In 1969, Busicom was enamored by the possibilities that miniaturization brought about through integrated circuits. It contacted Intel and asked them to design a set of integrated circuits (twelve to be exact) for a new line of programmable electronic calculators (Model 141-PF). Intel studied Busicom's design, and came up with an integrated circuit architecture closely based upon the 4004 microprocessor on which Intel was working. Intel's design used a mixture of three different integrated circuits containing ROM, special registers to store calculations, input/output ports, and RAM. In other words, whereas Busicom had specific programming ideas for this "thing" (it didn't have a name for it), Intel's engineers took Busicom's idea and made it better and more flexible for other programming instructions. Busicom's management agreed to Intel's new approach, and in 1971, Intel delivered chips with four integrated circuits to Busicom.

In mid-1971, Busicom had integrated the chip into its calculator, but the price of the calculator was too high to attract the quantity of customers needed. What to do? Decrease cost! Thus, Busicom asked Intel to lower its prices. Intel renegotiated the contract, but in so doing, Busicom made a strategic blunder—it gave up its exclusive rights to the chips. A few months later, on November 15, 1971, Intel announced the immediate commercially availability of the first microprocessor chipset family, the MCS-4 microcomputer instruction set (with a heavy influence from the Busicom design).

Figure 21—Busicom calculator (computer)

Because of the 1974 recession in Japan, Busicom became the first major Japanese calculator company to fail. Since it had signed away its rights to the Intel 4004 processor, it ended up with nothing to show for its innovative work in the microprocessor field. Looking back in speculation, the technology world would have changed dramatically if Busicom had started its own microprocessor development lab, or had not been so hard-nosed in its negotiations with Intel. If so, the world might have changed dramatically. Perhaps Tokyo would have become the "Silicon Valley."

Call Computer

Probably no more than a few people ever heard of this company, and one, Steve Wozniak (of Apple Computer fame), is certainly glad he walked away from it. Around 1974 (the actual date is lost to time), Call Computer was formed and owned and managed by Alex Kamradt. This company offered a time-sharing minicomputer. One of the people renting time from Kamradt was Wozniak. Wozniak was doing computer tinkering (e.g., trying to get programs to run) by using a TI Silent 700 or Teletype to dial in the host minicomputer, and the printout on thermal paper annoyed Wozniak.

Both of these dial-up systems by now had a microprocessor—which meant they themselves could be programmed to do smarter things. Plus, each had a keyboard and built-in communications hardware—things that meant he (Wozniak) would not have to figure out how to make work. Wozniak wanted to connect a CRT (monitor) to print out data instead of using the paper. Kamradt liked the idea presented to him by Wozniak and, with very little funding, Wozniak set about to make his idea a reality. The goal was to make these new hybrid machines, and then Kamradt would turn around and sell them to his customers.

Wozniak's new system was called the Computer Conversor. No photograph of Wozniak's creation could be found, but imagine the following two devices merged together—probably with the monitor physically sitting where the paper used to come out.

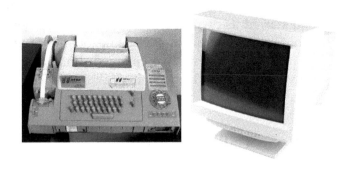

Figure 22—Teletype machine (with telephone capabilities) and a fairly generic CRT/computer monitor available in the mid-1970s

It is doubtful either one had a clear direction of where to take the Computer Conversor to market, although Kamradt did reportedly sell a few of them. With each sale, though, headaches arose—namely around support of the product. Wozniak was constantly tinkering and making modifications to the underlying hardware and firmware, so Wozniak's precious time (he was employed by HP at the time, and doing this work on the Computer Conversor was part-time) was not going to make a great new product, but rather was fixing what Kamradt had sold.

Wozniak and Kamradt decided to go their separate ways after only a few months. Wozniak eventually took his knowledge with him, and all of the features eventually made their way into the Apple II. Kamradt stayed in business for several more years, but time-sharing for processing data was over. Kamradt sold his company, and unfortunately, within a few years, was found murdered in Santa Cruz, California.

Centronics

Initially a division within Wang Laboratories (see Wang), in 1971, Centronics, based in Hudson, New Hampshire, was spun off as a separate company selling a specialized remote terminal for casinos and printers. One word summed up Centronics' dominance in the market, though: printers. It developed dot-matrix and line printers that were well respected throughout the computer industry. It also set many standards on how messages/commands were sent from a computer, and how a printer responded back with status messages. In other words, smarter printers were now the norm.

In 1970, before it became a separate company, the Centronics Model 101 was introduced. The print head was very creative in that by using a very tiny seven-wire solenoid impact system, they could cause the firing of little rods against a printer ribbon that then caused minute dots to represent a character. This was called "dot matrix" printing. The 101 was marketed as being able to print up to 165 characters per second.

Print heads and electronics (and final printer assemblies) were built in Centronics plants in New Hampshire, and Ireland manufactured the print heads, while other mechanisms were manufactured in Japan.

In 1975, Centronics teamed up with Tandy (see Tandy) and produced dot-matrix printers for Tandy to resell with its name.

Figure 23—Various Centronics dot-matrix printers

In 1978, the 6000 series "band" printers were introduced. This type of printer was unique in that it literally had a ribbon (or band) of all the usual characters used by computers at the time, which spun around and around in front of a ribbon. A microprocessor within the printer would keep track of where the band of characters were, and position the band where something needed to be printed. Sounds complicated, right? Yes, it was—lots of moving parts that could come out of adjustment. Still, it was a new idea, and it had some success for Centronics. By 1979, Centronics had original equipment manufacturer (OEM) contracts with other computer makers and revenues of over $100 million. The 1980s saw yet more printers, but Centronics experienced microprocessor programming errors (a nice name for "bugs"), which caused its printer sales to falter. Added to this was the competition from other printer makers, which affected Centronics' printer market share, and the fact that Centronics never could keep revenues ahead of costs.

Starting in 1982, Control Data Corporation (see Control Data Corporation) merged its printer division with Centronics and had enough investment to control Centronics, which it did until 1986. Then, CDC's financial interest in Centronics was acquired from them, and through legal maneuvering, Centronics was back in control of its company in 1987.

OEM partnerships and technology relationships were formed with other companies in the mid- to late 1980s, and revenues were steadily increasing. Unfortunately, more than one-third of its revenue (approximately $65 million) came from a partnership with IBM for Centronics to furnish the IBM 4214 printer. When IBM announced that it was discontinuing the 4214, Centronics suffered a serious financial blow.

Centronics also designed (and sold) printer interface connectors, which are still the standard today for many devices. In 1987, Centronics was bought by Genicom. In an odd company move, the execs of Centronics took the money from Genicom and purchased Ekco Housewares.

Chatitz

In 1970, this Rockville, Maryland, company introduced "Boris." Boris was a computer, but it only had one function: to play chess. What made Boris remarkable was that it talked to the user via a synthesizer. It came with an 8-bit Intel 8008 processor with its own power supply and 4K RAM. When it was turned on (via a console-mounted switch), it loaded instructions that accepted input from one of sixteen buttons. (Boris was self-contained in a 6.75-in. x 10-in. x 3.25-in. box.) It came with a separate chess board where a user had to move the actual pieces, and could visualize where Boris thought the pieces should be.

Figure 24—Boris

Obviously, it was limited in functionality and power, but it was a glimpse of the early ideas that were to come of what could be done with an Intel processor chip.

CII – (Compagnie Internationale pour l'informatique or International Company of Information)

To understand CII, one has to not only understand the computer climate in the 1960s (with France wanting to enter the nuclear age), but also any European country's overall sense of pride when an American company tried to dictate a country's future in the computer world. Companies such as IBM (along with a few others, namely UNIVAC and Control Data Corporation) were establishing footholds across France and other European countries, and if a French company wanted a computer, it had to pay whatever these big American companies wanted. From another perspective, the U.S. government was worried that France might use these high-speed computers to develop its own nuclear weapons—so computer sales were closely monitored, which more than likely irritated France even more.

To combat this heavy-handed attitude from the U.S., CII was created to pool both money and thinkers to figure out how to build France's own technology using integrated circuity technology. The French government, which was behind this movement, supplied funding for this venture. In return for this money, the government required a merger of three companies to form CII: 1) the European Society of Information Processing, 2) the European Company of Automatic Electronics (CAE), and 3) the Society of Electronics and Automation (SEA). Taking "French pride" one more step, the government also wanted to investigate building its own integrated circuits instead of relying on such American companies as Texas Instruments or Intel. In other words, France wanted to develop and market its own computers to stave off what it saw as the coming computer war. CII was an important part of that endeavor—and France, for better or worse, was now in the computer business.

CII did spur (and by some definitions, actually hamper) the growth of technology, but the bottom line is that it was trying to quickly figure out how to keep foreign companies from taking over the computer market in France. In the early days of CII (early 1960s), it ended up buying computers from American companies and renaming them (e.g., the Sigma 7 became the CII 10070, and the Sigma 2 became the CII 10020). In 1971, CII had its own models of a new generation of computers: the Mitra 15, the Iris 50, and the Iris 80 (with a true multi-tasking operating system). Code names were used internally, with the Mitra 15 known as the P1, the Iris 50 as the P2, and the Iris 80 known as the P3. CII was primarily installing its computers into universities and with the French military, and the requirements for these institutions required more than the simpler operating systems that were developed by other companies. CII, therefore, took the critical path of developing its own operating system.

The Mitra was a 16-bit minicomputer, and its marketing strategy was to be very modular in design so that it could adapt easily for what the customer needed (in terms of peripherals and software). The Mitra 15-20 was introduced in 1971. It was followed by the Mitra 15-21, the Mitra 15-35, and Mitra 125, the most powerful Mitra. The Mitra 125 supported bytes, words, double words, and byte strings as data types. Instructions could address sixty-four registers of 16 bits used as an accumulator, an accumulator extension, instruction counter, index, and base registers. Instruction operands could be addressed as immediate, indexed, and indirect. It supported thirty-two levels of interrupts, and the time it took to process an interrupt was measured from 3 microseconds up to 300 microseconds (the time variance depending upon the interrupt type).

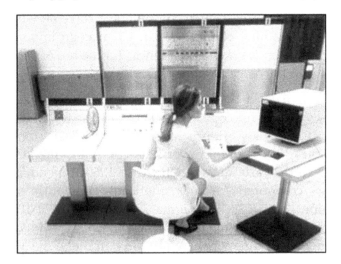

Figure 25—CII Iris 50

Optional features for the Mitra 125 included the following:
- Real-time clock
- Priority interrupts
- Floating-point arithmetic
- Continuous operation with 48V battery

The first Mitras were developed inside CII and code-named the "Gamme Q." Its memory technology was magnetic core (with an access time of 400 nanoseconds). The main cabinet supported up to 32K words and allowed for up to eighteen peripheral adapters. The control store used bipolar technology with capacity from 512 to 4096 words (each word being 16 bits). Bipolar technology registers had an access time of sixty nanoseconds (ns).

The Mitra 125's memory had an access time of 350 ns. It featured up to three micro-programmed I/O processors. The magnetic core memory was increased to 512K words, and included a memory protection at the word level. The number of registers was extended to 256 words. Up to sixteen Mitra 125s could be interconnected to other computers. The Mitras also supported myriad languages: COBOL 74, FORTRAN 66, FORTRAN 77, BASIC, QUERY, and LTR (a French-developed language for their defense agencies).

The Mitra was sold until 1980 by SEMS (which went on to develop more Mitra models, along with enhancements to the O/S). There also was a military version called Mitra 15M that was marketed by another company. A total of 7,929 Mitra systems were manufactured between 1971 and 1985, with the greatest majority of them being sold within France.

The Iris 50 minicomputer (announced March 21, 1971) had the following characteristics:

- 8-bit data
- Instruction set used 32-bit fixed-length instruction; addressing was relative to mod-64K segments (opposed to smaller mod-4K in S/360)
- Memory addressing limited to 256K on Iris 50 and 1024K on Iris 60
- Discs were fixed-length 256-byte sectors

The operating system was called Siris 2, and it supported a maximum of fourteen partitions (essentially fourteen spaces to run programs). Siris 2 was limited by its use of 16-bit system tables, and this was to be a major drawback as newer models were produced.

Also in 1971, CII started work on the Iris 60, along with a redesign of the Siris 2 O/S to use 32-bit tables. Keeping the concept of "partitions" in which to run jobs (which IBM had championed with its mainframe models), it developed a scheduler to run programs in priority order.

In 1972, though, more computer incest happened. CII signed an agreement with Unidata, and in the course of a few months the Siemens BS-2000 operating system was chosen to run the next generation of CII computers. With Iris 3 (P3) now scrapped from development, the witty software engineers and some marketing types simply renamed Iris 2 (P2) to Iris 3. Iris 3 was not compatible with the Iris 50 hardware, so two O/S versions had to be supported. It is confusing just to read — think about going to internal meetings and trying to figure out who was working on what!

The first Siris 3 O/S (with enhancements started before the Unidata agreement) was shipped in April 1973. At the end of 1974, both operating systems supported 100MB MD100 disk drives. The development of this O/S was managed by Jean Ichbiah, with Roger Briand responsible for the logic, and Claude Boulle for the actual programming.

Siris 2 was officially discontinued in February 1977. Siris 3, version 16 introduced support of shared discs between two systems (a significant leap in technology and programming skills), automatic recognition of new disks as they were added to the system, support of MD200 200MB discs, and the support of PENA-30 3200bpi tapes. The Iris 80 was now on the market, and it ran the Siris 3 O/S.

Two CII software engineers (Gerard Deloche and Michel Elie) had been lucky enough to work on the original

Advanced Research Projects Agency Network (ARPANET)[31] project while at UCLA in California in 1968. With this knowledge, they returned to CII and began work on their own version of how to connect computers together—not only within one family of products, but also different manufacturers. The result of the work was a success. Their new O/S was very unique in that it was the first operating environment capable of networking disparate computers to exchange data. The CII initially called this networking software Transiris. Eventually it became known by the catchy name of Distributed System Architecture (aka "DSA-ISO"), and was recognized in 1978 by the international bodies to form the new Open Systems Interconnection (OSI) model for data exchange (today known as the internet).

The CII also developed the ADA and SFER programming languages. Continuing to show its software expertise, in November 1973, it showed off its product capable of linking multiple computer systems together (two Mitra 15 machines in Paris, and one IBM 360 located in Grenoble, Switzerland); it called this product Cyclades.[32] In 1975, the CII successfully linked twenty-five disparate computers together between Rome, London, Paris, and Grenoble— their "internet" worked.

CII was certainly coming out with innovative ideas; however, it was being thought of as more of an engineering consortium than knowing how to market products in a business world. In other words, CII had a cash flow problem. The new French government, under President Giscard d'Estaing, decided it was tired of bailing out CII. On May 20, 1975, the merger of CII and Honeywell-Bull was finalized, and CII disappeared—but

---

[31] ARPANET is defined as a precursor to the internet that we know and love today. In reality, it connected a number of military computers together with a proprietary protocol and enabled users to send email back and forth. Still, this is basically what the internet is—except that any "proprietary" protocol is now "public" knowledge.

[32] They had started work on this in 1968.

not before laying some great foundations and raising the bar for computer systems to communicate with each other and sharing data.

Cincinnati Milling Machine Company

If there is one axiom in business that should be followed, it is "do what you do best." The Cincinnati Milling Machine Company (Cincinnati) of Lebanon, Ohio, was a manufacturer of electronics for control purposes. Think of devices that control, for instance, a gate to open or close when a certain event happens. Before the microprocessor, controlling anything was relegated to some type of mechanical trigger. The microprocessor changed that.

Picture going to a grocery in 1960. You take your item to the check-out person, some buttons were pushed on a cash-register looking machine, and your purchase was recorded. Move to today. You take your item to a check-out lane, you scan your item, and basically you are done. Microprocesses could do process control functions (e.g., run conveyor belts, monitor temperatures, etc.).

Most companies like Cincinnati bought a computer to do its process control work, but the company decided that since it made the electronic components anyway, why not take the next logical step and develop its own process control computer? In 1970, that's what Cincinnati did by introducing its CIP/2000 system. Its marketing claim was that its system was fast, reliable, and had a unique architecture, and since it embedded control right in the chip's (firmware), it was then five to ten times faster than other computers using software.

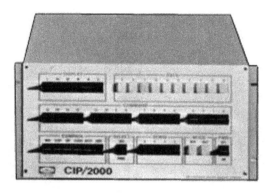

Figure 26—Cincinnati CIP/2000

The CIP/2000 was packaged similar to a Digital PDP/8 system, with myriad toggle switches and a panel of lights across the face. It was made to slide into a rack type of structure. Unfortunately for this company, although its system promised good performance and a good design, either because of bad marketing or from competition from bigger names in process control systems, the CIP/2000 never achieved much market share.

Most of this company was sold to a company named Unova, but a subsidiary in India still has the rights to some of the original products.

Cogar Corporation

George R. Cogar founded Cogar Corporation in 1974 after leaving Mohawk Data Sciences (MDS) Corporation, which he co-founded. Cogar had an interesting career, including as the head of the UNIVAC 1004 electronic design team. Using his technical skills and entrepreneur thinking, MDS was a success mainly because of Cogar's invention of the data recorder magnetic tape encoder (a fancy word meaning "writing") which eliminated the need for key-punches and punched cards by directly encoding data onto tape. Pause here and let this sink in. IBM had set the standard for collecting data with punched cards with little holes in them, and in so doing, it and other large computer makers had built an incredible business involving key-punch machines, card sorters, and card readers. Because of new ideas like Cogar's, IBM's world was about to change.

At his new company, Cogar also developed what he called the intelligent terminal.[33] This computer used the Motorola processor chip, had a built-in 5-inch character monitor, keyboard, and a floppy disk drive (similar to that which Apple would use a few years later). He called this computer the Cogar C4 (also known as the Cogar 4). The basic configuration had only 4K RAM, but it could be expanded to 16K. The system could be programmed using the Cogar Language Base, which was proprietary to Cogar. Users could connect directly to a remote host system (e.g., IBM mainframe), or could key data, have it stored locally, and later batch it to a remote host system. A printer, more disks, and more tape drives could be added. Nice options that Cogar offered were two business applications: data entry and general ledger.

The Cogar 4 system was very well designed, but for some reason lost to history, sales were dismal to say the least. In 1975, his company was acquired by Singer Business Machines (a division of Singer). They renamed the computer the Singer 1500. When International Computers Limited bought the Singer computer division in 1976, it renamed the computer once again—naming it the ICL 1500.

---

[33] Although he claimed this was the precursor to the world's first PC, his claim could easily be argued by many more—especially by such companies as Sycor.

Figure 27—Cogar 4

Cogar, a holder or co-holder of many engineering patents, and was a brilliant computer designer by any standard. Unfortunately, he seemed to be yet another engineer who didn't know how to run a successful business (of which there are many examples in this book). Not much was written about Cogar until September 2, 1983; that is when his plane went down somewhere in British Columbia, Canada. He was fifty-one years old, and his plane's wreckage has yet to be found.

COMPAT

In 1970, this company introduced the COMPAT 88-23 Batch Data Terminal and the ComFile Random Access Magnetic Tape Magazine. The overall purpose of the COMPAT 88-23 was to allow an operator to custom-build a data-entry screen and key in data, and whenever he/she wanted, cause the stored data to be sent via a dial-up connection to a host system. The system also could receive data from a host system.

The COMPAT 88-23 was programmable, and allowed for easy modifications of fields to reduce keying errors. It consisted of a keyboard with twelve programmable function keys and a CRT. The language used for programming this machine was called ComEnt Data Entry System. As data was keyed, it was stored on its magnetic tape product, which allowed random access. It had an internal modem that could transmit up to 2,000 baud.

The ComFile Random Access Magnetic Tape Magazine organized data into blocks. These blocks could be found through an index, and the records in the blocks retrieved individually once the block was read into memory. Each tape could store up to 64K.

Computer Devices, Inc.

In the early 1970s, the wonderful flat displays of today in laptops, cell phones, and tablets simply didn't exist. Instead, manufacturers either had TV-like CRT displays, or none at all—which is what this company opted to do. Computer Devices had two products: the CDI 930 and CDI 1030.

This company, located in Burlington, Massachusetts, wanted to market a portable data entry terminal, but thought a CRT display would be hard to package along with a keyboard—and keep the weight reasonable. (Although IBM, Olivetti, and others finally figured this in the late 1970s.) The CDI 930 was a typewriter-type device in a nice, sleek, enclosed case, and it used a 100-ft. x 8.5-in. roll of thermal paper for printing what was returned from a host system and to show the user what he/she was typing. It had a built-in modem that could transmit up to 300 baud, and it also had connectors for RS-232C (both serial and parallel capable). It weighed twenty-two pounds, and was 14 in. x 19 in. x 5.5 in.

CDI's marketing stressed the quietness of its device compared to similar terminals with a built-in printer. There was a very small market for these machines, but what small market it had disappeared when its competitors started selling terminals with monitors attached. I could find no specifications on the CDI 1030, but one can assume that it was a successor to the CDI 930 and probably had a faster modem.

Computer Display Systems

In 1972, simple character displays (like the words in this sentence) were the standard for most computers. Like a few others, this company saw a need for graphics processing (not just in displaying, but also editing and storing of the graphics).

Computer Display Systems developed the 6500 Graphic Display System targeting investment analysts (stock brokers), computer-aided design (we now know as CAD), hospital systems (e.g., heart monitoring), process control displays of graphs, business graphics (again, more graphs), and instruction where symbols are needed (e.g., geometry). With the 6500, one could either have a dedicated communications line or a modem to connect to another computer. Other products offered were the 6600 Television Display System, 6612 Display Monitor, 6611 Display Keyboard, 6648 Electrostatic Printer (which printed exact images that were being displayed), and the 6514 Trackball.

The 6500 Graphic Display System itself could support sixteen or thirty-two terminals, up to four trackballs, a printer, a disc controller and magnetic disk storage, and even a video camera interface.

It is worth noting more about the 6514 trackball. While not the mouse we think of today, this device did basically the same functions—except that the trackball was stationary, whereas a mouse moves around. The trackball allowed one to position the cursor in an exact spot on the display. (It also could be programmed to move to a certain location.) The dimensions of the trackball were approximately 6 in. wide, 8 in. long, and about 3 in. high with a sloped front. The ball was cradled on the top, and one controlled the movement of it by rolling it around. Think of a mouse turned upside down, and you get the idea of how it worked.

This company was based in Sunnyvale, California, and I could find no more history of this company past 1972.

Computer Machinery Corporation

As it is with several companies that came and went in the early to mid-1970s, not a lot of information is available about them. This company was based in Los Angeles, California, and manufactured and marketed a data-entry terminal that did not use magnetic tape storage (which was becoming the norm for many similar companies in this same market). CMC recognized that card readers (and cards themselves) were a dead technology, but the company also saw tape storage (either cassette or reel) as awkward for data entry and retrieval.

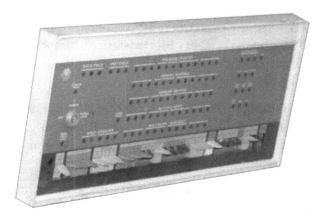

Figure 28—Computer Machinery Corporation terminal (front plate only)

Its product was marketed as a data-entry terminal that allowed connectivity to a host system, thereby bypassing the need to store data locally. Unfortunately for this company, many other companies also were competing in this market, and its competitors had more features for their systems. Whether because of lack of marketing or better competing products (or both), CMC's product never grabbed a foothold to sustain it as a profitable company.

Computer Operations Incorporated

Based in the southern California town of Costa Mesa, in 1970 this company produced a timesharing[34] system called Gemini. Unfortunately, the world was on the downward slope of the timesharing curve. Companies were starting to figure out that they didn't have to pay for a service bureau to process their data or run their applications when they could buy their own minicomputer to do the same thing faster and at less cost.

As with other small companies that simply disappeared, I could find no more references to this company after 1970.

Commodore Business Machines

The original company was started as Commodore Business Machines, Inc. (CBM) in 1954, in Toronto, Canada, by a very unique individual named Jack Tramiel. Tramiel came to America as an immigrant from Poland (and as an Auschwitz survivor). His first job was repairing typewriters and within a short while had signed a contract with a Czechoslovakian company to manufacture its typewriters. Lost to history is how and why he made his

---

[34] Timesharing systems did exactly as the name implies—they shared computer time. A company would buy a mainframe computer, establish communications connectivity to it (either through dial-up phone lines or expensive and dedicated circuits—or both), and sell (and invoice) the time that a person/company used on the computer.

way to Canada, but off Tramiel went to Toronto to start his new business venture. Competition in the mid-1950s came at a bad time for Tramiel, as Japanese typewriter imports put most North American typewriter companies out of business. Tramiel, always the entrepreneur, turned to making and selling manual adding machines. CBM was making a profit and growing, and in 1962, it went public on the New York Stock Exchange (NYSE).

Turning to the Japanese for a moment, after WWII they had an uncanny knack for finding markets and making products cheaper than were currently being sold. In the late 1960s, Japan started producing and exporting adding machines. CBM's main investor, Irving Gould, suggested that Tramiel travel to Japan and learn how to compete with these lesser-priced machines. Tramiel made the journey, but instead of returning with manufacturing ideas, he returned with an idea to produce electronic calculators (which were just coming into the market both in the U.S. and Japan).

CBM geared up production for a new electronic calculator line — including one with scientific functions (which is something we take for granted today, but at that time this was a superior feature). After CBM's typewriter sales had tapered off, CBM was soon very profitable again through calculator sales. In 1975, one of CBM's main suppliers, Texas Instruments, entered the calculator market directly and put out a line of machines priced at less than CBM's. CBM needed to cut costs and saw that a relationship with Texas Instruments did not make good business sense. So, in 1976, CBM bought MOS Technology, Inc. so it could ensure the supply of parts it needed.

Through the 1970s, CBM was starting to dabble in the small-computer market, and one of its first non-adding-machine consumer products (released in 1978) was a chess game called "Chessmate."

A smart man knows when to listen to others, and his engineering manager convinced Tramiel that calculators were dead as a product. Instead, the manager insisted that CBM should find out more about a trend called "home computers." In 1977, CBM had borrowed from Tramiel's earlier days of carting around portable typewriters, and came out with the Commodore Personal Electronic Transactor (PET). The PET had a full-travel QWERTY keyboard, 9-inch monochrome monitor, and tape recorder for program and data storage.

It had a 1 MHz processor with 8K RAM. The ROM was 14K, where an 8K BASIC interpreter resided. On the surface this might seem like a great and creative idea for this memory design, but unfortunately, the actual compiler/interpreter had some bugs and made programming a challenge. For example, its attempt at writing its own BASIC complier had some bugs such as: "10 IF F OR I=5, GOTO 20" caused a compiler error because "F OR" was interpreted as "FOR." Aside from the programming errors, which one can assume were eventually fixed, from this point forward, CBM would no longer be considered a maker of typewriters or adding machines, but rather as a true computer company.

In 1976, CBM reorganized into Commodore International Ltd., with its financial headquarters based in the Bahamas. Its base of operations, though, was West Chester, Pennsylvania, near the MOS Technology site. The operational headquarters retained the name Commodore Business Machines, Inc.

The PET computer line had a tough, all-metal case, and because of this, found a good customer in schools. CBM offered incentives for more schools to buy with marketing promotions like "buy 2, get 1 free." The company even ran ads promoting its machines as the "Teacher's PET." While it was a solid computer, it did not compete well in the home because its graphics and sound were not as good as other PCs coming into the market. CBM rode its PET wave until the early 1980s when it finally released its next generation. CBM would go on to market the VIC-20 PC for only $299; and thus became the first company to sell a million PCs.

Figure 29—Commodore PET

The Commodore 64 also was successfully introduced later. Then, competition came around once more. Texas Instruments, which had "deep pockets" (meaning lots of money), started a price war that took all PC makers by storm. To CBM's credit, it responded beautifully to this pricing challenge, and ended up selling close to twenty-two million PCs over the life of its products. CBM eventually cracked the $1 billion mark in sales in 1983.

In January 1984, Tramiel resigned due to intense disagreement with the chairman of the board and his investor friend, Irving Gould. Tramiel founded a new company, Tramiel Technology. For the next decade, Tramiel would compete head-on with CBM for computer business through acquisitions, price wars, and all-around good marketing by all parties.

By the late 1980s, the personal computer market had become dominated by the IBM PC and Apple Macintosh platforms. CBM was having trouble competing in quality and price, and therefore had an eroding customer base. Additionally, *The Philadelphia Inquirer's* "Top 100

Businesses" annual listing showed several CBM executives among the highest paid in the region — which didn't help its public and investor relations. CBM lost some focus on the computer industry as it tried to tackle the TV and gaming markets — both receiving unflattering press. Still, in 1990, it came out with the Amiga product line of PCs, but this machine was perceived as a "ho-hum" by the business world, and it never gained traction for the number of sales needed to sustain it.

In the early 1990s, all servicing and warranty repairs were outsourced to Wang Laboratories. By 1994, only CBM's operations in Germany and the UK were still profitable. CBM declared bankruptcy on April 29, 1994, and its assets were liquidated.

An interesting follow-up from *Byte* magazine, August 1994: "Commodore 's high point was the Amiga 1000 (1985). The Amiga was so far ahead of its time that almost nobody, including CBM's marketing department, could fully articulate what it was all about. Today, it's obvious that the Amiga was the first multimedia computer, but in those days, it was derided as a game machine because few people grasped the importance of advanced graphics, sound, and video. Nine years later, vendors were still struggling to make systems that worked like 1985 Amigas." Shame on CBM's management.

In September 1997, the Commodore brand name was acquired by Dutch computer maker Tulip Computers NV. In July 2004, Tulip announced a new series of products using the Commodore name. It also licensed the Commodore trademark and logo to the producers of a product called the C64 DTV. In late 2004, Tulip squeezed the last money it could from its original purchase of Commodore by selling the Commodore trademarks to Yeahronimo Media Ventures for €22 million.

Comshare Inc.

Incorporated in 1966 as Com-share in Ann Arbor, Michigan, somewhere lost to history is how the name morphed into simply Comshare in the late 60s — but it did, and that is what it became known as.

The University of Michigan had (and still does today) an excellent computer department in the 1960s. It had several mainframe computers on campus, but with the exception of only a few individuals who could actually touch them, if a student programmer wanted access to them, then he/she had to go to a computer lab and access one of the mainframes in a "timesharing" manner. (Basically, a student would key-punch his/her cards, and then have them read in at a special computer lab terminal — and then await the results of the compilation or testing. Believe it or not, for any company that wanted their own computer access but could not afford it, this was the norm for those companies in the U.S.)

Six students working in the University's lab came up with a business plan that would involve them buying their own mainframe and selling time (timesharing) to any subscriber. Comshare was thus born from practical experience and knowledge of how to set up a timesharing system.

Two miles south of the university in an office building also holding another startup called Sycor, Inc., Comshare started business. (See Sycor section.) Its mainframe machine of choice was the Sigma 7 from Scientific Data Systems (later bought by Xerox). Comshare became well known in the timesharing field as an excellent provider of access to a shared mainframe, and for their accurate job accounting software called "Commander II" (billing for actual time spent using the Sigma systems). The Sigmas came with the Berkeley Timesharing System that was developed at the University of California, Berkeley.

Comshare flourished for over a decade as one of the leaders in timesharing services — and then the mini-computer came into the market. What the mini-computer did was allow small and medium-sized companies for the first time to own their computer, thereby cutting the need to share a mainframe like Comshare was providing. Comshare knew it had smart engineers with expertise in the scientific area, so the company smartly, in a controlled manner, changed its business model to offer specialized software for scientific analysis. Once it established a base of customers to supply Comshare a stream of revenue, it knew it was on to something — so other specialized software sharing and analytics were offered for areas such as human resources, CPAs, trust services for banks, and telephone companies' billing and data-mining.

Comshare saw wild swings in the stock from $60 down to $2. Comshare never made what some would consider a lot of money (one of its highest revenue years amounted to around $13M), but it maintained a small staff and kept expenses low, thereby having net earnings around $1M a year. To Comshare's credit, it tried to change with the time, but in the end, businesses were doing more themselves and needed a "shared" computer and software less and less.

Around 1999, Comshare (the public company) went out of business. In 2006, a private company by that same name at the same old Comshare address was in business, but it is unclear what this company was selling. When contact was attempted, the last known number for the company was found to be disconnected.

Consolidated Computer

In 1970, this Waltham, Massachusetts, company sold a "data preparation" product called KEY-EDIT.[35] This product consisted of an odd configuration where data-entry people had to sit side by side because of the way the data entry stations were physically connected to the central processing unit.

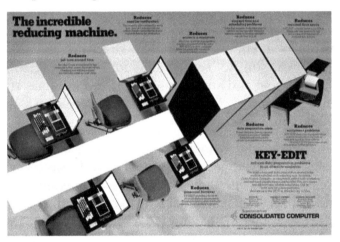

*Figure 30—Consolidated Computer's KEY-EDIT
data preparation product*

There were four data-entry stations, a CPU, and a Teletype keyboard/printer attached. It had built-in disk storage and a modem for host communication. The data-entry stations consisted of a typical alphabetic keyboard, extra programmable function keys, no numeric keypad, and no visual display like a CRT or even a printer. With a lack of competitive features, it is hard to fathom what the company and engineers were thinking, and it isn't hard to understand why the system never grabbed market share.

---

[35] Key edit means exactly that—data could be keyed and changes made to it if errors were found. This was a totally different way of processing data from punched-cards where there was no editing available. The point behind "key edit" was to save time and money for making any corrections to the data before it was sent off for processing.

Consolidated Computer Industries, Inc.

This Toronto, Canada, company was formed in 1970 by Mers Kutt (who, showing his acumen for understanding technology, went on to form two other computer companies within a few years of this one). Consolidated Computer Industries, Inc. (CCI) (not to be confused with the company Consolidated Computer) developed a data-entry system called the Key-Edit[36]. Key-Edit was a very low-cost terminal with a single-line display that was intended to address a need of being able to view on a screen what was being typed in. Up until this time, programmers had to key-punch their programs onto punched cards, and if a card was punched incorrectly, then the whole card had to be thrown away and a new one started. In a "Key-Edit" environment, if a wrong character was typed, the user simply had to backspace and correct it — thereby saving immense time (and thus money).

Although the Key-Edit was a slick idea for its time, it lacked an important feature — namely, after information was keyed in, what to do with it? Kutt at first assumed that some sort of communication link would be available to a central computer, thereby all one had to do was to "send" the data somehow (he hadn't really thought through this part of his new invention). In the real-world, though, sometimes the communication link was not available. Kutt then designed a way to capture and hold the keyed data locally — the "Key-Cassette" concept was born where data was stored on a cassette. Once the data was there, the information could be safely kept and/or transferred at any time to a central computer for work.

Engineers should never be marketing people (and vice versa, of course), as was shown in this case. Kutt wanted his Key-Edit computer to look like a calculator as much as

---

[36] This term, Key-Edit, became synonymous to with users being able to key in data and edit it—sort of like "Kleenex" is associated with the generic term "tissue." Not to be confused with the actual product called "KEY-EDIT" made by Consolidated Computer.

possible because he thought users were used to seeing a calculator instead of some new-fangled computer thing. Kutt's notes of the era state his company should "Try and use [an] existing calculator cover, display, modify power supply, and replace [the] keyboard." The replacement keyboard was a small odd model with thirty-two keys (not a full typewriter layout); each key was used to enter up to five different characters (a very complicated way to enter data). The display consisted of either thirteen or fifteen segmented LEDs. In 1978, CCI was out of business—still, one has to give Kutt points for creativity and seeding ideas for others.[37]

Control Data Corporation

Control Data Corporation (CDC) was a relative newcomer to the world of computers in 1957, but it had a tremendous impact by driving companies to build faster systems. CDC came into being through a series of events, mergers, and take-overs.

WWII had brought to the Washington, D.C., area teams of computer experts, mathematicians, and other "thinkers" to try and break codes used by Japan and Germany. It can be debated as to whether this team had much success (especially compared the brilliance shown by the folks at Bletchley Park in the UK), but the U.S. team had been formed of incredibly talented individuals. After the war, the U.S. Navy wanted to keep this group together to tackle the new threats it saw coming from communism—but how to do it?

Enter the owner of an aircraft company located in St. Paul, Minnesota, that was shutting down thanks to WWII

---

[37] Steve Wozniak (from Apple fame) bragged that in 1975 he was the first person to show a microprocessor system take a character typed in and have it show up on a monitor. Technically, Wozniak might be right if he defines a monitor as a CRT, but Kutt (and others) were doing something similar to this at least three years before Wozniak.

coming to a close (and thus its government contracts coming to an end). Through some arm-twisting and money from the government, the almost-out-of-business aircraft company found itself hiring a team of talented people from those about to be out of job in Washington, D.C. A new company, Engineering Research Associates (ERA), was formed soon thereafter (the name was chosen to better describe its work with research rather than with aircraft work). Out of this group came one of the first commercial computers that stored programs, the 36-bit ERA 1103. Because of the government's investment in this computer system, the U.S. Navy claimed ownership. Long and expensive legal battles ensured, and in 1952, ERA was sold to Remington Rand.

One of ERA's inventions was what was called magnetic drum technology,[38] and Remington Rand wanted it for its own computer line. (Computer incest alert: Rand soon merged with Sperry Corporation, which became Sperry Rand. The ERA division was then merged into Sperry's UNIVAC division, and Sperry/UNIVAC eventually merged with Burroughs, which then became Unisys.)

The ERA group continued to tinker on its own, and the proverbial excrement hit the fan when Sperry decided to move the UNIVAC II project to the ERA team instead of leaving it with the Sperry team who had developed the UNIVAC I. Infighting ensued between departments, and basically the ERA team decided it had had enough of working for a large corporation. So, in 1957, the ERA team left to form Control Data Corporation. The team moved its office to an old warehouse across the river from Sperry's St. Paul, Minnesota, laboratory. The ERA guys needed a leader, and William Norris was named CEO, with Seymour Cray named the chief designer. (Legally and

---

[38] For those accustomed to thinking of a disk drive in your PC as this little two-inch platter holding 1GB of storage, a magnetic drum was a vertical cylinder about 18 inches in diameter and about three feet tall. It had read/write heads (which had to almost constantly be monitored for clearance) stationed all over the device, and it held approximately 256K of data. We have certainly come a long way since then.

technically speaking, Cray was still wrapping up a project for Sperry and didn't join officially until a year after CDC was formed.)

CDC focused on its drum storage to support its business, but when Cray started to work at CDC, he had other ideas. Cray was an inventor's inventor—he liked to tinker with things and had a wealth of ideas he couldn't wait to bring to the world. Think of him as an older Steve Wozniak of Apple fame, but instead of tinkering with microprocessors and keyboards like Wozniak, Cray had big processors and all kinds of peripheral equipment to play with. Cray immediately built a small transistor-based 6-bit machine known as the "CDC Little Character"; this was a prototype of what he envisioned a larger transistor-based computer could be.

In 1959, CDC released a 48-bit transistorized version of the UNIVAC 1103, which CDC named the CDC 1604. (Either by coincidence or planning, the product number came about by adding the CDC street address "501" to the model number of the UNIVAC 1103). The 1960s brought more innovation, with Cray hell-bent on making the world's fastest (or in the vernacular of the day, the "largest") computer, and his ego and determination went on to make him a legend in the computer field. [39]

---

[39] Cray insisted on his own lab away from CDC—in fact, it had to be in his home town in Wisconsin, and no one, not even the CEO of CDC, could visit without an invitation. He insisted on these and other demands; otherwise, he said he would quit. CDC relented many times to Cray's quirky demands.

Figure 31—Control Data 1604

Cray and the head of CDC had an overly ambitious business desire to put the dominant player, IBM, out of business. They were touting that their product would be 10 percent faster than IBM's product and cost 10 percent less. As they would learn at great cost, IBM had its own marketing and development going on to counter any competition from CDC.[40]

In the late '60s and early '70s, CDC card punch and reader products followed, along with a line of printers. CDC, though was playing a "follow-me" game as far as it was concerned when trying to compete with IBM. CDC wanted to innovate, and was intrigued with a product from Rabinow Engineering that might leap it over IBM. Rabinow's product was called optical character recognition (OCR), which basically scanned a typewritten page and put it into digital form stored on a magnetic disk. CDC saw a tremendous opportunity for this technology, but it never caught on in the '70s. In 1976, after losing money on the investment, CDC shut down the Rabinow business. It ended up walking away from OCR

---

[40] In a (now looked upon) humorous attempt to compete with CDC, IBM announced to the world a new product, which was faster and cheaper than anything CDC had. The bad news to the world was that the machine didn't exist—it was a marketing ploy to stop CDC sales. CDC sued IBM and settled for $80M from IBM. The computer industry had just learned a valuable lesson that still echoes throughout the industry today—you can't announce a product that doesn't exist.

(and a lot of business when this idea caught on in the 1980s!). Through some odd business analysis, CDC thought that card processing was still a powerhouse market in which to contend, so it sought out companies with faster card processing machines, and more acquisitions and joint ventures followed. To coin the old adage, it would become one of the last great buggy-whip makers; punch-card processing, as most other computer companies were realizing, was in the process of being replaced by other technologies—and CDC lost a lot of money not realizing this sooner.

Another business in which CDC found itself was that of a "service bureau,"[41] which was a way of providing a computer service for those companies too small to afford their own computer system. In parallel to this, Cray was continuing his work on yet faster and more powerful computers. Additionally, other software development and specialized compilers were in the works at CDC, as well as improvements to its magnetic disk storage devices.

Faster and more powerful computers did emerge from Cray's work throughout the '60s, and this brings us to the 1970s where the STAR-100 and Cyber series made their debut. Jim Thorton led the development on the former using a new processor design called "vectoring."[42]

In 1972, CDC didn't have funds for (or didn't want to fund) two computer ideas: 1) computers for speed only, and 2) computers for the more commercial, business side

---

[41] A service bureau was an interesting business model. Whereas timesharing sold computer time on their mainframe computer, a service bureau would physically pick up/store/deliver punched cards/reports in addition to running the computer jobs on their computer. This service was perfect for those small companies who wanted to automate, but didn't want to go to the cost of buying their own computer.

[42] Imagine you're cooking hamburgers at McDonalds. Now, picture servicing one customer completely before even taking the order from another—and then starting and finishing that order before you get around to asking the new customer what she or he wants? Now, imagine if there were buns all lined up ready to slap on a hamburger as the orders came in. That's basically what vectoring is—it's having operating system instructions ready to go as the one currently being worked on finishes; it speeds up processing speed immensely.

of the market. Cray understood the dilemma, and so he opted to pack up and leave—taking a few key engineers with him. Cray knew there must be a market for fast computers, so that was his concentration from then on. His ego intact, Cray started his new company as Cray Research. CDC, though, was still a believer in Cray, and even an investor in Cray's company. With Cray gone, however, CDC concentrated on the STAR computer—and in 1974, it was marketed as the Cyber 203. CDC should have listened to Cray at least a little bit, or at least had its remaining engineers pay more attention. While the STAR system performed well enough in the lab, when it was sold and customers wanted to do a lot of business "stuff" on it (e.g., payroll, inventory control, etc.), it performed in a less than stellar fashion. In fact, it was so bad that Thorton acknowledged his defeat and left CDC.

Thorton went on to form Network Systems Corporation. CDC decided to repackage its older 6600/7600 systems under the Cyber product name, and with some price adjustments and a mixture of some of the new vectoring methodology for the processor, CDC made this its main product. The Cyber 205, for instance, had much better performance than the original Cyber system. In the meantime, Cray was using the same architecture as the STAR processor, but was achieving better speed. Cray Research was now marketing its own product called (ego drumroll please) the Cray-1.

Figure 32—CDC Cyber 70 Series

Sales of the STAR were weak, but the Cyber 200/205 gave Cray Research some competition. CDC still had excellent engineers on staff, and it embarked on custom/special projects for its clients. CDC produced what it called the Advanced Flexible Processor (AFP), which allowed it to be very creatively configured for strictly high-computational work or more general business work; this system was marketed as the CYBER PLUS system.

In addition to its computer work, CDC still had a division concentrating on building magnetic disks and tapes. In the mid-1970s, CDC was considered the world leader in this technology. In fact, in 1979, CDC celebrated the production of one million disks and three million magnetic tapes. This line of business provided substantial revenue to CDC overall. Also, CDC had been marketing a successful plant control computer; while it never sold a lot of these computers, it still represented a profitable arm of the company.

The end of the '70s drew to a close with competition coming from several other companies such as Tandem Computers, DEC, IBM, and others. CDC continued to produce new computer lines, as well improve its magnetic disk technology.

CDC decided to attack the high-speed computing market once more in '80s, and had some success by at least once claiming the world's fastest computer—even faster than the Cray products. By the mid-'80s, though, CDC was hemorrhaging money. It sold off divisions, and in the late '80s withdrew from the computer market completely.

By the late 1980s, CDC was still in need of money and sold off its plant control product line. With little left to manage and sell off, CDC concentrated on the service business and became known as the Ceridian Corporation. Ceridian continues today as a successful outsourcing IT company focusing on human resources. [43]

Courier Terminal Systems, Inc.

Based in Phoenix, Arizona, Courier produced the Executerm 60 terminal and the multi-station adapter (MSA), which enabled Executerm terminals to be clustered.

---

[43] As for Cray, he put up a valiant effort to produce a marketable, extremely fast computer. Unfortunately, as with a number of companies that were started by bright engineers, his lack of overall business acumen got in the way of making money. He never understood competition. His Cray-2 computer had mediocre success, and the Cray-3 found only a few buyers, yet he went ahead and marketed the Cray-4; it never found any buyers. Massive parallel computers, such as those coming from Tandem Computers, appealed to the business world (and at a cheaper price), and Cray could not understand why he was losing out in the market. Cray ran out of money and filed for Chapter 11 bankruptcy March 24, 1995. In February 1996, Cray Research managed a merger (actually a take-over) with Silicon Graphics, Inc. In 1999, that company then created a separate Cray Research business unit to focus exclusively on high-end supercomputing. Eventually, all assets of this business unit were sold to a Seattle, Washington, company named Tera Computer Company. In an odd twist of irony, Tera renamed the company Cray, Inc.

Figure 33—Executerm 60

The Executerm 60 had the following characteristics:

- 2265 and 2260 protocol (an IBM terminal protocol that was a precursor the later IBM 3270)
- Could be clustered with other Executerm 60s by using the MSA
- Could display either 240 characters (6 lines x 40 characters) or 480 characters (12 rows x 40 characters)
- Used a 7 x 8 dot-matrix for character displays
- Had a typical keyboard layout, numeric keypad, and toggles where one could alter the display, brightness, and communications protocol
-

CPS, Inc.

Based in Sunnyvale, California, this company produced and sold the Model 8001 color CRT monitor. Except for gaming systems, most terminals tied to a minicomputer could display only one color — it might be white, green, or amber, but usually only one of those. Minicomputer companies, though, were always looking for something to set its systems apart from others, and if it could offer something like a terminal with its system to allow different colors for data fields, then this would be a nice option to help clinch a deal.

The Model 8001 was sold as an OEM product to any minicomputer maker. It could display basic graphics (along with character displays) in red, orange, yellow, and green. The screen measured 21 inches diagonally.

Creative Strategies, Inc.

Creative Strategies (formed in 1969 in Palo Alto, California) provided marketing research (e.g., forecast estimates, where technology might be headed, etc.) to computer companies. Some companies during the 1970s threw caution to the wind and entered the market with little planning and sales forecasting other than what would fit on the back of a napkin. Creative Strategies was formed to help companies that wanted a more thorough understanding of the market, and needed help staying on the track to profitability.

As this book has documented, many companies (manufacturers of printers, semi-conductors, tape drives, magnetic disks, etc.) were coming into the minicomputer arena with a computer system or a "smart" peripheral that a minicomputer (or mainframe such as IBM, for that matter) needed. While not manufacturing or marketing computer products themselves, companies such as Creative Strategies provided focus for those who trying to enter the computer market. They served (and still serve) a critical function to those that would listen to them during the tumultuous 1970s computer era, and it is for this reason I chose to include them in this book.

Creative Strategies is still in business today, focusing on helping customers with strategic business planning.

Cromemco

Yet another Silicon Valley computer business, Cromemco was located in Mountain View, California, and was founded in 1974 after years of planning and asking "Do you think we can make this work as a company?" The exchange of ideas was between Dr. Roger Melen and Dr. Harry Garland, who finally got enough funding to kick off their idea to make a small, affordable computer.

Seeing the potential of Altair's MITS computer[44] being used for practical purposes instead of a "novelty" for hobbyists to play with, Cromemco developed a color video interface called the Dazzler. Next came an interface for a camera (and a camera itself) to be connected to the MITS. The camera was marketed as a device that could be used for process control, digital recognition, and other "industrial" use. Basically, these guys were on the leading edge of coming up with solid business uses for a microprocessor-based small computer system.

Other products followed, such as an 8K PROM board, 16K RAM board, seven-channel analog interface board, a gaming joy-stick, and a video interface board for connecting a standard TV to a MITS computer system (and later an IMSAI computer system). In 1976, it put its board-building expertise into creating its own microprocessor-based computer called the Cromemco Z-1.

Figure 34—Cromemco Z-1, Z-2, and Z-3

[44] Showing the dynamics of being located in the Silicon Valley where ideas fed off of other ideas close by, Altair shipped its second computer to Cromemco. Also, being located close to a new startup company called Zilog, Cromemco was the very first company to use Zilog's Z-80 microprocessor.

The Z-1 used a Z-80 microprocessor, came with 8K RAM, and had twenty-two slots for additional circuit cards. If the picture of the Z-1 looks eerily like an IMSAI computer, it is because it was the same chassis that IMSAI supplied to Cromemco.

In 1977, the Z-2 was released, but it was much easier to program than the Z-1—namely, all of the front switches were gone, and the cabinet started to resemble more of what a personal computer looks like today. The Z-2 had 64K of RAM, a parallel interface along with an RS-232 serial interface, and Cromemco's operating system, called CDOS.

More small personal computers followed: the Z-3, System One, System Two, System Three, and eventually the System 400, which was marketed as a "super" minicomputer because of its 32-bit operating system.

Cromemco was very successful in selling to the U.S. government, but never achieved the commercial success because of competition from Radio Shack, IBM, and others that were coming into the personal computer market. In 1987, Dynatech purchased all assets of Cromemco.

As a footnote to this company, little did it know that its Z-1 product had spawned an idea in a young man in southern California to develop a portable personal computer. (See G.M. Research section.)

Cummins-Allison Corporation

Cummins was founded in 1887. This company's niche was to produce banking equipment that would make a bank more efficient. Since banking was a very manually intensive job of balancing accounts and clearing checks, companies such as Cummins saw a potential market to help make these tasks more "automated."

After nine decades of establishing itself in the banking business, in 1973, Cummins merged with the Allison

Coupon Company, and soon thereafter the 4400 KeyScan Multimedia Data Entry System was born. Stop and think about how those millions of checks are cleared and processed daily. It's a lot of work, and in the early days was prone to errors.

Today, with better hardware and software, it is quite an easy task to scan a check and move funds to and from banking institutions. In the 1970s, though, check processing was still trying to find a good solution, and this is where Cummins-Allison excelled. Checks could be scanned into a computer, but what happened if a check was rejected for some reason? With the 4400, a clerk could bring up the problem check, update it, and send it on its merry way once again. This saved tremendous time when checks were processed in batches, because the batch could be corrected without rerunning the whole stack of checks.

Figure 35—Cummins 4400

The 4400 was actually a central processing machine, capable of allowing up to thirty-two workstations to be connected to it. Each workstation consisted of a cabinet, CRT, keyboard, and a network card.

Whether it was simply overlooked as a company to buy out or for whatever reason, the bigger computer companies left it alone. Today, Cummins-Allison is alive and well in Mount Prospect, Illinois, and has a global presence in supplying machines for currency counting, currency and coin sorting, currency scanning, check handling, casino-ticket processing, and programmable and customizable ATMs. From 1887 until today! The company must be doing something right—keep up the good work.

Daedalus Computer Products, Inc.

Daedalus was based in Syracuse, New York. In 1970, the company offered the Daedalus 711 Programmable Data Terminal. Like so many other similar products coming on the market, it was hard for it to find a large customer base—especially since its product didn't have a CRT. Rather, it had a roll of paper on which keyed data and host data could be downloaded and displayed.

The 711 had a built-in 100-character-per-second modem, which made host communications horribly slow. It supported up to eight peripherals, such as a printer, magnetic tape cassette, or other devices as more custom interfaces came available.

Figure 36—Daedalus 711

The keyed data was stored in memory, which is strange since memory was very limited in size. (The typical memory available for most similar systems was only 8K or 16K, but I could not find memory specifications for the 711, although it had to be relatively small and limited.) The marketing pitch for this system was that with custom programming, data was so properly edited when it was keyed that only limited data had to be transmitted to the host—thereby reducing communication costs. It is hard now to understand how communication speed was used as the basis for a system's design, but communication speed was indeed a key factor to how this system could be properly used.

Data100

Data100 was established in 1968 in Minneapolis, Minnesota, by former Control Data employees. (This conjures up Douglas MacArthur wading ashore in the Philippines exclaiming, "I shall return"; when bright people left a computer company, all they had to do was to wade in the water of money exclaiming, "I'm ready to try it again!") While it was a U.S. corporation, it also had a European factory located in Hemel Hempstead, England, for manufacturing and shipping. Later, this operation relocated to Cork, Ireland.

Before the internet and open connectivity to PCs via the hypertext markup language (HTML) came about, computers had their own proprietary way of communicating to printers and data entry stations that were remote from the central computer. In Data100's case, the company saw (along with a throng of others at about the same time) a potential market for products to compete with IBM products that did remote transmitting of data and data entry. Data100's first products were card readers and printers that adhered to the IBM 2780 and IBM 3780 protocols. These were known as remote job entry (RJE) stations, because they were simply protocols that opened up easy access to IBM mainframes from remote locations. If a company had a data input device that used the RJE IBM standard <u>and</u> it was cheaper than IBM's product, at least that company had its toe in the door to make some money — maybe not a lot as some would find, but still a little.

In 1968, Data100 came out with what it called the 70 Series products. Model 70 was for the IBM 2780 RJE emulation. This product was pre-programmed in the factory, and was limited in functionality and flexibility of adapting to different input formats. The Model 78 came out in 1971 and adhered to the IBM 3780 RJE protocol; this product could be programmed (by a Data100 proprietary language), thereby allowing a wider range of input formats to the IBM host computer. Both of these models had to be connected to the IBM for their input to be saved and processed by the IBM computer. The 70 Series supported multiple terminals, printers, card readers, and keyboards (no CRT attached).

The Model 74 was introduced in 1974 and had significant advantages over the previous models. This model allowed a data entry person to key in data, have it stored locally on a floppy disk, and at some later time have the data sent all at once (this was called "batch" processing[45]) to the IBM computer. This reduced connection costs, and was faster overall IF it was not critical to immediately process the data on the mainframe. The Model 74 consisted of a keyboard and a 256-character display.

In 1976, an improved (faster) product, the Model 76, was introduced. In 1977, the company introduced the Model 85, which could be programmed with IBM's RPG language in addition to Data100's proprietary language.

In addition to data entry devices, Data100 made card readers (Models 300, 600, and 1200), card punchers, paper-tape readers, printers, tape drives, and disk drives.

Figure 37—Data100 printer and punched-card processing system

The operating system used for its programmable data entry machines was called FML-11 (meaning Field Modified Level 11). This operating system was developed in-house, and was quite sophisticated for its time. It was

---

[45] To clarify the batch data concept: If a company doesn't care about knowing what inventory it has on hand until, say, the following day, then entering data, storing it, and sending and updating the database in batches a few times a day or even once a night might be fine. If, on the other hand, the business requires immediate knowledge of the products it has available to sell (e.g., airline seats), then an alternative to batching is needed—this was, and is, known as transaction or online processing.

interrupt-driven (meaning that higher requesting tasks could interrupt other tasks going on), allowed for multitasking (meaning that several jobs/tasks could be loaded and interleaved for execution), and it had its own device drivers for communicating with various input and storage devices. The programmable products had 64K of RAM.

Data100 was purchased in 1978 by Northern Telecom, which soon thereafter, had its products merged with products from Sycor, Inc. The company's name, although given up in 1978 in the U.S. because the company was purchased, was retained for use in Europe through 1983.

Datacomp Systems, Inc.

In 1970, Datacomp Systems, Inc., based in San Gabriel, California, produced a product that competed with the almost-end-of-life (from a user acceptance perspective) Teletype machine. Talk about bad timing.

Figure 38—Datacomp 404 (advertising certainly has changed)

The company's product was called the Datacomp 404. It was a clunky, noisy, keyboard-only, rolled paper only, data-entry terminal. To its credit, it did differ from its almost twin Teletype machine in that the 404 had a CPU that could be programmed using 16-, 32-, 48-, and 64-bit instructions. It also had a built-in modem; this meant that custom editing could be done by the operator, thereby supplying cleaner data to the host system. This system sold for $6,800.

Data Computing, Inc.

Based in Phoenix, Arizona, Data Computing, Inc. made a printer called the Typeliner, which could be plugged into the up-and-coming stand-alone remote terminals that people were starting to use for data entry. It could print at 100 lines per minute and supported the standard ASCII 64-character set.

Figure 39—Data Computing's Typeliner

In an ad that should have been offensive even in 1970 (but definitely could easily be categorized as that today), Data Computing featured a lone Native American seen on an open prairie examining a printout from its Typeliner product. The caption read, "Kick the smoke habit."

The Typeliner could be rented for $245 per month.

Data Computing Systems

Not to be confused with the previous company with a similar name, in 1970 this Santa Ana, California, company not only produced a high-speed, 600-line-per-minute remote printer, but also a card reader and card punch for IBM RJE connectivity work. It marketed its products as the CP-4 (meaning the fourth generation from its earlier products, which were sold less than a year earlier!).

Figure 40—Data Computing Systems CP-4 system

Datacraft Corporation (DC)

Incorporated in 1970 in Fort Lauderdale, Florida, this location would turn out to be fortuitous for DC (as witnessed by its eventual purchase by Harris in 1978). DC developed a line of minicomputers named the 6000 series. The DC 6024 featured an instruction cycle time of 600 nanoseconds, while the DC 6024/3 had a 1 microsecond cycle. Both of these models used a fixed word length of 24 bits, had core memory, a multi-bus architecture, five 24-bit special registers, and a console (typewriter type of mechanism).

Minimum memory was 8K of RAM, but could be expanded to 64K (in 8K increments). DC developed a unique approach to memory access from an application (which could be done in byte, word, and double word modes). In a configuration of more than 32K, memory was divided into what were called "sectors." A program could access up to 32K directly, or by using another sector identifier, it could add up to 32K more of addressable data space. What this allowed for was larger programs to be written to work on more complex problems.

Additionally, DC had offered the following peripheral products:

- DC 6001-1,2,3 console typewriters
- DC 6002-10,20 paper-tape readers
- DC 6003 paper-tape punch
- DC 6004-3 printer
- DC 6005-1 and 2 (card readers)
- DC 6006-2 and 3 (magnetic disk storage; 25MB and 29MB respectively)

Its base system came with a FORTRAN compiler and the company's own Assembler compilers (which supported 120 instructions and 500 operation codes). It had its own proprietary disk operating system.

Data General (DG)

Data General (known to many in the computer industry as simply DG) had one of the first computers to be dubbed a "minicomputer." Data General was started by four people: Edson de Castro, Henry Burkhardt III, Richard Sogge (all from DEC), and Herbert Richman (from Fairchild Semiconductor). Formed as a Delaware corporation in April 1968, Data General was located in Westborough, Massachusetts.

Data General came out with the Nova minicomputer (with a 16-bit operating system) product in 1969. As with all companies, demand for faster processors and competing products forced Data General to follow up the Nova with the Supernova and later, the Eclipse products. After being the chief engineer in charge of DEC's PDP-8 (meaning it had an 8-bit processor at its core) product line, de Castro had experience in designing a small computer.

The Nova was designed to be mounted in a vertical computer rack similar to the PDP-8 machines, but the Nova was smaller in height and ran considerably faster. Launched as *"the best small computer in the world,"* the Nova quickly gained a loyal following and provided a solid revenue stream for Data General — then legal issues bubbled up. Apparently, moving from one company to another and taking ideas with you was not looked upon kindly by the company from whence one came. And, if by chance a new product was produced that looked eerily similar to another company's product, then it made matters even worse. Therefore, Data General would start its first years mired down in lawsuits from DEC regarding the misappropriation of DEC's trade secrets. The 1970s were interesting from the standpoint that companies "borrowed" a lot of ideas from other companies (as what was done by Steve Jobs and Steve Wozniak at Apple after visiting Xerox). In a twist of irony, Xerox also "borrowed," as it found the Nova's operating system full of nice inspirations, and therefore the XEROX PARC folks integrated some of these ideas into their own products. The fact was that the Nova was a well-designed minicomputer that others were trying to emulate, and which Data General itself had emulated from others. Most companies played nice with each other in exchanging ideas — but in DG's case, DEC thought it had crossed the line. It was a very incestuous time, and there was a fine line between then and now as to what might bring on a lawsuit regarding copyright infringement. Eventually, DEC and DG worked out a compromise, which allowed DG to go forward.

With the initial success of the Nova, Data General went public (became a corporation with stockholders) in the fall of 1969. The last major version of the Nova product line, the Nova 4, was released in 1978. Nova was generating an annual growth rate of 20 percent for the company, and becoming a star in the business community; total sales for Data General in 1975 were $100 million. In 1977, Data General fell into the trap where it thought it understood the personal computer market—but it didn't. Like Napoleon not being satisfied with most of Europe and then attacking Russia (and ended up losing most of what his army had gained), this is what happened to DG. Instead of keeping its customers happy with its minicomputer product line, it put money into developing and marketing a PC called the microNOVA. This product failed to attract a customer base, and was a money loser for Data General.

Referring back to its minicomputer line, in 1974, the Data General Eclipse product line was introduced. It had many of the same concepts as the Nova (notably virtual memory and multitasking) and was carefully positioned to be sold to a small office environment. Therefore, the Eclipse was packaged as a floor-standing case resembling a small refrigerator.

Figure 41—Data General Eclipse

Production problems and questionable accounting (e.g., machines were pre-ordered, sales were logged, and some machines never delivered) led to more lawsuits in the late 1970s. Many customers sued Data General after more than a year of waiting, charging the company with "breach of contract"; some of its potential customers canceled their orders altogether and went to other companies for their computers.

In 1976, competition was gearing up to compete head-on in the minicomputer world. Tandem Computers, DEC, and others were carving out niches in the business market, and therefore Data General was about to find out that competition was going to be fierce.

Data General was one of the first companies to offer software that included its own email system, word processing, spreadsheet work, and other business-related tools—named the Comprehensive Electronic Office (CEO). Sounds similar to Microsoft's Office suite of products, doesn't it?

Data General also developed its own operating systems for its products: DOS, RDOS, AOS, AOX/VS, AOS/VS II, System V, and DG/UX. This meant that the company had the added cost of supporting not only several types of operating systems, but also versions within those types — all keeping the company's costs high. Data General also offered standard communication protocols such as X.25 and TCP/IP. It also supported standard programming languages such as FORTRAN, COBOL, RPG, PL/1, and C. Additionally, it had its own proprietary language — Data General Business Basic. Data General even developed its own database management system called DG/SQL.

Data General, like other 1970s companies, had a clean slate for almost all it wanted to do. One of Data General's employees, Robert Nichols, developed a proprietary language called PLN. With some inventiveness inside of this language, a programmer could accelerate microcode instructions more easily — thereby making application programs run faster. The language was packaged under the name "Data General Easy," but for some reason was never marketed properly. Another tool that Data General developed was called Interactive Data Entry/Access (IDEA); this made it easier for COBOL programmers to design a screen for data entry/display. IDEA could support twenty-four users by sharing a virtual code stack in RAM, thereby reducing the amount of computer resources needed to support this many users at once. It was developed and marketed as competition to IBM's CICS, but unlike IBM's product, IDEA did not catch on.

DEC announced a 32-bit architecture product in 1977, although its marketing folks were slightly more optimistic than the engineering department since this product didn't ship until February 1978. If one company can stretch the truth, why can't another? Since there was no love lost between Data General and DEC, DG responded to DEC by also pre-announcing its own 32-bit product! Data General, with its bravado, dubbed its machine to be the "world's best 32-bit machine"; internally, this product was code-named the "Fountainhead Project." When DEC's 32-bit product (known as the VAX 11/780) was finally shipped in February 1978, Data General's machine was not close to being ready. Showing ominous signs for internal production problems and users seeing good performance from the VAX 11/780, Data General's customers gave up waiting and went with the competition.

Then things got worse internally for Data General. They feverishly launched an effort for yet another 32-bit product and code-named it the "Data General Eagle Project." In 1979, internal turf battles over funding were intensifying when it was apparent that the Eagle Project would be ready for market before the Fountainhead Project. Rising costs and reduced revenues were becoming all too serious for Data General to continue with its current business model.

The Eagle Project, now given the marketing name of MV/8000, was documented in the book, *The Soul of a New Machine* (Kidder, 1979). According to Kidder, this product was a fairly well-designed machine with the feature of being backward-compatible with the 16-bit Eclipse product.[46] The author stated that this machine was equal to the VAX 11/780 in most aspects. But, again, timing was everything—and Data General had missed a great marketing opportunity by its failure to get the product to market sooner than it did.

---

[46] Being backwards-compatible was important to customers because it meant that their applications developed on a previous product could still run on the newer products, thereby reducing any reprogramming—and keeping the customers happy.

Figure 42—Data General MV/8000

Nevertheless, sales did slowly increase, and by 1984, DG recorded over $500 million in revenue. As a carry-over from the 1970s, Data General's proprietary video terminals would be among the first keyboards to adopt a wide three-pad layout (later standardized by the IBM PC). Still, just when some thought that DG might survive, quality control issues started to happen yet again. Some blamed this problem with poor quality control at the Data General factory in Mexico where the terminals were made and refurbished. Basically, DG had been looking to cut costs by bypassing higher American wages, and in return, it provided little oversight for the factory it had built in Mexico—there was lots of blame to go around.

Competition was hot for minicomputers, and DG kept trying to compete in this market even though its customer base was dwindling. PCs, now all running at least 16-bit instructions, took away DG's niche in the 16-bit minicomputer world; customers were finding that a box sitting on their desk was just as powerful as their DG minicomputer. DG, in what could be considered now as "Huh, are you serious?" decided to focus its sales force strictly on the Fortune 100 companies,[47] ignoring the small to medium-sized customers who had bought millions of dollars of its products over the years.

DG did eventually produce and market its own PC, named the Data General-One (DG-1) in 1984. Sales never caught on for this product as it was put on the market with a $2,895 price tag. Competition was looming at every turn in the PC market with PCs selling for half this price, and customers didn't see DG as being all that stable of a company to trust it going forward.

Today, everyone takes for granted "flat screens" (used in laptops, smart phones, smart watches, computer monitors, and TV screens). In the 1970s through the 1980s, the display everyone had to use was called a cathode ray tube (CRT). It was the only option available except for a new technology called "liquid-crystal display" (or LCD). There always has to be a first user of something, and unfortunately for DG, it chose to use an LCD "monitor" instead of the traditional CRT — and to call it a disaster might be an understatement. It was not backlit, had poor contrast, and was frequently accused by some as being a better mirror than a computer monitor. Some users resorted to using a flashlight in order to see the characters displayed. To be fair, an updated version of the DG-1 appeared later with a much-improved electroluminescent screen (a big word meaning "it's brighter"). But, as DG was finding out, testing was critical before products went out the door — and DG was not doing this. The new screen consumed so much power that the battery option was removed (it couldn't stay charged long enough to be practical), thereby making the DG-1 what I would call the only non-portable portable ever sold.

---

[47] Some companies, Data General being one, relied on selling products through companies known as resellers. Instead of Data General employing their own sales team, they left it up to the resellers to do the selling. The saying, "shaking hands with the devil" probably started this way.

DG went on to produce more products (most notably its AViiON[48] product line.)

The EMC Corporation acquired DG and its assets in 1999. The details of the acquisition specified that EMC had to take the entire company, and not just the storage product lines. EMC, though, didn't want the computers, so it ended all development and production of DG's computer hardware and parts — basically putting a stake through the heart of DG's customer base. Maintenance of the DG computers was sold to a third party, which also acquired all of DG's remaining hardware components for spare parts for sales to old DG's customers. Even the Data General internet domain name was sold in October 2009.

If it seems like there was a lot more written here than other companies in this book, it is because of two reasons. First, there are a lot of books written about Data General, and with each book read more interesting tidbits would be uncovered. Secondly, the engineers at Data General were a remarkable lot who did some very creative things, and therefore this section gives them recognition for their endeavors.

Dataindustrier AB

Based in Sweden, this company designed the ABC 80 system (with ABC representing Advanced BASIC Computer). Actual production of this system was done by Luxor, located in Motala, Sweden. It was marketed primarily as a gaming system.

---

[48] The name AViiON was a playful use of the first Data General product, Nova spelled backward. The "ii" in the middle represented the second coming of DG.

Figure 43—Dataindustrier AB's ABC-80

The ABC 80 used the Z-80 microprocessor, running at 3MHz, and could be purchased with 16K to 32K RAM. It had 16K ROM, a BASIC compiler, a keyboard (no numeric pad), a cassette tape recorder for data storage and programs, and (very importantly) no monitor (although it provided connections to plug in a TV). It used a Texas Instruments sound chip that could produce ninety-six sounds.

Data Products

Imagine a laptop, but instead of a nice, flat screen display, it had a roll of paper. That's what the Data Products PortaCom product was. It was nicely packaged in a typewriter-looking hard-shell case, and it even had a real, honest to goodness telephone positioned on top to the right of the paper roll. It had a full keyboard, numeric keypad, and built-in modem—all weighing slightly under thirty pounds (or about six times the weight of a current-day laptop).

Figure 44—Data Products PortaCom

It is easy to look back and scoff at this idea, but basically the technology didn't exist in 1970 for what we see in our laptops today. Still, this company saw a need for putting a portable device into the hands of people; and as clumsy as it was to tote around, it did accomplish its job. The PortaCom was, by all definitions, the forerunner of today's portable laptops.

Data Products was located in Woodland Hills, California.

Data Terminal Systems (DTS)

Yet another company to be spawned in the northeastern U.S., a Maynard, Massachusetts, company, Data Terminal Systems, introduced the Series 300 in 1970.

The company produced three models within the Series 300 line, and all were stand-alone cash registers that were really specialized minicomputers. All models came with a ten-key buffered keyboard, and could do split pricing, price extensions, and automatic tax calculations.

The Model 319 ($1,895) was hard-designed (meaning pre-programmed) for up to nine departments. The Model 315 ($1,795) could support up to six departments, and the Model 307 ($1,695) could support only two departments. All of these models had two video ports—one to drive a CRT for the clerk (included), and one to drive a CRT for the customer (optional). These machines were limited in what they could do (they could not be programmed), had a limited market (as compared to what Singer was selling), could store limited data, and had no communications controller or scanning capability. Their market aim was for the "mom-and-pop" shop that wanted some sort of computer to keep tabs of sales.

By the late 1970s, DTS had produced the Model 515, which was a more flexible point-of-sale system in terms of programmable department information and connectivity to a central system for data collection. By 1979, DTS and Wang Laboratories were together touting in ads the Wang 2200 coupled with the DTS 515 for small company point-of-sale data collection and processing.

DTS survived into the late 1980s (and maybe beyond, but no information could be found on them in the 1990s.) As a word of caution to those computer makers who make dubious claims about their software and hardware, in 1987 a lawsuit was filed by Cricket Valley Corp versus Data Terminal Systems. The lawsuit claims that DTS and Wang actually couldn't get their systems working as advertised. Judgement was ruled against DTS for over $78,000, and guess who stepped in with a solution for Cricket Valley Corp? IBM.

Datapoint

Datapoint—the original name was the Computer Terminal Corporation, but later changed when one of its products named Datapoint became popular—was founded in 1967 in San Antonio, Texas, by Phil Ray and Gus Roche. The original aim of the company was to make a small data-entry terminal with a display screen and keyboard to replace the clunky, older teletype machines. In 1969, the company raised $4 million through its initial public offering (IPO).

In 1969 and the early 1970s, Datapoint sold the 3300 terminal, which it marketed as a terminal to connect to computer companies offering timesharing for its mainframes. Seeing the versatility of the microprocessor, the company decided to use this technology in a smarter machine of its own design. The company's most popular product, the Datapoint 2200, was a terminal that could load various emulations of IBM and other mainframe terminals; these emulations were preprogrammed and stored on cassette tapes. Some users of the terminals chose to use them as simple programmable computers instead, thereby making the claim that it was the world's first PC—although other companies listed in this book could equally lay claim to this title because of their similar products.

Figure 45—Datapoint 2200

The Datapoint 2200 was a very interesting computer since it led to the development enhancements of the first 8-bit microprocessor. Datapoint had specific requirements for what it wanted the 2200 to do, and neither Intel nor Texas Instruments could accommodate the delivery date. Consequently, the 2200 was produced and released using the SSI and MSI[49] chip technology available. This decision

---

[49] Terms such as SSI, MSI, and LSI meant some number of transistors integrated into a computer chip; SSI meant "small scale integration," "M" meaning medium, and "L" meaning large (or lots).

turned out to be of significance in the computer industry, as it inspired (spurred-on might be more appropriate) Intel to hurry up and develop its 8008 microprocessor (around which other companies would then flock to build their standards and products). Four decades later, this standard is at the core of Intel's x86 family of processors (as well as AMD, another maker of CPU chips).

The 2200 allowed for an optional 8-inch floppy disk drive, which was the first commercial computer to include them. Additionally, the 2200 had its own word-processing software. Datapoint created its own programming language called the Datapoint Business Language, and had the unique idea (at the time) for allowing multiple 2200 users to share a common database. This product was called Mapped Intelligent Disc System (or, MIDS, by the user community). One of Datapoint's crowning achievements was the development of a network protocol that allowed multiple, stand-alone 2200 computers and printers to be tied together. Datapoint called its network ARCnet, and was marketed starting in 1978. As with other companies linking their machines together, the company was essentially creating its own internet years before the true internet was born. (An "internet" used internally by a company became known as an "intranet" years later.)

ARCnet was followed by ARCnetplus, which provided throughput of 20 Mbits per second, and yet another a very creative product called LiteLink.[50] Datapoint also developed and patented one of the earliest implementations to enable videoconferencing (calling it MINX, meaning Multimedia Information Network eXchange).

In 1975, Datapoint announced its Datashare product. This product was a clustered system similar in concept to

---

[50] LiteLink was similar to today's microwave communication "line of sight" technology. LiteLink was used to connect DataPoint systems that were located physically in other buildings; this technology worked fine as long as a flock of birds, rain, dust, etc. was not in the way.

Sycor's 440 and 445 systems. Datashare used the Datapoint 5500 processor and came with 48K of memory; it could have up to sixteen terminals connected to the main machine. It was programmed using Datapoint's Datashare proprietary language, BASIC, and RPG. The operating system offered virtual memory.

As the 1970s came to a close, Datapoint was clearly a Fortune 500 company in terms of gross revenue. Being a public company with both an image and stockholders to appease, Datapoint embarked upon questionable accounting sleight-of-hand tricks — and got caught. What happened was basically this: An order would be taken, but in some instances, money wasn't actually was paid yet by the customer — but Datapoint went ahead and counted this money as revenue. Picture a business quarter where the salespeople were pushing hard to close deals so they could get their fat commission checks. They would call the headquarters announcing their whopper of a deal, but...actually the customer had not spent the money yet — and worse, in some cases never actually committed to buying the Datapoint product. Datapoint announced these big sales on its financial reports. Datapoint, in its eagerness to please investors, never bothered to reverse these questionable deals if they fell through, so the sales stayed on the books. Couple this with auditors being shown the old shell game of the same physical inventory being moved from warehouse to warehouse in order to buy more time until sales could catch up, and you have a recipe for financial disaster. In other words, one lie was leading to another, and eventually the house-of-cards collapsed.

When some of the customers went broke before paying their bills, Datapoint finally was forced to reverse sales (or record substantial bad debts); this led to Datapoint showing an $800 million loss in 1982 — and that amount of money was a lot for any company to lose (especially in the early 1980s). Because of Datapoint's loose accounting practices, the U.S. Securities and Exchange Commission

(SEC) first ordered Datapoint to stop its accounting practices, and second, in a landmark decision set rules in place for all computer makers' sales/revenues to follow (which are still in place today).

In 1985, Datapoint was taken over by an outsider, Asher Edelman. In many circles, Edelman would be known as a "corporate raider," as his goal was to break up Datapoint and sell the assets as separate divisions to other computer companies — and in so doing make a lot of money for Edelman. There was nothing wrong with this from a financial perspective. From an engineering and moral standpoint, it was a dagger through the heart of a once vibrant, smart company. Datapoint was renamed (and spun off) its services as Intelogic Trace, Inc., which later declared bankruptcy from lack of revenues and high costs. In December 1999, all of Datapoint's patents for video communications technologies (along with all inventory and assets associated with the video business group) were sold.

On May 3, 2000, Datapoint filed for Chapter 11 bankruptcy, and by then all of their brilliant and creative engineers had departed into other companies or retired. On June 19, 2000, it sold the Datapoint name and its European subsidiary for $49.3 million. Today, on the north side of San Antonio, just up the road from the Taqueria Datapoint restaurant, is an office building and a street named Datapoint Drive. Many (perhaps all) people driving on that street have never known about the significant computer contributions the Datapoint company gave to the computer industry.

Delta Data Systems Corporation

Based in Cornwells Heights, Pennsylvania, Delta Data Systems produced three products in 1970: the TelTerm 1, the TelTerm 2, and the TelTerm 3.

The terminal market at this time was crowded with many similar products offering similar functionality. To set their products apart, companies sold their products as being able to display more data than the other companies. Most terminals had settled upon some number of pixels (usually white or green grouped dots) that was easily readable for a user. Delta Data Systems decided to use smaller pixels, and while this sounds like a good idea, being able to read four times as many lines on the same size CRT that everyone else was using made it hard to read.

Digressing slightly into the world of "character sets," each character in this sentence is a character. In the basic English language, most people think there are twenty-six characters, but to a computer, a lower-case "a" has to be processed (and thus displayed) differently than an upper-case "A." At first, Delta Data Systems' first machines could only display in lower-case, and it wasn't until enhancements followed almost a year later that they offered both lower-case and upper-case displaying of characters.

Delta Data Systems did offer some interesting technology in terms of being able to take a "page" from memory and with a button on the keyboard be able to display this new "page" of information very fast. (This was similar in concept to Four-Phase Systems' "Window into memory," and today, we accept the "page up" and "page down" functions on our laptops and PCs as standard features.) The early machines came with a built-in 9600 baud modem. Their memory could store up to 2K of characters. It was packaged as other similar terminals on the market, with its own custom cabinet, CRT, keyboard, and numeric keypad.

Delta's market was for either connecting to timesharing systems, or for process-control companies. (It was not meant for keying and holding a lot of data; therefore, it was not really geared for traditional business uses.)

It marketed the TelTerm 1 as a replacement for the Teletype (paper roll) machine. Also in its marketing, the company touted the fact that when the sixty-fifth character was entered, a bell would go off![51] The TelTerm 2 could transfer in blocks of data instead of a character at a time like the TelTerm 1 did. The TelTerm 3 was marketed as a replacement terminal for the IBM 2265 (i.e., it ran the IBM 2265 communications protocol).

All the products had the following options: built-in acoustic coupler or modem, external printer interface, and a cassette tape recorder interface.

Dicomed Corporation

Many have heard the phrase, "Xerox this for me," meaning, "make a copy," but another phrase less commonly used in the general English vernacular was, "Dicomed this image," meaning capture it, display it, or record it.

In 1970, some ex-UNIVAC employees recognized a possible market for capturing and displaying X-rays digitally, and formed Medical Computer Corporation, but after a trademark conflict, the name was changed to Dicomed Corporation. The initial founding members were Richard Hilden (president), Wayne Huelskoetter, John Grimaldi (engineering manager), and Richard Lundell (manufacturing manager). They were soon joined by Margie Poole (admin) and Stephen Posey (technician). These six people set about to change computer history.

This Minneapolis, Minnesota, company manufactured and sold the Dicomed 30 (D30) Image Display originally to display X-rays (but later marketed for all graphic uses). While most companies were displaying boring characters

---

[51] Typewriters would do this when you were typing and got to the edge of the margin you set; obviously the engineers at this company had a strong typewriter background that they couldn't shake.

in nice, neat little rows of characters (usually 80 characters wide by 24 lines), along comes this company marketing its ability to display pictures in a 1,000 by 1,000 format![52] Yes, it is hard to fathom that at one time only a few thought of being able to do this, and even fewer could design a machine and display to actually do it.

Using a concept called "photomation," half-tone (black and white) photographic images could be transmitted (albeit slowly) over a telephone line. Dicomed could receive these images, store them, enhance them (if needed), and display them. Their resolution claimed to be over one million points, and each point could be adjusted with sixty-four levels of intensity.

Figure 46—Dicomed D30 along with an unretouched display image (with permission from John Grimaldi)

Unlike CRTs of the time, Dicomed's was unique in that it didn't need refreshing from memory on a constant basis when it displayed the image. Instead, Dicomed developed a way to display an image on a special surface and retain it even when power was removed from the device; and then by applying heat to the surface, the whole image

---

[52] The D30 was followed by the higher resolution D36 image display at 2000 by 2000 pixels.

could be erased. Basically, it was like a small TV (it had a round screen—not square like other CRTs on the market). The first model, the D30, sold for $15,000.

In the early 1970s, image processing was not needed in the traditional business world. For others whose business was processing images daily, Dicomed found its machine being used to display medical images at the University of Missouri, data from space and moon pictures at the Jet Propulsion Laboratory (JPL), and sensitive data for agencies such as the Central Intelligence Agency (CIA) and National Security Agency (NSA). Dicomed went on to market the D172 and D173 digital magnetic tape controller units consisting of an Atron 601 minicomputer with either 7- or 9-track tape drives. These controllers were used to drive its displays (D30, D31, and D36), digitizers (D55, D56, and D57), and film recorders (D46, D47, and D48) when they were not connected to each other or interfaced to computer systems.

Competition was gearing up, though, for color graphic displays (and graphic software), but Dicomed also had linked its displays to DEC's PDP-11 minicomputer systems, which enabled small to medium companies to send and receive images, and to store and retrieve them. For processing a lot of images, such as those at JPL, CIA, and NSA, Dicomed interfaced most of its early film recorder models to the Cray mainframe computers.

The D48 film recorder could be interfaced with a DEC computer using Dicomed's own proprietary D148 operating system. Both black-and-white and color recording systems opened the door to other markets such as engineering drawings, computer output microfilm, computer animation, and graphic arts.

In the 1980s, Dicomed also added a line of artist and illustrator design stations (D38, Imaginator, and Producer) to capitalize on the emerging audiovisual markets that were already using its D48 color film recorders to generate 35mm colored slides for multi-media presentations. Most in the graphic arts and computer industry have heard the term WYSIWYG (what you see is what you get), but Dicomed was first to coin this phrase in its marketing to graphic artists. Translated this meant that the 35mm slide from the D48 film recorder would be an exact replica of what the artist saw on the Dicomed design station.

This may elicit a "ho-hum" today, since it is common to send a JPEG (or other image format) of pictures or scanned images to almost any PC. For an image to be included in this book, it was simply cut/copied and pasted in. But stop and think about the early 1970s, where just being able to display a row of characters such as "ABC" was the norm. To be able to display, store, and transmit an image was both exceptional thinking and technology that made it all happen. Ideas like this got others thinking about the possibilities of computers for other kinds of work rather than simply working with character data.

Over the life of the company, Dicomed produced more than fifty products related to video and picture capture, display, and recording on film—including digital video capture, digital cameras, and computer output microfiche systems. Dicomed alerted the world of what was possible with digital data of any kind.

In 1988 Dicomed, with over 200 employees, was sold to Crossfield Electronics, and over the next few years sales dwindled enough that production of the Dicomed models ceased. Dicomed had transformed and challenged an industry of black-and-white character-only displays to do more with processing image data.[53]

---

[53] For an interesting glimpse into the early days of this company, visit
http://www.dougplate/com/discomed/grimaldi.html

Dietz Computer Systems

Dietz Computer got its start in 1951 by an electrical engineer named Heinrich Dietz in the Ruhr area of Germany. Heinrich saw that electronic devices (e.g., calculators and such items coming into the market) were being marketed for business uses, but he wanted to make devices that could withstand the rigors of industrial (heavy-duty) use. In 1968, Peter Dietz (Heinrich's son) was the managing director of his father's company, and decided to form the company into Dietz Computer Systems.

Actually, the first Dietz minicomputers were first developed in 1963, but had limited sales — mainly because the company hadn't defined clearly what they were to be used for. IBM owned the mainframe market even in Germany, and a smaller computer to compete in that market just didn't make sense to many businesses. In other words, Dietz was ahead of the times because within another ten years minicomputers would be making a significant punch into IBM's sales.

In 1971, under Peter's direction, sales increased through an active marketing campaign — and the Dietz 600, 621, and 6000 models were phased into the market. By 1982, however, only 3,000 systems had been sold and installed — certainly not a large enough number to keep the company solvent.

Figure 47—Dietz 600

By 1979, other investors were infiltrating the board of directors and wanted to take the company in another direction—namely that of focusing on computer-aided design (CAD). They realized that more powerful computers being dubbed as "super minis" from the U.S. were coming on the market, so the Dietz minicomputer was being phased out from lack of internal funding.

By 1983, a Norwegian computer manufacturer had assumed an 80 percent ownership of the company, with Peter Dietz retiring from the firm. In 1986, full 100 percent ownership was made by the Norwegian company, and Dietz Computer Systems was officially named Norsk Data GmbH. The new company was based in Bad Homburg, Germany. In 1993, the company was dissolved, but patents on the CAD software were purchased by Intergraph (an American company).

Dietz Computer would become just a footnote in the history of computers, as its contribution to the minicomputer systems was limited in almost all aspects—but it did contribute greatly in two aspects. First, it (along with similar-sized computers coming out of England) made the industry aware that a smaller computer was a cost effective alternative compared to offerings from IBM. (Especially true for small to mid-sized companies.) Second, in the late 1970s, this company employed Hans

Langmaack of the Christian-Albrechts University of Kiel. Together, Dietz and Langmaack developed a new programming language called PASCAL. From this endeavor, work then started on simpler and more portable languages used for different computers, and from this, the C language compiler was developed.[54]

Digi-Log

Ah, if only Digi-Log knew what it had developed. In 1971, this Willow Grove, Pennsylvania, company marketed the TELECOMPUTER as a "portable video display terminal." Two products were marketed: Model 209 and Model 33. This device weighed seventeen pounds and consisted of a simple keyboard (nothing fancy, such as programmable function keys or numeric keypad), a built-in acoustic coupler, a 5-in. display (capable of displaying either a 40- or 80-character line length by sixteen lines, and only capable of displaying a basic 64-character set), and an electrical cord that had to be plugged into an AC socket. They claimed that it could be connected to any TV, although this was probably a stretch in marketing because most (if any) TVs then didn't have input jacks — so very creative interfaces would have had to have been used to make it work.

---

[54] Along with the programming languages Java and COBOL, the C language is one of the most portable computer languages used in the world today.

Figure 48—Digi-Log Telecomputer

Still, Digi-Log was on to something—namely, building a truly portable terminal. With better marketing and better engineering, maybe this company could have conquered the portable computer market—at least for a while.

Digital Computer Controls

Based in Fairfield, New Jersey, in the mid-1970s, this company produced the D-116 minicomputer. This system was a 16-bit system, offered direct memory access (DMA), and included an Assembler compiler, an editor, a debugger, and a BASIC compiler. It supported up to 64K of core memory, and could communicate with up to four peripherals.

No data could be found on its sales or marketing.

Digital Equipment Corporation (DEC)

Digital Equipment Corporation (or DEC, as it was affectionately known in the computer industry) eventually became the second-largest computer company in the world and made its mark as a leader in the minicomputer arena. It was, however, a long road to get to that point. Although I am including some basic background into the formation of DEC, there are many excellent books written about the founders of this company and the early days of its excellent products. All provide very entertaining reading for both technologists and business case-study writers.

As a brief introduction to the company, two engineers, Ken Olsen, and Harlan Anderson (in addition to a supporting cast of others) from the MIT Lincoln Lab in Cambridge, Massachusetts, had been working on computer projects for various markets (one being for the U.S. Air Force). As their contracts expired for their work, their attention turned to basically what could only be termed as "playing" with ideas and transistors. Some of their early work involved building an 18-bit computer and then a 36-bit version, both accessing an unheard of (at that time) 64K of RAM. Olsen and Anderson noticed that students had an interest in their work, and in 1957, they hit upon the idea of trying to start a company based upon their lab work.

After prudent rewriting and reviewing of their business plan a few times over, they decided their new business venture would be to first sell computer modules (that users could wire together however they wanted — sort of a precursor to the kit computers introduced in the mid-1970s), and then (if all went well with their first phase) DEC would build and sell its own assembled computer. DEC was officially in business with a $70,000 infusion of venture capital; its headquarters was in Maynard, Massachusetts.

In March 1965, DEC's first computer product, the PDP-8[55] was on the market. It is widely accepted by many that this product was the first minicomputer to be sold in the commercial market. It was not a mainframe like the big

---

[55] PDP meant "Programmed Data Processor." There was an earlier product called the PDP-1 on the market, but DEC did not own this copyright. DEC's PDP-1 sold for $120,000. The least powerful laptop (and most smartphones) available on the market today for only a few hundred dollars would easily outperform a PDP-1.

IBM systems, yet it could do almost all the things an IBM system did; it just wasn't as big (as in connectivity to other devices and storage of data). It was priced to be much cheaper than an IBM mainframe, and it took years for IBM to react to this market being taken away.

The two bright engineers and founders, Olsen and Anderson, were in the process of building an incredible dynasty, when in 1966 something happened that probably could have been worked out between many people. But engineers being engineers, tact was not Olsen's strong point. Olsen accused Anderson of being disloyal by discussing internal business issues with a board member, and with feelings hurt, Anderson left the company. He later said, "It was the greatest disappointment of my life that the falling-out occurred." Olsen was now in total control.

In 1970, the PDP-8 was replaced with a faster product called the PDP-11. DEC eventually recorded selling more than 600,000 of these products, thus establishing itself firmly as the leader in the minicomputer market.

DEC's next product was called the VAX-11, which had a 32-bit CPU at its core. It was a powerful machine in many aspects; therefore, a new name was coined to describe computers of this caliber—they were to be known as "super minis," and could easily compete with larger mainframe systems like the IBM 370. DEC sold over 400,000 VAX products, making it the second largest computer retailer (next to IBM).

The 16-bit PDP-11 had a major advance in how peripherals (e.g., tape drives, communication controllers, etc.) could be accessed. DEC called this design its Unibus. By separating these peripherals from the operating system kernel itself, other devices could be added fairly easily to this system—thereby making the PDP-11 quite a scalable system. This system also supported Bell Labs' UNIX operating system, as well as DEC's own DOS-11, RSX-11, and other versions of operating systems.

To say that DEC was prolific in marketing and development is almost an understatement. Here is a summary of its contributions just in the 1970s:

- 1970 – PDP 8/E, TU10 tape drive, PDP 11/20, VT05 terminal, MUMPS language
- 1971 – DEC System 10, PDP 11/35 and 45, RTM (PDP 16)
- 1972 – PDP 16/M, PDP 11/40, PDP 11/05, K10 processor
- 1973 – RSX-11D (real-time O/S), RT-11 (real-time O/S)
- 1974 – MPS (first microprocessor), RSX-11M (real-time O/S), LA36 DecWriter, KL10 processor
- 1975 – PDP 11/70, DecNet, VT52 and VT55 video terminals, PDP 11/34
- 1976 – 36-bit DEC System 20, TOPS-20 O/S, WPS-8 (word processing system)
- 1977 – PDP 11/60, DecStation, VAX 11/780
- 1978 – V1.0 Virtual O/S, DecSystem 2020, VT100 terminal
- 1979 – F-11, 16-bit microprocessor

Figure 49—DEC PDP-11 (Model 35)

While not marketed as a PC per se, in 1975, DEC released the VT55 Graphics Terminal. It had all of the basic features of a PC, and actually many more—which ended up pricing it out of the PC market for the masses. The VT55 offered automatic, upward line scrolling; graphic cursors for editing, and graph generation for x and y plotting of two 512-point graphs (offering two values for each x and y). The monitor could display 24 x 80 lines of characters, and also had a built-in modem that could connect up to 9600 baud. A most interesting feature of this machine was the design of a printer that was built in; the paper unrolled vertically on the right side of the machine. Showing off DEC's inventive engineering, if a user wanted a screenshot taken, all he or she had to do was hit a print button and out came a picture of what was displayed on the screen. The VT55 sold for $2,495.

DEC eventually was drawn grudgingly into the PC market. Their first one, the VT180, was introduced in 1980. This was after Olsen's quote in 1977, as follows: "There is no reason for any individual to have a computer in his home." Looking back, this testifies to the fact that Olsen did not grasp the changing trends in the computer industry. DEC eventually came out with three more PC models, but all were of a proprietary design, and the world wanted a more "open" product.[56] DEC's PC products could not compete financially with the cheaper PCs on the market, and they were later discontinued after losing millions for the company.

In 1984, DEC marketed a proprietary product called DECnet, which enabled DEC computers to be networked together to share information easier (similar to today's intranets.) While extremely fast (10 Mbits per second), it

---

[56] A prime example of this was that DEC required users to buy pre-formatted floppy disks from DEC for them to work in their PCs; the rest of the world could buy blank floppy disks and format them themselves for a lot less money than DEC wanted. Again, this shows that DEC was truly an engineering firm with great ideas, but was not strong on the business side.

initially had a hard time being accepted outside of the DEC world.

DEC was riding high with over 100,000 employees in the late 1980s. It was during this time that the company branched out its development into a wide variety of software projects, which were far from its core business in computer equipment. The company invested heavily in custom software development. About this time, the concept of "open" software was attracting the business world. What this term meant was that software could be easily ported (or used) between computer platforms with little or no alteration of the application. For instance, although it can be argued that all of Microsoft's Office products are proprietary to Microsoft, most (if not all) can be used across a wide spectrum of PCs. It was a time that companies were looking for "standards" to be set for software. Although many of DEC's products were well designed, most were designed to run on DEC only machines, so the business world mostly ignored them in favor of more "open" products. It would be worth your time to read more in other books about DEC during the 1980s, as it was a tumultuous time for DEC.

In June 1992, Olsen was replaced as the company's president. The new president (with CEO also in his title) was told by the board of directors to start dismantling DEC and to sell what assets it could. DEC had simply too many products and had lost control of what was being developed by the many internal groups. DEC was, by all definitions, out of control with the "tail wagging the dog" in too many instances.

DEC's savior was Compaq Corporation, who acquired DEC officially on January 26, 1998 (although unofficially the acquisition had started the previous June). Compaq, mainly a laptop, PC, and printer company, was sitting on a pile of cash and its management saw the purchase of DEC and Tandem Computers as a perfect complement to make Compaq the largest and most powerful computer company in the world. This turned out to be a financial disaster for Compaq, which did not realize the magnitude of DEC's sliding business share and the burden of having a company who didn't understand how to control expenses.

To DEC's credit, it pushed the minicomputer market further than any other company, and in so doing, advanced computer technology at a break-neck speed. DEC helped solidify programming standards (to be known as ANSI, meaning American National Standards Institute), and the ASCII character set, which survives as the International Standards Organization (ISO) 8859-character set. DEC was instrumental in using the C programming language and the UNIX operating system on its early PDP machines.

Using the domain name of dec.com, DEC was the fifth business to be connected to the internet. DEC also created one of the world's first internet search engines (think of Google, Yahoo, Bing, and others); it was called AltaVista and spurred on ideas for internet search engines and algorithms to find things faster.

Digital Group

By the time the late '70s rolled around, microprocessors were becoming less of a fun hobby to now being seen as a helpful business machine. Ahead of its time, in 1974, a company called the Digital Group was formed to develop a general-purpose PC. This company was founded by Dr. Robert Suding[57] and Dick Bemis, and was based in Denver, Colorado.

Before Suding started on his business adventure, he had been dabbling in the world of "kits" from his ham radio days starting in the 1960s. When Suding saw an article by

---

[57] Suding held his PhD in Latin—about as far removed from computers as one could have gotten!

Jon Titus about the Mark-8 minicomputer in *Radio-Electronics*, he ordered the assembly instructions and circuit boards from Titus and began hunting for the actual parts to build the system. The instructions were basically a reprint of the magazine's article in addition to the schematics and board layouts. Suding did figure it out eventually — fixing several errors in the circuit board design and reasoning out missing interconnections from the diagrams. Being proud of his accomplishment, Suding announced over his ham radio set that anyone wanting to see his creation should pop over the following day. A small crowd appeared, as it showed the pent-up desire and enthusiasm to see what was possible now and the possibilities going forward with these "new-fangled" microprocessors. Very few had actually explored to the depth that Suding had, and the audience was curious. (One of the attendees was Dick Bemis, who would later team up with Suding as Digital Group was formed.) After showing off his working Mark-8, Suding realized that he had done little more than assemble a bunch of parts and put together a very primitive computer with few practical features. He saw both the Mark-8's shortcomings and at the same time figured that he could build a better one. In fact, Digital Group's first product was not a piece of computer hardware, but actually an article titled "*Packet Number 1, Extensions and Modifications to theMark-8*," which was essentially as the name describes — suggested improvements to the Mark-8 kit.

In early 1975, the first hardware products from the Digital Group were introduced. These products were the Texas Instruments-1 (a cassette tape interface) and an 8-line by 32-character width video interface card. In September 1975, Digital Group introduced its first complete computer system offered as both a kit or assembled. (To say that it was assembled is actually a misuse of the word, though, as the assembly referred to the circuit boards only; it was left up to the hobbyists to buy their own cabinets and power supplies, and determine the interconnections.)

Their first assembled computer was well thought-out, and the other generations over the next two years improved even more. For example, to get its operating system to boot, when Digital Group's users turned on the power switch, the computer was ready to load the operating system from a cassette player (with no more user interactions). The operator only had to press the "play" button on the cassette device, and the operating system or other software would load into the computer itself. While this might sound archaic by today's standards, this approach was very innovative. A cassette interface came standard with Digital Group systems, and could load programs at 1100 baud. The system also came with a keyboard and video interface (although what people had to do to attach something to those interfaces was another issue[58]).

A basic Digital Group system had a processor card with 256 bytes of ROM and 2K of static RAM, a video/cassette card, and an I/O card. The physical cards could fit into a large standard or small mini-motherboard, with the standard one accepting up to three memory cards, and the mini one only accepting one additional memory card. A low-current power supply was offered at a reasonable price, with a choice of +5V suppliers. The cabinet was optional at first, as Digital Group expected its new owners to get creative and build their own nice box out of whatever materials they wanted. Digital Group had its own I/O bus design and did not use the (starting to be) standard S-100 bus. Keep in mind why this was so: when Digital Group started, the S-100 bus did not exist. Suding had almost a clean slate from which to start designing his computer—so if he wanted his I/O bus to be built a certain way, he simply built it that way.

---

[58] For instance, a normal TV didn't have a nice HDMI or a display interface cable port, so if one wanted to make a TV work as an interface, the owner had to hack into the TV by very creative means.

Digital Group's final product was called the Mini Bytemaster, which was introduced in February 1978. This system was quite exceptional in many aspects; for instance, it included a single, internal mini-floppy (5¼ inches) drive (160K formatted capacity), and a high-resolution, 9-inch video monitor. The machine also sported the newly designed Digital Group motherboard with improvements that made adding interface cards easier.

Figure 50—Digital Group Mini Bytemaster

Suding felt comfortable with what he had done to build a good, basic microprocessor system, and for providing components and instructions for people to make their own systems. Unfortunately, Digital Group was built on the cusp of new hardware coming on the market—namely denser memory chips and faster microprocessors. What Suding did was to continue offering his original components <u>and</u> offer these newer components for those wanting a little more capacity and power from their systems. He was an engineer, not a business guy.

While Suding tinkered with his design, Bemis had assumed the role of marketing manager, personnel director, shipping manager, and any other management hat he wanted to wear. Unfortunately, Mr. Bemis didn't seem to have the skills or time to devote to his duties, and the company was quickly suffering from his lack of business acumen. So, what occurred was an inventory nightmare for his fledgling company; some components were not available when needed, and other components were over-purchased and ate up unnecessary inventory costs.

Interest was high for the Mini Bytemaster, but Digital Group had cash-flow problems. For instance, cash received from one sale was used to buy parts for the next systems being built. Things were tight at Digital Group, and getting tighter. Trying its best to struggle on, some systems were shipped along with a note in the box that read, "We ran out of 'part x'; it is backordered and we'll ship it at a later date." Bad PR followed, even though Suding was accumulating literally thousands of requests for more information on the products, and received actual orders for several hundred systems.

Unfortunately, only about thirty to forty Mini Bytemaster systems were ever made. According to Suding, most of the machines were delivered to friends and cash-paying customers. In other words, if you wanted one, you had to know someone who knew someone. Design shortcomings can be overlooked in some aspects, as Suding was still struggling with moving from a hobbyist's mentality to a commercial model. What cannot be excused was how the company was run in terms of marketing, inventory control, shipping, revenue accounting, etc. All of these shortcomings spun the company out of control from a financial perspective, and in October 1979, the last of its assets were sold and Digital Group closed its doors. It was too bad, as this company was on to something that computer hobbyists wanted.

Dimensional Systems, Inc.

This mid-1970s Lexington, Massachusetts, company is, perhaps, an odd company to include — mainly because I was torn because it only slightly contributed to the 70s.

Being in the same general area as DEC, one can picture some marketing and engineering "geniuses" in a bar discussing how they could manufacture and sell cheaper core memory — specifically for the PDP-9 system that DEC was selling. It was decided (perhaps after a few drinks) that a company should be formed.

Dimensional Systems produced a product called the DMS-9 Core Memory Module. Issue #1 — core memory was at the end of its useful life, as most minicomputers were now using RAM chips. Issue #2 — The PDP-9, while a nice small system, would soon be replaced with other systems. Issue #3 — When you have only a few ideas for products, it's tough to compete in the market.

This company's contribution (and why I included it in this book) was that it actually served as a warning to other companies coming into the computer business: keep ahead of technology and don't try to market something that people no longer want or need.

Electronic Data Systems (EDS)

Electronic Data Systems was founded in 1962 in Dallas by Ross Perot. Perot had been a salesman for IBM and saw first-hand state governments and companies (even large ones, including banks with supposedly big computer departments) struggling to get applications developed. He dropped out of selling for IBM and started selling for himself and his new company, EDS.

EDS would go on to be one of the largest "service providers" in the world — and in so doing, make Perot worth billions of dollars from the underlying principle idea of providing quality work. (And promising security of customer data second to no one.)

During the 1970s, EDS was expanding its business to go after other markets (namely insurance services and credit unions), and in 1975 its gross revenue was over $100 million. Later on, EDS expanded even more by tackling international markets. EDS was proving a software "services" company (not just a hardware company) was capable of making money in the computer arena; basically, it was proving the importance of software to drive hardware sales.

In the 1980s, EDS expanded into new markets, and its profits grew. GM (the automobile company) liked what it saw for EDS' money-producing potential, and ended up buying EDS in 1984 for $2.5 billion. Perot stayed on with GM, but left soon after the merger, after being offered a very large "golden handshake" worth hundreds of millions of dollars. Perot did well for a one-time IBM salesman who turned an entrepreneurial idea into a multi-billion-dollar corporation.

GM eventually divested itself of EDS, and EDS was again running its own show. At least until 2008—when HP bought it, and the EDS name ceased to exist.

Electronic Laboratories, Inc.

In April 1970, a very primitive version of a laptop was introduced to the world. Electronic Laboratories, located in Houston, Texas, brought to market the data-kap 806.

This device had only a numeric keypad (with a few special characters added) and a cassette drive/recorder, and was packaged in a small metal box with a hinged top. The overall dimensions were 7 in. x 9 in. x 4 in.; it had rechargeable batteries (that didn't have to be removed for charging); and it weighed six pounds. The cassette could hold 100,000 bytes, and could record in BCD, ASCII, or EBCDIC in variable-length words.

Figure 51—Electronic Laboratories data-kap 806

The company marketed this device to businesses that wanted a way to track inventory in retail stores, warehouses, and manufacturing plants, and in places where inventory counting needed to done in a more computerized manner instead of by paper and pencil. When done in the field or plant, the user brought the cassette back to another computer that could read it, and then more processing could be done with that data. It was on the right path to the portable personal PC—it just didn't have the technology at the time to make it better.

Electronic Memories, Inc.

Incorporated in 1961, this company was located about 300 miles south of the fledgling Silicon Valley. Hawthorne, California, was the home of Electronic Memories; its products were related to magnetic core memory.

A patent search for the company reveals various kinds of magnetic core memories and testing tools for these types of products. As is pointed out throughout this book, the trend was for small packaging in PCs—and even mini-computer makers with larger cabinetry saw the wisdom of making their machines smaller. In other words, core memory boards were simply too large to fit into a PC, plus magnetic core memories were more difficult to manufacture, which made semiconductor "chips" the memory of choice for computers. Apparently Electronic Memories either could not make the transition to semiconductor memory, or was behind the ramp-up time and money needed to compete. Whatever the case, Electronic Memories disappeared by the early 1970s.

EMR Computer

Based in Minneapolis, Minnesota, this company built and marketed the EMR computer systems. In 1970, small to medium-sized companies hadn't quite figured out the minicomputer yet — meaning, what was the cost to not only buy their own system, but also the operations and programming costs that went along with it? Hence, IBM sold remote terminals and printers to connect to a host IBM system, and other companies (such as EMR) decided to cash in on this timesharing model also.

Up until this point, if companies wanted a number of devices connected to a host system, they either bought peripherals from that large company (e.g., IBM, Burroughs, Sperry, etc.), or bought a hodge-podge of devices from various sources. EMR's market push was to offer a series of products that competed with the large companies, or solved the problem of a company trying to find the right printer, CRT terminal, etc., to connect a host system. The EMR system consisted of an "intelligent" front-end that was called the EMR Data Communications System. This unit then allowed connections to other EMR products like a high-speed printer, magnetic tape drives, programmable terminals with CRTs, Teletype machines (no displays, but rolls of paper), paper-tape readers/punches, and other small peripherals.

English Electric

English Electric (later marketed by ICL) came into existence in the mid-1960s in the UK. The company marketed a clone of the RCA 501, calling it the KDP10. Other models came out (such as the KDF8), all designed to compete with the IBM systems enjoying so much success. Its market, as the company saw it, was Europe—including parts of what was called "Eastern" Europe at the time (i.e., Soviet bloc countries). It had no plans to market its products in the U.S.

English Electric's marketing, though, was not as well established as that of IBM, and English Electric's models System 4-10, 4-30, 4-50, 5-52, 4-62, 4-70, 4-72, and 4-75 never caught on. Their marketing names meant that the higher the number, the more users it could support. The 4-10, for instance, was a small stand-alone computer that was meant for remote data-entry, while the larger 4-75 was the mainframe into which the smaller systems could connect. The models making up the middle were scaled-down versions of the 4-75 in terms of disk drives and memory.

Systems 4-50 and 4-70 were intended for real-time applications (e.g., process control). Each system had four processor states, and each had its own set of general-purpose registers (GPR). Although some states did not have all sixteen GPRs, its inventive design avoided having to save registers when switching between processor states.

The System 4 could be supplied with medium-speed or high-speed card readers, which could read eighty-column cards at 800 or 1,435 cards per minute (depending upon the model). Cards with fifty-one columns were read at 1,170 or 1,820 cards per minute, again, depending on the model. A high-speed paper-tape reader (1,500 characters/second) was available, as well as a card punch, magnetic tapes, printers, and removable magnetic disc platters (providing a maximum of almost 8K of storage).

The operating system was creative in that it allowed multi-programming. English Electric's engineers, though, didn't understand much about storing data on disk. For instance, they figured out that buffering 80 bytes of data into a block and writing that block was much more efficient and faster than writing a record at a time. While working well in English Electric's lab, in a real-world scenario where the customers' applications were sometimes complicated, the System 4 failed to perform as well as promised. In 1971, its disc supplier, ICL, rewrote the I/O modules to be more efficient (e.g., block sizes increased to 384 bytes), and performance increased quite considerably.

In 1963, English Electric bought Leo[59] Computers Ltd., and subsequently came out with the Leo II and Leo III. The Leo I holds the distinction of being certified as the world's first business computer (in 1951), doing tasks such as inventory and payroll processing. The Leo III had a multi-tasking operating system capable of running up to twelve programs at the same time.

In 1964, English Electric acquired the scientific and commercial computer rights from the Marconi Company. For a brief moment, the much larger company was English Electric Leo Marconi Computers Ltd. To extend its presence in the computer space, in 1967 Leo merged with Elliott Automation. To complete its picture of its lineage, in 1968 English Electric merged with ICT in 1968, and from this the company ICL was formed.

The astute reader may wonder why this company is included since its most significant computers were developed before 1970. The answer is this: British computers, of which English Electric was a major player, supplied ideas, patents, and smart people who would seed other UK computer development into the 1970s and beyond.

---

[59] Leo was an acronym for Lyons Electric Office.

Entrex

Located in Burlington, Massachusetts, Entrex marketed a product called the System 580. In 1976, this system was trying to position itself as a database system instead of having to connect to a mainframe (e.g., IBM) to get data. Similar in concept to Tandem Computer's, Entrex wanted its computer to act as its own database machine, which meant that its minicomputer supplied a database that could be accessed locally by terminals connected to the system.

Unlike Tandem Computers, which offered a database that could scale to billions of bytes, the System 580's database started at 1MB and could only grow another 29MB in size. Another key difference in the database approach between Entrex and Tandem Computers was the use of the relational model (Tandem Computers) versus the ISAM model (which IBM used, and which Entrex followed.) ISAM databases turned out to be less scalable than the relational models, and Tandem Computers used this thinking to exploit smaller companies wanting to grow their databases — whereas Entrex could not.

Entrex's terminals were called DATA/SCOPE keystations. The System 580 also offered a magnetic tape drive for backing up a database.

Eugene Dietzgen Company

As you probably have gathered (or will gather from continued reading), companies were kind of loose in calling their machines a computer. The Eugene Dietzgen Company, based in Chicago, Illinois, came out with the Dietzgen Desk-Top Computer in 1970.

It was, by all definitions, a calculator, and sold as one even though its advertising used the word "minicomputer."

This calculator not only had the typical numeric keypad, but also a bank of keys for special characters and programmable function keys. It was about twice the size of an old desk phone, had a digital read-out (using Nixie tubes), and had an attached card reader. It advertised that it had ten memory registers, which means it probably was using the Intel 8008 processor, but the exact specifications are lost to time. It weighed twelve pounds, and used LSI circuitry.

Figure 52—Dietzen Desk-Top Computer

Programming this machine was the fun part. Via the use of keys on the keypad, a program of up to 128 instructions could be entered and stored. Another way to load a program was via the attached card reader. This company would sell you special cards, and tell you how to punch holes in them from which to create your own program (again, up to a limit of 128 instructions). By using the cards to store your program, one could easily load new programs without the tedious task of keying the instructions in via the keypad.

This is a prime example of companies searching for a use for the Intel processor and still having a foot anchored firmly in 1960s thinking. Still, Dietzen was actually on to something in the world of personal computing that was years away. Basically, the company was selling this computer to replace a reliance on mainframe computers for processing of scientific data.

Evans & Sutherland Computer Corporation

In 1968, David C. Evans and Ivan Sutherland had the idea of not only displaying an image/graphic, but making it move in an almost three-dimensional manner. In 1970, terminals that could display graphics were limited mainly because of the processing power needed at the terminal to move pixels around, but Evans and Sutherland saw a viable business doing this work. (Although Dicomed had a powerful image-processing "terminal," Evans and Sutherland thought they could compete on price.) By buying General Electric's flight simulator division and forming a partnership with a UK company (Rediffusion Simulation), they were on their way to producing and marketing their first commercial product.

Picture an airplane approaching a runway. As the airplane comes in closer for a landing, the airport's dimensions should change to show the approaching runway. If the airplane pulled up or banked, then the airport's perspective should change with it. Evans & Sutherland developed the LDS-1[60] to handle simulations like this. While this might seem archaic and rudimentary at the time, this was a new way of using computers that few had considered for an individual user. (Obviously, a microprocessor was used in this cabinet/display/keyboard configuration, but I found no specifications.)

---

[60] Since the company is located in Salt Lake City, I will let you determine the association of this product name to the location at which it was developed.

Figure 53—Evans and Sutherland LDS-1

More products followed in the 1980s; Evans & Sutherland is still located in Salt Lake City, Utah.

Exidy

Based in Long Beach, California, this company was a video game company that in 1978 produced a wonderfully packaged small computer called the Sorcerer. Its claim to fame was a computer game called Death Race. This game had excellent graphics and set the competition on its heels while it tried to play catch-up to this exciting game. The system itself looked to the Commodore PET and the Radio Shack TRS-80 as its competitors (which was strange in a way, as both those systems were actual business computers that could also run games, whereas the Sorcerer was sold as a gaming system.)

The Sorcerer included both graphics and color; it used the Z-80 microprocessor and ran at 2.6 MHz. It came with 4K RAM, but could be expanded to 48K RAM. It had a full keyboard and a numeric keypad, and offered a cassette drive for storage.

Figure 54—Exidy Sorcerer

In 1978, the personal computer and gaming market was getting crowded in the U.S., so with a stroke of brilliance (at least initially), the company saw the foreign market as being more open for sales. While continuing domestic sales, it concentrated on exporting where it found it could charge twice the domestic price. One of its main importers was Liverport Ltd. of the UK.

Fabri-Tek

While some companies were looking at the minicomputer to change how businesses thought of connecting to a mainframe (e.g., IBM), some were content to play with IBM (plug into an IBM and look like another IBM peripheral). Enter Fabri-Tek with its LCM 207 and LCM 207-20 products.

Instead of an IBM customer having to buy IBM's somewhat expensive products, companies like Fabri-Tek were offering less expensive components. The LCM 207 was touted as being faster and offering more storage than IBM. This machine offered a 2.5 microsecond cycle time, and could store from 5MB to 20MB. The cabinet was approximately 6 ft. tall, 2 ft. deep, and about 5 ft. wide. (This was all core memory, which took up a lot of space;

today a 16GB chip fits in the palm of your hand.) The LCM 207-20 used the same cabinet as the LCM 207, but could only store 2MB of data.

Figure 55—Fabri-Tek LCM 207

Additionally, Fabri-Tek sold add-on core memory boards that could fit into Digital Computers, HP, and Data General computers. Fabri-Tek was located in Minneapolis, Minnesota.

Fairchild Camera and Instrument Corporation

Fairchild is a name usually associated with military products and aviation, but in the 1970s, it ended up in the commercial-game market with a microprocessor-based product. The road to that product, though, took an interesting path.

The Fairchild Aviation Corporation was originally formed in the 1920s to make instruments for aircraft, and eventually developed sophisticated spy camera equipment mounted in aircraft. In fact, they were so good at what they did that in 1944, they changed their name to Fairchild Camera and Instrument Company.

While their military contracts were sustaining their growth, some forward-thinking marketing person had the brilliant idea of using the company's vast electronic skills to start dabbling in the commercial market. The late 1940s and early 1950s saw this company successfully bringing to market X-ray machines and a product for the printing industry that immensely eased typesetters' use of fonts and sizes. Their new strategy for growth was taking hold.

Electronics was their forte, and what better way to increase their market than to hire some much smarter folks! William Shockley[61], a man who ran a successful electronics business and who many called a genius in the electronics arena, was brought on board. He immediately brought with him seven PhD electrical engineers from his old company, and Fairchild sat up a division for them called Fairchild Semiconductor.

Successes followed in the commercial market, and the 1970s rolled around with the microprocessor starting to catch the eye of many (as shown throughout this book) with "how can we use this?" Fairchild was no different— except that they had a large company behind them to help with product development and marketing.

Enter a man named Jerry Lawson who had the idea of developing a microprocessor-based gaming system using replaceable game cartridges instead of "one-hit wonders" like Atari's Pong. Given the go-ahead to take his product to market, Lawson did exactly that. Fairchild marketing people seemed to want to justify their existence by coming

---

[61] I would be remiss if I did not point out the brilliance of Shockley. He and one of his engineers, Robert Noyce, could easily be called the inventors of the integrated circuit— at a minimum the co-inventors with another person. Instead, through shrewd timing and arm twisting, Jack Kilby of Texas Instruments got the credit—and a Nobel Prize for his contribution to the world. I don't mean to take anything away from Kilby, who was also a brilliant electrical engineer; rather, the awarding of the patent for the integrated circuit should be marked with an asterisk to at least make people read more about the competition between Texas Instruments and Fairchild.

up with the creative name of the Fairchild Entertainment System. Although clever and descriptive, it was a mouthful for a buyer. The name was dropped and the Channel F was used instead of the previous name. ("F" stood for "fun.")

The Channel F was based on Fairchild's own 8-bit microprocessor, and had 64K of RAM. It consisted of two controllers (which creatively fit in its own compartment under the lid of the unit). A cable connection on the back allowed it to be connected to a TV or computer monitor. The original idea was to allow a keyboard to be connected to it, but the idea was scrapped to focus on gaming. Like Atari with their 2600 system, both of these companies were sitting on a gold mine; both had the essence of a personal computer — they just didn't recognize it.

Although the Channel F beat Atari's 2600 gaming system to the market, Atari had name recognition. The Channel F went on to sell a respectable 250,000 units, while the latecomer Atari 2600 ended up selling 30 million units. Fairchild saw the writing on the wall for their Channel F, and stopped production in 1983 after sales dwindled because of competition.

Figure 56—Fairchild Channel F

In 1979 this company was sold to Schlumberger, an oil and gas exploration company. In 1987 Schlumberger spun off this company to National Semiconductor.

Ferranti

In 1882, Sebastian Ziani de Ferranti established his first business — Ferranti, Thompson and Ince, located in the UK. Ferranti was focused on developing alternating current power distribution stations to electrify his country. In 1885, with a partnership change, the company simply became known as S. Z. de Ferranti, and subsequently as Ferranti-Packard.

Through the decades up until the 1950s, Ferranti was involved in power generators, radar development, aircraft electronics, and other electrically related components for business and military.

WWII brought about a need for computing for various war uses (e.g., code breaking, trajectory calculations, etc.). In the late '40s, Ferranti teamed with UK universities to develop computers. The Ferranti Mark 1, completed in 1951, was the first outcome from this effort.

Figure 57—Ferranti Mark 1

Keep in mind that up until this time, computer manufacturers were encoding the characters they typed in to mean anything they wanted them to mean — they could care less about how other computers stored their data. For instance, the character "A" might be represented as "00011000" in one computer, but "11110000" in another. This is all fine and good except when one wanted to move data from one machine and process it in another.

In 1956, Ivan Idelson at Ferranti developed the idea of coming up with a standard for this character representation, and in so doing originated what was called the Cluff-Foster-Idelson coding of characters on 7-track paper tape. *This work helped solidify what we know today as the American Standard Code for Information Interchange, or ASCII.*

The Ferranti-Packard firm arose with the merger of Ferranti Electric Limited and Packard Electric Limited in 1958. More computer development and partnerships followed, but its computers were not competitively priced nor did they perform that well (speed-wise) in the market. By the mid-1960s, Ferranti's management wanted out of the computer business and to sell the computer division.

A merger was consummated in 1963 with International Computers and Tabulators (ICT), thus finally becoming the Large Systems division of ICL in 1968. After studying several options, ICT selected the previous Ferranti model FP 6000 as the basis for its ICT 1900 series line; this system sold into the 1970s. Ferranti only sold five of these FP 6000 systems, but after the acquisition by ICT, approximately 3,000 of them were eventually sold—verifying that indeed, Ferranti had designed a nice computer to compete with IBM.

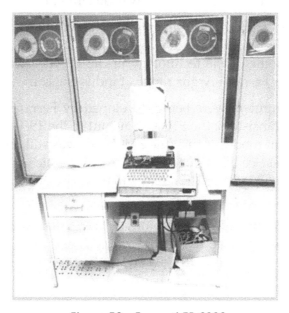

Figure 58—Ferranti FP 6000

Ferranti wanted its computer to set the company apart from the other makers of computers from the U.S. (which were also dominating sales throughout most of Europe). While all computers up to that time executed one program at a time (at least within a "partition," which was a discrete area set aside for a program), Ferranti wanted something more flexible. What it developed was a way for multiple programs to run at the same time; of course, this meant keeping track of a program's data in memory (32K of core memory), so some very sophisticated operating system programming was done to accomplish this. The company employed some very bright software engineers.

The FP 6000 was a very scalable machine in that it had sixty-four hardware channels that could accommodate almost any sort of peripheral device attached to it. It used a 24-bit word with a twenty-fifth bit for parity checking. It originally came with a magnetic memory drum to hold "memory" needed for the processor itself, but with the advent of more condensed memory, the drum was replaced, and now all memory was on circuit boards.

ICT excluded Ferranti from entering the commercial sector of computing, but Ferranti was free to sell to the industrial market. Some of the technology of the FP 6000 was later used in its Ferranti Argus range of industrial computers.

More computers were being developed by Ferranti using discrete transistors; the F1600 came out in the 1960s, and a descendent model of this (the FM1600E) was still reported to be in service by the UK's Navy in 2010 (which probably says more about the UK's Navy than about the computer itself).

Ferranti continued modestly into the 1980s. Through some its divisions (via acquisitions), Ferranti found itself in legal hot water. By the late 1980s, Ferranti had no positive cash flow, and in 1993, declared bankruptcy.

Four-Phase Systems

Four-Phase Systems was founded in February 1971, and was located in Cupertino, California. One of Four-Phase Systems' founders was Lee Boysel, who had worked at Fairchild Semiconductor designing metal oxide semiconductor (MOS) chips. Boysel suggested to Fairchild that a small, departmental type of computer (meaning it could support up to approximately sixteen users) could be designed and built from a small number of MOS chips. Trusting in his judgement, Boysel was made the manager of the MOS design group. Wanting to branch out on his own with his ideas, Boysel, along with two other engineers, did exactly that.

In October 1968 Boysel and his small team had initial plan to manufacture its own chips. Fabrication of these, though, were (and is) expensive—so this work was sent to a company named Cartesian (which, coincidently, was founded by another engineer from Fairchild), while Boysel concentrated on getting the computer built. Out of this engineering came one of the first microprocessors, the AL1 – beating Intel and Texas Instruments to the "commercial" market. The reason I put quotes around "commercial" is that even though Four Phase sold their systems commercially, they never had the time or foresight to ask themselves "I wonder if anyone else would want to use the AL1?" Intel, on the other, saw a true commercial market for their microprocessor and marketed it thusly.

Four-Phase's first system could connect to users to their central system, and eventually it could be expanded to connect up to 16 users. Their first system was shown at a computer conference in late 1970, and it was received well enough that Four-Phase started taking orders. By June 1971, Four-Phase had four customers, and by March 1973, it claimed 131 customers using a total of 347 of its systems. One of its peak years (if not the peak year) was 1979 in terms of revenue when it hit $178 million.

Figure 59—Four-Phase computer system

The AL1 used a 24-bit word size with 8 bit slices. The CPU fit on a single card and was composed of three arithmetic logic (AL1) chips, three ROM chips, and three random logic chips. A memory card used Four-Phase's proprietary 1K RAM chips. The system also included its own video controller from which to drive (map displays) up to thirty-two terminals from a memory buffer. Four-Phase called this mapping, "A window into memory", where storing and retrieving/displaying data was extremely fast because of this design.

Their initial customers found their "window into memory" a nice feature as it kept down RAM cost needed for each terminal. In other words, the connected terminals to the central CPU needed fewer physical parts. Being able to connect up thirty-two terminals, though, turned out to be a theoretical limit. Users found that when more than sixteen terminals were all sharing the "window into memory," each terminal slowed down. When customers complained of this design flaw, they were told to buy another system. While this marketing approach was having mediocre success, other companies were developing more scalable systems that could connect more terminals to their central computer (or in some cases, a cluster of computers all communicating and sharing information very efficiently).

Four-Phase had carved out an early niche for its systems, but its non-scalable design turned out to be a dead-end street. Four-Phase was sold to Motorola in 1982 for an exchange of $253 million in stock.

In the early 1980's there were several microprocessor competing with Intel. Intel then claimed (in their marketing literature) "Buy Intel – we were the first developers of the commercial microprocessor!" Ex engineers and management of Four Phase took exception to this bravado and sued Intel. The court agreed with Four Phase founders – that the AL1 was a true microprocessor and that Intel had to change their marketing claiming to have the first commercial microprocessor.

Friden, Inc.

Founded by Carl Friden in San Leandro, California, in 1934, this company was named the Friden Calculating Machine Company; it made electromechanical calculators. (Eventually, the name was changed to Friden, Inc.). Over the course of the next three decades, the company made typewriters and simple electronic calculators.

In 1957, Friden purchased the Commercial Controls Corporation of Rochester, New York. What this provided to Friden was a machine (actually a revolutionary invention) called the Flexowriter teleprinter. This machine not only printed out copies of a stored document, but also allowed the user to change parts of the text if changes were needed. The Flexowriter teleprinter could be attached to Friden calculators and driven by programs punched on paper tape to produce invoices and other form letters, which had customers' names and invoice amounts filled in automatically. Taking this idea one step further, Friden eventually expanded into production with early uses of transistorized computers.

In 1965, Friden was purchased by the Singer Corporation, but continued operation under the Friden brand name until 1974. The only computer to come from this merger was the System Ten, which was marketed as a small business minicomputer. The Singer System Ten (also mentioned in some literature as the System 10) was a small-business computer introduced in 1970. It featured an early form of logical partitioning of applications that could be run at the same time. It was a character-oriented computer, using 6-bit characters and decimal arithmetic. This system could be programmed with either Assembler or RPGII. Additionally, Friden developed software products that were used as tools for data layouts for updating files and generating reports. The System Ten was somewhat of a success in that there were an estimated 8,000 licenses sold for it by 1979.

Combining microprocessor and new technology ideas (e.g., CRT display), Friden went back to its roots to enhance its calculator line.

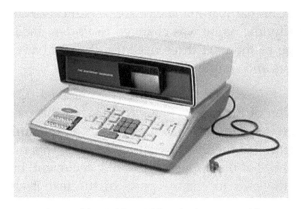

Figure 60—Friden 132 calculator machine

The computer operations of Singer were bought by ICL in 1979. ICL continued to market the system as the ICL System 10, and in the early 1980s introduced the System 25 as an upgrade. The Singer/Friden Research Center in Oakland, California, was moved to Palo Alto, California, where it remained in business from 1965 through 1970.

Computer incest alert: In 1973, the Cogar Corporation was acquired by Singer Corporation, then by ICL, and then by Friden. The machine (called the 1501) that was the core of this relationship was a small point-of-sale terminal used in gas stations. The application had to be loaded from a tape drive, two of which were attached. There was a connector on the rear of the machine that allowed connectivity to printer, disk drives, or tape drive.

Fujitsu

Since its founding in 1923, Fujitsu has been an innovator in commercial and consumer electronics. Fujitsu's early days saw the company understanding the power of electricity to drive innovation, so it set out to develop generators, electric motors, and then eventually telephones and telephone switching systems.

In 1954, Fujitsu manufactured Japan's first computer, the FACOM 100. In 1961, it announced an enhancement to this machine by redesigning it to use all transistors; this product was called the FACOM 222.

In 1959, though, a turning point occurred when the new president, Kanjiro Okada, decided to put more (and substantial) funding into the research, marketing, and development of its brand of computers. He didn't dissolve the other products it produced, though, as Okada saw these products helping to sustain Fujitsu's overall growth. He predicted (accurately as it turns out) a future in which high-speed telecommunications with the aid of computers would be essential for both businesses and consumers.

Fujitsu was now developing a line of FACOM computer products. Working in conjunction with its telecommunication product lines, it succeeded in developing submarine coaxial cable systems and practical applications of fully digital transmission systems. In 1968, the FACOM230-60 was introduced, and it cemented Fujitsu's creativity and innovation by offering all integrated-circuit logic boards, the world's first two-CPU multiprocessor system, and a new operating system. The year 1968 also brought significant banking software products, most notably one that allowed online deposits to Dai-Ichi Bank (currently Mizuho Bank). Both of these products not only put Fujitsu at the top in Japanese computers and technology, but gave a significant boost to the Japanese banking world.

In the '70s, Fujitsu had reached a fork in the road with its computers. The world was enamored with IBM, and with this came what was called the "IBM standard." In other words, companies liked IBM products, and if a company wanted to compete with IBM, it had to look and feel like an IBM. Any company, though, that wanted to continue with IBM-only products confronted a big drawback — price. IBM knew it had products that people wanted, and it priced its products accordingly. Fujitsu's computers were well liked by many companies in the Asia area, but its systems were "proprietary" in nature, and this meant that the IBM applications that others liked would not run on the Fujitsu models. What to do?

First, as a stop-gap (explained further on), Fujitsu worked out a marketing agreement with the Amdahl Corporation to rebrand and resell its IBM-compatible system (the Amdahl 470V/6) in 1975 throughout Asia. At the time, however, Fujitsu wanted its own IBM-compatible mainframe machines (not an Amdahl version). The FACOM M Series was the outcome; it was designed to help existing users of Fujitsu computers migrate to IBM-compatible machines.[62] Sales soared in 1976 and onward with each new release of the next generation of this series. The FACOM M-190 was released in 1976, and the FACOM M-200 in 1978.

---

[62] Japan was similar to other countries that wanted to control their own computer fate instead of relying on IBM to dictate their direction. Both Hitachi and Fujitsu were doing their best to design their own IBM competitive computers, and when Fujitsu signed their marketing agreement with Amdahl, IBM apparently finally got worried. IBM met with Gene Amdahl in the mid-1970s and told him that Amdahl's contract with the Japanese could have a detrimental effect on the U.S. national security. The reality was that the Japanese computer companies were having a detrimental effect on IBM's sales. I can find no outcome from this IBM/Amdahl meeting, but I can assume that Amdahl ignored their plea and continued his relationship with Fujitsu.

Figure 61—Fujitsu FACOM M-190 (with permission from Information Society of Japan)

Although not an innovator in the sense that Fujitsu had developed a startling new computer technology, it did have a solid marketing department with sales and support in place. The 1970s showed that Fujitsu could compete head-on with the other computer makers in the world, and it showed that it had a firm grasp of how computers could be (and had to be) integrated with high-speed telecommunications needs. In 1978, Fujitsu came out with its own 4-bit microprocessor — the MB8843.

In the '80s, Fujitsu introduced its own IBM-compatible PCs, although it can be said that its focus on its mainframe computers made it lose focus on the home computer revolution — and in doing so, it lost ground in this market. But by 1995, Fujitsu had picked up its market share in the PC business, and was now thought of as a major player in this business.

Via well thought-out partnerships and acquisitions, Fujitsu today is a multi-faceted company involved with consumer products, telecommunication products for businesses, consulting services, scanners, software, and, yes, a commitment to making quality and high-speed computers. Their latest computer product is called the K. This computer is capable of processing 10 Peta floating point mathematical operations per second. (A Peta is equal to 10,000,000,000,000,000 — 10 quadrillion!)

General Automation, Inc.

General Automation, Inc. was founded in 1967, and based in Anaheim, California. While many computer companies in the 1960s and 1970s were started strictly by engineers, General Automation was one of the exceptions. As Steve Jobs needed Steve Wozniak, it was the same in this company where a keen business mind needed a smart engineer. Burt Yale was salesman and marketing executive from Honeywell. Larry Gorshorn was an engineer from a small company called Decision Control, Inc., and together they founded General Automation. Unlike Apple, though, who had Jobs and Wozniak mostly in sync with marketing and engineering, in my research it seems that this was not case with these two fellows. Gorshorn like to build and tinker with things (like Wozniak), but Yale concentrated on sales — and not so much on the other business side of things (like controlling expenses and building a product that businesses would buy).

These guys saw a need for a commercially viable product to compete in the process control space (think nuclear power systems or pipelines that need to respond to events NOW!). Their first machine, an 8-bit "Automation Computer," debuted in 1968, as a real-time data collection and control system. As more powerful 16-bit computers came to market, General Automation incorporated this new processor technology into a new line of products. Its products were selling well, but engineering costs were quite high. By 1970, the company had sales of $5 million, but it also owed $5 million to creditors and for general ongoing expenses. In other words, the company's net worth was zero dollars.

In 1970, Ray Noorda was brought in as a consultant to try and figure out how to turn the company around. In May 1971, Noorda was named executive vice president of General Automation. (Noorda had a degree in engineering and had worked at General Electric prior to coming onboard. In 1984 he became CEO of Novell, Inc. — a software and service company based in Provo, Utah.)

In 1971, the company doubled its sales to $10.6 million. For the first time in its history, it showed a net profit instead of a net loss (although the profit was a modest $3,000). But Noorda's strategy was working, and by the end of 1972, sales had increased to $16 million and net income to $1.56 million. In 1973, sales doubled again to $30.4 million. Noorda was named president of the company in December 1973. From 1973 to 1974 sales again doubled to $61.4 million. In terms of gross revenue, General Automation was now the fourth largest minicomputer company in the world. Noorda also had taken the company public, thereby raising more needed capital.

Rapid sales growth is one of the greatest tests of a president of any company. While having lots of money coming in is nice in many aspects, there is a tendency at some companies not to watch where the money is invested — and so it was at this company.

One anecdote I found illustrates the chaos that Noorda and the other upper managers had to deal with inside the company. Yale, one of General Automation's founders, had a heart attack and left the company, leaving the international operations unsupervised. No successor had been named, and no manager had stepped up to take over. Noorda invited an old GE colleague, Jack Davis, to have breakfast in downtown Anaheim and to discuss General Automation's woes. Davis was offered the job of getting control of the international business, and off he went. After one of Davis' follow-up trips to Europe, Davis told the following story to Noorda: "The guys in Europe had been running totally out of control. They had nobody to report to. So, what these folks would do was either call in sick or just disappear. I got over there and found a guy in France, an American expatriate, building a new home. He hadn't been in the office more than half a dozen times in the last six months. He left a message with his secretary to call him if anybody needed him." General Automation was definitely a company out of control — contrary to what Noorda was being led to believe by some of his managers.

In 1975, a new generation of products being built by the company was behind schedule. When the products finally came to market, the technology was fast, but didn't catch on with sales. The mid-1970s saw a light recession, and funding was drying up for money from outside investors. As spending was reduced in the markets, General Automation was in trouble — sales came in at a paltry $5.5 million in 1975. Internal management and the board of directors' finger-pointing started, and Noorda ended up leaving the company.

Figure 62—General Automation SPC-16

General Automation had carved out a niche for "automation" computers — computers that monitored events in real-time. What it failed to do was to keep an eye on the competition with the adaptation of less expensive components. There was also a lack of knowledge, in general, about how to run a company, with its many facets of engineering, sales, and support closely intertwined.

In the mid-1980s, General Automation had completely sold off its minicomputers that did real-time monitoring, and had come out with a line of business computers, called Zebra, which ran the Pick operating system; each system could support up to 256 users. It also could accommodate up to five Motorola microprocessors when fully configured. Not to be deterred from conquering the world market, General Automation signed an agreement with AWA Computers of North Sydney, Australia to launch a major marketing and sales campaign for the Zebra line of business computers in the South Pacific area. The computer systems, although made according to General Automation specifications, were to be sold under AWA Computers' brand, a division of AWA Ltd. Few sales were generated from this venture.

The *Australia Times* wrote in August 28, 1986: "General Automation computer maker is in the middle of a massive turnaround effort...it has signed a marketing and distribution agreement with an Australian company that could be worth more than $15 million over the next three years." Unfortunately, the infusion of revenue didn't help much, and in 1987, General Automation was dissolved.

General Electric

As the old adage goes, "so close, but no cigar." I am including GE in this book because it was right on the cusp of the 1970s computer revolution – and to illustrate what happened to companies that wanted to compete with IBM, but then realized they couldn't. Some companies fought the IBM battle to the bitter end and ended up losing everything; in GE's case, it was so diversified that when it figuratively (and literally) did pull the plug on its computer line, the overall company survived quite well, and is of course, still alive and kicking from its headquarters in Fairfield, Connecticut.

General Electric had developed its own line of proprietary computer products from the 1950s through the early 1960s. It was grouped in fine company and mentioned in the same breath with companies such as IBM, Burroughs, Control Data Corporation, Honeywell, RCA, UNIVAC, and NCR.

GE was competing for IBM customers. In 1964, IBM brought out the System/360 line of products. GE attempted to compete by coming out with its "GE Compatibles 200" line. Basically, the GE system was a "me too" system with little advantages to IBM other than price—and the IBM salesforce was ready to compete with that also. IBM customers (and potential GE buyers) weren't buying into GE's version of the IBM 360, and sales never did make the product line profitable. In 1970, GE sold its computer division to Honeywell leaving GE to concentrate on aircraft engines, consumer products, and other industrial products.

GE contributed to the computer era in two areas. First, GE created (along with the Bank of America) the concept of using magnetic ink character recognition (MICR) standards used on checks today. Second, it created a very sophisticated database product to use on its computers. (It only worked on its computers, so it wasn't portable like today's SQL is.) Its product was called the Integrated Data Store. Similar in concept to IBM's hierarchical linking of data files to together, GE could spread its data around on different random-access devices (while still maintaining a link between the data files), supplied access to it via COBOL or FORTAN, had lots of utilities for querying and maintaining it, had random access directly to any data file, and on an ongoing basis, automatically reorganized the data so that it was stored efficiently. This is yet another example of a product ahead of its time and the company not understanding what it had.

G.M. Research, Inc. (aka GMR, Inc.)

What do garlic and a laptop computer have in common? It turns out quite a lot—and it shows how ideas and inspirations spring from different places. When my research started and I began digging into 1970 computer companies, I found two one-sentence references in two separate documents for this company. As I tried to find out more about G.M. Research (GMR), I kept hitting a dead end from simply a lack of anything being written about it. But I kept researching because I was intrigued by the fact that the owner of the company claimed to hold the first U.S. patent for a portable computer. My sleuthing eventually led me to James Murez—the inventor I was looking for. Through emails and phone interviews, I was able to finally answer, "What was this company?" To start with the basics, GMR was located a little south of Los Angeles, California, in Carson, California, and was incorporated in that state on Friday, August 25, 1978, by Murez.

A little more now on garlic. Murez's family had a large garlic farm in southern California, and like all farmers, needed to sell their product. At the time, though, garlic was one of those commodities thrown in loose with the other vegetables in a supermarket. The senior Murez, Joe, convinced a supermarket that he could increase sales (thereby benefiting both parties) by packaging the garlic into little bags and putting them on a rack to be sold separately. It worked, and the Murez garlic market was booming.

As a teenager, James worked in the garlic packaging plant and was fascinated by the machinery needed to produce the product. Tinkering and improving on the technology was a common day in the plant for Murez. In the mid-1970s, computer clubs and companies were forming to show how microprocessors could be built and used for real work. Whether it was a spark from visiting a local computer store (aptly named, The Computer Store, in close-by Santa Monica) or just his inventive nature (or both), Murez set out to build his own computer.

The idea for building a portable one was not quite there yet—another spark was needed for that. In his small house on Santa Monica Beach, Murez would tinker, solder, test, and then drive a few weekends a month to a friend's house in Santa Barbara (about 100 miles away) where they would continue their work. Necessity again proved to be the mother of invention. Murez was worried about someone breaking into his beach house and stealing the Z-1 computer he had bought from Cromemco, so he would pack all of the parts into his car every time he made the drive to Santa Barbara. Tiring of carting this huge box, a TV, and other parts into and out of his car, he hit upon the idea of making the computer more portable—and thus, work was now focused on putting a keyboard, video display, memory, CPU, floppy disk drive, and power supply into some sort of all-in-one enclosure that could be carried around more easily.

In 1978, GMR produced its first product called the Micro Star. According to Murez, the Micro Star was never intended to be released as a commercial product per se, but rather to serve as a prototype to get everything to fit and work together properly before a "production-ready" system was started.[63] The result was a product ready to sell; it was named the Small One. This machine was not only a PC, but was indeed a "portable" one—and it was beautifully built with all kinds of wonderful hardware and software options.

---

[63] To show Mr. Murez's creativeness, he took the Cromemco motherboard and cut it into three pieces to make it fit and work inside his smaller enclosure!

Figure 63—The Small One, and the Small One on a stand

Specifications for the Small One were as follows:

- Using an S-100 bus, it came with three boards and five empty slots for expansion
- Z80 microprocessor
- 14-amp power supply
- 9-in. CRT display
- Implosion protection shield
- 77-character keyboard with numeric keys, plus four programmable function keys
- Hinged, detachable keyboard
- Retractable carrying handle (!)
- Optional carrying cover
- Space for an optional 5-in. mini-disk
- Space for three I/O ports on the back
- Reset/power controls on the back
- Cooling fan (advertised as "super" quiet)
- Fit into a 20¼ in. x 8 in. x 16 in. cabinet
- RS-232 communications port (optional)
- Color plotter (optional)
- Screenware Pak 1 operating system (standard)
- Screenware Pak II operating system (optional for graphics processing)
- Graphic software emulation of TEKEM

- Color graphic upgrade
- Optional light pen

Obviously, this was an impressive PC, in addition to being a portable one. The weight was approximately thirty to fifty pounds depending on options. The Small One came with the GMOS operating system, and offered a database management system, a word processor, compilers (PASCAL, BASIC, Z80 assembler), and other utilities. However, not only could the Small One be used for business work, but with optional video cards and drivers, it allowed for very detailed graphics for more scientific work. Many of these systems were sold to government agencies as custom built/delivered from the factory.

Murez received the <u>first</u> U.S. patent for a portable computer.[64] He filed for his patent on June 11, 1979, and it was granted on March 30, 1982. Unfortunately, from what I could gather from the patent itself, it was rather specific in some areas, and too loose in others — basically because Murez did not have the funds to hire more than a part-time lawyer (Murez's words). Murez exhibited his PC at the 1980 IEEE WESCON trade show in a new category "computers," as well as at the first Comdex Computer Show in Las Vegas. Other companies with an eye for making a portable also attended these shows, and in a strange set of coincidences within only a few years Compaq, HP, IBM, Olivetti, Kaypro, and Osborn (to name a few well-known companies) came out with their own versions of a portable PC that looked eerily like the Small One. None of these companies offered to pay Murez

---

[64] Looking nothing like the small, five-pound version we fold up and tuck under our arm today, this portable's patent description is as follows: "The present invention permits use of a single enclosure which satisfies the needs of portability as it is closeable into a suitcase-style cabinet with a tractable carrying handle. Specifically, the keyboard enclosure is hinged to the main frame enclosure in such a manner that it is possible to fold the keyboard up against the main frame and to latch the two together. It is, therefore, an object of the present invention to provide for a computer housed in a closeable, suitcase-style cabinet. Another object is to provide for such an enclosure, which is easily deployable into operation."

any money for his idea or royalties — still GMR was hanging on.

Figure 64 - Other portables competing with the Small One in the early 1980s; from left to right: Osborne, Compaq, and IBM

Another model, the GO-512, came out in 1979. This model was almost identical to the Small One except that it offered a graphics option which allowed 512 x 512 resolution on the display. Using only one video printed-circuit board (PCB) from Scion Corporation, this reduced the need for daisy-chained video boards that other companies used to make a high-resolution color display.

Here are some examples of how software was now used to increase hardware sales. One of the most impressive systems GMR developed was a joint project with Bolt, Beranek and Newman (BBN) in Cambridge, MA. The machine was called the CAT system, which stood for Computer Automated Testing. It was basically a psychometric testing system to be used by the U.S. Department of Defense (DOD) for enlisting people into the armed services. The DOD project created a question pool that was stored on a Small One's 5MB hard drive (which was a wire wrapped prototype by Shugart). A person who was taking the test would be asked some number of questions in one category until he/she started to give wrong answers, at which time the system would change to another subject, until it was determined exactly what the person was capable of doing. The entire system had to be capable of being set up by a retired school teacher, who might have to walk up a flight of stairs with it to administer it on the second floor of a school gym under times of, as the DOD put it, "full mobilization," meaning if and when the U.S. was at war and recruiting is a very high priority. Sounds pretty simple today with a laptop, but this was not feasible with any other PC on the market then, as they were simply not "portable" enough.

The CAT system introduced several advancements in the development cycle of the GMR systems. BBN was working on switching packet protocols at the time (today it is called the internet) and wanted the system to be able to wake up and transmit test scores to central systems in the middle of the night. The need for this software now drove the need for more hardware inside the Small One. A piggyback PCB was developed that allowed the emerging Ethernet specification to function in 1981. The first switching power supplies GMR developed also were created with the CAT system in mind. They had an input power range of 12-85VDC or 100-250VAC at 50-400 Hz, so basically, they could be plugged into anything from a car to an airplane or the wall outlet anywhere around the world. (The CAT system was described and shown on the cover of the BBN Annual Report in 1982.)

As the personal computer market was being inundated with public offerings from Tandy/Radio Shack, HP, and IBM, the niche that GMR had created in high-end, custom, low-production markets was drying up. The IBM personal computer introduced a new circuit board design that was incompatible with the S-100 design and the CP/M software GMR had developed. Retooling was out of the question with limited financing and the growing competition in the marketplace.

In 1984, another small business was about to understand what it was like to compete with IBM. The Olympic Games were coming to Los Angeles. In early 1983, BBN and GMR made a presentation of the CAT system to the Los Angeles Olympic Organizing Committee (LAOOC). The demonstration showed how GMR's portable computers could be used to sign up volunteers around the city. It was a perfect match for both companies. Unfortunately for GMR, IBM was the computer sponsor for the Olympics, and it quickly inserted its own machines instead of GMR's. Whether this GMR contract with the Olympics could have sustained GMR's business is questionable however, because IBM and others were competing with their own portable versions. In total, GMR produced approximately 1,000 Small Ones before closing up its business in approximately 1983.

There is a happy ending to this brief story about the first portable-computer maker. Murez was hired as a technical consultant to the LAOOC, where he met his future wife Melanie Goodman, a linguist who organized and ran the LAOOC Interpreter Services department. Murez, his wife, and two children remain in the Los Angeles area, where he continues to develop new ideas, including high-tech, mixed-use live/work architecture and software for many different applications. (By the way, that is Mr. Murez on the cover.)

Gould, Inc.

Located in Cleveland, Ohio, the graphics division of Gould manufactured and marketed the 4800 Electrostatic Printer.

In 1970, even though Gould's printer could print text, it also could do a lot more, which made it expensive over simple character printers. This printer could print up to 412K characters per minute, and could print any image sent to it. As quirky as it might seem, it allowed connectivity to it via a land line, radio interface, and even a microwave receiver.

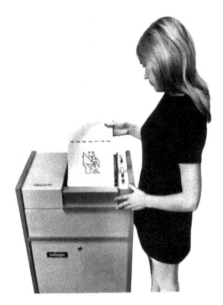

Figure 65—Gould 4800 Electrostatic Printer

GRI Computer

GRI got off to a rough start that had nothing to do with technology, but everything to do with simply trying to come up with a legal name for its company! Located in Massachusetts, founder Saul Dinman came up with the name of General Research Corporation and went public with it. Alas, it did not have its legal department (which probably consisted only of Dinman) do enough research with competing names already in the market—two other companies, General Research and General Radio, caused GRI grief with naming rights. Working it out, GRI was eventually in business in 1968.

Dinman came from DEC where his engineering skills found him as one of the designers of the DEC PDP-8/S model. GRI's first product, the GRI-909, was introduced in 1969. In 1970, it sold for $5,650, and had from 4K to 32K of memory. The GRI-909 had a Teletype machine for input and output (as a printer stand-in), a paper-tape reader, and paper-tape punch—a very basic system. The GRI-909 had a printed-circuit board for the backplane, making it unique at the time. This system was targeted for process control applications, and because of this, it was very Spartan in its design. In other words, it was not meant to be a business computer doing general business applications, so it lacked nice features like being easy to program and having interfaces for peripheral devices.

The GRI-99 came next, and with it came better enhancements to the operating system (which was developed in-house). A later model called the GRI-919 came out last.

After a successful run at selling its line of process control computers, GRI was purchased by venture capitalists in North Carolina, who then turned around and sold the assets to other companies.

Groupe Bull (Bull)

On July 31, 1919, an engineer named Fredrik Rosing Bull filed a patent for a "combined sorter-recorder-tabulator of punch cards." (Let this sink in for a moment, as this was decades before IBM expanded on this idea.) This machine had been commissioned to be built with money from the Norwegian insurance company Storebrand. In 1921, Storebrand was pleased enough with this invention to have it deployed into its overall operations. In 1922, Bull increased its sales by finding another customer to buy its machine; Bull had doubled its customer base, and the France-based company was off and running.

Over the following years, new product enhancements came out, management changes ensued (along with company name changes), and partnerships (most notably General Electric, Honeywell, and NEC—all of whom just happened to be doing their own computer development). Bull was finding itself a leading electronics company by the time the 1960s rolled around. Bull, though, was noticing (along with the French government) the inroads IBM, Honeywell, UNIVAC, and other American companies were having on the computer industry throughout France. Bull was driven by the possibilities of making money by competing against IBM, whereas the French government was simply irritated that IBM was hurting French pride — that French companies were using computers that were, well, not French. Both the French government and Bull set out to at least take some of the computer business back for French companies. To understand what was going on and to understand Bull fully, though, one has to understand another entity called CII (and vice versa). The following products were listed under Bull's umbrella:

- CII Iris 50 (1970)
- CII Iris 60 (1972)
- CII Iris 80 (1972)
- CII Mitra 15 (1972)
- GE 600 series (1965)
- Honeywell H200 (1970)
- HB 2000 (1973)*
- Micral (1973)
- Mini6 (1978)
- GE 58 (1970)
- CII HB 64/40 (1976)
- CII HB 66/60 (1976)
- CII HB 61 DPS (1978)

* Honeywell-Bull was importing the Honeywell computer and rebranding it to keep the French government happy.

In reality, Bull was assisting the CII consortium with some research dollars, and in return Bull could help in the marketing of these computers. By the mid-'70s, not only were French companies having a hard time competing with IBM, but also American companies who were facing the IBM juggernaut. Honeywell needed help marketing in Europe, and on May 12, 1975, the merger of CII with Honeywell-Bull (Bull) was announced by the French government. Bull was to receive marketing preferences in certain countries, and the French government gave them a preference on selling computers to (drum roll) the French government!

Figure 66—Groupe Bull Iris 80

In 1977, Bull realized that software was becoming more and more important to its hardware sales, and thus started programs to help accomplish that goal. They started work (with Honeywell's nod of understanding and working with CII software engineers) on what was known internally as unified control processor (UNCP), which would ultimately be known as Datanet. Datanet was a common way for the computers from all three companies (Bull, Honeywell, and CII) to have their computers communicate with other. Datanet was very similar in many aspects to what we today call the internet. Also in 1977, it introduced software (originating from CII) that would communicate to newer magnetic tape peripherals. Additionally, the company introduced new disk drives and software to communicate to them.

Bull was doing quite well financially, with reported earnings of 3,788,000 French francs, and employing over

18,000 people. In this timeframe (1978, to be exact), Bull had taken the original operating system developed by General Electric (which was named the General Electric Comprehensive Operating Supervisor, or GCOS) and with modifications was offering it as GCOS8 for its own Bull platforms.

Bull continued its hardware sales (through partnerships with both Honeywell and CII), and kept on its path for creating new systems-related software components. Up until 1982, Bull was a private company, but in that year, the French government took almost all French computer companies and made them property of the government. In 1994, Bull was allowed to be privatized once again. Today, Bull has a worldwide presence, and is active in many sectors of commerce.

Gulton Industries, Inc.

Gulton (specifically the Gulton Computer Systems Division) wanted to build a less expensive, but reliable, data-entry terminal. Teletype, with its very noisy roll of paper and hard-to-use keyboard, had been a standard for many years for slow data-entry use. For some reason, companies like Gulton could not imagine a data-entry terminal without a roll of paper, and since CRTs added extra cost, the roll of paper for displaying data was continued by Gulton on its terminal. The Gulton LG 10/30 was born in 1970. Unlike the Teletype, which was dumb (it could not be programmed), at least the Gulton could be programmed with limited function keys.

Figure 67—Gulton LG 10/30

The company also offered the LG 10/30 ASR, which had an attached magnetic tape reader/writer. Gulton was based in Hawthorne, California.

Harris

Harris laid down its roots as the "Harris Automatic Press Company" in Niles, Ohio, in 1895. Over the next sixty years, it didn't veer too far from its core business, as it perfected lithographic processes and printing presses. Rich in cash and seeing a need to expand its business, Harris acquired Gates Radio (which produced broadcast electronics) in 1957, and Harris' role in the world was about to change.

Through more acquisitions, such as PRD Electronics located in Brooklyn, New York, Harris found its electronics division growing and producing more profit. In 1967, Harris purchased Radiation, Inc., which developed antennas, integrated circuits, and other electronic components used in America's space program. Radiation's headquarters was in Melbourne, Florida, and since management considered the year-round weather there more pleasant than in the northern Ohio area, Harris packed up and headed for sunny Florida.

With smaller but important acquisitions, more profit rolled in. With more profits came the need to invest it — no use sitting on piles of money if you can't spend it. In 1969, Harris acquired RF Communications and Farinon (both involved in the microwave industry).

Enter Harris into the 1970s. Through its acquisitions, it picked up people who were knowledgeable of the revolution going on in the world of small microprocessors. One such acquired company, Datacraft Corporation, had developed its 6000 Series (which Harris dubbed its "departmental" size computer). This product consisted of a cabinet for its 24-bit operating system CPU, and other smaller cabinets for disk drives and tape drives. The company's computer would support many users on a proprietary communications network, and provide word processing and other basic business needs. Its play was to find a niche for its product that was in competition with IBM's remote processing workstations. Either through copying the Datacraft 6000, or inventiveness on Harris' part, Harris came out with the COPE 1600 minicomputer.

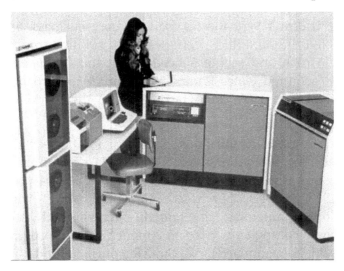

Figure 68—Harris COPE 1600

Harris went on to develop its Series 500 and SLASH 6/7 products. The problems with Harris' computers were twofold: 1) They were not easily expandable. At this same time, for instance, Tandem Computers was marketing a similar type of minicomputer, but Tandem's could easily grow to thousands of processors, and it provided completely fault-tolerant architecture. 2) Harris had turned into an engineering company, and in its ads at the time for its 6024 product, it stressed the engineering that went into its product rather than the business need it filled.[65] In other words, Harris misread the market (although initially getting a foothold in the market) and found itself losing its customer base. Although the company realized it had good ideas in engineering, in 1981, it shut down its business minicomputer line.

One of Harris' significant contributions was the invention of the programmable random only memory (PROM) chip. Before this, computers had to load (or "pre-burn" as some called it) their code into chips. PROMs revolutionized the industry by allowing vendors to buy blank chips, and then custom-load them with code as changes in the code were necessary (e.g., if bugs were found in the previous code, or the device to which they were communicating changed its message formats, etc.).

By the 1980s, Harris had chosen to get out of the minicomputer market and concentrate on its core electronic component niche. (As a side note, after a run of over close to a century of printing involvement, Harris' management saw its printing business take more of a back seat to its electronics; in 1983 the printing division was sold.) Harris continued to acquire more businesses related to the "electronics" industry, and fine-tune its business to focus more on communication equipment, avionics,

---

[65] A comparison on company philosophies can be made between Harris and DEC. Both were "engineering" companies in a sense, but DEC chose to keep making minicomputers (and arguably good ones, at that). While not understanding the business market well, Harris realized it was not a good marketing company and chose to focus on its engineering. Today, while Harris is still in business, DEC is not.

commercial broadcasting, and specialized government needs. Harris is still in business today.

Hazeltine

In 1970, this Little Neck, New York, company manufactured and sold the Hazeltine 1760 terminal. It had its own processor, a keyboard, and a monitor — all actually nicely packaged together. For all practical purposes, it looked similar to any current PC.

Figure 69—Hazeltine 1760

The 1760 in the product's name signified the number of characters it could display. It allowed for split-screen formatting and editing (which was a leading feature at the time), and came with a keyboard with "insert" and "delete" keys. (It's hard to picture a keyboard without these keys today, but in 1970 these simple functions were an added bonus for an operator.) The cursor's position could be programmed. The Model 2000 (which could display 2,000 characters) superseded the Model 1760.

Heathkit

Heathkit, located in Saint Joseph, Michigan (or Benton Harbor as some resources reported, but both being close by on the western shore of Michigan), was a company that originally was for the true hobbyist. In 1978, it had been in business for fifty years, and during the latter part of these five decades, it had started to publish a magazine that listed all kinds of electronic gadgets for sale. The company understood electronics, and had time to look around and see what others were doing with computer "parts." People playing with processor chips were fairly common (for computer-oriented-thinking folks) throughout the U.S. With this information in hand, Heathkit leaped into the world of personal computers.

Heathkit marketed enough parts and peripherals for some inventive folks to build their own small computer system. The first system was called the H8, meaning Heathkit 8-bit CPU, which was based on the Intel 8080A processor. It was marketed as a training computer, but the context was not entirely clear. What kind of training? Programming? Data entry? Soldering? The company's ad didn't say.

Their other computer system was the H11A. This system was based on the Intel 16-bit processor chip, and with its circuitry based on DEC's LSI 11/2, the company promised the system could run thousands of existing applications and software already developed and on the market.

Both the H8 and H11A could be purchased assembled or (for those brave souls) as a kit. The marketing was very creative, as it seemed to steer buyers to the kit instead the assembled versions. The reason this was done was for maintenance. Here is a quote from Heathkit's ad: "The knowledge you gain in building your Heathkit computer is invaluable—for service if it is ever needed, for quick troubleshooting and correction, and just for understanding the workings of the machine."

To continue its link to DEC, Heathkit offered its own peripherals that were compatible with DEC own peripherals. These peripherals included:

- H9 CRT terminal, this had a standard keyboard with programmable function keys, and a built-in CRT monitor
- H10 paper-tape reader/punch; (why it included the paper-tape machine is a mystery, as by 1978 this type of media was all but dead)
- ECP-3801 cassette storage recorder/player
- WH14 line printer
- Floppy-disk storage system
- Dot-matrix printer

Figure 70—Heathkit family of products

In many aspects, Heathkit computers were a "me-too" type of system and never grabbed much of a market share. Still, if someone wanted to build his or her own inexpensive computer (with promised good documentation), then this was an option.

Hewlett-Packard Company

As with several companies that eventually ended up being involved in the computer industry, the Hewlett-Packard Company (HP) had its roots with limited funding ($538) and having a garage as its development area. In 1935, Bill Hewlett and Dave Packard (both engineering graduates of Stanford University) decided to form a company that made electrical testing equipment. Up until 1957, Hewlett-Packard was a private company getting by engineering a small set of dependable products. (There are excellent books written about HP in its early days.)

HP grew, and because it now had a lot of electronic equipment, one could argue that the company was in general unfocused and in need of a direction. Some of its early products included electronic test equipment such as signal generators, voltmeters, oscilloscopes, frequency counters, thermometers, machines that kept time standards, wave analyzers, and many other instruments. One of the overriding traits of HP's products, however, was the company's accuracy and precise measurements — something that the electronics industry needed as TVs were coming onto the world stage.

Another reason one could tag HP with the label of "unfocused" was because of it spinning off divisions, only to buy them back again. There was a failed partnership with a Japanese company that also added too many people to the HP payroll—again, with some questioning about whether HP knew where it was going.

In the late 1950s and early 1960s, HP bought some DEC's minicomputers to work with its own instruments. Instead of continuing this relationship with DEC, HP knew it had smart engineers on staff, so it assigned some of them to design their own minicomputer. Rather than use someone else's processor, HP also decided to manufacture its own. The results were the models HP 2100 and HP 1000 series, debuting in 1966 – and keeping in production throughout the 1980s. Both of these systems used what HP called their "real-time operating system," which meant that their optimum use was for real-time process control functions. In 1968, HP came out with a version of a "personal" computer (the HP 9100A), although HP was leery of using the term "personal computer" for two reasons: 1) Few in the world understood what this term meant, and 2) IBM had started to use the term "personal computer" in its ads, and since HP's cabinetry didn't look like the IBM product, HP was afraid that people wouldn't know what it was. The answer? Call it a calculator, of course! Although primitive to what anyone today would call a PC, this product had integrated circuits, a CRT monitor, magnetic card storage, a printer, and keyboard that was a cross between an adding machine and scientific calculator (it had no alphabetic keys). It sold for approximately $5,000.

HP produced the HP 9100 (models A and B), as a programmable desktop calculator in 1968, and in 1971 came out with the 9810, which was programmable with small magnetic cards.

In 1972, HP produced the first handheld scientific calculator (the HP 35), then a programmable version, the HP 65, in 1974, and the first symbolic and graphic calculator in 1979 (the HP-28C).

A series of true desktop computers started in 1975 with the 9815,[66] a cheaper 9805 series, then the 9825 series in 1976, and the 9855 series in 1979. All of these products used BASIC as their programming language, and used a proprietary magnetic tape for storage.

HP developed its line of minicomputers called the 1000 series, then with continued enhancements came out with the HP 2100 series (which had started with the 2116 and ended at the 21MX). The 21MX was renamed to 1000M, the 21MX/E to 1000E, and later on the 1000F was introduced. The 1000F came with a floating-point processor included and support of the FORTRAN language (which itself supported matrix calculation and trigonometric functions).

---

[66] In a strange coincidence Steve Wozniak was torn as to whether to present his idea for a PC to his company (HP). But, after he did present his idea to HP's management, they gave him a "thanks, but no thanks" for sharing that with them. Soon thereafter, and after more tinkering in Job's garage, Apple was born. Timing and creativity was everything – for both Wozniak and HP.

HP rode its successes in the minicomputer family to bigger and faster versions of its HP 3000 and later with the HP 9000.[67] Using its expertise, HP produced many lines of printers,[68] which contributed greatly to its revenues starting in 1984 until today.

Figure 71—HP 3000

Seemingly forgetting the problems of not being focused from its earlier days, HP ventured into marketing its own brand of TVs, digital cameras, scanners, personal digital assistants (PDA), and other "touchpad" types of devices. What HP seemed to do was to follow computer fads that made the rounds in the 1990s instead of being inventive and truly creating its own products. Most of its products died an inglorious death by lack of demand (and quality, which HP had once held as one of its foundations). Unable to focus on creating products to compete with IBM, HP eventually bought Compaq Inc., which only a few years before had acquired Tandem Computers Incorporated and DEC. The acquisition of Compaq gave HP new patents

---

[67] Please see the section on the ASK Group and how it spurred HP 3000 sales.

[68] HP's proliferation in the printer business is so well known that today many people refer to HP as "the printer company."

and products it could once again use to compete with IBM. In 2008, HP bought Electronic Data Systems (EDS), thereby adding the potential for sale of more services.

Today, HP's main office is in Palo Alto, California. Its U.S. operations are directed from its facility near Houston, Texas. Additionally, it has offices in most of the countries in the world.

Hitachi

The Hitachi company was formed as an electric motor repair and manufacturing shop in 1910 by an electrical engineer named Namihei Odaira in Ibaraki Prefecture, Japan. His first product was the country's first five-horsepower motor (used in ore mining). No one at the time could imagine how this little company would grow to be one of the largest in its country, but it did. In 1920, Hitachi Ltd. was formed, and four years later it was making and selling its first direct-current electric locomotives. Ninety-five years later, Hitachi is manufacturing bullet trains that travel over 150 mph.

From the 1920s until today, Hitachi has developed large, electrical equipment, monorails, software for reservation systems, elevators, nuclear power plants, digital/optical inventions, and eventually made its own computer systems. Hitachi was in the middle of basically anything that had to do with electrical devices. For instance, in 1965 it introduced the HITAC 10 and HITAC 5020 computer. These systems were of limited commercial use, though, because it was basically used for manufacturing to do engineering calculations. Of significance, however, was the fact that it was the second generation of Hitachi's computers that used all transistors as circuitry, and the whole machine was of the company's own design.[69]

With a focus still on engineering work, the HITAC 5020 was designed and manufactured primarily to perform calculations relating to science/engineering or scientific management, but it also was appropriate for business calculations. Along with the processor came developments of special display devices, and other peripheral equipment (e.g., magnetic disk storage).

The 1970s brought significant development for the company, as it developed a SCADA application to provide real-time monitoring of the bullet trains. In 1971, Hitachi developed what was considered a huge triumph in the computer industry by coming out with a one gigabyte magnetic storage device. Today, it is not uncommon to think of this as a small size, but in the early 1970s, other manufacturers' computers' storage held a small number of megabytes; a 20-megabyte disk was considered large, and Hitachi had exceeded this fifty-fold.

Serious computer development followed for Hitachi in 1971; this is when it started work on its about to be very successful M-series product line. IBM, as has been noted throughout this book, was a juggernaut when it came to convincing companies to automate with its (IBM) computers. Hitachi wanted to compete in this business and was convinced it could make a computer that could do this. The M-series was basically designed with the IBM 370 architecture in mind. For instance, having the same design as the IBM 370 for the input/output interface meant that peripheral equipment (e.g., disk drives, tape drives, etc.) could be moved easily from IBM to Hitachi.

---

[69] The instruction system of the HITAC 5020 was based on the "FABM" concept (where F stands for Function, A for A-register (accumulator), B for B-register (index register), and M for memory). The concept behind this design was that instructions to handle A, B, and M were made in a uniform fashion; both the A and B registers to be the same and either could be accessed by other instructions, thereby providing slightly more processor speed.

In November 1974, the M-180 was announced. This was followed by the M-170 in May 1975, the M-160II in November 1975, and the M-150 in February 1977. The high-end (meaning lots of memory and storage) M-180 turned out to be excellent for telecommunications work and for handling large amounts of data. Because it was a fast machine overall, it found its way into more universities for engineering calculation work.

The M-170 was an improvement over the M-180 in that it provided yet more storage, and the processor had improvements. It found usage in both real-time processing and the processing of large batches of transactions.

Figure 72—Hitachi M-170 (with permission from Information Processing Society of Japan)

The M-160II's main feature was its particularly high cost-performance; meaning that as yet another improvement to the M-series product line, customers got significant performance for the investment (compared to, say, what IBM was offering).

The M-150 was developed for companies that couldn't afford the higher priced M-series machines. Basically, it was a scaled-down M-160II with fewer disk drives and less memory capacity.

In general, an M-series computer could be configured with the following:

- One to two CPUs
- 1MB – 16MB of main memory
- Up to 64K of buffer memory
- Up to 16 channels for I/O peripherals

In 1976, Hitachi succeeded in sending and deciphering the world's first digital/optical transmission. Essentially, digital commands were passed to a device of Hitachi's design, light pulses were sent in fiber optic cable, and on the other end another Hitachi device interpreted these patterns and converted them into digital commands for processing. Today, we take optical connection technology for granted—in 1976, it was an event that revolutionized how computers could communicate with other computer devices.

Hitachi introduced a high-speed amino acid analysis machine, along with higher resolution electron microscopes, small color cameras, and other related, but not especially focused computer products.

The HITAC M-series 200h was released in 1979. This family consisted of the 220D, 220H, 220K, 240D, 260D, 260D, 260H, 260K, 280D, and 280H products. These products consisted of the following configurations:

- M-220D—CPU (1), main memory (1MB - 8MB), I/O channels (3 – 5)
- M-220H—CPU (1), main memory (1MB - 8MB), I/O channels (3 – 5)
- M-220K—CPU (1), main memory (2MB - 8MB), I/O channels (3 – 8)
- M-240D— CPU (1), main memory (2MB - 16MB), I/O channels (3 – 8)
- M-240H—CPU (1), main memory (2MB - 16MB), I/O channels (5 – 8)
- M-260D—CPU (1), main memory (8MB - 32MB), I/O channels (8 – 32)

- M-260H — CPU (1), main memory (8MB - 32MB), I/O channels (8 – 32)
- M-260K — CPU (1), main memory (8MB - 32MB), I/O channels (8 – 32)
- M-280D — CPUs (1 – 4), main memory (16MB - 64MB), I/O channels (8 – 32)
- M-280H — CPUs (1 – 4), main memory (16MB - 64MB), I/O channels (8 – 32)

Hitachi's contribution to the computer revolution was that of innovative design of its operating system, disk drives, optical connectivity between computer systems and peripherals, and creative packaging/bundling of its systems to attract customers.

From 1980 until today, Hitachi continues to come out with yet faster computers, faster trains, faster and smaller disks, thermal power generation, software, computer consulting, construction equipment, elevators, power tools, and other business and consumer products.

Honeywell International, Inc.

Honeywell had its start at the dawn of the electricity age in the late 1800s. Keep in mind that at that time there were generally two ways to heat a building or house — either with wood or coal. Coal mines all over the world were in peak production and forests were being cleared because of the demand (for both their heating and building properties). There were few options to control the warmth from a coal furnace — basically you had to watch the furnace constantly to adjust the heat output, or let it run low and then add more coal. To use the old adage, "necessity is the mother of invention," and so it was in 1885. Albert Butz invented a device called the "damper flapper," which was a primitive (by today's standards) thermostat for coal furnaces. Egged on by this success, Butz created electric motors and more ideas to control furnaces. Butz went on to form the Minneapolis Heat Regulator Company in 1886.

Twenty years later, Mark C. Honeywell founded Honeywell Heating Specialty Co., Inc. in Wabash, Indiana. Honeywell was doing well competing with (and complementing) Butz's company, but Honeywell was now the larger company of the two. Thus, in 1927 Honeywell purchased Butz's company, with the new company now called the Minneapolis-Honeywell Regulator Company. Honeywell kept his position of president of the merged companies, and W.R. Sweatt was named its first chairman.

Sweatt's (followed by his son Harold) led Honeywell in some capacity for seventy-five years, and during that time took Honeywell from a rather small, regional company to a large global enterprise. One of the projects it oversaw was something that many take for granted today—a thermostat that controls when one's furnace comes on and goes off. One of the ways that Sweatt pushed innovation was via the annual "H.W. Sweatt Engineer-Scientist Award." This award was for any employee in recognition of his or her outstanding technical ability and contribution to a significant technical accomplishment for the company and their profession; this act of recognition would be fruitful as the world of computers came about.

In 1961, Honeywell went through a new sales model, which placed an emphasis on profits instead of strictly sales volume. International presence was increased as the new president, James Binger, wanted his company to be a world leader in its business. As the company branched out into more electronic components (importer and reseller of Pentax cameras, defense components, aerospace electronics, and a little computer development), Binger officially changed the company's corporate name from Minneapolis-Honeywell Regulator Company to Honeywell.

One of Honeywell's major contributions during the 1950s and 1960s was an automated control unit that could control an aircraft through various stages of a flight (now known as the "auto-pilot").

Honeywell stepped into the computing pond via a joint venture with Raytheon called Datamatic Corp. Raytheon sold its share to Honeywell, and from watching IBM and others seemingly have a monopoly on computing, Honeywell fell into the trap where it saw potential business in this area — not realizing just how hard it was to compete with IBM. Honeywell officially named its computing division the Honeywell Information Systems Division. The first computer to come out of this division was called the Honeywell 800, which was renamed later to the Honeywell 1800. In 1962, Honeywell purchased the computer maker Computer Control Corporation (AKA "3Cs"), and gave this new group its own division named the Honeywell's Computer Control Division. Honeywell now had its hands in the business end of computing and in the control systems area (e.g., aiming rockets). These computer company acquisitions officially made Honeywell part of a group known in the computer industry as "IBM and the Seven Dwarfs."[70] Later, when their number had been reduced to five, the "seven dwarfs" became the BUNCH (an acronym made from the initials of Burroughs, UNIVAC, NCR, Control Data Corporation, and Honeywell).

In 1963, Honeywell was selling its Honeywell 200, which competed with a small IBM system called the IBM 1401. The 200 was sold until the early 1970s, when it was made obsolete by faster computers.

Now we finally come to Honeywell in the 1970s. In 1970, Honeywell bought General Electric's computer division. In the early 1970s (and even to a large extent today), most computer companies were fighting the same technical problem — how to store data. IBM, Burroughs, UNIVAC,

---

[70] Because of its size, IBM was "Snow White," while the "dwarfs" were the seven significantly smaller computer companies: Burroughs, Control Data Corporation, General Electric, Honeywell, NCR, RCA, and UNIVAC.

and others had developed their own way to do this, but of course each product was proprietary to that company. Honeywell, the French company Groupe Bull, and Control Data Corporation formed a joint venture called Magnetic Peripherals Inc. (MPI) to develop a more generic storage device that could be used by different computers (and, of course, produce revenue for MPI). Within two years, MPI became the world leader in 14-inch disk drive technology.

Continuing its involvement in computing, in 1970 Honeywell took over responsibility of GE's Multics operating system.[71] Multics had its roots at MIT, GE, and Bell Labs, and had many redundant hardware components built in. Phone companies and other companies needing process control liked this operating system (as well as the way it could be easily expanded by adding more processors, memory, and disk storage).

Around this timeframe (in mid-1969 to be exact), the Honeywell 316 came out, and was a popular (from a sales perspective) 16-bit minicomputer. It was part of the Series 16, which included the Models 116, 316, 416, 516, and 716 (which continued to be sold through the 1970s). These products were used for process control, real-time data acquisition and control, laboratory systems, and timesharing needs. This machine was used by Charles H. Moore to develop the first complete, stand-alone implementation of the Forth programming language. The same machines were used as the ARPANET interface message processors (IMP).

Honeywell 316 operated at 2.5 MHz. It was initially released with a capacity of 4K – 16K RAM (which eventually could be expanded to 32K). The basic processor had a single interrupt signal line, but an option provided up to forty-eight interrupts.

---

[71] UNIX borrowed many of Multics features and even the naming of their same commands.

In addition to a front panel display of lights and toggle switches, the system supported a Teletype Model 33 ASR teleprinter/input device and a paper-tape reader/punch. In general, most (if not all) of the Honeywell family of computers could access card readers and punches, line printers, magnetic tape, and both fixed-head and removable hard disk drives.

A rack-mounted configuration weighed around 150 pounds and used 475 watts of power. Honeywell advertised the system as the first minicomputer selling for less than $10,000.

The Honeywell 316 has the distinction of being the first computer displayed at a computer show with semiconductor RAM memory. To help sell the 316, Honeywell provided up to 500 software packages that could run on it. A FORTRAN IV compiler was available, as well as an assembler, real-time disk operating systems, and system utilities and libraries.

Figure 73—Honeywell 316

A strange relationship occurred when Honeywell and Neiman Marcus, the department store chain, teamed up in 1969 to offer the "kitchen computer." There was a fascination that people had about computers, but the masses thought of computers only for large companies — and this product wanted to change that thinking. Using the Model 316 minicomputer as a base, and stripping aside things such as a tape drive, communication lines, card reader, etc., the Honeywell Kitchen Computer was born. This product was essentially a keyboard and printer, and was advertised for $10,000. It included built-in recipes that were supposed to attract affluent women to buy these computers to impress their guests. It even had a built-in cutting board! Contrary to the hype, I could find no evidence that any Honeywell Kitchen Computers were ever sold. Take a look at the next picture and ask yourself, "Would I buy one of these for my kitchen?"

Figure 74—Honeywell Kitchen Computer

Although the Kitchen Computer was a lark in many aspects, it did represent the first time a computer (not just calculators) was offered as a "consumer" product.

By the 1980s, Honeywell was continuing its growth in the computer industry with purchases such as Incoterm Corporation, being known for its involvement in both airline reservations system networks and bank teller markets, as well as software innovations for the first Digital Process Communications protocol (for smart transmitters used in process measurements). In 1989, as Honeywell's focus was less on business computers, it sold its computer division to Groupe Bull (which was briefly named Bull HN, and then simply Bull).

General Electric announced in 2000 that it would attempt to acquire the $21-billion-valued Honeywell. The merger was cleared by American authorities, but was blocked (because of the potential of the merged companies to stifle competition) by the European Commission in 2001.

The current Honeywell International, Inc. is actually the product of a merger between AlliedSignal and Honeywell, Inc., which occurred in 1999. Although AlliedSignal was twice the size of Honeywell, the combined company chose the Honeywell name because of its brand recognition. However, the corporate headquarters were consolidated to AlliedSignal's headquarters in Morristown, New Jersey, rather than Honeywell's former headquarters in Minneapolis, Minnesota.

Today, Honeywell is a Fortune 100 company, and shown in 2012 as seventy-seventh in the Fortune 500 America's ranking. Honeywell has a global workforce of approximately 130,000, of which approximately 58,000 are employed in the U.S.

IMLAC Corporation

Located in Needham, Massachusetts, this company saw a niche for graphic display terminals. Most companies were happy just to be able to display numbers, alphabetic letters, and a few ordinary symbols such as a period. Since IMLAC was located close to MIT, DEC, and other area engineering companies, it saw a need for users to be able to display mathematic formulas, intricate electronic circuits, blueprints, and other graphic needs (perhaps borrowing an idea from Dicomed).

In 1972, it produced the PDS-1D, an "interactive graphics display computer," and sold it for a whopping $10,000. (Light pen included!) It was, for all practical purposes, a minicomputer. It had one display monitor; a keyboard and numeric pad; a 16-bit, 4K RAM (expandable to 32K) CPU, and it ran FORTRAN. As options, it offered magnetic disk, magnetic tape, cassette drives, cursor positioning device, and a joystick.

While not a huge company from a gross revenue perspective, IMLAC sold enough to continue more research and development. Over the next six years, it produced a product called the DYNAGRAPHIC™ System. This was basically an expansion of the PDS-1D with the capability of supporting up to thirty-six graphic terminals. Users could share their graphic displays with others in their network. In 1978, IMLAC had eight sales offices throughout the U.S., and another in the UK. By this time graphics were becoming more common from Microsoft Windows programming and through Apple products, and IMLAC started to lose its market share. I could find no reference of the company after 1978.

Incoterm Corporation

This corporation was brought to life on June 4, 1970, in the Sudbury, Massachusetts, area by James F. Upton and Jean Noel Tariot. The company name was derived from INtelligent COmputer TERMinals. Its products included a line of banking systems (including software), ATMs, intelligent controllers, and passenger airline reservation and ticketing systems. Incoterm offered what it called intelligent clustered terminals; these allowed entities such as banks, airports, and other client environments to do certain functions and operations independent of a mainframe connection. It is hard to fathom today what the early commercial airlines faced when dealing with reservations, but imagine a gymnasium-sized facility where dozens of people answered phones and updated reservation lists that someone had to find on someone's desk. What Incoterm did was design airline reservation software, minimize communication costs, and do away with slow response times from the mainframe as some data could be stored and accessed locally.

Figure 75—Incoterm products

Incoterm held patents for a "cash dispensing machine" (ATM), banking software, and three specialized types of card readers.

Clients of Incoterm included Security Pacific, Barclays, Wells Fargo, United Airlines, TWA, Delta Airlines, American Airlines, and the Florida Department of Motor Vehicles. Honeywell bought Incoterm in 1977 (although it retained its name as a wholly owned subsidiary of Honeywell through the mid-1980s) to compete in both the airline reservations system networks and bank teller markets.

Infomark

In 1977, Infomark, an Exton, Pennsylvania, company, introduced its DMS-24 system. This system was designed specifically for order entry and inventory control, and it was actually a Data General Nova 3 minicomputer coupled with Control Data's disk drives. It also came with a 100-line-per-minute printer and one console terminal. The basic configuration consisted of 32K RAM and 10MB of disk space. It could be expanded to 256K RAM, 320MB of disk space, and twenty-four CRT terminals.

Figure 76—Infomark DMS-24

Infomark modified the operating system to focus on five modules: data preparation, online access to stored data, unattended batch processing, high-volume/real-time data updating, and security (against loss and unauthorized access of data).

Its database control module also was very inventive because it was a central point of access to the data, meaning that no one could access the data without going through the database control module — which in theory could provide a very secure database. The bad part of this "you must go through me approach" to the data meant that it was a potential bottleneck for throughput.

As stated above, this system was targeted for basically two audiences, and thus the third key element that Infomark brought to the market was software packages (applications) tied directly to its hardware products. The basic DMS-24 system sold for $35,000.

Inforex

By the time the mid-1970s rolled around, the world was moving away from punched cards — and those who clung to this old way of thinking were doomed with antiquated ideas and technology. In 1970, though, punched cards still held a place for processing data, so when companies like Inforex came along with new ideas, it was an outlier on the punch card bell curve.

Based in Burlington, Massachusetts, this company developed its Intelligent Key Entry system. It consisted of a cabinet, which held the processor, a 7- or 9-track magnetic tape, a modem, a magnetic disk, and connections for eight keyboard terminals.

Each terminal had a standard keyboard, tabbing, column duplicating, and other functions a keypunch operator was used to doing. The company's thinking was that it didn't want to throw the users into the new world of keying to a disk instead of a punch card by not letting them do traditional keypunch actions. As a user typed in data, the data was collected on a central magnetic disk, and this data was then made available to any other user at any other terminal. Any user from any terminal could initiate a data transfer from the central processor to a remote/host server.

A nice feature for users was that a terminal was capable of learning a new format for keying in data. The new format was stored on the central processor's magnetic disk, and then this format was available to any other user on any other terminal. Users weren't limited to eighty characters as with a punch card, but rather variable length records of up to 125 characters were allowed.

The monthly rental was $50 per terminal, or $960 for the complete system (including eight terminals).

Information Management Sciences Associates, Inc.

Information Management Sciences Associates, Inc. was founded by Bill Millard in 1972, in San Leandro, California (his home doubling as his world headquarters). Although San Leandro was across the bay from the "Silicon Valley," it was close enough to keep tabs on what was going on with the other things happening in the world of microprocessors. In 1973, Millard (with a slight change to the original name) formed IMS Associates, Inc. Its success was to be built on opportunity and out of frustration. Being primarily a consulting company, IMS was contracted to build some sort of small "workstation system" for a General Motors new-car dealership.

The planned system would consist of a "control" unit that had a number (undefined at the time) of "workstations" connected to it, which could all share data somehow. IMS thought it could buy the parts it needed from Altair, but when delivery kept being postponed for the equipment, IMS stopped the project. Instead, IMS looked internally for someone to build its computer (which, it turned out, was all it had to do, as well as find additional engineers across the San Francisco Bay; this was what was so incredible about working in or near Palo Alto and Cupertino.)

In October 1975, IMS ran an ad in *Popular Electronics* magazine announcing the IMSAI 8080 computer. In the brief description of its product, it noted that it came unassembled, but that all the boards were the same as for the Altair 8800 (which had recently been released and sales were doing quite well, at substantially more than the IMSAI's price of $439). Two months later, IMS sold its first 50 IMSAI computer kits (and of course the price went up;

$599 for unassembled and $931 assembled — makes one wonder how it arrived at this odd number, doesn't it?). As a kit, a buyer got a cabinet and a bunch of parts — including a processor chip; it did not include a keyboard or monitor. One could program it, though, by toggling switches on the front panel. But this was tedious, and one wrong toggle at the wrong time could mean your whole program was corrupted and you had to start over. Still, to show the pent-up demand for someone actually being able to own a computer, IMS sold its kits, but later sold the same components pre-assembled (for more money, of course). It was available with 4K, 8K, or 12K memory, and came with BASIC. It also had interfaces for video, teletype, printer, and other I/O peripherals (e.g., card reader, paper-tape reader, etc.). For $1.00, a person could order a brochure describing how the IMSAI worked.

Figure 77—IMSAI 8080

The IMSAI 8080 computer was an improvement on the original Altair design in several areas. First, it was easier to assemble; the Altair required sixty wire connections between the front panel and primary circuit board holding the processor. Rather, the IMSAI was designed with what is termed a "backplane," which had eighteen slots into which circuit cards could be placed. Second, the IMSAI had a larger power supply to handle the increasing number of expansion boards used in most systems that users were building. IMSAI's advantage was short-lived, as MITS (the maker of the Altair) took note and marketed the Altair 8800B, which now had the same features as the IMSAI. The Altair 8800B was introduced in June 1976.

244

Competition was alive and well, and it kept pushing others to make something better.

In 1975, IMS announced something very exciting in the computing world that was outside its personal computing market. Its new product was called the Hypercube. Available in three models, it consisted of some number of IMSAI computers that were assigned tasks by a central microprocessor acting as a "control" terminal (e.g., a complicated database query from IMS' 108 Intelligent Disk System), and when the answers were done by the computers, it reported back to the main system. In other words, spread out a problem on multiple machines and have them all work on the answer together. The Hypercube II ($80,000) had 32 microprocessors, the Hypercube III ($400,000) had 132 microprocessors, and the Hypercube IV ($1,280,000) had 512 microprocessors. A special operating system called the Hypercube Operating System (HOS) was developed for the Hypercube products.

(To get an idea of what an IMSAI looked like in use, in the 1983 movie *War Games*, an IMSAI 8080 used a telephone to connect (break into) a government mainframe computer.)

In 1976, as IMS more and more found itself making things rather than consulting, the name of the company was changed to IMSAI Manufacturing Corporation. Enter a problem that was very subtle at the time: the 1970s (and into today) saw people experimenting with "social enhancing" programs. Sort of like Facebook, but done face-to-face instead of through postings. Communes, sweat lodges, and other activities might come to mind, but another one was called EST. You can do your own research into this craziness, but suffice it to say that it encouraged discrepancies (disagreements) between executives and staff (or husband and wife, or basically between any two people) to be hammered out until an agreement is reached — or someone runs off screaming. A documented story has it that Millard enjoyed EST so much that it was assumed he worked for the people doing the EST seminars. One of the interesting things about EST is

245

that one either buys into it — or doesn't. Millard battled with his engineers about building a computer, but Millard didn't agree that the task might be impossible — so in some ways he "ESTed" his company into a downward spiral. EST, as Millard found out, didn't work well with a bunch of hard-nosed engineers.

In short span of a little over two years, between 17,000 and 20,000 IMSAI units were eventually sold (with an additional 2,500 sold under the Fischer-Freitas name). By 1977, the market for the IMSAI 8080 was declining, and Millard decided to take the company in another direction. In addition to the manufacturing business, he wanted to go into the retail business. To accomplish this goal, he established Computer Shack, a chain of franchised retail stores (the name was changed to ComputerLand following pressure from Radio Shack).

Here is where problems began in earnest. ComputerLand retailed not only the IMSAI product, but also computers from other companies, including Apple and others. The IMSAI 8080 sold poorly in comparison to the others in its stores, so IMSAI developed the IMSAI VDP-80. As a slap in the face to Millard, many franchise dealers refused to retail newer IMSAI product because of its performance compared to other personal computers in the market. With Millard pouring money into the expansion of his ComputerLand businesses, money was drained from any R&D for his computer products. In October 1979, IMS filed for bankruptcy.

IMS' trademarks were acquired by Thomas "Todd" Fischer and Nancy Freitas (former early IMS employees who undertook continued support after the parent company folded). Their new company, officially formed in October 1978, was called the Fischer-Freitas Company. ComputerLand stores continued to do well in 1984, but the franchises became independent following a series of bitter and costly legal battles with Millard.

Infoton

In 1970, Infoton, a Burlington, Massachusetts, company sold a self-contained semi-intelligent terminal (meaning that it couldn't be programmed per se, but could offer more controls than a comparable IBM 3270 terminal).

Figure 78—Infoton Terminal

It consisted of a standard keyboard (with cursor arrows), modem, and a CRT monitor. It was all contained in one nicely packaged cabinet and sold for $1,495.

Intel Corporation

Intel Corporation was founded on July 18, 1968, in Mountain View, California. The name itself is an abbreviation of the words **Int**egrated **El**ectronics, which is a beautiful summation (in the author's opinion) of what this company did then and still does today. Although this book is about what the creative minds did <u>with</u> the microprocessors, it would be a disservice not to include a brief description of what Intel itself did during the 1970s — and discuss how it tried to venture into the world of making PCs. As with IBM, Apple, Microsoft, and others, excellent books are available about Intel's early days; delve into those books for more insight and intrigue about the early days at Intel. The following, though, is a brief summation of this creative company.

Before I describe more about Intel and its microprocessor, it is important to point out that, before Intel, there were three other microprocessors developed. One was called the MP944 and was used in the Grumman F-14 Tomcat fighter jet in late 1969 and early 1970. For over two decades this information was classified, but finally the company Garrett AiResearch was shown as the developer of this chip. Hopefully one can understand that unless one wants to develop a fleet of jets and sell to the public, this microprocessor was not meant to be used by the masses – rather it had a very specific and limited use.

Figure 79 -MP944 microprocessor
with supporting memory and I/O boards

Another microprocessor was developed by Texas Instruments in 1971 and called the TMS1000.

Figure 80 - Texas Instruments TMS1000
(shown approximately at its actual size)

Unfortunately for Texas Instruments (apparently not understanding the market it could conquer with this product), it chose not to commercially release it until 1974.

By then it was too late and Intel and Motorola were capturing the microprocessor market.

A third microprocessor pre-dating Intel's commercially available one was developed by engineers at Four Phase. (See more detail under that company elsewhere in this book.) Four Phase had developed a microprocessor to be used on their own commercially available systems. They called it the AL1. Similar to the Texas Instrument story above, Four Phase was myopic as they didn't see more of a "let's make a microprocessor and sell to the masses". Rather, Four Phase was focused on using the AL1 just in their systems, and they never attempted to sell the AL1 by itself.

Before I get into Intel's early dominance of the microprocessor world, a description is needed. Intel took the idea of an integrated circuit (IC), and reduced it even more to make one "component" consisting of the following parts (in 1971):

- Arithmetic logic unit (ALU)
- Instruction register/decoder
- Program counter
- Registers
- Timing and control unit

In other words, it took a bunch of IC's that were connected literally by small wires and instead connected the IC's by very, very, very small copper etched pathways that were so small that that it took a very powerful microscope to see them. A microprocessor is programmable, meaning that it can be made to execute a known set of commands (called an instruction set) and give a result.[72]

---

[72] For a description of how a microprocessor is designed and works, refer to John Clark Scott's excellent book, *But How Do It Know*.

*Figure 81—Intel 4004 microprocessor
(actual size about 1.5 inches long)*

A development team consisting of Ted Hoff, Stan Mazor, and Frederico Faggin was brought together to work on the microprocessor development. The fruit of their labor was announced on November 15, 1971—and the world changed with the commercial release of the Intel 4004 microprocessor.[73] The 4004 had 2,300 transistors,[74] was capable of executing 60,000 instructions per second, used 4 bits for data transfer, and, of course, be programmed. It sold commercially for $60. An interesting side note is that TI produced a manual regarding how the 4004 worked. This manual sold more copies than were sold of the actual microprocessor chips themselves—showing how people were excited to know more about this wonderful technology.

A mere five months later (after the 4004), the Intel 8008 was announced. This microprocessor used 8 bits for data transfer (which basically meant it could do things faster, since fumbling with registers to hold bigger numbers was not needed as much), and was available in either a 500 KHz or 800 KHz machine cycle rate, giving a speed of 45,000 to 100,000 instructions per second capability. It could handle interrupts and address up to 16K RAM (but only indirectly by loading an address into a register), and had eight "in" ports and twenty-four "out" ports. Direct addressing was remedied in the Intel 8080 microprocessor.

---

[73] Read more about Busicom, discussed earlier in this book, to get a more complete picture of the microprocessor's early days.

[74] The latest Intel Microprocessor holds over 56 million transistors!

The first 8080 had a flaw, in that it could only drive low-power TTL devices.[75] Once the "bug" was uncovered, an updated 8080 (called the 8080A) came out very quickly. This microprocessor used interrupt processing logic the same as the 8008, memory addressing was increased to 64K, and I/O ports were increased to 256.

In 1972, Intel showed $2M in profit. In 1973, the company showed $9.2M in profit. In April 1974, its 8-bit 8080 microprocessor was released and at year-end, the company showed profits of $19.8M. The microprocessor and memory chip production was good for Intel. And then . . . OPEC (an oil cartel in the Middle East) declared higher prices for crude oil, and this had a ripple effect throughout the business world. Companies started scaling back their purchasing, and one part of this was for computer technology.

Before delving into more Intel firmware and other software contributions, I want to mention Intel's involvement (well, sort of) in the actual PC market. On the surface one could reasonably say that of all companies poised to corner the PC market, it would be Intel — after all, it owned both the 4004 and 8008 microprocessors. In 1973, Intel came out with a product called the Intellec 4/40 (4-bit CPU). It was not meant to compete on the open market in the PC space; rather it was meant for internal development use, and anyway, in actuality, there was no such thing as a PC market — it simply didn't exist. However, it was on par with the kits on the market at the time — only this product was assembled.

Not taking "no, we don't want it" as an answer from the market, Intel went on to release other Intellec models. In 1973, the Intellec 8-80 (an 8-bit computer) was announced. In 1975, the Intellec 800 was released, and in 1977, the Intellec Series II was completed. The Intellec Series II

---

[75] Transistor–transistor logic (TTL) is a class of digital circuits built from bipolar junction transistors (BJT) and resistors.

(Model 230) included an 80-character wide by 25-line CRT, a full ASCII keyboard (detachable), and dual double-density 8-inch diskette drives, which provided more than 1MB of storage.

Figure 82—Intel Intellec 4/40 System

Intel had produced its own operating system called ISIS. ISIS supported the Assembler, FORTRAN, and PL/M languages. Language development, though, was only the tip of the iceberg for what Intel was doing. A summary of its development efforts included: bipolar RAM and ROM, SRAM, bipolar logic circuits, serial memory, DRAM, EPROOM, memory systems, bipolar bit-slicing, compiler linkage tools, peripheral interfaces, single-board computer, editing software, bubble memory, and developer tools. In other words, Intel found itself as not only being in the microprocessor development arena, but also developing products such as PCs, which it needed in-house for development work—and which could possibly be marketed. So, what happened?

Why didn't Intel lead the market in PCs? As stated above, there was no such thing as the PC market, so Intel probably did not know what it had for a product. As the 1970s were coming to a close, Intel was still on a development streak with faster and faster chips (and faster and better designed PCs), and the demand for its microprocessors was increasing, while competition was knocking at its door for PCs. In this timeframe, Siemens (a Germany-based company) also was trying to break into the microprocessor market. To quickly get a toehold in this area, Intel gave Siemens the right to sell the Intellec Series II as the SME-800. I could find no further reference to sales figures for the Siemen's SME-800, which means in all likelihood it didn't sell well — but it doesn't mean that Siemens didn't learn technical aspects of it for its own development.

I will leave it to you to follow up with more reading about Intel from the 1980s onward, but suffice it to say that Intel finally dropped out of the PC market; it was simply not its focus as a company. Today, Intel remains a dominant player in the production of microprocessors and other related components. Their name root — Integrated Electronics — continues to suit the company perfectly.

Intelligent Systems Corp.

In 1977, this Norcross, Georgia, company announced its Compucolor II system. It had built-in graphics, and was marketed as an "all-in-one" computer. By this, the company meant that it included a motherboard, monitor, keyboard, and floppy disk drive. It used the Intel 8080 microprocessor. The monitor could display 28 lines by 128 characters wide, graphics, and supported eight colors. The system came with 8K of RAM, but could be expanded to 32K. An odd feature was the fact that three different types of keyboards could be ordered. Another interesting fact (and what could be considered by some as strange and odd) was that initially this system came with an 8-track tape deck (similar to those units in stereos and audio systems in the late 1960s), and held approximately 1,000 bytes of data.

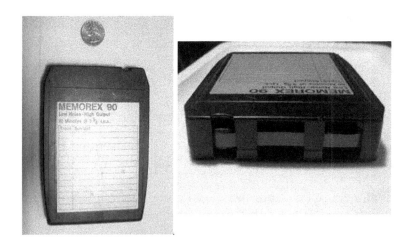

Figure 83— 8-track magnetic tape cartridge

Eight-track tapes were very unreliable for two reasons: 1) manufacturing quality of the cartridge itself, and 2) the reader technology that picked up the magnetics from the tape itself. Because of this unreliability they were soon replaced with a more standard (at that time) 5¼-inch floppy drive.

Figure 84—Intelligent Compucolor II

By 1978, when Intelligent Systems Corp. announced its Intecolor 3621 product, Apple had figured out how to display color graphics in its well-packaged systems. What this meant was that just as color TV changed the viewing habits of millions, computer users were getting used to expecting color in their displays. The 3621 offered a color-graphics terminal with a 13-inch screen, which could display 32 lines x 64 characters. It came with a fully integrated keyboard with a numeric keypad and seventeen programmable function keys. The 3621 sold for $3,300. References were found for more products in the 3600 product line, but no specific product information other than the 3621 could be found.

Interdata

In 1970, Interdata advertised its third generation of computer products, starting with a TTY type of terminal as its first product in a product line that consisted of six products—one of which was a clustered minicomputer. The company also claimed to have an extensive suite of software.

Within a short time after Intel released its 16-bit processor chip, Interdata introduced its 7/32 and 8/32 32-bit minicomputers. There is a claim made by some that these were the first 32-bit minicomputers brought to the market, but since no actual release date of the 7/32 and 8/32 could be found, it is uncertain if this is a fact. The 8/32 allowed user-programmable microcode, which meant that if some user knew what he or she was doing, the operating system could be altered.

The 7/32 and 8/32 systems were fast compared to other 16-bit minicomputers in the market. Primarily, these systems were used for process control and simulation systems. The company offered communications software (IBM 2780 and 3780 protocols) that enabled it to communicate easily with an IBM system.

The operating system in the 7/32 and 8/32 was Interdata's proprietary OS/32. The UNIX operating system was ported to the platforms in 1977 by Wollongong University and Bell Labs. Outside of Digital Computers' systems, Interdata's system was one of the first to run UNIX.

Interdata was acquired by Perkin-Elmer in 1973, and in 1976, the systems were sold as Perkin-Elmer products in Perkin-Elmer's Computer Systems Division. In 1985, this division was sold to Concurrent Computer Corporation.

In Interdata's 1970 ad, it said, "From the only 3rd generation small computer manufacturer to being the leader in a growing field." The company gave it a good run, and survived another five years. While it could have been considered a leader at one time, it didn't turn out to be enough of a leader to sustain a share of the market. The company was based in Oceanport, New Jersey.

International Business Machines (IBM)

IBM, headquartered in Armonk, New York, had its roots deep in other companies before becoming the IBM of today. As with other large companies discussed in this book, there are excellent detailed books available about IBM. This section contains a summary of the company.

In the early 1900s, people were just starting to need the results from the tabulations of lots of data. Data about people arriving to and leaving from work, train schedules, and census information are a few examples of what companies and the U.S. government wanted to track in a more precise and speedier manner. Today, with few exceptions, most assume that compiling data is mundane and trivial—not so in the early 1900s. IBM was, as they say, in the right time at the right place (in industrial America) to invent something that was needed by businesses. In 1911, the Computing Tabulating Recording Company (CTR) was formed from a merger of the Tabulating Machine Company, the International Time Recording Company, and the Computing Scale Company. CTR adopted the name International Business Machines in

1924, using a name previously designated to CTR's subsidiary in Canada and later in South America.

Jump ahead to the 1960s (where along the way IBM was enjoying much success in punched card processing business.) The computer industry was dominated by the BUNCH (Burroughs, UNIVAC, NCR, Control Data Corporation, and Honeywell) — and IBM. These companies, along with excellent mainframe type of computers being built in the UK and Japan, were making what was then considered the only type of computers that companies would ever want. Namely, these companies approached compiling programs and running job batches in a slightly different manner, but their common thread was that they were all big computers — and big usually meant expensive. IBM had perfected the use of punched cards,[76] and had built an industry around punching, sorting, and processing them. The BUNCH members (and again, computers from the UK and Japan) followed this path somewhat, but several of them had started to use magnetic tape and paper tape more than punched cards, and were in general experimenting with other storage media to try and set themselves apart from IBM. Although IBM embraced the transistor, it had its own CPU chip manufacturing lab, so it didn't really care much about the small din regarding the commercial and cheaper CPU microprocessor chips being designed by Motorola and Intel.

IBM was considered the antithesis of the barefooted, sandal-wearing computer geeks from the Ann Arbor, Boston, or Cupertino areas. The free-thinking guys and gals who wanted to play with the Atari, IMSAI , and other kit makers didn't care much for IBM, and vice versa. Coupling these free-thinkers with business visionaries such as James Treybig, Alan Kay, Steve Wozniak, Bill Gates, Steve Jobs, and pretty much anyone from the

---

[76] The first usage of a card that could tell a machine what to do was done in the early 1800s in France.

Homebrew Computer Club, and the world was about to change—leaving IBM behind in many regards and opening up incredible competition about which IBM had never worried about up until then. (For those on the edge of their seats wondering if IBM survived this assault, the answer is "they did"—but they learned a lot in the process.)

This section on IBM is relatively short compared to what you might be expecting. After all, IBM is THE computer in many people's view, so why not write a lot about it? The answer is this: During the 1970s, IBM had little to contribute except for a standard it was about to set in the PC area, and the reason it was able to do this was simply because of its clout via its size. IBM had developed mainframe computers called the 360 and 370 series, and these systems were bringing in huge amounts of money to IBM—so why change? Many computer companies in the 1970s believed that the IBM 370 was the system to which they should aspire.

In 1971, IBM released the floppy disk, which would become the defacto standard for personal computer storage for the next fifteen years. It allowed users to exchange information easily, to back up data from their primary disk storage, and for software manufacturers to sell and distribute software easier. The floppy disk was a piece of thin plastic coated with a thin magnetic film; this was then encased in a paper envelope that had a small slit through which the disk could be accessed. The hardware (floppy disk drive) would position a head over the disk and read or write data at the location to which it was being directed. It was inexpensive (approximately $1 – $2), and because of its floppiness in design, could withstand the rigors of being tossed around and not broken. This simple device would go on to help revolutionize the personal computer market.

Figure 85—Floppy disk

In 1973, the IBM Palo Alto Scientific Center developed a portable computer prototype called SCAMP (Special Computer APL Machine Portable) based on the IBM PALM processor with a Philips compact cassette drive, small CRT, and full-function keyboard. SCAMP emulated an IBM 1130 minicomputer so it could run APL programs. (In 1973, APL was generally available only on mainframe computers—most desktop-sized microcomputers offered only BASIC.) Because SCAMP was the first to emulate the computer language APL's performance on a "portable,[77]" single-user computer, *PC Magazine* in 1983 designated SCAMP a "revolutionary concept" and "the world's first personal computer." (This was obviously a big stretch of the truth, but it did help sell a lot of magazines.)

In 1973, the IBM SCAMP prototype had been developed in IBM's Palo Alto Development Center. While not commercially brought to the market, it created enough buzz within IBM that in two years IBM had their first commercial "portable"[78] computer called the IBM 5100. (Other companies had developed a "portable" type of computer, but either they didn't offer it in the commercial market, or they simply weren't accepted enough to get a foothold like IBM did.) IBM referred to its PALM processor as a microprocessor, though it used that term to mean a processor that executes microcode to implement a higher-level instruction set, rather than its conventional

---

[77] Today most people think of a portable of weighing around 4 pounds. These early portables were nicknamed "luggables" because all weighed over 30-50 pounds.

definition of a complete processor on a single silicon integrated circuit.

The 5100 offered 64K of RAM and 284K of ROM. The 5100 was sold as an "intelligent terminal." The 5100 was IBM's first effort to introduce a personal computer, which meant that IBM envisioned it to be put on a desk and could be custom-programmed to do specific tasks for the user. The 5100 had all of the components integrated into one cabinet; it had a 5-inch monitor, a tape drive, a keyboard, and optional BASIC compiler (and/or APL interpreter). It also had two serial interfaces, an IEEE-488 interface, an optional matrix printer with optionally 80 or 120 lines per second, and an external tape drive. The 5100 weighed in at fifty pounds—certainly putting it at the extreme definition of a "portable" computer.

Figure 86—1973 IBM SCAMP (prototype) on left; 1975 IBM 51000

As the world was starting to communicate more from computer to computer, the thought that fraud might eventually start to occur finally caught IBM's attention. In 1977, the company announced standards for commercial encryption and decryption of messages. This standard was called DES.

In 1978, IBM introduced the IBM 5110, available as the Model 1 or Model 2. (IBM was never known for its creative marketing nomenclatures.) It used a cartridge to hold data, but these cartridges were not compatible with other computer systems—so data could not be moved easily (if at all) from a 5110 to something else. User complaints caused IBM to add support of 8-inch floppy disk drives, which made everyone happy except, of course, the people who developed the proprietary data cartridges that no one wanted. The 5100 and 5110 never caught on enough to satisfy IBM's sales requirements, and eventually the 5150 replaced the 5110. The 5150 also was known as the IBM PC. An inventive year for IBM, 1978 was also when it announced technology that merged laser printing with electrophotography—a fancy word for digital pictures.

Figure 87—IBM 5110

Also in 1978, IBM announced what it called a "mid-range" computer—meaning not really a minicomputer, and not as large as its mainframe 370 models. Jumping back to 1971, IBM worked on a new model to store data into files (also known today as SQL tables), and link data between multiple files with values. For instance, an entry for "Joe XYZ" could easily be moved around in a file and the underlying file system also would be able to locate it quickly; this, in a nutshell, is called a "relational database." Jumping forward again to 1978, the System 38 was IBM's first commercial use of the relational database on its systems. Other computer systems also were using the relational database model of storing data, and it was soon to be adopted as one of the best models for storing data ever devised.

As a side note: It was (and is) rare that a program never has a bug and needs corrections, and IBM software designers came up with a very creative way to see what was going on inside their code as it was executing. A programmer could press a special key on the front panel, and as a sort of back door[79] into the system, the display would switch to show the first 512 bytes of the main memory, instead of the normal output. This allowed all of the registers to be visible during execution to help resolve problems. (Tricks like this caught on and debuggers got a lot better from then on.)

Just as IBM was the dominant player in mainframes (and introduced its mid-sized System 38 series), a few years later, it also became the leader in the personal computer market segment—this would turn out to be both good and bad for the company. IBM's strategy was fairly simple: sit back and see what the PC fuss was about, and when ready, then and only then enter that market. In 1981, it pounced and set was to be known as the "IBM standard." IBM went on to develop more innovative products, and today, IBM is still a strong name in computer technology and in providing consulting/services. (From its inception, IBM had been led by its founder, Thomas Watson, and then his son, Thomas Watson, Jr. In 1973, the reins were finally handed over to a non-family member, Frank T. Cary.)

International Computers Limited (ICL)

International Computers Limited (ICL) was formed in 1968. It was part of the UK's push to create a British computer industry that could compete with major

---

[79] It was not uncommon then, nor uncommon today, for programmers to build in a secret way to display the contents of what is actually going on inside of a CPU; some of these back doors are harmless and are strictly used for debugging, but some back doors can allow all kinds of bad things to happen to a computer if a programmer wanted to do this.

manufacturers (read between the lines: "non-UK"). Its formation was that of a merger of International Computers and Tabulators (ICT), English Electric Leo Marconi (EELM), and Elliott Automation.[80] Taking note of the French government, which backed its country's computer research, the British government eventually held a 10 percent stake after providing a $32.4 million computer research and development grant.

ICL inherited two main product lines: the 1900 Series of mainframes from ICT, and the System 4 from English Electric Computers (EEC). The new board of directors flip-flopped on which computer system to retain, as ICL's sales and development costs could not sustain both. In this turmoil, board members resigned in frustration after disagreements on which direction ICL should be going.

One of the interesting creations to come out of ICL is the GEORGE operating system.[81] This operating system was said to be very popular to British programmers at the time for its functionality and ease of use. Another significant feature to be developed by ICL was the notion of being able to move programs from computer to computer (meaning any one of several ICL models then being sold) without recompiling the program. IBM had not solved this problem then, and even today many computer makers have not figured this out. To move a program from one IBM machine to another meant that the source program had to be found, fed/moved to the other IBM machine, and then compiled (and hope that it worked properly on the new machine—as there were possibilities that because

---

[80] The water gets muddied a lot because of mergers. For instance, Elliott Instrument Company (actually founded in 1804!) got funding in the 1950s from England's National Research Development Corporation, and Elliott made arrangements with National Cash Register Company Ltd, which sold Elliott's computers as the Elliott 405 or NCR 405. Elliott changed its name to Elliott-Automation in 1957, and in 1967 merged with English Electric Company, and then the computing functions were sold to International Computers Ltd; eventually this was sold to BAE Systems.

[81] For further reading, refer to
http://en.wikipedia.org/wiki/GEORGE_(operating_system). There were four versions, with each one adding more functionality than its predecessor.

of incompatibilities in the different operating systems on both IBM machines the programs might not run properly). In this author's view, it seems that ICL didn't know what amazing technology it had in this invention, as it never exploited this feature to potential IBM customers.

In 1976, ICL acquired the international (non-U.S.) part of Singer Business Machines (which at this time was selling the System Ten, a small business computer). The acquisition led sales away from the UK and provided a presence in other markets such as manufacturing and retail. ICL later developed the System Ten into the System 25, and used this product to provide inroads into more retail areas.

A cute little system acquired in the acquisition was the model 1501. This was a system developed by the Cogar Corporation, acquired then by Friden Singer, and finally by ICL; it was used as a stand-alone terminal and data capture in petrol stations throughout Germany.

Figure 88—ICL 1501

ICL bundled its software components under what it called the "superstructure" label. It included in this a reference to compilers, data management tools, and transaction processing software. It did not include the operating system in this bundle, as that was a major separate component to its computers.

ICL developed the following superstructure components:

- IDMS(X) Integrated Data Management System — A standard (at the time) database, which was ported from the IDMS system
- TPMS(X) Transaction Processing Management System — A transaction processing monitor
- DDS (X) Data Dictionary System — Used for describing database records
- QuickBuild — A package of tools for building applications
- Querymaster — A query language for IDMS databases and indexed-sequential files

These products were actually leaders in the field, and why ICL never exploited the wonderful superstructure feature is a mystery. ICL's computers supported the following languages: S3 (a derivative from ALGOL 68), COBOL, SCL (a job control language), FORTRAN, PASCAL, SFL (an assembly language), and C.

Throughout the 1980s, ICL continued to develop many different-sized models of computers to attack different market niches. With sales waning, the company was ripe for picking — and in 1990 Fujitsu purchased an 80 percent stake of ICL. Finally in 2002, Fujitsu acquired the company completely, and any computers still being sold were rebranded as Fujitsu International Computer Logistics Limited.

International Data Sciences, Inc.

In 1970, the following advertisement was run by International Data Sciences:

"With all the different keyboard data preparation systems now on the market, you know which one of them a typical operator still prefer[s]? The slow, ugly keypunch. Because she knows it, and even if she hates it, she's afraid to change to something unfamiliar. A womanly reason."

With marketing like that, I'm sure its competition wasn't worried. International Data Sciences, based in Providence, Rhode Island, sold a product called the LIBRA. It consisted of a desk with a large pull-out drawer with a magnetic tape peripheral that wrote/read data, which the operator keyed in using the keyboard on top. The display wasn't a CRT like we think of, but rather a very small one-line display showing the operator what she (or he) had typed in.

As with other companies trying to compete with IBM for a slice of the revenue pie, it was trying something new — and one has to give it kudos for that. Unfortunately, creating a huge desk with a magnetic tape and a small display was not in keeping up with (or surpassing) the competition. Other companies had floppy drives and cassette drives that made for better and less expensive machines. In other words, the timing was bad for the market this company was after.

Figure 89—International Data Sciences LIBRA

ITEL

While not an innovator and contributor with new software or hardware ideas, ITEL is nevertheless included for its contribution to competition in the 1970s. ITEL was basically a computer leasing company—it was so good at this that it worked out deals whereby a company could lease IBM mainframes cheaper than companies could lease them from IBM. It was a Delaware corporation, with at least one sales office in Kansas City, Kansas. Information on this company is scarce, so there is no certainty as to where its main office was located.

ITEL wanted to keep leasing IBM systems, but IBM started to pay more attention as some of its leases slipped away. IBM wanted to figure out a way to beat ITEL with creative financing of its own for the customers. One of the creative deals ITEL struck was with National Semiconductor and Hitachi in 1977 for them to build IBM-compatible mainframes branded as Advanced Systems. ITEL ended up signing deals for the shipment of 200 of these systems. ITEL then increased its investment in this IBM-compatible computer, as it saw it as another way to beat IBM.

But IBM was not going quietly into the night, and thus spun into high gear to beat ITEL. A few companies played a game in the 1970s whereby they would pre-announce a new product to not only scare their competition, but also to hopefully give pause to competitors' customers and have them wait before making a purchase. IBM was not a company to be trifled with, and when it announced that it was coming out with a technologically superior computer, it had the desired effect of causing ITEL's customers to put their orders on hold; ITEL was now sitting on a lot of inventory it could not sell or lease. Hitachi agreed to cut back on its shipments of Advanced Systems product to ITEL, but National Semiconductor forced ITEL's hand by making ITEL continue to buy National Semiconductor's systems. ITEL's president resigned in 1979, and National Semiconductor took over ITEL.

ITEL was renamed the National Advanced Systems (NAS) division, and it continued assembling and selling IBM-compatible systems. IBM sued National Semiconductor in 1983 for using stolen IBM secrets, and finally National Semiconductor threw in the towel and gave up selling and leasing its IBM-compatible systems. In summary, what ITEL provided to the industry in the 1970s was a creative way to compete with IBM — albeit in ITEL's case, it was a short-lived venture. Still, it kept IBM on its toes with the computer market and made IBM alert to new competition.

Jacobi Systems Corp.

Of all the wonderful computer company ideas to come out of the 1970s, a few odd ones bubbled up. Located in Van Nuys, California, Jacobi Systems marketed the MINITS 1 System.

For those non-mathematically inclined people, a Jacobi algorithm is "a real symmetric matrix reduced to the diagonal form by a sequence of plane rotations." The folks at Jacobi must have known what this meant, because they wanted to offer a timesharing system for people who wanted to work on such calculations, but couldn't afford their own computer.

Jacobi Systems didn't invent anything new per se — the company assembled a computer server (its source remains an unknown), and attached some communication controllers to it so people could literally dial in to it and run their FORTRAN programs. Jacobi's spiel was that because the MINITS 1 was so inexpensive, a company could sell timesharing time more cheaply than its competition. And then — this is where its marketing really kicked into high gear — when your company started rolling in so much money from the timeshare business, you could afford to go buy your own IBM or Sperry mainframe! (Yes, this was actually part of its psychedelic-themed marketing literature in 1970.) If nothing else, Jacobi Systems contributed to case studies on why a solid business plan is so important before starting out.

Jacquard Systems

Jacquard Systems was founded in Santa Monica, California. This company developed software and two small computer systems in the late 1970s through early 1980s.

The J100 Videocomputer was basically a prototype and could support one user, the J500 Videocomputer was more production-ready and also meant for one user, the J505 Videocomputer, could connect two users, and the J1000 Videocomputer was a shared system that could connect up to four J500 systems. The J1000 sold for $15,000.

The J500 was nicely packaged in a trendy cabinet with keyboard (with 20 programmable function keys), two floppy drives, one to four optional hard disk drives, and a parallel 12-bit printer. It came with 32 PROMs giving 128K of memory storage (where all programs were stored), supported sixty-four kinds of interrupts, and used the AMD 2900 microprocessor. The following picture was the best I could find (there was another better-quality picture in a museum that claimed it was a Jacquard 500, when in reality it was not), and it doesn't do justice to the overall size of this system; it was huge at 14.5 in. high, 24.5 in. wide, 17.25 in. deep, and weighed a whopping ninety-five pounds.

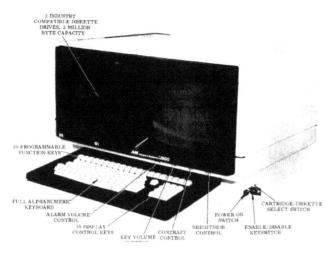

2 INDUSTRY
COMPATIBLE DISKETTE
DRIVES, 2 MILLION
BYTE CAPACITY

20 PROGRAMMABLE
FUNCTION KEYS

FULL ALPHANUMERIC
KEYBOARD
ALARM VOLUME
CONTROL
16 DISPLAY
CONTROL KEYS
KEY VOLUME CONTROL
CONTRAST
CONTROL
BRIGHTNESS
CONTROL
POWER ON
SWITCH
ENABLE/DISABLE
KEYSWITCH
CARTRIDGE/DISKETTE
SELECT SWITCH

Figure 90—Jacquard J500

The systems were sold with the Jacquard word processing product Type-Rite, and the Jacquard data management product called Data-Rite. (From Jacquard's instruction manual, the user had to type "$TYPIV" and wait sixty seconds for the Type-Rite application to load and run. Can anyone imagine having the patience to wait that long today to run, say, Microsoft Word?) As an option, Jacquard also sold a unique legal software package call Tomcat. What Tomcat did was take a court reporter's log (from a magnetic storage log), and then, by using a database of 60,000 English words and 100,000 "root" words, could translate the cryptic court reporter notes into something more readable.

In the early 1980s, Jacquard was acquired by AM International. Within a span of two years, AM International was acquired by a company calling itself ATV Jacquard, Inc.

Kantronics Company, Inc.

Using his IBM engineering skills and formal electrical engineering education, in 1971, Phil Anderson set out to build a successful tech company. Kantronics was born and headquartered in Lawrence, Kansas. The first product was a controller box designed to check the assembly of car wiring harnesses; it was a successful venture. With that product going well, the company designed and built a small minicomputer called the PDAC, whose market focus was to be for education and laboratories — basically those small entities that needed a low-cost computer.

The PDAC could be mounted into a rack, and the O/S had a limiting twenty-two basic instructions (which meant that complex programming could not be done — or at a minimum made programming harder). It allowed indirect addressing, and had a 2.5 microsecond CPU cycle time. It came with a console terminal for controlling it, and up to eight I/O modules (tape drives, printers, communication lines, etc.) could be driven from the system. The PDAC didn't become a household name, and was scrapped.

Still, the company branched out into manufacturing packet modems and paging controls with good growth. In 2009, Kantronics LLC, based in Olathe, Kansas bought the assets of Kantronics Company, Inc. The new Kantronics sells wireless computer modems, digital data controls, custom protocols, and GPS location and status reporting devices and software.

Kenbak Corporation

People had many wonderful ideas in the 1970s for a computer product, but the more I researched this company and John Blankenbaker, the more impressed I became with the sheer creativity.

Blankenbaker gained knowledge of computers and digital circuitry while working at Hughes Aircraft in the 1950s and 1960s. Companies began understanding how a multi-user system could be built, but outside of the "hobbyists," few grasped the feasibility of having a "small computer" for the masses. Working in yet another California garage (this one was in Los Angeles), Blankenbaker designed and invented his own vision of what a personal computer could be.

Because engineers are not usually great marketers, Blankenbaker needed a catchy name for his computer. In the early 1970s, Kodak (the camera and film company) was a well-known entity. After a discussion with his wife, it was decided between them that a name similar to Kodak might attract attention. So instead of calling his computer a Blankenbaker, better judgment won out, and using only a part of his last name (Blan**kenbak**er), the Kenbak-1 was born. In 1971, the first one of only forty ever made was sold and shipped to a customer. The purchase price was $750, which by itself might have limited sales since that was a lot of money to spend on something that few could understand—but other factors also weighed heavily against it, as described below.

What made the Kenbak-1 unique was that it never had a one-chip CPU like what Intel had developed with its 4004 or 8008 microprocessors. Being a creative fellow, Blankenbaker decided to bypass the whole microprocessor chip thing and design his computer using a series of digital circuits.[82] The Kenbak-1 was an 8-bit machine and offered 256K of memory (Blankenbaker defined his byte as being 8 bits wide). The instruction cycle time was one microsecond, but all memory fetches had to be executed serially, which substantially slowed down the overall running of a program.

To use the machine, it had to be programmed with a series of buttons and switches. The only instructions available were: ADD, SUB, LOAD, STORE, AND, OR, LNEB, JUMPS, SKIPS, SETBITS, SHIFTS, ROTATES, NOOP, and

---

[82] Digital circuits that do logic gate functions, amplifying, etc. are generally grouped under the nomenclature of TTL—which means transistor–transistor logic.

HALT. The SHIFT, NOOP, and HALT required one byte, and all of the other instructions required two bytes. Output consisted of a series of lights. It didn't have a printer, keyboard, punched-tape reader, or card reader. Obviously, the Kenbak-1 was seriously lacking in user-friendliness and practicality. Technically, it could be programmed, and it sat on your desk, so in a loose definition it was a "personal computer."

To grasp exactly what Blankenbaker had built, take a look at the following picture.

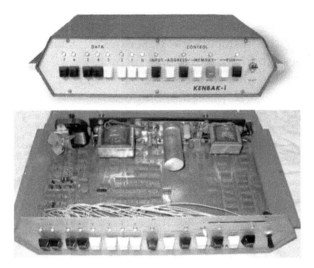

Figure 91—Kenbak-1 (with permission from John Blankenbaker)

He intended to make a machine that was low-cost, small (about 20 inches wide), and more educational in nature, rather than to make himself a millionaire. He envisioned his machines in university labs where bright engineers could get excited about the potential uses for such a computer. He offered no software, such as a high-language compiler like BASIC (mainly because this was years away from being developed!), so to program it required the machine language instructions listed above. Still, he was aware of the practicality of having a program stored for re-use, so his computer had to be able to do this. The logic board contained all of the 132 integrated circuits. The front panel had lights and switches, which were connected by wires to the logic board. The clock of about 1 MHz was generated by a multi-vibrator (which is a fancy word for something to generate a "cycle" so that the next instruction can be triggered to be executed).

Over the company's two years of existence, Blankenbaker played around with different configurations of the toggle switches and buttons to try and make it more user-friendly. (If this reminds you of the joke about rearranging deck chairs on the Titanic, then you understand this conundrum correctly.)

Programming the machine was difficult to say the least—not the actually programming logic per se, but rather the entry of the instructions into the computer. For instance, data, instructions, and addresses were entered by first clearing the Input register with the Clear key and then setting the individual bits. Then, it got worse. For instance, if one wanted to read the contents of memory including the A, B, X, and P registers, the address was set and then the Read Memory key was used. All of these operations were done while the computer was halted—so one didn't know if the instructions worked or not until the RUN key was used. The computer could be stopped with the Stop key, and holding the Stop key and the Run key at the same time would cause the computer to execute one instruction.

In 1973, Blankenbaker folded his company, and the production of the Kenbak-1 stopped. Today, there are supposedly fourteen of these computers still around. If you are lucky enough to be at the Computer Museum in Nova Scotia, Canada, you will see seven of them. So, was it a computer? It has my vote. I would not have paid $750 for it—with no keyboard or monitor—and I cannot think of any practical use for it, but a lot of other "computers" coming on the market didn't have an obvious use either (including the Apple I). I believe the Kenbak-1 could legitimately be classified as one of the first personal computers (if not the very first one) created. Good job, Mr. Blankenbaker.

Kennedy Company

While most companies were using round magnetic tape for back-up storage, this Altadena, California, company offered a magnetic cartridge during the late 1970s—think of it as an oversized cassette tape. Its product was called the 330 Digital Cartridge Recorder, and used 1/4-inch tapes from the 3M Company.

The unit was small and could sit on most surfaces close to the minicomputer. It was bi-directional and could move at 25 inches per second for reading and writing, and had a 90-inch per second rewind rate. It offered a 40K bits per second transfer rate.

Kennedy Company sold these devices to minicomputer companies and personal PC makers so they could back up and restore data.

Kienzle Apparate (Apparatus)

Kienzle Apparate GmbH was formed in 1928, in Villingen-Schwenningan, Germany, as a spin-off of the Villingen Kienzle clock factories. The men forming this new company were intrigued by developing a better taxi meter, as it already had a rudimentary version developed since 1905(!). The business continued its success by using the clocks as a starting point for the further developments of control and measuring instruments for farm tractors and automobiles. Their most important invention at the time was a device called the tachograph, which showed the performance of any engine. (Today we know this as a tachometer.) In 1934, ownership was fully in the hands of Dr. Herbert Kienzle.

During the financial crisis of the 1930s in Germany, many people were without jobs. Kienzle, though, either by luck or political savvy, kept his company going and provided jobs — and was earning points with the people about to take power in Germany. When WWII broke out, Kienzle's company found itself providing electronic products to the Wehrmacht. Products included its tachograph for aircraft and tanks, as well as other gauges for aircraft. (Rumor had it that Kienzle's expertise and products were used as the foundation for Germany's Enigma Machine, although I could not find confirmation of this.)

After the war, almost all German aircraft had been shot down, so there was little market for aircraft gauges — especially for the now out-of-business Luftwaffe. Kienzle reverted to its roots by focusing on producing automotive gauges, and with its introduction of one of the most hated machines of all time — the parking meter!

Keinzle found itself employing smart, creative people who saw a need for more office machinery, so electronic calculators (employing the new integrated circuits just starting to catch on) allowed Keinzle a foothold in that business. Keinzle then took its next step in the business market by producing a small office computer called the model 200. It was limited in almost all ways in functionality as we think of computers today, as it concentrated on bookkeeping registries. Still, it was a computer — just focused on specific tasks.

Figure 92—Kienzle Buchungsmaschine (bookkeeping machine)
Model 200

By the end of the 1960s, Nixdorf (another German company) was now producing a more powerful computer. Kienzle thought that it had a complete package for small companies — bookkeeping machines, data storage, and a small minicomputer. But sales of the Kienzle 800 (also known as the Kienzle Komputer) failed to generate much revenue for Kienzle. Jochen Kienzle and Herbert Kienzle (sons of the founder) were now running the company, and decided to team with Nixdorf to develop meteorology measuring equipment.

During the 1970s, Keinzle, in addition to the core automotive and other measuring gauges, held on to the small computer market — but it was a money-losing part of its business. In 1981, Keinzle sold its computer business to Mannesmann AG. Eventually, DEC bought the patent rights to the Keinzle Komputer, but even with money rolling in for support of the machine it was a money-losing business. In the mid-1990s, DEC (itself losing money) pulled the life support plug on the Keinzle Komputer. As an epitaph, this little company would be glad to know that its automotive gauges turned out to be so well-designed that even today, parts and even whole gauges of its designs exist in many fine automobiles — and that its parking meters are still hated everywhere. Alas, its foray into the world of computers did not contribute anything meaningful except to spur on competition with and growth by the competitors. Focusing on electronics other than computers, Kienzle is alive and well in Germany today.

Lear Sigler

While many companies in the early 1970s were developing "intelligent" terminals (that could do special formatting and data editing), along came Lear Sigler with its "dumb" terminal. In fact, the name of its product was the Dumb Terminal. Lear Siegler came about from a merger of the Sigler Corporation in Los Angeles, and Lear Avionics, Inc. in Santa Monica, California.

Their market plan was solid — why compete in the smart terminal space with so many other companies when some companies simply needed a good old basic, nothing fancy, data-entry terminal? And that's exactly what Lear Sigler built.

Figure 93—Lear Sigler Dumb Terminal

Companies could adapt their own protocol to it, as Lear Siegler provided easy-to-read and use programming manuals. It did have a microprocessor in the terminal itself, but with the exception of 4K of memory, it could not store a lot of data, and had no way to connect to a peripheral device other than a communications line.

It offered a basic 24-line x 80-character-wide display, a standard keyboard with 16 function keys, and cursor control. The Dumb Terminal was priced at $895.

The company went on to produce two "smarter" terminals — neither one was a key-to-disk type of terminal, but they could be programmed from a host machine with special control characters sent to it. These control characters could cause a field to blink, be underlined, etc. Lear Sigler also produced a line printer that could be attached to its terminals.

Lear Siegler was acquired by URS Corporation in 2002.

Liverport Ltd.

Based in Cornwall, UK, this company primarily imported the well-packaged Exidy Sorcerer system.

Figure 94—Exidy Sorcerer computer

It added extra ROM-PAC cartridges for more games, and a floppy drive to the system before reselling it. This was a prime example of a system that had all of the necessary components of a "PC" (keyboard, monitor, RAM, floppy disk storage), but instead was sold as a "gaming" system and not a business computer.

Lockheed Electronics

When many think of Lockheed, they think of it being involved with aircraft development. While that is certainly true, to get to that point the company had to develop a lot of electronics. Based in Los Angeles, California, the Data Products Division of Lockheed developed a product called the System III.

In 1974, the System III was marketed as a distributed computing system. What this meant was that it held its own database and that users didn't have to connect to a mainframe to get data. It had up to eight terminals connected to the system, and could then pass on data to a host system as it wanted—or not pass it along if the data was meant for local use only. It had an RPGII compiler, and claimed it was ANSI-compatible for most RPGII source programs (which meant good portability of programs to and from the System III).

Each terminal had a keyboard with numeric keypad, a video monitor, and floppy disk storage. All of these features were packaged in a sleek one-piece shell. Each terminal also could support an optional printer and a card reader that supported either 80- or 96-column cards. The System III main unit had its own shared disk storage and could support line printers. It came with a disk operating system.

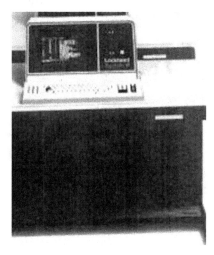

Figure 95—Lockheed System III

By the mid-1970s, other systems could be expanded to thousands of processors and terminals, so products like the System III quietly fell out of favor because of its limitation in expandability.

Logic Corporation

In 1970, this Cherry Hill, New Jersey, company marketed its LC-720 computer system. The LC-720 was a "key-disc" system where an operator at a terminal keyed in data that was stored on the LC-720's central control location.

Up to sixty terminals could be connected to the LC-720, with each capable of entering different formats of data (which was compatible with IBM's EBCDIC data format). The data stored on the LC-720's magnetic disk could be randomly accessed by a user from any terminal. The LC-720 also could store data on an IBM-compatible 7- or 9-track magnetic tape, which meant that its data could be backed up easily and/or sent to IBM for processing. While most companies were content to have a system that could send data to an IBM, because of the way Logic Corporation stored its data, this meant (at least theoretically) that an IBM user could access data directly on the LC-720.

Logitron, Inc.

To see this Cambridge, Massachusetts, company's ad for its Logiport/1 in 1970 is at first awe-inspiring, and at the same time (with the benefit of forty years of hindsight) think, "You were so close! Why didn't you see the potential?"

The Logiport/1 was a true "portable terminal." (Notice the careful wording — nothing mentioned about "portable computer.") Weighing in at around twenty-five pounds, it was heavy. With a carrying handle, it was all nicely packaged in a very sleek, hard-plastic case (with a fully enclosed lid), and it contained a keyboard and an easy to read, large CRT display. Pretty good so far, but here is where the fun stopped.

The Logiport/1 had no battery, so it had to be plugged in to use. It was not intelligent from the perspective that it could not run its own standalone applications. Rather, one had to use its built-in modem, find a phone line, and dial in to a host system.

Figure 96—Logitron Logiport/1 (and with carrying case)

Here was a company slightly behind the technology curve, but yet ahead in thinking about what a portable "computer" could do. If it could have lasted a few more years when color graphics, faster processors came out, and floppy disks or cassette tapes could be used for programming and backup, the company possibly could have led the PC portable field. Still, this company was on to something in the area of "portable"; it simply couldn't (and didn't) carry it far enough.

Management Assistance, Inc. (MAI)

Management Assistance, Inc. (MAI) was founded in 1957 by Georg Horgae and Walter R. Oreamuno.

Horgae and Oreamuno realized, along with the rest of the business world, that IBM was a dominant computer player (as you will read time and again in this book). IBM was very smart in its marketing and would get businesses hooked on its technology. Then, within a relatively short time IBM would come out with a newer model—convincing its customers to upgrade (and spend more money). It worked like this for IBM: It would either sell a company a computer, or lease them a computer with an option of buying it outright at one-third the original selling price.

Horgae and Oreamuno had the idea of re-leasing a computer to businesses. What they did was look for those IBM leases about to expire, acquire the computer for the one-third the price, then turn around and either re-lease it back to the company or find a new company to lease it; this obviously would work well if they could find leases of the used equipment. Unfortunately, after a while they found themselves with a warehouse of outdated computers that no one wanted. "Making lemonade out of lemons" is basically what MAI did. If its customers who wanted the latest technology didn't want their older computers, then MAI found customers who did. This idea of re-leasing older computers was new in the computer business, but it caught on quickly after MAI started this business model.

By the time 1970 rolled around, though, MAI's business model was in financial trouble. While the company had $60 million in revenue, it also had $140 million in debt and a net worth of negative $28 million. In 1971, MAI Chief Financial Officer Raymond Kurshan took over as president of the company. Kurshan realized that something radical had to be done to turn around the company if it was to be saved. By this time MAI, through acquisitions, had several subsidiaries under its wing — one, the Basic/Four Corporation, located in Tustin, California, caught his eye.

Basic/Four was one of the first independent entries into the small business-computer system arena. In 1971, Basic/Four launched a line of business-computer systems for small to medium-sized companies. Basic/Four was an interesting company from the standpoint that it didn't really manufacture any computer from the ground up per se, but rather bought components and assembled them into small turn-key computers (including an operating system). The computers primarily were marketed to handle inventory control and general accounting, but in reality, it could do many business functions – if someone could write the software for it, that is. The operating system was a proprietary version of the Dartmouth operating system. The original Basic/Four models were now called the MAI 400 and MAI 800 (where 400 = four users, and 800 = eight users). The MAI 500 (1972) was capable of attaching up to eight workstations that could share information. (Think "very small internet.") By 1975, Basic/Four's revenue had grown to $43 million, and it was contributing around two-thirds of MAI's total earnings.

Additionally in 1971, MAI offered an IBM-compatible standalone display station. The IBM model was the IBM 2265 and sold for $14,625. The MAI model was the MAI 2265 and sold for $8,250. MAI bought these systems ready-made from a company called Atlantic Technology Corporation. As options, MAI offered a smaller case, some graphics, and a built-in printer. It also contained two keyboard keys – INSERT and DELETE – that the IBM didn't offer.

Toward the latter part of the 1970s, MAI began to focus on adding software to its hardware offerings. In 1977, the company acquired Wordstream Corporation, which produced word processing systems and IBM-compatible CRT terminals. Over the next several years, MAI introduced several business software packages (called Business Basic) that ran on its models. In the 1980s, software "packages" that did custom business functions (e.g., scanning lanes at supermarkets that added up your purchases and gave you a receipt when done) were on the market. Basic/Four was one of the first companies to examine how technology could help small businesses to do real business applications. To that end, it set about developing software packages that could be resold to hundreds or thousands of small businesses.

In 1978, the Z-80-based MAI DataWord I was introduced. This was marketed as both a word processing and data processing computer. What was interesting about this machine was that it came with a 15-inch monitor, which was quite huge for that timeframe. In 1979, MAI launched DataWord II, which was a DataWord I except that this new machine came with a letter-quality printer. The price of the DataWord II (with printer) was $12,500.

Competition was heating up though with Apple and an upstart company called Microsoft. MAI brought out a new workstation for its shared connectivity system, and put a word processing application on it. But its Wordstream was not as full-featured as Wang Laboratories' word processing system and Apple's similar product. After less than a year on the market, MAI gave up on Wordstream.

Figure 97—Top: MAI IBM 2265, MAI ATC 2265, MAI portable
Bottom: MAI "dumb" terminal, MAI 1200

MAI shipped its 10,000th computer system in 1980; the '70s had been good to the company. In 1980, it was marketing a system called the Spectrum 80. This system was interesting because of a very inventive idea—while most companies had the operating system drive the applications and database access, the Spectrum 80 had MAI's database management system (called FMC) drive how data was accessed. It was a novel idea, but it didn't allow scalability very well. In 1982, the Z-80-based MAI S/10 personal computer was released.

At this time, the market for business computers began to shift radically during this time, as many small companies turned to cheaper, newly available PCs—instead of the minicomputers like Basic/Four's, or for more expandable systems that could support thousands of users. MAI was caught in the middle, it seems. Smaller firms were starting to come out with low-priced PCs, buying standard applications or tools, and adding both hardware and software as needed. Although Basic/Four was still generating nearly two-thirds of MAI's revenue, it was becoming less profitable. For 1980, Basic/Four earned $14 million (a 39 percent drop) on sales of $304 million. The division's leadership was changed, and the 1980s proved a disaster for Basic/Four amid proxy fights over management, yet more competition, the cost of doing business, loss of market share, attempts at taking over other companies (and the bad press that ensued), and generally all-around bad business decisions.

Attempts to turn around Basic/Four failed (and were not helped by a never-ending change in management). After losing $182 million in 1992, a group of banks took control of Basic/Four's assets. Still, Basic/Four was holding on after its bankruptcy filing, and actually reported revenue of $115 million in 1993. Expenses, though, coupled with yet more competition and bad marketing finally led to the demise of Basic/Four. In 1994, MAI closed its doors.

Micro Computer Machines

Started in 1971 in Toronto, Canada, this company had interesting roots mainly because it was one of three related computer companies started locally by a very creative fellow named Mers Kutt.

Kutt had already achieved some success with another company, Consolidated Computer Limited, which he had started in 1970 (also in Toronto). Kutt was following Intel's work on the Intel 8008, which was due to be released in late 1971. Kutt signed an agreement with Intel early on to ship him its 4004 processor, a development system, and an EPROM programming machine at no charge. Micro Computer Machines' plan was to build a lot of small computers, and in so doing make Intel a lot of money. Kutt was nothing if not a salesman.

In April 1973, Kutt visited Intel and discussed the 8008's progress with Intel's developers. The next month, Micro Computer Machines received one of the earliest SIM8-01 kits (a development kit for putting the processor on a motherboard—and then making it all work). Work began in earnest, and the outcome was what is now known as the "M/C," which was one of the world's first personal "microcomputers." In the time between designing what Kutt called the key-to-cassette hardware and software tools and receiving the SIM8 kit, he had modified his design to support a full keyboard, and an improved display (using the Burroughs Self-Scan 32-character display). It also supported the APL programming language.

This company had little success with the SIM8 development kit, so it decided to build its own motherboard (using the Intel 8008 processor chip, of course). The company was working to get APL running on the new processor, as well as a FORTAN language emulator it was calling INTERP/8. A mockup of its new system using the Intel 8008 chip was displayed publicly on November 11, 1972, at the Micro Computer Machines' offices in Kingston, Ontario. In May 1973, the system was given a custom fiberglass case and shown at the APL Users' Conference in Toronto. The completed design, with its new injection-molded case, made its debut to the press on September 25, 1973.

The machine consisted of a wedge-shaped metal box about half a meter on the side, with a keyboard at the front, a cassette tape recorder(s) in the middle, and a tiny one-line plasma display at the top. Kutt's product, the MCM/70, (also known as the MCM 70) looked quite a bit like a Commodore PET with the monitor removed and replaced with the smaller display.

The MCM/70 included the APL and a nice battery feature, which would save data in case of a power failure (including someone turning off the machine by mistake without first saving his/her work). Although it weighed in the neighborhood of twenty pounds (nine kg), it was by all definitions a "portable PC" - Kutt just didn't know it at the time, plus he failed to put a carrying handle on it. The MCM/70 was available in various configurations of RAM, and zero, one, or two cassette drives. The basic unit, Model 720 with an 80 kHz 8008, 2K RAM and no cassette drive sold for $4,950 Canadian. (Approximately the same then in U.S. dollars.) The high-end model, the 782, came with 8K of RAM, and two cassette drives; it sold for $9,800 Canadian.

The first manuals contained this personal note from Kutt to future customers:

"But the simplicity of the MCM/70 and its associated computer language...make personal computer use and ownership a reality...Enjoy the privilege of having your own personal computer."

The first packaged systems were shipped to dealers in autumn 1974; this date certainly competes with others claiming to be the first PC available in the world.

With a combination of "Now what can we do with this?" being asked by the business world and poor marketing by Micro Computer Machines, the MCM/70 failed to sell as forecast. In 1975, it was rebranded as the MCM/700, and another sales campaign ensued. In 1975, Micro Computer Machines also released a punched card reader, plotter, and programs that did spreadsheet types of work. In 1976, a faster computer, the MCM/800, came out. This computer had 16K RAM, and included the ability to drive an external monitor. Virtual memory was supported on all of the machines, although using cassettes for storage made it somewhat impractical as swapping (writing and reading) by the operating system was extremely cumbersome and slow. The MCM/700 was sold under the creative name "Sysmo" by a French company called...Sysmo!

The MCM/900 model was released in 1978. This machine was faster than the MCM/800, had 24K of RAM, and included a monitor. Playing the renaming game (thinking the buying public couldn't put two and two together), it announced the Micro Computer Machines/1000 (also known as the Micro Computer Machines Power) and released it in late 1979. Both the MCM/900 and MCM/1000 supported the HDS-10 Disk Server (another product it produced). The HDS-10 included an 8.4MB, 8-inch Shugart hard drive; an 8-inch floppy disk drive; and a 64K Zilog Z80 processor that controlled disk access). This multi-layer design of separating applications from the database was years ahead of what others would eventually figure out. To sweeten this design, Micro Computer Machines would allow up to eight MCM/900s or MCM/1000s to be plugged into one HDS-10 Disk Server.

Figure 98—MCM/700 and MCM/900

While being on the leading edge of the computer revolution going on in Canada (and in the world, for that matter), venture capitalists (including banks that needed terminals to connect to their mainframe systems) didn't understand the computer market that well, and, therefore, were loath to invest in Micro Computer Machines.

Meanwhile, in the U.S. venture capitalists were flocking to the Silicon Valley area to get in on the action. By the late 1970s, Micro Computer Machines was facing a number of new home computer systems with the same sort of power as its own machines (but priced significantly less). In 1982 or 1983 (the actual date has been obscured from lack of information on this company), Micro Computer Machines went out of business.

Micro Instrumentation and Telemetry Systems (MITS)

Since this company claimed to have the first microcomputer (although others could easily make this same claim), I've provided a little more background on how this company came to be. It started with Ed Roberts and Forrest M. Mims III, who decided to use their electronics background of working in a weapons lab to now produce (sell) kits for model-rocket hobbyists. In 1969, Stan Cagle, Robert Zaller, Roberts, and Mims founded Micro Instrumentation and Telemetry Systems (MITS) in Albuquerque, New Mexico. From this location, it started selling radio transmitters and instruments for model rockets.

While its kits sold well to a select group of model-rocket enthusiasts, it's hard to sustain business growth with such a limited offering. The November 1970 issue of *Popular Electronics* featured the new MITS kit, marketed as Opticom (which would send voice over an LED light beam). Mims and Cagle by this time was losing interest in the kit business, so Roberts bought out his partners. His first product (sans previous partners) was a calculator kit. Another company, Electronic Arrays, had just announced a set of six integrated circuit chips that would make a four-function calculator. Roberts contracted with Electronic Arrays to supply him with these small circuit boards, and using these, the MITS 816 calculator kit was born — and featured on the November 1971 cover of *Popular Electronics*. This calculator kit sold for $175, or $275 assembled.

Despite the high cost, the calculator was a success and was followed by several models with more functions. For instance, the MITS 1440 calculator was featured in the July 1973 issues of *Radio-Electronics*. It had a 14-digit display, memory, and a square-root function. The kit sold for $200, and the assembled version was $250. MITS later developed a programmable unit that would connect to the 816 or 1440 calculator and allow a simple program to send it instructions (of no more than 256 steps, though).

MITS was quietly branching out with a line of test equipment kits in addition to calculators. To keep up with the demand, in 1973 MITS moved into a larger building in Albuquerque. The problem with being a growing small company is that sometimes the company keeps doing things with a small-company mentality — and in MITS' case, soldering things by hand had gotten the company behind in volume and in quality. To make its products better, it installed a wave soldering machine and an assembly line at the new location — and this helped tremendously in reducing manufacturing errors. Orders were closer to being shipped on time, and in general MITS was enjoying its moment in the sun.

Things were going along relatively smoothly for MITS when it was financially devastated by something happening outside of its control. Competition had come to the small "computer" market. Texas Instruments developed its own calculator chip and started selling complete calculators at less than half the price of MITS' models. MITS was now in debt to the tune of $250,000, and Roberts saw his forecasted revenue shrink to zero.

Something else was going on that would change the computer landscape. *Popular Electronics* merged with *Electronics World* (retaining the name *Popular Electronics*). A change in an editorial staff rarely agrees with anyone, especially when two publications merge—and this was no exception. Many existing contributors and department managers/editors left and started writing for a competing magazine, *Radio-Electronics*. *Radio-Electronics* now had some of the best writers chomping at the bit for tidbits and stories about what anyone was doing with the Intel microprocessor.

In 1974, Art Salsberg entered into the picture, becoming editor of *Popular Electronics*. Salsberg's goal was to reclaim the lead in writing about current and future electronics projects. He knew a little about what "big" computers could do, but he was interested in what he was reading about the possibilities of smaller computers. One of his writers, Don Lancaster, dug up a story on how an ASCII keyboard could be attached to a computer; this was published in *Popular Electronics* in April 1974. The July 1974 of *Radio-Electronics* ran an article on the Mark-8 8008-based computer. Now, the race was on to find more interesting small-computer stories before another publisher could write about them.

A *Popular Electronics* editor, Les Solomon, knew MITS was working on an Intel 8080-based computer project, and asked Roberts for more detail so it would be ready for its January 1975 issue. While hooking up a typewriter and making it connect to bare, printed circuit boards was fun for some, it was not easy to get it all to work—and when done, it wasn't much to "ooh" and "aah" over. Solomon wanted a complete kit in a professional-looking enclosure that he could show his magazine buyers.

The typical MITS product had a generic name, such as the Model 1440 calculator or the Model 1600 digital voltmeter. Ed Roberts was wrapped up in getting a kit put together to sell that looked nice, so he basically said to Solomon to "come up with whatever name you want for it." The Altair computer was about to be born.

Rumors persist on how this name came about. Solomon told an audience at the first Altair Computer Convention

(March 1976) that the name was inspired by his 12-year-old daughter, Lauren, who suggested the name after a *Star Trek* (TV series) destination (actually Altair Six).

Another story going around during this time was that the computer was originally going to be named the PE-8 (*Popular Electronics* 8-bit computer), but Solomon and his other editors thought the name lacked a marketing slant to it, and said (according to some), "It's a stellar event, so let's name it after a star." McVeigh suggested "Altair," the twelfth brightest star in the sky.

However the name came about, it stuck. Altair was now the official marketing name. Roberts and Bill Yates finished the first prototype in October 1974, and shipped it to *Popular Electronics* in New York; however, it never arrived due to a strike by their shipping company. Solomon already had a number of pictures of what the machine would look like, so those, along with a small write-up on how it worked, got to Solomon. The computer shown on the magazine cover was nothing but an empty box with switches and LEDs on the front panel—nothing on the inside at all (so much for truth in advertising). As it turns out, the first officially finished Altair computer had a completely different circuit board layout than the prototype described by the magazine. The January 1975 issues appeared on newsstands a week before Christmas 1974, and the kit was officially (if not yet practically) available for sale just in time for that special gift to someone special.

In 1974, the price of an Altair kit was $395, or a multi-disk built system could be had for under $10,000. (How much under I am not sure, as this is verbatim from its ad.)

Roberts was familiar with the microprocessors available in 1974, and he didn't think his Altair using the Intel 4004 or Intel 8008 was powerful enough. As Captain Kirk on *Star Trek* would holler when being pursued by evil aliens: "Scotty, I need more power!" Scotty: "Captain, I'm giving it all she's got!" (This was about to be a common theme throughout the microcomputer and minicomputer companies — people with grand ideas for more applications and features, but being limited by the CPU's speed and features.) New ideas required faster computer hardware, and the lack of this had a devastating effect on many companies. It turns out the National Semiconductor IMP-8 and IMP-16 required external hardware, and the Motorola 6800 was still in development, so Roberts chose the 8-bit Intel 8080 microprocessor. At that time, Intel's main business was selling memory chips by the thousands to large computer companies; it had little experience in selling quantities of microprocessors to one business. When the 8080 was introduced in April 1974, Intel set the single unit price at $360. Roberts had experience in buying quantities of calculator chips, and with excellent negotiating skills he was able to negotiate a $75 price for each 8080 microprocessor chip. At least, the Altair could now be priced at a "fair" price to small businesses, while allowing MITS to make a respectable profit.

As with many things, timing is everything — and the introduction of the Altair 8800 fit this description perfectly. For over ten years, many colleges and universities had required science and engineering majors to take a course in computer programming. Two of the prominent languages were FORTRAN and COBOL, and there was a new one called BASIC. This meant that there was a sizable customer base that knew about computers. In 1970, electronic calculators rarely were seen outside of a laboratory, but by 1974, consumers had started buying them (mainly thanks to Texas Instruments' attractive pricing). Arcade video games, such as Atari's Pong, also introduced computers to the general public, although many players could not appreciate the fact that a microprocessor was behind the ball floating back and forth across a TV screen. The Intel 8008-based computer systems available in 1974 could do basic functions, but they were not powerful enough to run fast enough to support a high-level language like BASIC. The Altair, with the Intel 8080 chip, though, had enough power to actually be useful, and was thus designed as an expandable system that opened it up to all sorts of ideas and applications.

Roberts forecasted to his loan officer at his bank that he could sell 800 computers, while in reality they needed to only sell 200 over the next year to break even. When readers got the January issue of *Popular Electronics*, MITS was hit with orders it did not anticipate (thereby making its banker very happy). In February 1975, MITS received 1,000 orders for the Altair 8800. The quoted delivery time was 60 days, but because of a lack of staffing, slow lead times on parts, and manufacturing issues in general, a typical order took several months to be filled. Unfortunately, Roberts was now up to his neck in production issues, and his ideas for more options and gadgets were put on hold. MITS claimed to have delivered 2,500 Altair 8800s by the end of May 1975; this number grew to over 5,000 by August of the same year. MITS had fewer than twenty employees in January 1975, but by October 1975 had more than ninety.

The Altair 8800 computer pricing ($439 unassembled or $621 assembled) was just a break-even sale for MITS. To make any significant profit, it needed to sell additional memory boards, I/O boards, and other options. The system came with only "1024 words" of RAM. The BASIC language compiler for its machine was announced in July 1975, and it required one or two 4096-word memory boards and a special interface board. In other words, the basic Altair 8800 was limited in functionality, but with a few more options, such as the following, it could now be considered a viable, commercially acceptable, real-life small computer. Note the two prices below — one reflects unassembled and the other assembled:

- 1024-word Memory Board - $176 or $209
- 4096-word Memory Board - $264 or $338
- Parallel Interface Board - $92 or $114
- Serial Interface Board (RS-232) - $119 or $138
- Serial Interface Board (Teletype) - $124 or $146

- Audio Cassette Interface Board - $128 or $174
- Teletype Model 33 ASR N.A. - $1500
- 4K BASIC language (when purchased with Altair, 4096 words of memory and interface board) - $60
- 8K BASIC language (when purchased with Altair, two 4096-word memory boards and interface board) - $75

MITS had no significant competition for the first half of 1975. Its 4K memory board used typical RAM technology, which meant that all contents in memory was lost if power was lost. That, along with other small design problems, started to creep up on Roberts. The delay in shipping optional boards and the problems with the 4K memory board created an opportunity for outside suppliers. Seeing an opportunity to make some money because of MITS' production problems, Robert Marsh (an Altair owner himself) came along. He designed a 4K static memory board that was plug-in compatible with the Altair 8800 and sold for $255 (compared to MITS' price of $338). His company, Processor Technology, turned out to be one of the most successful Altair-compatible board suppliers. [See Processor Technology.] The July 1975 issue of *Popular Electronics* promised Processor Technology could supply an interface and PROM boards (which retained memory contents if power was lost) in addition to the 4K memory board. Processor Technology would later develop a popular video display board that would plug directly into the Altair.

In the first design of the Altair, the parts that were needed to make a complete machine would not fit on a single circuit board containing the microprocessor. Instead, the machine consisted of four boards stacked on top of each other. Another problem facing Roberts was that the parts needed to make a truly useful computer weren't available, or wouldn't be designed in time, for the January launch date. So, during the construction of the second model, he decided to build most of the machine on removable cards, reducing the motherboard to nothing more than an interconnect between the cards (and a "backplane" was thus born). The basic machine consisted of five cards, including the CPU on one and memory on another. He then looked for a cheap source of connectors, and came across a supply of 100-pin edge connectors. This random purchase of these connectors was dubbed the S-100 bus by Roberts, and was eventually acknowledged by the professional computer community and adopted as the IEEE-696 computer bus standard.

The Altair bus consisted of the pins of the Intel 8080 directly soldered (or plugged into) a board known as a computer backplane. Getting it out the door quickly was paramount, so good internal board designs took a back seat at times — which led to disasters such as shorting from various power sources of differing voltages being located next to each other inside the enclosure. Another oddity was that the system included two unidirectional 8-bit data buses, but only a single bidirectional 16-bit address bus. (One can only guess that the company had older 8-bit parts it wanted to use, but couldn't figure out how to move them to a 16-bit architecture.)

The Altair shipped in a two-piece case. The backplane and power supply were mounted on a base plate along with the front and rear of the box. The "lid" was shaped like a C, forming the top, left, and right sides of the box. The front panel was copied from another computer startup called the Data General Nova minicomputer; this panel included a large number of toggle switches to feed binary data directly into the memory of the machine, and a number of red LEDs to read those values.

Figure 99—MITS Altair 8800

From a practical and "mechanical" perspective, programming the Altair was hard. While writing instructions for the machine were fairly easy, the entering of them into the computer was arduous. The programmer had to toggle switches to positions corresponding to an 8080 microprocessor instruction (known as "operations code," or opcode for short) in binary (0's and 1's), then had to use an 'enter' switch to load the code into the machine's memory. If a mistake was made in entering the opcodes, the programmer had to start all over. And if the machine was turned off, there was no assurance that the program would be saved. In other words, the Altair was officially a small computer sold to the masses, but it was very hard to program and lacked peripheral devices (e.g. a keyboard, printer, and monitor) to make it very useful. Roberts was already hard at work on additional circuit cards, including a paper-tape reader to make programming instructions easier to enter and to reboot the machine faster if power was lost. Additional RAM cards and an RS-232 (a communication standard) interface to connect to a proper Teletype terminal were about to be released as options.

Two other guys, Bill Gates and Paul Allen, entered into the picture. If there was a decade in which to be interested in computers for either of them, this was it. Roberts expressed his interest in buying a programming language from them, and Gates and Allen started work on putting the final touches on one they had been using. Using a self-made simulator for the 8080 on a Digital PDP-10 minicomputer, they finished it up and Allen flew to Albuquerque to deliver the program on a paper tape. Gates and Allen called the language Beginner's All-Purpose Symbolic Instruction Code (known to many as simply BASIC), and was marketed by Altair as "4K BASIC." The first time it was run, it displayed "READY"; then Allen typed "PRINT 2+2" and it printed "4." The game Lunar Lander was entered in and this worked as well. Altair now had an easy-to-use programming interface, and Gates and Allen had sold their first software. Gates and Allen then formed Micro-soft (which was the original spelling of the larger company now known the world over as Microsoft).

By 1977, MITS was the leader in this new market that no one had officially named yet. It had the Altair 8800 models A and B, a Motorola 6800 microprocessor-based computer, and peripheral products. Plus, it had a network of dealers set up to sell and service. It ran ads consistently in magazines, and seemed that the company was poised to corner the "personal computer" market. As you see many times over in this book, engineers and "idea" people don't necessarily make good business people.

Roberts gave a man named Richard Brown the entire east coast of the U.S. as an exclusive territory. Brown and his partner planned to franchise computer stores up and down the coast under the name The Computer Store (which, as it turns out, was never officially registered as that name). Brown sold only a few franchises. Meanwhile, other computer retailing stores opened, which would have sold Altairs if they could have gotten them. Instead, they sold other computer making kits and assembled computers that were now competing for market share. Because of Brown's lack of business acumen, his competition was flourishing.

To make matters worse, Roberts insisted that his small dealers could only sell Altairs; however, he could not supply enough computers to keep the dealers in business. In addition, MITS continued to sell directly to end users even after its dealer network was in place. A marketing mess rapidly ensured.

Bill Millard and Ed Farber of IMSAI took advantage of MITS' sales model debacle. These two guys would allow anyone who would put up $2,500 and a promise to buy twenty-five computers in a year to become a dealer. In retrospect, Roberts might have been able to salvage his franchising operation, but cash flow problems kept his attention on a day-in and day-out basis. When Pertec offered to buy MITS, Roberts took his lumps and losses and retired from the computer business.

To digress slightly, Pertec was well established by the late 1970s after carving out a market to sell disk drives and other computer peripheral equipment. [See Pertec.] Pertec knew that MITS was moving a lot of disk drives for the company, so why not cut out the middle man and own the company outright? And that's what it did. Unfortunately, it did not understand the current buyers of the Altair very well. Pertec saw the name "Altair" as being associated with hobbyists, and it wanted to produce something more commercial and appeal to a larger market (i.e., the business world). Soon after Pertec bought MITS, it dropped the Altair name, thereby getting rid of one of the best-named brands in the fledgling personal computer market. By 1980, sales of the Altair had been surpassed by Apple and other faster PCs.

As for Ed Roberts, he retired to the state of Georgia. In 2013, an Altair 8800 clone was introduced for enthusiasts who wanted to recreate the Altair 8800 experience, but with modern hardware. The clone carried the same price as the original Altair 8800.

MIT Digital Systems Laboratory

This was a difficult "company" to document, since it never existed—and it never officially created a marketable product. Still, it was worth writing about. In 1975, an MIT student, David Emberson, constructed an early microprocessor-based portable computer.

Emberson's "product" (and I use that term loosely since it never made it into production) was based on the Motorola 6800. Constructed literally in a Samsonite suitcase measuring 20 in. x 30 in. x 8 in. in size and weighing approximately twenty pounds, it had 4K of RAM, a serial port for a modem, a keyboard, and a 40-column thermal printer taken from a cash register. It was unofficially known as the MIT Suitcase Computer.

The only surviving model is currently in the collection of Dr. Hoo-Min D. Toong. Below is a very rare photograph of this early example of a "portable" computer.

Figure 100 - MIT Suitcase Computer

Mitsubishi

The Mitsubishi company ranks as one the oldest companies in this book, as it was first established as a shipping firm by Yatarō Iwasaki in 1870. In 1873, the name was changed to Mitsubishi Shokai. The company dabbled in insurance (for the shipping vessels), purchased a shipyard, and even started its own bank in 1919. In 1917, Mitsubishi produced Japan's first production-line automobile, which was a copy of the Ford Model A that was sold in the U.S. Automobile and engine growth (especially aircraft engines) was substantial for it through the end of WWII.

After the war, Mitsubishi participated in Japan's unprecedented economic growth. Mitsubishi created companies to focus on specific areas such as Mitsubishi Petrochemical, Mitsubishi Atomic Power Industries, Mitsubishi Liquefied Petroleum Gas, and Mitsubishi Petroleum Development. Additionally, Mitsubishi continued to be involved by design and purpose with consumer goods, data communications, computers, and semiconductor development.

In 1970, Mitsubishi's electronic division produced the MELCOM 700 series through a technology-sharing agreement with the American firm XDS. The MELCOM 700 series consisted of the MELCOM 750 and MELCOM 770 models. One of the strengths of this system was that it was marketed as being able to support four data processing types at the same time: batch processing, timesharing processing, real-time processing, and remote batch processing. While the MELCOM 700 line of minicomputers was excellent, it still was not accepted as being big enough to compete in the IBM market. At the same time, Mitsubishi was seeing a demand for large computers from within its own manufacturing divisions, and Mitsubishi thought that if it needed large computers, then other companies must also. In other words, it wanted in on this market, and saw its continued development in the computer market as a way to eventually compete head-on with IBM.

Figure 101—Mitsubishi MELCOM 700 (permission granted by Information Processing Society of Japan)

The MELCOM 700 line of computers allowed up to 128 users to access and use the computer simultaneously. This functionality included dynamic relocation of programs and high-speed, fixed-head magnetic disk program virtual program swapping; it had a data transfer rate of 3,000 Kbytes per second. The system had main memory of up to 512 kilobytes, and up to eight I/O channels for accessing peripherals. Its main memory was unique in that it broke it up into eight separate areas in order to reduce any bottlenecks for access to it. Basically, what it allowed was memory to be accessed in one module while the next module's address was being pre-fetched and ready to present data to the processor. This interleaving of memory access was a creative way to speed processing up. The main memory's cycle time was 0.85 microseconds, but with interleaving as designed by Mitsubishi, the main memory operated with an effective cycle time of just 0.56

microseconds. The operating system was called Universal Processing System (UPS).

As with the UK, France, and Germany, there was a lot of pride in having your country develop a great computer. And just as those countries assisted monetarily to help in some way, Japan's Ministry of International Trade and Industry contributed also. Japan had (and has) a unique environment where companies could work together to arrive at a common goal. The goal here was simple — develop a computer that could compete with IBM and be more adept at processing Japanese character sets. Mitsubishi teamed with Oki Electric, and the outcome was the COSMO series Model 700, released in 1974. This was a smaller model (in disk size and memory) than the MELCOM 700, but it offered something very unique — it maintained backward compatibility to the MELCOM 700 series. What this meant is that all applications developed on the COSMO would run on the MELCOM.

The Model 700 offered a virtual memory operating environment, which allowed many large programs to execute within the processor. Its specifications were as follows:

- 32K – 1024K of main memory
- 132-bit word length, but read from memory in 64 bits
- 8-bit error correction code
- Cycle time $0.9\mu s$
- CPU with
    - Fixed-point binary numbers (word, double word)
    - Logical numbers (bit, byte, word, double word)
    - Virtual memory allocated to each user
    - Direct and indirect addressing
    - Sixteen general-purpose registers (three of which were index registers)
    - Two floating-point registers

- I/O devices available
- Removable magnetic disk of 50MB, 100MB, and 200MB (transfer speed: 806K/s, average access time: 38.3ms)
- Cartridge magnetic disk of 10MB
- Fixed-head magnetic disk of 1MB (average access time: 8.3 ms)
- Magnetic tape
- Card reader
- Line printer

The system came with two service processors and two sets of system consoles; this was done to provide redundancy. The operating system was called UTS/VS.

Mitsubishi enhanced its operating system to enable it to handle any mixtures of Japanese characters, kanji (Chinese characters) and kana, and true Japanese language data for batch and transaction processing. This is extremely important to comprehend, because up until this time the Mitsubishi users had to acquaint themselves with the traditional ASCII "American" character set. *With the Mitsubishi enhancement, the Japanese computer users could work in their native language.*

In 1976, the COSMO 700II and the COSMO 900 were jointly announced. The COSMO 700II used higher-density chips, and therefore consumed less energy, plus it could have up to 3MB of memory. Copying some ideas from Tandem Computers, this system also implemented battery takeover in case of a power failure. The COSMO 900 used multiple CPUs, and implemented a shared memory concept across all of them; and it could address up to 4MB per CPU. After this, the water is murky regarding who owned what and the marketing rights to the COSMO series. The COSMO 700III and COSMO 700S were announced in 1979 by Mitsubishi. These computers had a unique design where the traditional processor architecture (e.g., system control, arithmetic processing, input/output processing, and communications control) was broken up by placing them in separate processors (which used high-speed fiber-optic buses to connect to each other). Even though there were multiple processors in a configuration, they were tightly coupled in that they shared a common memory scheme. The maximum main memory capacity was 4MB.

As the 1980s rolled around, new models such as the COSMO 800III and COSMO 800S were announced with more speed on overall improvements. Today, Mitsubishi is a huge company that consists of a multitude of independent companies, such as an auto manufacturer, nuclear power work, chemicals production, fiber optics and imaging development, consumer products, banking, solar development, and many others. The company no longer develops commercial computers, although it continues to leverage its computer work by having its engineers involved with the many facets of electronics today. The names of most, but not all, of its companies contain the word "Mitsubishi." Many of the companies use the three-diamond Mitsubishi mark, but none calls itself simply "Mitsubishi."

While never achieving a system that gave IBM much competition, it did market an excellent system that took some business away from IBM (especially those mid-size companies), and it kept IBM on its heels for relying too much on its traditional mainframe systems.

Modcomp

In 1978, Modcomp (a Fort Lauderdale, Florida-based company) announced its Modcomp CLASSIC 7860 "super" minicomputer (the company's words, not mine). By the end of that same year, it came out with the CLASSIC 7870 system. What was both odd and funny about its ad was that since the company had developed a system earlier in the year, Modcomp now could lay claim to being an experienced computer maker now on its second-generation system! How's that for positive spin? It is not a stretch for the astute business major to assume that the company could have just as easily written: "We screwed up so badly on our first machine that we quickly had to build its replacement."

Modcomp claimed a 125-nanosecond memory cycle time. It aimed both of its systems to the scientific, engineering, and process control environment, and because of this could take some shortcuts in the operating system to focus on that kind of work instead of business transactions (and the supporting software to run those business applications). The bottom line was that these systems were fast, and could outperform the DEC's 11/70 and VAX, Interdata's 8/32, and PRIME's 400 (verified through independent benchmarks at the time).

Both the 7860 and 7870 had a very inventive way of processing 16-bit, 32-bit, and 64-bit instructions — something that few had figured out. The operating system also performed pipelined instruction processing, which meant that more instructions could be processed in a given window of time. Both systems supported the FORTRAN programming language.

Figure 102—Modcomp 7870

The 7860 and 7870 were large (physically) compared to most minicomputers in the market. They came with one operator console, a high-speed line printer, a magnetic disk cabinet, a tape drive cabinet, and other cabinets to hold the memory, more disk drives, and the CPU. From one end to the other, it took up approximately 25 feet in linear space, and all cabinets stood approximately 6 feet tall.

Mohawk Data Sciences Corp. (MDS)

MDS was formed in 1964 in Herkimer, New York, by several engineers who had left UNIVAC. The idea of forming MDS came from George R. Cogar who had an idea for a better way to enter data into a computer. (In this era, remember that punched cards were the standard for entering data into a computer.) IBM had developed the standard for what were called keypunch machines,[83] and if anyone wanted to play with IBM, then they had better support punch cards. A keypunch machine physically punched holes in a small cardboard card, and then this card was read by a device called (what else?) a "card reader." (IBM didn't invent the punch card, but to show the clout of IBM, they became known as the "IBM punch card" to many.)

---

[83] I wanted to be very clear to use the word "standard"; the act of using holes in a card and using that as data was invented by Herman Hollerith as a way to help New York City gather and process statistics in the late 1880s. Hollerith, though, was technically not the first with this idea, as weaving looms could be programmed in the early 1800s using this same idea.

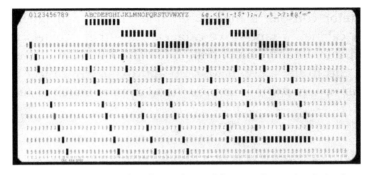

Figure 103—Example of punch card (approximately six inches long and three inches wide)

MDS' idea was to allow data to be written to a magnetic tape, and then read as input to the computer, thereby bypassing the whole concept of punch cards. This is one of those, "Why didn't I think of that?" times that some people in the 1970s started asking themselves. MDS' first product was called the Data Recorder.

The product caught on quickly as a powerful product to compete against IBM's domination in data entry. MDS had ideas to expand its product to do more, and with the revenues flowing in from the success of the Data Recorder, MDS acquired Atron Corporation. Atron had developed a minicomputer called the Atron 501 Datamanager, and MDS needed this type of system (a computer that could control several "data entry" machines and store the data in batches) to take it to its next market.

Figure 104—Mohawk Atron 501

The Atron 501 was renamed the MDS 2400, and was sold as a "Peripheral Processor." The MDS 2400 had 4K of RAM, but was expandable to 32K. MDS wrote its own emulation of the IBM 2780 and 3780 protocols, and this allowed the MDS 2400 to emulate both IBM printers and data entry keypunch machines. In other words, the whole awkward world of dealing with punched cards was about to change. The MDS 2400 was expandable (for added cost) to allow up to four input/output channels,[84] with each channel being able to support up to sixteen devices (again, any combination of printers or data-entry devices).

Once the keyed data was ready to be processed, a dial-up link was made to the host IBM (or to another maker's mainframe) via built-in 9,600 baud modem. Overall, it was

---

[84] Think of a channel as a highway in and out of city (or in this case, a computer). On each road there could up to sixteen houses or businesses. Each house or business was given a house address consisting of basically what road it was on and what house number it was on that road. If the city wanted to send something to one of the houses (or a house had something to send to the city), it used the road and house number. Computers work the same way with the concept called "channels."

an excellent idea that propelled the industry to think of new ideas.

As with many small startup companies like MDS, though, it failed to plan for "what do we do next?" Companies such as Sycor, Datapoint, and Data 100 had taken the MDS idea and were making faster, programmable systems that left MDS behind the technology curve. MDS had no answer, plus its location in New York might have played against it when trying to attract bright engineers who were keeping abreast of the changing computer landscape. MDS was successful early on with one idea, but it needed an infusion of new ideas—and men and women graduating from the University of Michigan, MIT, Stanford, and others were not keen on moving to Herkimer. By 1984, revenue (which had never been stellar) fell, and MDS closed its doors.

MOS Technology, Inc.

Started in 1969 as a subsidiary of Allen-Bradley (which had its hands in many aspects of electronic componentry), MOS Technology's focus was on metal oxide semiconductors (ergo the name MOS). It was located in Norristown, Pennsylvania, where the company did both the designing and fabrication of the chips.[85]

Texas Instruments was a leader in the various kinds of chips then being used in computers and other electronic machines, which needed smaller and specialized chip functions. MOS Technology meant to give TI users a choice. For instance, in an early 1970 ad, MOS offered chips that functioned as shift registers, counters, encoders, programmable, clock driving, sequence timing, digital transponder, and ROM.

---

[85] It used an address in Valley Forge, Pennsylvania, in its marketing literature.

By 1975, MOS had seen and read enough about the Intel microprocessor that it knew it could build its own. The problem with fabricating a chip on a wafer of silicon was that because of either imperfections in the silicon itself or in the manufacturing process, more than 50 percent of the final chips produced were flawed and could not be used — adding to the cost to make good chips. MOS' bright engineers came up with a way to actually fix a fabricated chip after some flaws were detected in it; this caused a profound effect on the company being able to offer a microprocessor chip at a lower cost than both Intel and Motorola (both of which very quickly lowered their prices to compete with MOS).

MOS' first microprocessor was called the 6502, and the MOS KIM-1 was marketed to highlight MOS' entry into the computer market. The KIM-1 was not a kit, but a fully functional computer — without a keyboard, storage, just 1K of RAM, and only 2K of ROM. The price was right, though, at only $245.

Figure 105—MOS KIM-1

Commodore Business Machines, which up until now was making calculators, entered the picture. But both MOS and Commodore were taking their licks by competing with TI on price, and in general the chip market was slow for sales.

MOS' big break (which could now be seen as both good and bad) was when they convinced Commodore to use the MOS 6510 microprocessor in Commodore's new line of computers. Commodore ended up buying a majority stake in MOS—thereby officially changing MOS Technology, Inc. to Commodore Semiconductor Group.

Commodore went out of business in 1994, taking the Commodore Semiconductor Group with it (at least for a while). Ex-management of MOS took over the remnants of their old company, and renamed it GMT Microelectronics. GMT was making solid revenues on new products, but in 1999 it was forced into liquidation because of considerable pollution violations, and thus fines imposed by the U.S. Environmental Protection Agency (EPA).

Motorola

This company started life as the Galvin Manufacturing Corporation in 1928, with a name change to Motorola in 1947. Riding on the wave of transistor technology, in 1955 it opened a plant for that production in Phoenix, Arizona.

Motorola's vacuum tubes, transistors, and integrated circuits found usage in everything from retail products (e.g., portable radios) to military and commercial telecommunications areas. Having smart engineers and watching the Intel wave of small processors hit the market, Motorola began work on its MC6800 microprocessor in 1972, which was then marketed in 1974. The 6800 (as it was known throughout the industry) was an 8-bit microprocessor, which included serial and parallel interface ICs, RAM, ROM, and other supporting chips.

A feature that set the 6800 apart from Intel was that it required only a single five-volt power supply. Its instruction set was similar to DEC's PDP-11 (consisting of seventy-two instructions with seven addressing modes). Although it was an 8-bit microprocessor, with creative addressing it would address 64K of RAM. The first 6800 had a clock frequency of up to 1 MHz, but later improvements moved this to 2 MHz, which was very impressive for the mid-1970s.

Motorola provided an assembly language development system. The company also developed a desktop computer called the Motorola EXORciser; this machine was basically meant to be used for prototyping and debugging new microprocessor designs, and was not available to the public. As peripherals were getting smarter (e.g., a tape drive could buffer up data before writing to the magnetic tape, therefore speeding up operations), Motorola saw these peripheral makers using their processors more and more. In other words, microprocessors were needed to communicate with other microprocessors inside the same computer system.[86] In 1977, the MC6802 was introduced, and it included 128K of RAM and an internal clock oscillator on a chip.

In 1979, the Motorola 6800, with a 16-/32-bit CISC microprocessor, was introduced. It was designed and marketed by Motorola Semiconductor Products Sector. Intel and then Zilog were having success in the 16-bit microcomputer market, and Motorola wanted a piece of the action.

The 68000 grew out of a 1976 project at the MACSS (Motorola Advanced Computer System on Silicon). The goal of the project was to develop an entirely new architecture from a clean slate (meaning that it was not

---

[86] All new cars have this same setup. There is an ECU (Electronic Control Module) that acts as the central processor on the car, and around the car are other microprocessors that control acceleration, braking, GPS, etc.—all communicating back to the ECU; this technology is behind "driverless" cars.

backward-compatible to anything that the 6800 did). When the dust settled, though, more reasonable minds prevailed, and the 68000 did retain a bus protocol compatibility mode for existing 6800 peripheral devices. (Meaning that 6800 -compatible peripherals could still communicate with a 68000 based system.) The 68000 CPU registers were 32 bits wide. In February 1980, the 68000 chips were available with speeds of 4 MHz, 6 MHz, and 8 MHz.

The 68000 became a major competitor to Intel, as the 68000 was used in Apple products, Atari, and others. While Motorola continued its success in many electronic areas, in 1999 Motorola spun off its analog IC, digital IC, and transistor business to ON Semiconductor of Phoenix, Arizona. In 2004 Motorola spun off its microprocessor business to Freescale Semiconductor of Austin, Texas.

Before I move on from this company, it is important for the reader to understand Motorola's contribution to the "smart phone" world we are in now. Human communication over any distance has been key throughout history. When Gugliemo Giovanni Maria Marconi figured out that radio waves existed and Alexander Graham Bell could transmit a voice over a wire, the world was about to change.

During the 1950's and 1960's, police had proprietary networked phones installed in some metro areas, and wealthy people could have a portable phone installed in their limousines. (As with the police proprietary networked phones, these worked on the same scheme – the public could not access that network.) In the late 1960's and early 1970's, Motorola and Bell started sharing the idea "would it be possible to create some sort of 'open' communication that would allow portable phones for anyone to use?

In 1974, the world's first "cellular phone" was announced. It would be another ten years before it would be sold to the public, but during this time Bell and Motorola perfected their idea of "open cellular towers" which any "cellular phone" could access. The Motorola phone was called the DynaTac (short for Dynamic Total Area Coverage).

Figure 106 - Motorola DynaTac and typical smart phone

The DynaTac (shown on the left) weighed over two pounds, stood nine inches high, could only story 30 names/phones numbers, could not text, had an LCD readout, and of course could not store or execute "applications" like the smart phone shown on the right can do. The DynTac sold for close to $3,000, and it used a precursor of the commercial Motorola 6800 microprocessor. From these two very inventive companies wondering "could we put a microprocessor into a hand-held phone and would people buy it?" we have the amazing "smart" phones of today.

And Motorola wasn't done yet with its commercial creativity and inventiveness that would change the world. Before the 1970's, every vehicle manufactured used what was called a carburetor to deliver gasoline to its engine. The carburetor had existed for seventy plus years with only improvements along the way – and it still was a mechanical device prone to tuning quirkiness. In the mid 1970's, the Ford Motor Company and Motorola collaborated to develop a microprocessor controlled device (using the Motorola 6800) as a replacement for the carburetor. Welcome to the world of Electronic Fuel Injection (EFI) that would change the automobile world forever. Today every automobile uses EFI to provide programmable tuning that allows better gas mileage and engine performance.

National Cash Register Company (NCR)

NCR has its roots as the National Manufacturing Company. It was located in Dayton, Ohio, and founded in 1879. The name changed to National Cash Register Company in the late 1800s. (The name officially became NCR in 1974, but for simplicity's sake, I will refer to the National Cash Register Company as NCR from here on.) NCR started out doing calculations on its invention of the mechanical cash register. As the turn of the century approached, NCR had a near monopoly on the cash register market.

The company kept tinkering with the cash register, and added an electric motor making it faster for users to enter transactions. (Instead of pulling a large lever to total entries, a button accomplished the same task—just like slot machines evolved and work today.) NCR was inventive in many ways—namely by its creation of a national salesforce working on commission and selling by business function—not just on the wizardry of the machine itself. Because of this sales strategy, NCR grew with its own product sales and through acquisitions of its competitors. (The aforementioned was added only to show how NCR was trying to keep up with the times and competition, which were changing rapidly.)

NCR was drawn into the banking world mainly because banks liked its products; if a bank wanted to "automate," NCR was becoming the default for banking machines. Banks required a lot of customer calculations to be done accurately. Additionally, banks were starting to automate their check processing instead of using the traditional way that involved a lot of human handling of the checks. During WWII, NCR was tapped by the U.S. government to help develop high-speed counting machines. After the war was over, NCR found itself drawn into the world of computing just because of what it had developed, both with its bank customers and with the government.

One of its main electronic creations was the Class 29 Post-Tronic machine, marketed in 1956.[87] NCR had figured out a way to put a magnetic stripe on pieces of paper, encode them with data, and then read them as the paper floated from bank to bank. Partnering with GE, NCR built and marketed the NCR 304. This machine was a transistor-based computer that processed what was (and is today) called magnetic ink character recognition (MICR). Of course, to keep up with this technology, each bank would need an NCR machine, so NCR saw its sales soar.

Other models came out during the '60s, and in 1970 the Century 200 was released. The Century product line introduced the CRAM storage device, which was essentially a huge storage of data on magnetic disks instead of using magnetic tapes. The Century 300, a true multiprocessor computer, soon followed. In 1976, the Criterion series was announced. The Criterion was NCR's first virtual machine system, which meant that it could not only run many programs at the same time, but these programs also were not limited to a physical memory size (at least theoretically).

---

[87] In 1953, two of its Dayton chemists submitted a patent for "Pressure responsive record materials." It was marketed as NCR paper. Keep in mind that up until this time, if anyone wanted to make a copy of a piece of paper, a messy carbon sheet had to be inserted between the original and the copy. NCR solved this, and today we simply call it a paper copy without ever having to dream of using a carbon sheet.

Figure 107—NCR Criterion 8570

Computers had been thought of as big and expensive, and NCR's business plan set out to change that perception. In the late '70s introduced the NCR 605 minicomputer for smaller needs (actually a model of what it called its 7400 series). Also, in the late '70s, NCR was making POS machines and ATM machines and riding the wave of this new demand for banking transactions.

During the 1980s, NCR introduced more computer products, ATM machines, PCs, and assorted banking devices that increased the speed of check handling (along with other banking requirements).

NCR gradually gave up its minicomputer business for three reasons: 1) It couldn't (or didn't want to) compete with the faster computers on the market, 2) They were late to the market as other minicomputer makers were staking out a competency in that area, and 3) It wanted to concentrate on its core competency—namely, to focus on one the banking market (after all, this is where NCR had its roots). One of its concentrations was on building more programmable ATM machines for custom use. On September 19, 1991, NCR was acquired by AT&T Corporation (NCR's largest customer) for $7.4 billion. Money losses ensued for AT&T with its purchase of not only NCR, but also other computer companies. In 1995, it sold its "microelectronics and storage" division to Hyundai (a Korean company). NCR, though, sort of existed inside AT&T in concept only—namely, NCR still had a "consulting force" intact. AT&T didn't see this as making money for the company, so in 1996 it officially changed its AT&T Global Information Solutions to NCR in preparation for a spin-off.

On January 1, 1997, NCR re-emerged as a stand-alone company. From this time until today, NCR has had many ups and downs (a lawsuit and judgment against it by the U.S. government had a serious effect on the stock price), and several acquisitions of smaller firms that made banking equipment beneficial to its bottom line. NCR remains focused on the banking industry in various forms of automation from ATMs, teller processing, check processing, and funds transfers from financial institutions to others.

A little trivia about NCR: One of NCR's early salesmen, Thomas J. Watson, wanted to instill enthusiasm with the employees, so he installed the motto "THINK" around its offices. Wanting more of a challenge than selling cash registers, Watson left to start IBM. When Watson left NCR, one of the first things he did was erect the "THINK" motto around his new digs, and today the motto lives on with the IBM culture and in sales ads.

National Semiconductor

National Semiconductor was yet another company to come out of the northeast area of the U.S. Located in Danbury, Connecticut, it was started by Bernard Rothlein with seven other people on May 27, 1959. Its focus was to make semiconductors, which was a natural for the company since the founders just so happened to have come from Sperry Rand Corporation's Semiconductor Division.

Unfortunately for this new company, Sperry Rand didn't like the new competition—especially since Sperry Rand claimed that National Semiconductor was using patents that Sperry Rand owned. While battling patent infringement issues in the courts in the mid-1960s, National Semiconductor was acquiring more companies and key people (both engineering and marketing) from other companies. The semiconductor business became very incestuous with people jumping to and from companies on a regular basis. To make deals sweeter for potential employees, company promises of stock ownership, paid sabbaticals, and other enticements were part of many employment packages. In 1967, National Semiconductor relocated to Santa Clara, California.

Why the fuss with semiconductors? What is a semiconductor? First, a deep understanding and an appreciation of quantum physics is needed. I don't have this knowledge, so I urge you to do your own research on that topic. I do know how they are used. Mainly, they make laptops and cell phones extremely portable – and they make things like jet airplanes and spaceships possible. A semiconductor moves electrons – it "conducts" them along a path. Insulators are required to keep things moving properly; advanced reading will tell you that different materials conduct electricity/electrons depending upon influences such as heat. Semiconductor companies spent a lot of research time and money figuring this out. The earliest semiconductors were huge by today's standard for what they could properly conduct on a small scale. With new engineering and micro-electronics for manufacturing, today's memory chips hold many gigabytes, whereas fifty years ago only a few megabytes were possible.

What National Semiconductor contributed to the computer industry in the 1970s was twofold: 1) It, along with other companies such as Texas Instruments, drove competition and thereby increased the density (and thus the speed) of chips, and 2) it spread its knowledge around the world, which in turn spurred on development in many areas. By the time the early 1970s rolled around, National Semiconductor already had operations in Hong Kong,

China; Greenock, Scotland; Fürstenfeldbruck, Germany; and Singapore. In 1972, Malaysia was added, and Bangkok, Thailand; and Bandung, Indonesia, were added in 1975. Manila, Philippines, came along in 1976, as well as other plant sites in the U.S.

Many case studies can be (and probably have been) written about what happened to National Semiconductor in the '80s, '90s, and the years following. One fact was that National Semiconductor's products were being easily copied and reproduced (without permission from National Semiconductor) by some Asian manufacturers. Add to this, many internal management changes, more acquisitions, higher than anticipated manufacturing costs, loss of orders, and fierce competition...and it was a disaster looming. Again, you are urged to research what was occurring inside of National Semiconductor during this truculent period, but suffice it to say it was not pretty. Plant closings ensued and spin-offs occurred on a regular basis to bring in cash, but eventually enough was enough. In 2011, National Semiconductor ceased to exist when it was acquired by Texas Instruments.

NEC (Nippon Electric)

In 1898, Takeshiro Maedo and Kunihiki Iwadre formed a partnership to establish a company called Nippon Electric. The intent of the company was to manufacture, sell, and maintain the potential telephone market (including switchboards) throughout Japan. It took a few years for the government to catch up and establish standards for this, but eventually, it all settled down and NEC was making a name for itself in the telephony business (not only in Japan, but in exporting to China, Korea, and other places).

Over the next seventy years (during which time WWII intervened), NEC found itself a leader in Japan's need for telephone infrastructure. Computers, of course, were being integrated into the telephone networks to make call switching and routing faster and more reliable. NEC's early computers were the NEAC-1101, NEAC-1102, and NEAC-2201.

NEC was now a well-thought of telephone company, and sales to Europe were growing. During the 1960s, NEC had fully integrated computer technology with most (if not all) aspects of electronic communications. In 1978, NEC moved into the U.S. market by acquiring a semiconductor manufacturing company, Electronic Arrays, Inc. (located in California), and opening up a plant in Dallas, Texas, to manufacture electronic telephony switches.

Also in 1978, NEC released a minicomputer to compete in the growing minicomputer market. The first system was the MS10, which could only address 64K of memory. The MS30 soon followed, allowing addressing of 256K. Through some very creative software engineers, the MS50 came out, which allowed addressing of 1MB. All of these systems offered floating-point arithmetic, had twenty-six registers, could support sixty-four levels of interrupts, and applications were priority-driven inside of its NCOS1 operating system. For some reason, memory parity checking was optional in the MS30, but standard in the other two. The following picture shows the technological progress from the MS10 system to the MS50.

Figure 108—NEC MS10 (top) and NEC MS50 (bottom)
(permission granted by Information Processing Society of Japan)

In 1979, NEC beat IBM to the market by announcing a PC called the PC-8001; this was to be followed by more PC models in the 1980s, along with the SX-2 in 1985 that was called by some the world's faster computer.

By 2010 NEC held a substantial market share of all PCs sold in Japan. Its dominance in commercial computers grew—one path was through a partnership with the Chinese company, Lenovo, and the other was through developing and marketing faster minicomputers (which were fast and large enough to compete with mainframe systems).

While not especially inventive in new discoveries in the world of computers, NEC did figure out practical and beneficial uses of computer technology to help the growing world of communications.

Today, NEC is a flourishing giant in the communications area and innovation in the world of high-density chips, discoveries such as carbon nanotubes, smartphone technologies, geo-environmental research, cryptography research, and much more.

Nixdorf

Nixdorf had its roots in work done as the Laboratory for Frequency Metrology (1952 - 1968). The company officially came about as Nixdorf Computer AG in 1968, and lived until 1990. Eventually, Nixdorf became Siemens Nixdorf Information Systems in 1990, then Siemens Nixdorf Retails & Banking Systems GmbH in 1998, and finally Wincor Nixdorf as it is known today.

Heinz Nixdorf was a student in Frankfürt am Main, Germany, working for the Remington Rand Corporation. He found himself working on projects related to the newly invented integrated circuits, but his company hadn't quite seen the benefit of tying this in with its mechanical calculating machines. Frustrated by this myopia on the part of his company, Nixdorf took his idea of integrating more electronics with machines to a consortium of electricity-generating companies. In 1952, intrigued by his ideas, these companies granted Nixdorf a 30,000 DM (Deutsch mark) investment and a laboratory in which to develop something new. He called his company RWE, and located his lab at the Rhein Westphalia power station in Essen, Germany.

The remainder of the 1950s found Nixdorf and his meager staff developing electronic interfaces to traditional mechanical devices, and in 1958, it produced what it claimed was the first electronic calculator with a built-in printer.[88]

Expanding his staff and his own ideas, Nixdorf looked at the computer market in which IBM basically had a

---

[88] Granted, this probably does not go down in history alongside the creation of fire, but in some room in 1958, a bunch of nerdy engineers were probably throwing a party.

monopoly. Small and medium-sized companies had few alternatives other than to pay a connection service to an IBM mainframe, as smaller computers were too expensive and complicated to manage for themselves. Nixdorf knew that a small machine could not compete with this "mainframe" technology, so he decided to attack this need by offering a simple-to-operate and reasonably priced computer. In 1967, RWE produced the Nixdorf Universal Computer 820 (eventually called simply the Nixdorf 820). Revenues began providing a nice profit, and in 1968 Nixdorf Computers AG (now called) acquired the Cologne-based Wanderer-Werken company for the purchase price of 17.2 million DM. The headquarters was moved to Paderborn, Germany, and in 1972, the company established sales offices in the U.S. and Japan.

From 1974 until 1984, Nixdorf developed a family of microprocessor-based terminals called the 620, using the Argos data collection software product. This system was a way for clerks to enter data similar to how it was done on IBM's 3270 data-entry machines; in addition to entering the data, the data was collected and sent to a centralized system (the Nixdorf 820) for processing and storage.

The Nixdorf 820 computer was produced and marketed from 1968 until 1979. The Nixdorf 820 was unique in the computer industry as custom software was offered depending upon the customer's needs. (The downside of this approach was that many custom software packages had to be supported by a large staff of Nixdorf personnel.) The Nixdorf 820 was very attractive to small and medium companies; these companies realized they could achieve automation without expensive ties to an IBM mainframe. The Nixdorf 820 was sold from a price range of 30,000 DM to 200,000 DM.

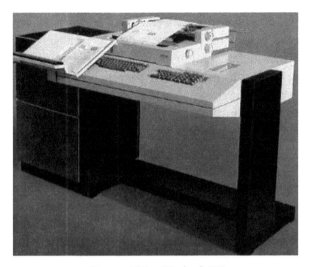

Figure 109—Nixdorf 820

The Nixdorf 820 was superseded by the Nixdorf 840 (from 1973 to 1979). This system did everything the 820 did, plus it allowed for direct data processing and data transmission from input devices (meaning data didn't have to be stored and batched for processing, but was processed as a business transaction at the point of entry). It also used dot matrix printers as output devices.

The Nixdorf 880 (from 1972 to 1975) was its first system with magnetic disks serving as memory. The Nixdorf 880's life was cut short by money and development people who were focused on the Nixdorf 700 family point-of-sale (POS) intelligent cash registers from 1971 to 1981 (with names such as the 705, 710, and 720). These systems had their own microprocessor, redundant power supplies, and other hardware to protect from a power failure.

From 1975 to 1979, the Nixdorf 8811 was a follow-up to the 880. This new machine allowed a phone connection to transmit data between computers. In this timeframe, Nixdorf also released an ultra-quiet printer, an alphanumeric keyboard with a 55-character set, proprietary data-entry terminals called the Nixdorf 8812 and Nixdorf 8862, and the Nixdorf 8815 word processor.

All of these systems and products eventually evolved into other products and were marketed into the 1980s.

The Nixdorf 8820 terminal system (from 1975 to 1984) was a programmable system for data collection and a management system for the terminals connected in a cluster. These systems used floppy disks as a read/write media. These devices found an excellent use in shipping departments for inventory control.

The Nixdorf 820 and 840 computer systems finally ended up evolving into the Nixdorf 8830/35 (sold from 1974 to 1982). These latter systems were more compact in design because more compact chips were used as memory and for other uses inside the overall cabinet holding the electronics.

The Nixdorf 8840 word processor system (from 1979 to 1990) was developed and marketed for processing documents — and it had few other uses. (Imagine buying a computer that only ran Microsoft Word.) The Nixdorf 8840 had an electronic writing pen in addition to a keyboard. Data was saved on a magnetic disk on a central computer to which each Nixdorf 8840 was connected. Each Nixdorf 8840 could have a printer attached, and up to ten copies of a document could be printed.[89]

Nixdorf 8862 and Nixdorf 8864 terminals came out in 1976 and 1975, respectively. Primarily, these were terminals designed for a specific use; the 8862 was designed for order queries, and the 8864 was used with banks for account processing. Following on this success of specialized terminals, Nixdorf eventually developed more products such as the 8870/G and 8870/Uh for general accounting, payroll process, and data collection and processing. Both of these devices could serve as a single workstation, or could manage up to twenty workstations.

---

[89]But what if you wanted more copies, you may ask? It is hard to fathom a limitation like this today, but at the time, some engineer in some department thought that this would be a good number to use.

In 1977, the 8870 system came out, and this allowed custom programming for specific tasks (instead of buying a separate product for different tasks). The Nixdorf 8870 used a Nixdorf product called COMET for this custom programming. Nixdorf's hope was that since companies would be developing custom coding for their machines, the customers would be less prone to leave the folds of Nixdorf—and based on the increase in sales for the 8870, that strategy worked for a while.

Nixdorf was surviving quite well mainly because it adapted the 88xx Motorol microprocessor chip and by using AT&T's UNIX operating system, which was becoming more commonly known in the computer world. Additionally, Nixdorf had been expanding into specialized data-entry terminals and software made for banks. In 1978, Nixdorf had 10,000 employees, and was approaching 1 billion DM in sales. More on the founder, Heinz Nixdorf; he believed that camaraderie was important throughout his company, and to reinforce this belief, he established a networking model for all employees. His goal for this networking was to transfer knowledge between employees, and in so doing, achieve a long-term value for the company. Things were going well for Nixdorf—so well, in fact, that in 1978, Volkswagen AG offered to buy the company. Nixdorf refused the offer. Sales eventually rose to 4 billion DM, with over 23,000 employees. On March 17, 1986, Heinz died of a heart attack while at a computer fair in Hanover and died.

Klaus Nixdorf succeeded his father in running the company. Eventually, Nixdorf was acquired and folded into other larger companies. Today, the Nixdorf 820 is no longer manufactured, sold, or supported, but the roots of Nixdorf's involvement in the banking industry (especially throughout Europe) changed how banks saw automation. Nixdorf was extremely prolific in its ideas and products — and Heinz Nixdorf would have been proud of his networking personnel model. Primarily, Nixdorf was (and is today) known as a computer, POS, ATM, and telephone company.

North Star Computers, Inc.

In October 1977, this Berkley, California, company (later simply known as NorthStar) produced a series of PC parts, and then later its own line of PC products. One of its early successes was a low-cost floppy-drive system that could adapt easily to the then standard S-100 bus that most PCs were using. Its other early product was a custom circuit board that could do floating-point calculations for the 8080A microprocessor (and later provided support for the Z80A).

Business schools around the world should take note of what happened to this company. NorthStar was making a reliable one-sided floppy drive and software to read/write to it—but some brilliant person in the computer world thought, "Why not write on both sides of the floppy drive?" Indeed, it was a fine idea, and NorthStar jumped on this idea as it didn't want to be left out. Unfortunately, when it made the pre-announcement that it was also going into the dual-sided floppy business, its inventory for one-sided floppy drives built up since its customers wanted the newer floppy drives. Business majors can figure out what happened next; this "pre" announcing had a devastating effect on sales. Eventually (and slowly) sales recovered, but it took a long time.

Its first PC product was the NorthStar Horizon. It could be purchased as a kit or assembled, and it used the Z80A microprocessor. It had 16K RAM, two 5¼-inch floppy drives (the company's own, of course), ran either the CP/M or NSDOS operating system, came with its own NorthStar Basic compiler, and found a marketing niche for sales to universities. This system sold for $1,599 assembled.

Figure 110—NorthStar Horizon

In 1983, the company introduced the NorthStar Advantage system, which could run the MS-DOS operating system, and a server version running either DOS or Novell NetWare for its operating system. It used the Z80A microprocessor and ran at 4 MHz. The NorthStar Dimension server system followed, but market share and sales were dwindling. In 1984, the company closed shop.

Ohio Scientific

By the time 1978 rolled around, Apple had changed (and challenged) the world in thinking about inexpensive, higher-resolution graphic displays. Ohio Scientific, located in Aurora, Ohio, saw the desire for graphic displays and developed the C2-4P terminal. It sold this as a portable system, but it wasn't the definition of a laptop as we know them today. Rather, all it meant was that it could be moved fairly easily from room to room. It was approximately 18 in. wide, about 12 in. deep, and stood about 18 in. high.

Figure 111—Ohio Scientific C2-4P

The C2-4P came with 8K of ROM for the operating system, and another 4K of RAM for programs, which could be developed with the BASIC language that was included. It had a standard keyboard, a color monitor, and an external cassette drive for recording and playing back data. (The company's ad stressed that the keyboard supported both uppercase <u>and</u> lowercase.)

The display could only display 32 rows by 64 columns wide, and had an overall resolution of 256 x 512. Following similar programming techniques like Four-Phase had done, the system provided mapping to/from the display directly to memory. The system had a bus architecture that had four slots for cards; two were reserved for the processor and memory cards, and two were open for expansion (e.g., a sound card).

Oki Electric Industry

This company has its roots in 1881 as the first telephone maker in Japan. (Telecommunications is still key to its success today—135 years later.) The founder, Kibataro Oki, reverse-engineered Alexander Graham Bell's telephone and came up with a prototype that worked — and from this he started manufacturing his new product.

Jumping ahead eight decades, in the 1960s this company responded to the growing business desires for computing by developing an early general-purpose computer called the OKITAC-5090. Oki found its niche by developing color and monochrome printers, dot-matrix printers, and FAX machines. In 1972, Oki founded Oki Data Americas, Inc., in Mount Laurel, New Jersey, and this spurred on tremendous growth for both the parent and its subsidiary. Another thing that set Oki Electric printers apart (especially in Japan) is that they could print "English" alphanumeric, Kana (Japanese characters), and Kanji (Chinese characters).

Figure 112—Oki Electric Electro 800-lines-per-minute printer (with permission from Information Processing Society of Japan)

While many (especially in the U.S.) remember this company as a printer company (just as Xerox is lumped in with copiers), Oki also made the following minicomputers:

- 1969 – OKITAC 4300
- 1971 – OKITAC 4300E/S
- 1972 – OKITAC 4300C
- 1974 – OKITAC 4300B
- 1980 – OKITAC 4300A

These systems never achieved much of a market share, mainly because they were limited in memory addressing and used a non-commercial (proprietary) microprocessor.

Today, this Tokyo, Japan, company is a multi-national corporation, making ATMs, telephone systems, and other electronics.

Olivetti

Before I describe this remarkable company, I would like to set the stage and give a nod (actually a bow) to the amazing detailed engineering that Italian scientists accomplished in the early 17th century. From telescopes, barometric and hydrometer measuring machines, to simple weighing machines, Italy was going through a technology spurt. Here are two examples of early Italian macchina calcolatrices (calculating machines).

Figure 113 – Pre-1650 and 1664 Italian calculators

With this rich country history of inventiveness as a background, in 1908, in the small town of Ivrea in the Piedmont area, nestled next to Switzerland in northern Italy, Camillo Olivetti bought a building that would be the basis of a worldwide corporation for over a hundred years. Camillo was an electrical engineer by trade (which was rare, because electricity was in its infancy) and had an idea—to not only build typewriters, but to build them with proud Italian workmanship. Three years later, the

M1 typewriter was presented in an exhibition in Turin, Italy.

WWI slowed down production (as wars always seem to do, unless one is producing guns). Most of his employees were drawn into fighting either for or against someone, as Italy (and especially northern Italy) could easily choose alliances with Austria/Hungary, Turkey, France, England, Germany, Serbia, Croatia, Russia, or any other country of its choice. In other words, shooting bullets took precedence over making typewriters. It was not an easy time to be an Italian man in his twenties. Still, the Great War finally ended, and Olivetti had survived. In 1920, sales of the M1 were enough to employ 200 workers. In 1925, he dispatched his son Adriano, to the U.S. to learn more about production line efficiencies — and this was to pay off handsomely as demand for more Olivetti products increased.

Similar to a few other paternalistic owners, Olivetti treated his employees with great care (after all, many of these employees had been loyal to him during a lot of conflict within their country.) For instance, he offered his workers health insurance, kindergarten care, maternity care, and education assistance. This care for his employees would serve the company well in years to come. Another way that Olivetti rewarded loyalty (this time to the general area in which the company was located), was that he insisted that local workers be hired before outsiders were considered.

During the 1930s, unrest was coming back to Europe along with unemployment and inflation, which was rising to incredible heights. Tack onto this anti-Jewish sentiment being shown in Germany by Hitler and his Nazi organization, and it was about to be another hard time for Camillo Olivetti (who had Jewish roots) to figure out how to save his company. By luck or fate, this is where being in the Piedmont area came into being helpful. In 1938, at the age of 70, Camillo turned the company over to Adriano. By 1940, Olivetti employed approximately 800 workers.

Germany had invaded Austria, and it was only a matter of time before Italy was drawn into yet another war.

While Hitler's orders to Benito Mussolini (installed by Hitler to rule over Italy) were explicit about instituting anti-Jewish programs, Mussolini was too busy with other matters to give that area much attention. As the war waged on in Rome and other strategic Italian battle fronts, little Ivrea (as it turned out) was fairly much ignored. Olivetti's company survived, and in the 1950s, Olivetti had enough revenue to own offices in twenty-one countries, with sales of over 65 percent outside of Italy. Its products were then typewriters, calculators, and adding machines.

In 1959, Adriano was leading the company, and had his workers developing something new for Olivetti: the Olivetti Elea 9003 computer. Developing computers and risking your company's funds (and heading a large corporation in general) is a risky endeavor, and whether this or some other stress caused Adriano's deadly stroke in 1960, no one will know for certain. Another bad event struck Olivetti quickly when its new president, Giuseppe Pero, died soon after taking over the reins. If there was a time in Olivetti's history where it was teetering on the brink of survival, it was then. By 1964, the company was in financial turmoil, so jobs were cut along with wages for those left working. Things were not looking promising for the company.

Finally, Olivetti got management in place once again and one of the new president's first acts was to separate the company into two divisions: 1) non-computers (typewriters, calculators, etc.), and 2) computers. One of Olivetti's innovation, the Computer Programma 101 (also known as the Perottina or P101), was very well designed and selected by NASA to assist in its calculations for moon landings. It didn't look like a computer as most would envision one, but it contained most of the components of a computer. (However, it didn't have a microprocessor; instead, transistors and other electrical components were creatively mounted on its own custom "processor" board). It could be programmed, and the programs were stored on small, odd-looking plastic cards.

Figure 114—Computer Programma 101

Sales grew, and revenue increased fivefold. In 1970, the computer division accounted for 20 percent of total Olivetti revenue; by 1977, it amounted to 43 percent of revenue. Additionally, in the 1970s Olivetti was producing bank teller terminals, emulating IBM's remote job-entry software, and other more intelligent CRT displays.

As for computer products per se, Olivetti understood the need for computers to run a company, but saw two major obstacles for developing its own centralized, larger computer: 1) entrenched competition from IBM, and 2) a large R&D investment. What Olivetti settled for was a niche market of specialized and high-speed calculation machines, ATMs, and banking terminals. The 1970s were passing the company by when it finally invested in the hot PC market. Under product names such as the Thomson MO6 and Acorn BBC Master Compact, Olivetti was not only making a PC, but also a "portable" PC (if weighing more than twenty pounds qualifies for a portable, that is).

In 1986, Olivetti took over the office machinery and computer manufacturer Triumph-Adler (then owned by the Volkswagen Group). The reason Olivetti gave at the time for buying this money-losing company was that it wanted the distribution network Triumph-Adler had established.

During the 1980s, Olivetti was the second-largest PC supplier in Europe after IBM and the second-largest computer manufacturer in the world, with 71 percent of Olivetti's revenues now attributed to the computer line of business. Then, competition hit with a resounding thud, and Olivetti had to cut cost. The company began buying more and more components from Japan and Korea to cut costs.

Not to pick on the Koreans and the Japanese, but companies in these countries were looking for a fast way to compete in the world market; what better way to do this but figuring out what (and how) your competition was making—and then making it cheaper? Not too long after the outsourcing of parts was started to Asian countries, cheaper knock-offs (some even with the Olivetti name imprinted on them, but not an Olivetti product) were being sold for less than $200. Olivetti had learned an important lesson about counterfeiting and piracy, and it eventually cost the company its computer business.

In 1995, Olivetti stopped all in-house computer work and, in 1997, stopped all support and sales of its computer products. The 1990s and early 2000s saw Olivetti taking over other companies and having parts of them spun off. Olivetti was making telephone systems, ATM systems, and other banking terminals. In 2003, after four years of wrangling, Olivetti succeeded in taking over the telephony giant Telecom Italia (located 250 kilometers south, in Rome). In an odd twist of name changes, Olivetti became a subsidiary of Telecom Italia. In March 2010, Olivetti re-entered the computer market by announcing the Olivetti Olitab tablet.

It would be an injustice to Olivetti to let it be thought of as just another company with ho-hum products (including even office furniture). Olivetti not only wanted to produce quality and competitive products, but also wanted to add some pizzazz to the boring look of typewriters and its computers. Designers from the Ulm School of Design, along with talented Italian designers, had given Olivetti what it wanted. In 1983, the magazine *Der Spiegel* wrote, "Olivetti products were the most elegant products of the machine age." Behold the following example of a beautiful, pre-computer age "word processor" by Olivetti.

Figure 115—Olivetti typewriter (Valentine model)

Olson

If the phrase "bad timing" could be applied to any company, it was Olson. In 1978, kit computers were on a downward spiral, as nicely packaged microcomputers were coming on the market at a fairly reasonable price. Olson, though, thought there was still a market left for hobbyists, and thus came out with the Olson 8. The model MP-200 ($499) was a "build-it-yourself" system, and the model MP-210 ($750) was fully assembled. It had 1K of PROM memory, and programming could be done by toggling switches on the front panel and watching the lights blink.

It had no keyboard, no monitor, and lacked peripherals (but one could buy those separately, of course, from other companies). Other than that, it was the perfect home computer. Olson was located in Akron, Ohio.

Omnitec

Owned by Nytronics Corporation, in 1970, Omnitec was on the tail end of the Teletype[90] era. Omnitec thought there was still a market to compete against Teletype machines — little did it know that few people wanted those machines, as new technology was about to make them obsolete.

Omnitec produced two products. The first was an acoustic coupler (where an old-style telephone speaker/receiver could be positioned) that attached to an actual Teletype machine. It sold for $345. This allowed the Teletype to be more portable and to dial in to a host system from remote locations. The Teletype machine weighed close to thirty pounds, so it wasn't exactly a "portable" terminal, as we think of them today.

Figure 116—Omnitec portable

Omnitec's other product was an actual replacement for the Teletype. Weighing in at a mere twenty-five pounds, it sold for $1,500 and included a 63-key keyboard, rolled-paper printer, and a built-in acoustic coupler for dialing in to a host system. The machine itself looked interestingly

---

[90] Teletype created a very noisy, slow, keyboard data entry, and had a rolled printer-paper terminal. For all its shortcomings though, it was reliable and a true workhorse for many computer makers. Mostly, it served as an operator's console, although it could be used for regular data entry if an operator had the patience.

like an IBM Selectric typewriter only with slightly different packaging.

Perkin-Elmer

Perkin-Elmer was founded in 1937 by Richard Perkin and Charles Elmer as an optical design and consulting company. In 1944, Perkin-Elmer entered the analytical instruments business.

At this point I need to introduce a company (central to Perkin-Elmer's history) called EG&G (which began life in 1934 in a Boston garage). EG&G was named after MIT professor Harold Edgerton (a pioneer of high-speed photography), his graduate student Kenneth Germeshausen, and another MIT graduate student, Herbert Grier. This group of people developed high-speed photography that was used to image implosion tests during the Manhattan Project. After WWII, the group continued its association with the burgeoning military nuclear effort, and formally incorporated Edgerton, Germeshausen, and Grier, Inc. in 1947.

During the 1950s and 1960s, EG&G was involved as a nuclear testing contractor for the Atomic Energy Commission. Subsequently. EG&G expanded its range of services, providing facilities management, technical services, security, and pilot training for the U.S. military and other government departments. EG&G was purchased by Perkin-Elmer in the mid-1960s.

Time to introduce yet another player in the Perkin-Elmer history — Interdata, Inc.. This computer company was founded in 1966, and based in Oceanport, New Jersey. It eventually produced minicomputers based upon both 16-bit and 32-bit processors. With forgettable names that sound more like wrench sizes than a computer name, the Model 7/32 and Model 8/32 were born. The 8/32 was a more powerful machine than the 7/32, with the interesting feature of allowing user-programmable microcode (to allow the alteration of the operating system if someone was so bold). In 1973, Interdata was purchased by Perkin-Elmer, with Perkin-Elmer continuing to market the Interdata minicomputers using the Interdata name. (Interdata originally operated as a wholly owned subsidiary of Perkin-Elmer, with Interdata retaining its management.)

The 7/32 and 8/32 became the computers of choice for companies wanting fast computers to process real-time[91] information (e.g., CAT scanners, flight simulators, seismic analysis, etc.). The computers behind the first Space Shuttle simulator consisted of thirty-six Perkin-Elmer 32-bit minicomputers.

The operating system for the 7/32 and 8/32 was Interdata's internally developed and marketed OS/32. In 1977, the UNIX operating system was ported to the 8/32 at Bell Labs, making the 32-bit Interdata machine the first non-DEC computers to run UNIX.

In 1976, Perkin-Elmer decided to make Interdata a division within the bigger company, and gave this new division the name of Computer Systems Division (CSD). In 1985, CSD was sold to Concurrent Computer Corporation, and both Perkin-Elmer/Interdata minicomputers were no more.

In 1979, Perkin-Elmer sold a product called the IR Data Station. This product was specifically designed for analyzing chemicals in an infrared spectrum. While obviously having a limited audience, it was sold to universities and the U.S. government. Also in 1979, the Perkin-Elmer 3220 (32-bit processor) system was

---

[91] Most people think of real-time as meaning "now," as when you type in an internet address, the web page gets returned quickly. But, real-time to computers means that when something is detected, drop everything else you were doing and act on this event NOW! If a nuclear reactor develops a leak, a computer somewhere had better be monitoring this and take immediate action. Real-time processing is also known in some circles as Supervisory Control and Data Acquisition (or SCADA).

announced. It came with FORTRAN VII and was aimed at more of a scientific (simulations) user base than anything else.

It was a typical minicomputer in many aspects, though, as it had a central processing unit that could connect up to thirty-two users, and up to 255 different programs could be executed simultaneously in the operating system.

Figure 117—Perkin-Elmer 3220

In the late 1980s and early 1990s, most of the EG&G divisions were sold off to other interested parties. In an odd twist of events, in May 1999, EG&G purchased the Analytical Instruments Division of Perkin-Elmer for $425 million, also assuming the Perkin-Elmer name. At this time, EG&G was based in Wellesley, Massachusetts.

Perkin-Elmer, Inc. today is a U.S-based multinational corporation focused on the business areas of human and environmental health. Additionally, Perkin-Elmer produces analytical instruments, genetic testing, diagnostic tools, medical imaging components, software, and other products.

Pertec Computer Corporation

Pertec Computer Corporation started life in 1972 from the acquisition and evolution of the Peripheral Equipment Corporation (PEC). PEC, located in Chatsworth, California, designed and manufactured peripherals such as floppy drives, tape drives, and other hardware components for computers. After the acquisition, Pertec and its disk drives and tape drives sold well — especially to big companies such as IBM, Siemens, and DEC.

Pertec manufactured multiple models of 7- and 9-track half-inch magnetic tape drives. These products had densities of 800 and 1600 characters per inch (CPI).

By the mid-1970s, Pertec was antsy to get in on the computer revolution it saw going on all around it — especially a few hundred miles north in the Palo Alto area. At the same time, it didn't want to disrupt its cash cow with its peripheral business. The company's answer to this was to split into two companies: Pertec Peripherals Corporation (PPC) (which remained based in Chatsworth, California), and Pertec Computer Corporation (PCC), which was located in Irvine, California.

PPC was to be focused on computers, and what better and quick way to tackle this market than by buying a computer company? In 1976, PPC bought out MITS for $6.5M. MITS owned the small and limited marketable Altair computer, but it also owned the BASIC language compiler. Or so PPC thought. In reality, MITS didn't own BASIC, but was simply licensing it. So, selling computers (even with Altair enhancements done by PPC's engineers) at $400 a pop would take a long time to recoup its investment into MITS, especially when other companies, such as Apple, Commodore, and Radio Shack, were now gearing up with faster and slicker packaged systems. In the world of marketing, timing is everything — and PPC's was horrendous.

In 1978, Pertec (through its PPC division) came out with the PCC-2000, which was a true computer of Pertec's own design. This computer was based on two Intel 8085 series microprocessors: one controlled the processing of applications, and the other was dedicated to I/O control. In reality, the marketing of this machine left something to be desired, as prospective customers weren't sure of its purpose. Being a fairly robust computer performance-wise, it was intended by some within PPC to be sold as a minicomputer, as it could have up to four less intelligent computers attached to it.

Figure 118—Pertec PPC-2000

The applications would run on the "host" PPC-2000, and the dumber workstations would share the host machine's processing abilities. The host computer had four RS-232 ports on it in addition to an internal console for management duties. Additionally, the host had two 8-inch floppy drives, each capable of storing 1.2 megabytes, and could connect to two Pertec twin 14-inch disk drives (don't forget, Pertec was first and foremost up until this time a maker of computer peripheral devices). Storage of a total of 22.4MB was possible. The host machine had a choice of operating systems: MTX, MITS DOS, CP/M, and BOS (which was sold only in the UK for some reason). The bottom line was that the PCC-2000 turned out to be a really expensive PC, or a small clustered computer with limited scaling and functionality — depending upon how one wanted to define it. Its sales were dismal compared to what Pertec needed for revenue.

Not giving up, Pertec decided to make the computer bigger with the hopes of attracting a larger customer base (although that marketing approach never worked for them). The PCC-2100 data entry system came out next. This computer could support up to sixteen coaxial-connected terminals, had two D3000 disk drives, and one T1640 tape drive. This computer competed directly with the IBM 3270 clustered units, which allowed data entry by users (usually within a small physical area, such as a department within a company). Data was keyed in, and then the data was sent to the host IBM for processing. The PCC-2100 had more success than the PCC-2000, although its sales alone could not sustain this division.

In 1978, the Pertec XL-40 was introduced. This computer system had its own 16-bit processors built using the Texas Instruments 3000 or AMD2900 as the core components. It had up to 512K RAM and I/O controllers with direct memory access for tape units, floppy and rigid disk units, printers, a card reader, and terminals that could be connected to it. It was a much better-performing model than the PCC-2100, and it was more scalable in components (and user workstations).

The Pertec XL-40 came in two configurations. One featured four T1600/T1800 Pertec tape units, two floppy disk units (Pertec's models could be used, but for some strange reason, Pertec was also making IBM's drives), and four disk drives (they could be Pertec or Kennedy, another manufacturer). The other configuration offered larger disks (both manufactured by other companies, in this case Kennedy or NEC), five printers, a card reader, four SDLC communication channels, and thirty proprietary coaxial terminals (Model 4141 with 40x12 characters or Model 4143 with 80x25 characters). As with the PCC-2100, this computer was marketed to replace the more expensive IBM clustered data-entry computers. It ran its own custom and proprietary operating system, called XLOS; this

347

operating system was a little ahead of its time in that it embedded database work for online transaction processing in its code. (The downside of this was the company had unwittingly constrained its operating system for scalability.) The XL-40 also was marketed in Europe by Triumph-Adler under either the TA1540 or Alphatronic P40 name.

In the early '80s, Pertec's computer market share was not gaining ground. More models followed, but finally Pertec sold off its computer division to its European partner, Triumph-Adler. Pertec sold off the remaining parts of its struggling business, and in the mid-1980s, had little left to sell; it was literally a shell of the former company, and quietly closed its doors. One of the legacies it left was its magnetic tape interface, which was adopted as the standard for many companies that needed to connect external tape storage with their computer systems.

Philips

Koninklijke Philips N.V. (Royal Philips, commonly known simply as Philips) is a diversified technology company headquartered in Amsterdam, The Netherlands. Philips was originally founded in 1891 by Gerard Philips and his father Frederik Philips. It made carbon-filament lamps and anything else it could produce that was a tie-in with the new-fangled invention called electricity. Today, Philips is one of the largest electronics companies in the world and employs around 122,000 people across more than sixty countries.

Philips was always inventing and improving on ideas it saw going on in America. Vacuum tubes, electric razors, better light bulbs, radios, and other ideas kept it competitive and with a strong balance sheet.

Multiple chapters (perhaps even a complete book) could be written on what Philips wanted to do to expand its radio business — and I briefly touch upon it here just to show Philips' creativity and ingenuity. Philips wanted to sell its radios to remote areas, but providing electricity to some of those areas was lagging by governments. What to do? It would be nice to generate electricity, but building power plants were expensive—something that Philips certainly didn't want to undertake.

Stepping back for a moment into the early 1800s (1816 to be precise), a Scottish man named Robert Stirling invented what he called the "hot air" engine. (A friend convinced him that the name Stirling Engine sounded better, thus the name was unofficially changed; today such an engine is called by either name.) Basically, a Stirling engine generates power from a heat source (e.g., wood or coal), and via a closed system of gases it alternates from hot to cold compressions it generates a pulley or some external drive mechanism. It doesn't put out a lot of power, but it is truly a simplistic system that actually does what it is supposed to do.

Jumping back to the early 1930s, with a few modifications Philips found that he could get the Sterling engine to generate up to 200W of electricity! Coupling this power with the engine's extremely quiet running, it was suited perfectly for what Philips wanted to do—namely power radios (that Philips would sell, of course). Therefore, in the 1940s there was a revival of the Stirling engine, as Philips not only installed Stirling engines, but also sold radios that consumed that power. It was a brilliant idea. Philips' work on improvements to the Sterling engine ran through the 1970s.

WWII came and went, and through significant slight-of-hand maneuvers to keep out of harm's way, Philips stayed in business. Jumping ahead two decades (which saw continued growth of Philips), the company introduced the very successful compact audio cassette tape in 1963. (It was at first marketed as a dictation machine, but later was adapted to play music.)

The 1970s brought about more innovation and marketing of the cassette, video tape recording, and LaserDisc players. Philips was an electronics firm at heart, but still understood the power of the computer chips coming into the market—it just wasn't sure what to do with them. Instead of jumping into the market and developing a business computer system (and misreading the personal computer market entirely), Philips chose to use the computer chip for something less than a computer. Ergo, the G7000 (aka Philips Videopac G7000) was born. This product was a video game console and came out in 1978. The G7000 was only marketed in Europe under this name; in the U.S. it was sold as the Magnavox Odyssey or Philips Odyssey, and in Brazil as a Philips Odyssey.

The G7000 had an Intel 8048H processor with a clock speed of 1.79 MHz. The processor had 64K of RAM, but only half was allowed for game loading, as the other half was used for the operating system itself. As an option, a 6810 RAM chip with 128K could have been purchased, thereby increasing a game's speed and supplying more options (e.g., better graphics). Integrated in the processor was 1K of ROM. It also produced a video resolution of 256 x 192 pixels with eight possible colors, and had a monophonic sound channel.

Figure 119—Philips G7000

350

A special feature of the device was the built-in keypad. The two joysticks looked like an analog controller, but it was an ordinary digital 8-Wege Steuerknüppel (8-way joystick) with a fire button, such as the Atari 2600. The G7000 had a built-in power supply, as well as consoles with an external power supply unit. The G7000 console had a power switch, except in the French version, which for some odd reason did not have one.

The next version to come out was the Philips G7200; this product included all of the features of the G7000 except it had a black-and-white monitor in the same housing. The games were stored on a plug-in module called a Videopac.

Many competitive products, such as the Atari 2600, were coming on the market, and Philips came out with yet more improvements to its products (e.g., the Philips G7400, marketed in 1983) to try and keep market share. Slowly, though, Philips had decided to return to its core competency of consumer electronics. In the mid-1980s, Philips stopped production of the video game consoles. What it missed (and the world failed to realize) was that its consoles had everything a PC had — except it could not be programmed. Instead, Philips relied on the pre-programming of the video games to drive its sales, never realizing that if it allowed its customers to write their own games (or business applications) that its market could have conceivably grown into the home computer market.

In 1991, the company's name was changed from N.V. Philips Gloeilampenfabrieken to Philips Electronics N.V in Europe. At the same time, North American Philips was formally dissolved, and a new corporate division was formed in the U.S. with the name Philips Electronics North America Corp. From that time until today, various spin-offs, acquisitions, and name changes have taken place for Philips. Today, Philips is involved with medical devices and many facets of consumer electronics, and is a thriving company thanks to innovation that started over a century ago.

Polymorphic Systems

This Santa Barbara, California, company was founded in 1976, and developed and first marketed a custom CPU board for people wanting to build their own computer around that. In 1977, it was making its own computer system called the System 8813.

The System 8813 had a keyboard (no numeric keypad); a small, square CRT display (measuring approximately 6 inches on each side); and the CPU itself, which resided in a separate cabinet that also could hold up to three large floppy-disk drives (each capable of holding 90K bytes). It used the Motorola 8080 microprocessor, and could be expanded from 8K to 56K RAM. It could display graphics in addition to characters (16 lines by 64 characters across), and the company's marketing aimed it at scientists, educators, lawyers, accountants, medical professionals, and business managers. It had its own proprietary disk operating system called EXEC, a text editor, and BASIC compiler. The base price $3,250.

PRIME Computer, Inc.

PRIME Computer, Inc. (also known as PRIME, or PRIME Computer) was based in Natick, Massachusetts, and produced a series of minicomputers over its lifetime (from 1972 to 1992). The company was started by seven founders, some of whom worked at MIT on the Multiplexed Information and Computing Service[92] (Multics) project. Although Multics was, by every

---

[92] Multics was designed in 1965 to be a timesharing computer system (literally giving any user a slice of time to run his or her application or test); it was tried and tested within MIT, and became the way that all students and faculty connected to a computer network. Its design incorporated security and other features that made it viable to other industries outside of academia.

definition, a mainframe operating system (large, centrally located, with many users connecting to it via proprietary software), these PRIME founders were interested in what the new microprocessors could do for small businesses. Another way to put it — it wanted to avoid trying to compete head-on with IBM.

In 1972, PRIME produced the PRIME 200, and one of the initial systems of this product line was installed at Kean University. In many aspects, this machine was basically a clone of the Honeywell 316 minicomputer. PRIME's first "non-cloned" computer was the PRIME 100. (I'm not sure why the first one was the 200 and not the 100, but I'm sure the PRIME marketing department knew what it was doing).

The next PRIME system, also similar to the Honeywell's 516 (cloning worked once, why not again?), offered a 32-bit operating system instruction instead of the 516's 16-bit. PRIME developed its own operating system and called it DOS[93] also referred to as PRIMOS 2,[94] and not to be confused with MS-DOS or PC DOS). The PRIME 100 differed from the PRIME 200 in that the former had no memory parity checking,[95] nor did it offer floating-point calculations. It only offered FORTRAN, BASIC, and assembler compilers.

In 1974, PRIME came out with the PRIME 300. It offered 6MB (!) of disk storage and 32K to 512K of RAM. The operating system was being refined, and now was named DOSVM (also referred to as PRIMOS 3). This operating

---

[93] PRIME DOS should not be confused with Microsoft's DOS (MS-DOS), which is totally different. To be legally correct, there was PRIME's DOS, and then there was MS-DOS.

[94] PRIMOS was originally written mostly in the Fortran IV programming language with some Assembler sub-routines. Subsequently, the PL/P and Modula-2 languages were used in the operating system language. A number of new PRIMOS utilities were written in SP/L, which was similar to PL/P.

[95] A word about parity checking—when bits travel from point A to point B, sometimes things could happen to, well, make the bits appear in a different order (or just lose a bit here and there). This is not good in the world of computers, so "parity" checking is a way to ensure that data is verified from point of transfer to the point of receiving.

system was one of the first minicomputers to offer virtual memory capability. Offering floating point calculations for multiple users, it was well accepted within mathematics departments at universities. This machine could support up to thirty-one users, and sold for about $165,000.

The PRIME 400 was introduced in 1976; this machine had an execution rate of 0.5 MIPS. It had 8MB of RAM and 160MB of disc storage, and ran the PRIMOS 4 operating system (the PRIMOS name was now specifically used for the operating system).

The PRIME 450, 550, 650, and 750 were the next products to be sold. The PRIME 550 had an increase in performance by running at 0.7 MIPS, had up to 2MB of RAM, could have 500MB of disc storage, and a 9-track tape unit.

The PRIME 750 was considered a major upgrade for both PRIME and its customers. This product had a 1.0 MIPS processor, 2x8MB of RAM, 1,200MB disk storage, and a 9-track tape unit. This was very performance- and price-competitive in the market, and was dubbed a "super" minicomputer because of its speed (it offered 32-bit instructions.) It was a favorite at universities, as witnessed by its installation at Rensselaer Polytechnic Institute (RPI), Rutherford Appleton Laboratory (RAL), University of Paisley, Leeds University, Scripps Institution of Oceanography (SIO), University of Rhode Island, University of Manchester Institute of Science and Technology (UMIST), and the CADCentre in Cambridge.

During the 1980s, PRIME continued to offer faster processors, along with its own proprietary version of an "intranet" (allowing PRIME computers to share information with each other), larger disks, its own processor chip (called the EXL-316), and a modified version of an operating system called UNIX (which was being adopted as a standard throughout the computer industry). The company was successful in terms of revenue and profit in the 1970s and 1980s, peaking in 1988 at number 334 of the Fortune 500. In 1985, the company was the sixth largest in the minicomputer sector, with estimated revenues of $564 million, PRIME's attraction grew outside of the universities, with banks using the PRIME Info database product.

PRIME was heavily involved with Ford's internal computer-aided design (CAD) product—the Product Design Graphics System (PDGS). Ford's design engineers used PDGS for auto body design. In the 1980s, PRIME had the world's largest integrated CAD system, spanning the U.S., Japan (Mazda was Ford's subsidiary/partner), (Cologne) Germany, (Dunton) England, and (Geelong) Australia. What this meant was that designers in all of these locations could work together on a common design fairly easily (assuming they all used similar PRIME systems).

It is not an understatement that in the 1980s bad management decisions caused PRIME to lose its focus. PRIME ended up betting the company's future that it could lead the world in CAD systems. As the old adage goes and can be witnessed by other companies' successes and failures throughout this book, "timing is everything." PRIME neglected to see the wave of high-powered PCs coming—and companies no longer had to be connected to one central system that was expensive like PRIME's. By concentrating on the CAD business (which it would eventually lose), it could not keep its banking customers, who now moved to computers that were designed with more transaction processing. PRIME also was now plagued by its earlier decision to develop its own processor. Intel was producing a faster chip that many in the industry had embraced as their standard, and PRIME could not/would not spend more money to make its own processor faster to keep up with Intel. (Digital Computers was also learning this painful lesson around the same time.) To show how bad this was, not a single PRIME computer was subject to U.S. export controls because its processors were deemed too slow for the U.S. government to care if they fell into the hands of hostile powers.

In the late 1980s, PRIME was learning that customers liked applications that did real business work. It was one thing to offer a fast computer, but if few applications ran on it, then why would businesses buy it? PRIME acquired the marketing rights to an application called OAS from ACS America Inc. It was one of the pioneer systems that used electronic mail, and it had a global email directory of names. The bad news was that it only ran on PRIME products—and businesses did not want to invest in its technology just to do email. Another questionable decision by PRIME was to develop its own word-processing product. As before, its timing was horrendous, as this development cost the company a lot of money, and when done, no one wanted to buy it because of better, less expensive solutions already in the market.

The computer design and manufacturing portions of the company were eventually shut down and the company was renamed Computervision. In 1992, Computervision sold PRIME Information to Vmark Corporation. In 1998, it was bought by Parametric Technology Corporation. The remainder of the company became a support organization for existing customers.

Processor Technology Corporation

In April 1975, Gary Ingram and Bob Marsh launched this company in Berkley, California. Seeing a lack in quality with the MITS' 4K RAM boards, these guys figured they could make a better one—and sell it to MITS customer base (which was growing rapidly). Two key people were bought on-board: Lee Felsenstein and Gordon French. Both of these gentlemen had their roots in the Homebrew Computer Club, and they were the right people to understand the power of the microprocessor.

More memory and I/O boards (including a video display module) were to come out later on—but for now, the magazine world was spurring on the popularity in kits and "intelligent" desktop computers. *Popular Electronics* was always looking for more articles to increase its sales, and this company, Processor Technology, was asked if it could put a computer together for the magazine. Marsh agreed, and the July 1976 issue of *Popular Electronics* highlighted the Sol-20 personal computer.

Figure 120—Sol-20

The first units were shipped in December 1976. A major difference between the Sol-20 and many other machines of the time period was Processor Technology's built-in 2 MHz video driver (which allowed it to be attached to a monitor, although it didn't ship with one). The Sol-20 had a main motherboard mounted at the bottom of the case, and five slots connecting to an S-100 bus. The motherboard consisted of the CPU, memory, video display driver, and I/O circuits. The case included a power supply, fan, and keyboard. Optionally, it sold software and a cassette tape player/recorder. The case was painted blue, and the sides of the case were solid, honest to goodness, oiled walnut!

This company was said to have made approximately 10,000 Sol-20 personal computers between 1977 and 1979, but those numbers might be highly inflated since marketing was not this company's strength. All of its products were available either fully assembled or as kits.

Gary Ingram and Steven Dompier wrote the original software utilities.

The Video Display Module 1 (VDM-1) was the original video display interface for S-100 bus systems. The board generated 16 lines with 64 characters in each, and allowed displaying in both upper and lower case. The VDM-1 used 1K of system memory, and mapped characters directly to it as they were typed or read from the memory and sent directly to the monitor; it also supported a feature we take for granted today, but scrolling in 1975 was a nice added feature.

The following products could be ordered from Processor Technology:

- S-100 bus with VDM-1 support
- 3P+S – Input/output Module 3 Parallel plus one serial board
- 4KRA – 4K static memory board
- 8KRA – 8K static memory board
- 16KRA – 16K DRAM memory board
- 32KRA-1 – 32K DRAM memory board
- CUTS – Tape I/O interface board, CUTS format and Kansas City standard format
- 2KRO – EPROM memory board
- Helios II disk memory system
- SOLOS operating system
- CUTER – Monitor program and cassette tape loader
- ASSM – 8080 Assembler
- BASIC/5 – 5K BASIC programming language
- Extended Cassette Basic (8K) – BASIC Interpreter
- ALS-8
- PTDOS – Operating system for use with the Helios II Disk Drive
- EDIT – 8080 editor

- 8080 Chess – chess game
- TREK-80 – Star Trek-themed game
- GamePack 1 – Collection of games - Volume 1
- GamePack 2 – Collection of games - Volume 2

As you can see from the list, this was a lot of products for which a small company had to provide support in regards to order processing and manufacturing. Also, as with many technologists trying to act as their own marketing department, the company started faltering on many fronts. In other words, it didn't keep an eye out for competition, costs, and revenues—small things that eventually build up and can easily put a company out of business. In May 1979, Processor Technology closed its doors.

Producers Service Corporation

Almost every minicomputer needed a way to back up its data—and if it didn't and if its disk storage data was lost somehow, how to recover it? The answer was to back up the data to magnetic tape. This Glendale, California, company produced a stand-alone tape system for minicomputer makers; this product could sit on a table and could accommodate 7-in., 8½-in., or 10½-in. magnetic reels. The system could read, read/write, and read after write. It offered a unique power failure feature where data would not be corrupted if power was lost during a write operation.

Their product was simply called the PSC Low Cost Tape Transport.

Quantum Science Corporation

This is one of only a few companies included in this book that did not produce software or hardware. Still, I believe it is important to include it as it shows how one company was attempting to make money from the chaos that was occurring in the computer industry in the early 1970s. Quantum Science Corporation offered written studies. With offices located in Palo Alto, California, (to be close to the heart of the action), and in New York City, New York, (for marketing), the company produced studies that explained the virtues of using a minicomputer for data entry/editing, printing, storage, and data communications. For a mere $450 (as one of its ads stated), it provided the results of a six-month study it had independently done on minicomputer users.

Office space in New York City and Palo Alto was expensive even then, and this would mean a lot of $450 reports would have to be sold to keep the lights on. Nothing can be found of the company being in business too long after 1971. If only it could have held together for another fifteen years, it could have been at the forefront of the "consulting" phase that eventually took hold in the computer industry.

Radio Corporation of America (RCA)

This company had a somewhat odd (yet very interesting) start in business after WWI. Basically, General Electric was urged (with some arm-twisting by the U.S. government) to buy the American Marconi Company. It did, and then formed RCA in 1919.

From the first days of business, RCA was focused on communication products—namely radios, then record players, TV studios, color TVs, and most anything that had to do with sound and video. Jumping forward about forty years, RCA had created a research and development lab located in Princeton, New Jersey. Out of this lab came many innovations and ideas, including one that would change computers by the creation of what was called complementary metal-oxide-semiconductor — or better known as CMOS.[96]

Computers were a logical next step for RCA, since it was related to communications (albeit with data instead of sound and video, at least at that time in history). Computers were seen as another line of business to RCA as providing more revenue. In the mid-1960s, RCA marketed the Spectra 70 Series (Models 15, 25, 35, 45, 46, 55, 60, and 61) to compete with the IBM 360. The Spectra 70 was compatible with IBM hardware (meaning that it could replace most IBM computer modules and peripherals), but its software was <u>not</u> compatible with IBM. What this meant was that most of the programs would not execute as previously written on IBM and, therefore, had to be modified a little (or perhaps a lot in some programming circumstances) to run properly on RCA systems. Why RCA chose this path of incompatibility is perplexing.

In the mid-1970s, its engineers were fully committed to competing in the full computer spectrum, and in 1976 it produced its own microprocessor called the RCA CDP1802. It was an 8-bit computer, and used a unique architecture different from Intel. RCA's engineers convinced their management that they could now design and market their own computer. The result was the COSMAC VIP. (COSMAC stood for Complementary Symmetry Monolithic Array Computer.)

To call the COSMAC VIP (also called the VP-111) a computer was a stretch (especially in the mid-1970s when PCs were starting to take form). As you can see in the picture, it is hard to envision this as a "personal computer," but indeed it was. It had a microprocessor (the RCA version), and could be programmed — albeit very slowly with the small keypad on the board.

---

[96] CMOS refers to a particular style of digital circuitry; in a nutshell, once the IC was invented, others (such as RCA) came along to make improvements to it.

Figure 121—COSMAC VIP

Still, RCA marketed this as a true computer and noted that as soon as it was assembled (!), it would be a joy to behold and play with (paraphrasing RCA's marketing literature). All one had to do was supply power to it (it had no power supply built on the board), figure out a way to connect it to your TV (which RCA hoped was one of its own, of course), and then sit back and watch as two numbers could be added together and displayed on the TV.

Other "personal" computer-related RCA products followed:

- VP-580 – expansion keyboard
- VP-550 – super sound board
- VP-565 – EPROM programmer board
- VP-711 – the VP-111 (but enclosed in a blue, plastic case)
- VP-700 – tiny BASIC ROM board
- VP-114 – on-board 4096-byte RAM expansion
- VP-560 – EPROM board
- VP-570 – 4K RAM expansion board
- VP-590 – color board
- VP-595 – simple sound board

Eventually larger (and more competitive mainframe-class computers came out of RCA, and their Series 2, 3, 6, and 7 of computers competed with the newer IBM System/370. All of the RCA computers ran RCA's real-memory operating systems called DOS and TDOS. The Spectra 70/46 and 70/61 and the RCA 3 and 7 also could run RCA's virtual memory operating system (VMOS, originally named TSOS, which meant Time Sharing Operating System).

While its mainframe class of computers was well designed, RCA could see that it was not making enough inroads into the computer market. A decision was made by RCA's management to return to its core (non-computer) products and to sell off its computer division and customer base to Sperry Rand.

While RCA had a minor success with its microprocessor (namely for NASA uses), the other RCA "computer" products were hardly a blip in the PC market, and after only a few years, they were no longer marketed. In 1986, GE took over RCA basically because RCA was ripe for the picking with financial difficulties. GE then continued to spin off RCA technologies to other companies around the world, and today RCA patents are scattered everywhere and are used in many audio and video technologies.

Raytheon

Its roots started as the American Appliance Company in 1922. In 1959, the Raytheon name was adopted, and the company found a home in Waltham, Massachusetts. In 1972, the company listed its home office as Santa Ana, California.

Raytheon found out early that in addition to the consumer products it was producing (such as washing machines and refrigerators), the federal government had a lot of money to spend on projects to support military and space endeavors. By concentrating on developing systems for the moon missions, Raytheon became strategic in the U.S.' race into space.

In the early 1970s, Raytheon announced the Raytheon 703 IC systems computer. This was a 16-bit minicomputer aimed for the industrial, engineering, and scientific control market. It could be expanded up to 32K RAM, had an instruction cycle of a little more than 900ns, direct I/O, four programmable registers, and an instruction set of 74. It could have a paper-tape reader/punch, line printer, magnetic disk, digital plotter, digital-to-analog converters (Raytheon's own MINIVERTER and MULTIVERTER products), and magnetic tape peripherals. It came with FORTAN IV and Assembler languages, a Teletype console, a direct I/O bus, and a cabinet in which everything but the console terminal could reside. The price was from $10,000 to $19,000.

In 1975, Raytheon announced its PTS/1200 minicomputer system. It consisted of six Raytheon intelligent terminals, a high-speed line printer, a smaller dot-matrix printer, and two cabinets (which held the power supplies, processor, disks, and memory). This system was marketed as a distributed processing system that held its own database, and could store up to 20MB of data on the centrally shared magnetic disk. It also offered IBM 2780 and 3780 protocols.

Figure 122—Raytheon PTS/1200

Competition was tough in the minicomputer market, and while the PTS/1200 was a nicely packaged system, it was limited in expandability which, therefore, limited its market. Since Raytheon had established an excellent track record in the scientific area, why mess with a good thing? So, it focused on its computer work for the scientific market instead of the business market. Currently, Raytheon has around 63,000 employees worldwide, with revenues of approximately $25 billion. More than 90 percent of Raytheon's revenues are from military contracts.

Before moving on, I want to acknowledge the efforts of one its employees, Raymond Tomlinson. As any email user knows, the accepted format of an addressee is "name@.domain name." Tomlinson had been working with the ARPANET team (the U.S. government's first attempt to link computers together). Just as spreadsheet software was the catalyst needed to show how PCs could be useful, Tomlinson looked at the ARPANET and questioned, "How could this thing be useful to the ordinary user?" Aha, he reasoned—what if we could use it to send messages between people? Eventually, he wrote email software in the early 1970s, and today, every time you type in an email name, marvel at how simple it is to do—especially for the little, nondescript "@" symbol. Thank Mr. Tomlinson for that small but helpful contribution for making email easier to use.

Realisation d'Etudes Electroniques (R2E)

Realisation d'Etudes Electroniques (translated from French into English as "Achievements of Studies Electronic") was founded in 1972 by Andre Truong (who was of French Vietnamese background and lived in Paris). R2E was formed as the result of an interesting meeting of men wanting to provide small computers for true business applications (which was, by the way, several years ahead of the Silicon Valley whiz kids).

Truong had developed a small computer using the Intel microprocessor, but it was being used to measure dirt volumes (before and after a rain). François Gernelle (the "idea" guy) worked for a company called Intertechnique. Gernelle had kept up on the microprocessor news from Intel, and he went to his management wanting to build a small business computer. Gernelle experienced what Steve Wozniak went through at HP when he presented his idea for a small business computer—he was turned down. The history is murky as to how Gernelle actually met up with Truong, but Gernelle went to work for R2E around the first part of 1972.

After Gernelle caught Turong's attention, the two of them set out to make a business computer that did more than just measure volumes of dirt. Unlike the hobbyists who were trying to figure out what to with this new thing on the market called a microprocessor, these guys had a vision. They saw companies tiring of being tied to large timesharing and mainframe systems, and thought that even the up-and-coming minicomputer makers were missing the mark. What they envisioned was more of a "personal" use of the computer to do whatever the user wanted it to do. R2E wasn't quite sure what to call this small-computer market, but some would claim what it developed was the first personal computer based on a microprocessor. (Other companies could make this same claim equally, as development was going on ferociously in the U.S. I will leave it to you to award this distinction to this company if so desired — keeping in mind that it beat Apple and others by at least two years.)

Their development began in earnest in July 1972, on a classic shoestring operation. It wasn't started in a garage like Apple and HP, but rather in a basement under a house in a Paris, France, in the suburb Chatenay-Malabry. The prototype (which eventually became a product), was called the Micral-N ("micral" is slang for "small" in French); it was a personal computer and was delivered a mere six months later on January 15, 1973. The price of this machine was slightly over $1,000. In March 1973, Gernelle received a patent for this system. (Gernelle relates the story that his computer was about the price of a Citroën 2CV car. The 2CV was the "people's car of France; just as the Volkswagen "Beatle" held that claim in Germany, the 2CV was quite a remarkable automobile in many ways. People were beginning to be willing to spend the same amount of money on a computer as they did on a car — this showed the value businesses placed on having their very own computer!)

As stated earlier, to be called a personal computer, it needed the following qualities:

- Be small (which was relative given the comparative sizes then as compared to today's sizes)
- Be able to do what the user wanted it to do; not limited to, say, doing strictly calculations like a calculator does

- Have a microprocessor as its brain
- Not meant to be shared (meaning, not tied in by need to a central computer, or other users sharing its resources (such as memory and disk)
- Be affordable
- Be easy to use

Figure 123—Micral-N

The Micral-N met the above requirements. It was well received throughout France, as it found itself being used for motorway tolls and the cash registers in supermarkets. Referencing an interview with Gernelle in July 2010, by 1981 his company had sold 10,000 Micral-N systems. R2E was about to come up against its first hurdle—what sells in France might not be allowed in other countries such as Germany or the UK. Every country was setting its own standards for power supplies, electrical shielding, and other rules—all in the name of consumer safety. Also, since the Micral-N was rushed out the door, enhancements soon followed to make it more stable. What this all meant was that now R2E had multiple versions of the Micral-N to support.

The Micral-N was powered by the Intel 8008. It was clocked at running approximately 50K instructions per second, and was working at 500 KHz. The machine had MOS memory, parallel and serial interface cards, and a bus architecture, which theoretically meant that most I/O peripherals, such as disk drives, tape drives, etc., could be connected to it easily. The bus itself was on a separate back panel, and had a 74-pin connector (which R2E called the Pluribus—get it? Plural, as in more than one, and bus, well, for the bus itself). A total of fourteen boards could be plugged into a Pluribus, where each board could be customized to communicate with something hanging off the end of it (e.g., a disk drive). With two Pluribuses, the Micral-N could support up to twenty-four boards. R2E developed its own custom boards for its Pluribus; these included a processor board, memory boards, channel boards called a "channel-stack," communications adapters, digital I/O boards, analog I/O boards, floppy disk, hard disk, and magnetic cartridge controllers.

The operating system software was written on an Intertechnique Multi-8 minicomputer, using an Assembler cross-compiler. Once the operating system, SYSMIC, had been written, it was fed into the Micral-N with punched cards, with a Teletype used as an output device. Later, the O/S would be enhanced and become the Prologue multi-tasking operating system.

An 8-inch floppy disk reader was added to the Micral-N in December 1973. In 1974, a keyboard and display were added; in 1975, a hard disk became available; and in 1979, the Micral 8031 D (the latest model) was equipped with a Seagate 5¼-inch hard disk (which provided a whopping 5MB of storage).

The Micral-G and Micral-S models used the Intel 8080 microprocessor (running at 1 MHz). The Micral-CZ model (also called Series 80) using the Zilog Z80 microprocessor came out in 1979. The Micral-M model was an amazing machine in its own right, as it could have up to eight Micral-S machines configured together. Each Micral-S in a Micral-M had its own local memory, but could share common memory across all microprocessors; each Micral-S had a copy of the operating system loaded into its memory. This architecture of sharing processors with other processors was very unique in the computer industry. The last Micral model was called the 9020.

The Series 80 (or CZ) came with 32K RAM (64K max), two 5.25-inch floppy-disk drives, monochrome monitor, integral keyboard/keypad, and BASIC as the programming language. As options, one could get an external 10MB removable hard-disk drive, graphics display upgrade, and a tabletop monochrome monitor.

R2E sold about 90,000 units of the total Micral line, so from a sheer volume perspective one could say it was a success. The numbers hid an important fact, though — most of the machines were being used in a limited market (e.g., highway toll booths, engineering labs, supermarkets, and process control). In November 1975, R2E and Warner & Swasey Company signed a contract where the latter was to be the exclusive manufacturer and marketer of the Micral line throughout the U.S. and Canada. Keeping with what it understood about the R2E market in France, Warner & Swasey marketed the Micral for applications such as engineering data analysis, accounting, and inventory control. In June 1976, both companies jointly displayed at the Micral-M National Computer Conference in the U.S.

The 8080-based Micral-C was introduced in 1977; this product was sold as an intelligent CRT terminal designed with two purposes — word processing and automatic typesetting. It had two Shugart SA400 mini-floppy drives, and a panel of control and sense switches below these drives. It could be programmed in business application language (BAL) and FORTRAN. In late 1977, R2E wanted to increase its North American sales, so it set up an American subsidiary in Minneapolis, Minnesota; it named this company R2E of America.

The Micral-V Portable was announced in 1978. It ran two compilers: Assembler and FORTRAN, and it used the Sysmic operating system. In 1981, R2E was bought by Groupe Bull. Starting with the Bull Micral 30 (which could use both Prologue and MS-DOS), Groupe Bull transformed the Micral computers into a line of PC compatibles. François Gernelle left Bull in 1983.

The 1980s was filled with angst from within with some R2E managers wanting to continue developing their own proprietary line of PCs, while some wanted to follow what was becoming the "IBM" standard. R2E of America, headed by Truong, chose the IBM clone route (which Bull marketed as the BM-30). With sales starting to lag for the Micral line, R2E officially closed all operations in 1985 after selling its operations and patents to Bull.

Philippe Kahn, a programmer for the Micral, later went on to head up Borland (which released Turbo Pascal and Sidekick in 1983).

In the late 1990s, Truong claimed that he alone invented the first personal computer. A lawsuit (filed in France) developed from this, and the French courts ruled against Truong (actually declaring him "the businessman, but not the inventor"), and giving the sole claim as inventor of the Micral personal computer to Gernelle and the R2E engineering team.

Redactron

This company was founded in 1969, but didn't go into production until 1971. Evelyn Berezin, truly a woman ahead of her time competing in a computer world dominated by men, built this company in Long Island, New York.

Berezin's computer background was solid from years of work with IBM, but she also was a pragmatic person who saw wasted time and effort in something as simple as correcting a typed document. She thought that there had to be a better way to do this. In her brilliant mind she visualized a device called a "word processor" — basically, processing documents from initial writing to editing and sharing. Other companies (Microsoft for one) would build on these ideas and go on to create multimillion dollar companies.

Examining this company in more detail shows the computer competition of the 1970s and how other companies "borrowed" freely from others' ideas. In 1971 Redactron came out with its first machine and called it the "Data Secretary." It would be a disservice to both Redactron and Berezin not to give them credit for coming out with what could be called the first "word processor." It could not only edit, correct, cut, and paste words (basic characters—no graphics), but also store and retrieve a document. To be fair, it was not a fancy setup, but rather an inexpensive re-use of existing technology. The first machine was a box of semiconductors and wires that stood about 40 inches tall, an Intel 4004 microprocessor, and an IBM Selectric typewriter sitting on top. It did not have a display monitor.

Figure 124—IBM Selectric Typewriter

The typewriter was electric, and had its own semiconductors that made the keys easier to press and offered other nice features (such as backspace and correct) that were hard to do with manual (non-electric) typewriters. It was noisy—but in a cool, electric way. Berezin figured out how to marry the IBM Selectric to the programmable Intel microprocessor so typed characters could be stored and later retrieved for editing. Then, she made the Selectric print it with a command from the keyboard itself. It wasn't fancy, but she was on to something that helped process documents.

Berezin was unique in the technology/management world. She not only had a keen, logical engineering mind capable of inventing new ways to approach a problem, but she also considered herself as having a solid entrepreneurial spirit who understood business.

In 1972, The New York Times' business writer Leonard Sloane wrote: "Miss Berezin, a serious, soft-spoken individual, nevertheless talks at times like a systems engineer (which she is), a sales executive (which she is) and a proponent of a sophisticated product (which she is). She is also obviously a woman on the senior level of a field where her sex is still a rarity at any level."

Berezin had designed numerous single-purpose computer systems from technology (e.g., calculations for maximum firing ranges of large guns,) to business needs (e.g., distribution data, accounting systems, and banking transactions).

She ran the company's first ad in 1971 — not in computer newspapers or magazines, but rather in "MS," a magazine focused on women's issues. She knew her audience, and it worked.

More refinements came, and eventually, in 1976, the Data Secretary 2 was introduced.

Figure 125—Data Secretary 2 with Evelyn Berezin

The Data Secretary 2 was a true word processor, rich with features to edit, store, retrieve, print, and share documents easier than anyone else believed possible. (Within only a few years, Microsoft, Apple, and several others would build on these ideas to come out with their own versions of word processing.)

Redactron's Data Secretary 2 was selling quite well—so much so that it caught the attention of Burroughs. Burroughs bought Redactron in the fall of 1976, and made Berezin the president of the Redactron Division of Burroughs. Approximately 10,000 Data Secretary units were sold at an average cost of $8,000 each. (Keep this in perspective with today where a laptop and software costing no more than $500 can accomplish the same and more.)

"Why is this woman not famous?" the British entrepreneur and writer Gwyn Headley asked in a 2010 blog post. "Without Ms. Berezin there would be no Bill Gates, no Steve Jobs, no internet, no word processors, no spreadsheets; nothing that remotely connects business with the 21st century." That might have been a stretch on his part for many reasons (namely the internet was way out of her area of expertise), but he did make a good point in that she had been overlooked for advancing the use of microprocessors in the world of document processing.

Berezin died on December 10, 2018, after leading companies and mentoring other women for over 40 years on how to excel in the business world. Good job, Ms. Berezin.

Remcom

With only one product in 1970, Remcom was at least trying to keep IBM on its toes. The bad news for Remcom was that, well, it only had one product. The Remcom 2780 had one market—to compete with the IBM remote line printer and card reader that ran the IBM 2780 protocol.

The Remcom 2780 claimed that it:

- Was twice as fast as IBM's similar remote line printer
- Could also read punched cards at 300 or 600 cards per minute
- Could do data compression for both receiving and transmitting
- Could buffer up to 1,200 bytes before transmitting
- Sold for less than the IBM model and had less maintenance cost

Remcom was based in Garland, Texas.

Roland Corporation

What is a good, catchy song without a great drum beat in the background? In general, companies from Japan were very inventive in all areas of manufacturing; they were hungry to compete in the world markets. When the microprocessor came on the market (with a big push from another Japanese company named Busicom), this Osaka-based company saw the potential of how to use it to first make rudimentary sounds, then the allow a user to program a machine to make custom sounds.

Before the microprocessor, inventors figured out ways to make electric guitars and organs produce sounds with basic electronics. But with exception of a dial to control pitch or volume, these sounds were inflexible in their function. The founder of Roland, Ikutaro Kakehashi, had his roots in the non-microprocessor world of sound, but he saw the possibility the microprocessor could bring—

and thus the Roland Corporation[97] was formed on April 18, 1972.

With inventive and creative people such as Tadao Kikumoto Roland set out to change the world of music for the hobbyists and amateurs. In other words, he wanted to put inexpensive tools in the hands creative people so they could enhance and create music. Out of their lab came a prolific line of products: TR-77 (aka Rhythm 77), TR-33, and TR-55 (these were drum-producing sounds only); then the true synthesizers SH-1000 (1973), JC-120 (1975), RE-201 (1976), and the MC-8 MicroComposer (1978) came next.

I am including the TR-808 in the book because 1) it was started in development in 1979, and 2) it had (and still has) a tremendous impact on music with musicians even today using this machine for its creative sounds.

The Roland Corporation was instrumental (no pun intended) in setting computer standards to connect PCs to sound generating products. In the early 1980s, Roland's Musical Instrument Digital Interface (MIDI) altered the world when it came to setting communications protocols, interfaces, and connectors needed to pull together PCs and other sound-producing equipment (e.g., keyboards).

Roland, employing over 3,000 people, is still in operation and offering products in music streaming and sophisticated synthesizers and instruments for the music industry.

---

[97] Kakehashi wanted a non-Japanese sounding name for his company—something that would have more international appeal. A story goes that he looked in an American phone directory and chose the name Roland at random. The name was easy to pronounce with only two syllables, plus he could find no other "music" company starting with the letter "R."

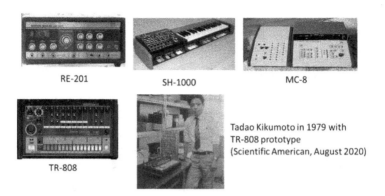

RE-201   SH-1000   MC-8

TR-808

Tadao Kikumoto in 1979 with
TR-808 prototype
(Scientific American, August 2020)

Figure 126—Roland Corporation equipment

In 1978, another company, Texas Instruments, 6,000 miles away was also coming out with a micro-processor based, programmable sound machine. The Texas Instruments device was Speak and Spell. It is hard to say if companies were borrowing ideas from others, or if engineers simply hit upon the same ideas at roughly the same time. But the fact was that ideas were blooming with the capabilities of the microprocessor, and now engineers were figuring out how to make them talk.

Rolm Corporation

Founded in 1969 to supply computers that would withstand the rigors of military use, Rolm Corporation eventually spread into other offerings. After years of slow but profitable growth, a public offering was done in 1976.

Four engineers—Gene Richeson, Ken Oshman, Walter Loewenstern, and Robert Maxfield—started the company. The name Rolm came from the initials of their last names.

Rolm used the Data General operating system as the basis for its custom military computer systems. They offered models 1601, 1602, 1602B, and 1603. As the model numbers increased, so did the amount of memory, more communication capabilities, and faster processors (32-bit vs 16-bit).

In 1977, Rolm saw (as did most) the Japanese controlling the telephony market via computers adding features over basic telephones talking from point A to point B. Rolm decided to attack this market and was quite successful (mostly in the U.S.). Their products in this area consisted of the 7000, 8000, and 9000 series, with the 9000 supporting both fiber optics and copper- connected communications. These systems were meant for the CBX (Computer Branch eXchange), and PBX (Private Branch eXchange), which added nice features such as voice mail, multi-party calling, etc.

Rolm was holding its own in both the "military"[98] and telephony market, and in the early 1980s, IBM bought Rolm. IBM ended up separating both product lines, and eventually sold the Rolm product line.

Sanders Associates

Sanders Associates, founded in 1951 and soon thereafter located in Nashua, New Hampshire, took its name from one of the eleven founding members, Royden C. Sanders, Jr. After earlier work developing circuit assemblies and specialized printed wiring boards for military and other government agencies, the company produced two products that fit into the burgeoning computer market — the Sanders 720 and the Sanders Series 800. Both systems provided data entry where data could be verified for things such as range values and numeric/alpha checking. The intent of these systems was to allow only "valid" data (unlike data that could contain typos and other data entry keyed errors) to be sent over communication lines to a host computer system (e.g., IBM, Burroughs, Sperry, etc.). Each system had its own storage and each controlled a

---

[98] That term is actually a misnomer because a few customers outside of the military were buying the systems for their capabilities of being abused (e.g., knocked over) but still continuing to work.

small number of actual display terminals. Data stored on the 720 or 800 could be retrieved, added, deleted, and updated locally.

The display terminal came as one unit consisting of a keyboard with numeric pad, a communication card, and a CRT that looked like a small TV screen turned on its side. (In other words, as most displays at the time were standardizing on a 24- or 25-line monitor with 80 characters wide, Sanders Associates thought just the opposite — and it never really caught on.)

Figure 127—Sanders 800

In 1986, Lockheed Corporation purchased Sanders Associates.

Sanders Data Systems, Incorporated

Making its home in Burlingame, California, in the early 1970s, Sanders Data Systems was doomed from trying to market some products that were part of a dying time, or products that were not fast enough to keep up with newer products coming out by competitors. Basically, what Sanders attempted to do was to buy component parts and package them into a small business system.

In 1972, Sanders offered the following:

- Microprocessor cabinet; it held a 16-bit CPU operating on 8-bit data, and memory of up to 4K words. The cabinet itself was approximately 12 in. high, 15 in. wide, and 4 in. deep; its face consisted of over forty toggle switches!
- Series 800 programmable terminals; these could stand alone or be clustered with up to thirty-two others that would be controlled by the microprocessor (described above).
- Magnetic disk transport; held up to 5MB of data, and was in a cabinet about the size of an old phonograph player.
- Card reader; held up to 300 cards (80 or 51 columns) in its hopper.
- The 3130 line printer; could print up to 200 lines per minute.
- Dual cassette tape transport; each cassette held up to 300,000 characters, and could accommodate variable record lengths of up to 2,048 characters.
- Modems; allowed speeds of up to 1,200 baud.

The target market was obviously very small businesses that simply needed a way to input data and store minimal amounts of it. The microprocessor was not expandable for growth, and as mentioned, the company had tied itself to older technology that was now becoming obsolete and, therefore, not saleable. Add multiple sales offices across the U.S. and two in Europe, and it isn't hard to see why Sanders Data Systems didn't make it.[99]

---

[99] Efforts to contact someone at a current company called Sanders, Inc. (also located in Burlington) to see if it was linked to the 1970s company by a similar name failed when no emails or phone calls were returned.

Scientific and Engineering Computers, LTD.

In 1971, this Northampton, United Kingdom, company, located about sixty miles north of London, resold the Dietzen Desk Top Computer. [See Eugene Dietzgen Company.] Scientific and Engineering Computers advertised this machine as a "mini computer," but what it literally meant was that it was a "mini" computer. The following is a picture of the product.

Figure 128—Dietzgen Desk Top Computer

Scientific Control Corp.

Large, successful companies were full of bright engineers in the 1970s. Usually, but not always, these bright engineers felt a loyalty to their company—but in Carrollton, Texas, a few engineers with a product idea left Texas Instruments and started their own company. On October 1, 1968, Scientific Control Corp. (SCC) was formed (although it had become a public company in December 1967, issuing stock for $7.50 a share). There was no reason for this company to be located in this small Dallas suburb other than the fact that Texas Instruments was close by—thereby seeding this company with engineers.

SCC marketed several products from the early 1960s until the mid-1970s. In 1968, the 4700 (its 16-bit minicomputer product) was announced; it could support up to sixteen local terminals, store data locally, and then send it to a host via a dial-up connection. Additionally, SCC had a line printer and card punch/reader, which could be attached to the 4700. The 4700 product was aimed for the scientific market and not for traditional business processing. It had core memory, which was supplied by Electronic Memories, Inc. [See Electronic Memories.] The 4700 sold well for SCC into the early 1970s.

In 1969, SCC released its SCC 6700 Time Sharing Computer. In one of the documents describing the internal workings of this machine, SCC paid homage to the University of Berkeley for sharing with it Berkeley's own timesharing research, and for sharing its work on the Advanced Research Projects Agency (ARPA) in general. SCC went on in its literature to describe how it had made improvements to the timesharing software. The SCC 6700 could have one or more multiple CPUs running in parallel. (I could not find what the maximum number of CPUs could be, though.) Each processor could execute its own instructions without interrupting another processor—although all processors shared a common memory. Each processor communicated information to another through an inter-process bus architecture. Data was stored memory in 2K words; instruction length was 24 bits. This system could support up to 256 users, and execute up to 5,000 instructions per second. It supported a card reader, line printer, and an acoustic coupler for a dial-up mechanism.

In May 1969, the DCT-132 remote batch terminal was brought to market. This product was an intelligent terminal (it could be programmed), could store data locally to it, and then transmit that data to a host machine via a dial-up modem of up to 4,800 baud. In August 1969, SCC announced sales of 100 of the machines for $2.4 million—$24,000 for one terminal was expensive even then!

The Series 670 also was produced, but little detail was available regarding its characteristics.

Because of unknown circumstances, this company fell upon hard financial times. In November 1969, it filed for Chapter 11 bankruptcy — which should have been the end of SCC, but it didn't give up. In January 1970, it opened its doors once more and shipped $653,000 of products within the first twelve days (either showing that there was a demand for its products, or that it finally shipped products that were on the books before the bankruptcy filing).

In 1974, things continued going downhill for SCC, financially speaking. Sales were down, forecasts were much lower than actual, and expenses were eating up any profit. They held on until 1977 before disappearing as a legal entity.

Scientific Data Systems(SDS)

Scientific Data Systems (SDS) was founded in September 1961 by Max Palevsky (a veteran of the Packard Bell and Bendix companies) and eleven other computer scientists. SDS was a believer in the IC and, therefore, was one of the first to use silicon wafer transistors in its computer design. Instead of tackling the business market, which IBM, Burroughs, and others had staked out, SDS wanted to carve out its own niche by concentrating on larger scientific workload machines — coincidently, several other companies had their eyes on this market as well. Even though the company was sold to Xerox in 1969, the company was close enough to the '70s to make a big impact; namely, on Xerox with SDS' Sigma product line.

Much of SDS' success came from its use of silicon-based transistors in its earliest designs, and in its 24-bit SDS 910 and SDS 920 computer models. The SDS machines shipped with a selection of software, including its own designed (and optimized) FORTRAN compiler for the SDS products. In a single pass of the compiler, for instance, it could compile programs (in 4K, 24-bit words) without the need for secondary storage. For scientific users writing small programs, this was a real boon and dramatically improved development turnaround time.

The 910 and 920 were followed by the SDS 9300 in June 1963. The 9300 included a floating-point processor for higher performance. The performance increase was dramatic; the 910/920 needed 16 microseconds to add two 24-bit integers, and the 9300 needed only 1.75 microseconds. The 9300 also increased maximum memory from 16K words to 32K words. More models followed in the '60s, and each brought higher performance (with lower costs) to the customer. And here is where its computer work was starting to have an impact on the world.

SDS had been studying the IBM success phenomenon closely, and could see that IBM was so big that it was driving new standards that it (IBM) was setting on the world. For instance, the IBM System/360 used a 7-bit ASCII character standard, but now it was pushing the 8-bit as the new standard. SDS wanted its machines to compete head-on with the IBM System/360, and make it fairly easy for IBM customers to move to its platform. Though not fully compatible with the 360, it did use similar data formats—namely the EBCDIC character code—and multiple registers rather than an accumulator. In December 1966, SDS shipped its new Sigma series, starting with the 16-bit Sigma 2 and the 32-bit Sigma 7. Both of these products used common hardware internally (thereby reducing manufacturing costs). Various versions of the Sigma 7 followed, including a new Sigma 5 and redesigned Sigma 6. (The Xerox Sigma 9 was a major redesign with instruction "look-ahead" and other advanced features.) The Sigma range of products was a very successful for SDS[100] even though it had only about one percent of the total U.S. computer market.

In 1969, Xerox bought SDS. When this purchase occurred, about 1,000 Sigma models had been sold. By the time Xerox closed its computer division down in 1975, about 2,100 were sold.

In 1979, an attempt was made to restart SDS with former SDS engineers. They introduced a microprocessor computer system called the SDS-420. This machine was built on a 6502A-based processor design with up to 56K of memory and a proprietary operating system called SDS-DOS. It also included the BASIC programming language. The SDS-420 featured a dual single-sided, double-density (400K per side) floppy drive, Model 70, manufactured by PerSci of Santa Monica and Marina del Rey, California. The SDS-422 model offered a dual double-sided, double-density floppy drives. Other hardware options were a 6551-A USART and a proprietary network SDS-NET, which used an 8530 SDLC/HDLC chip and software (patterned after the early Xerox 3.0 Mbit/s Ethernet and transceivers). The 400 Series was primarily used for word processing and business services; it was not a scientific machine like the old Sigmas. The company sold about 1,000 of the 400 Series machines worldwide.

SDS went on to develop its own networking standards, faster models, and custom software for legal and medical usage. With sales lagging and costs increasing, SDS finally closed its doors in 1984.

Scientific Electronic Biological

Scientific Electronic Biological (SCELBI) was located in Milford, Connecticut, as a personal-computer hardware

---

[100] The first node of ARPANET (a precursor to today's internet) was established by Leonard Kleinrock at UCLA with an SDS Sigma 7 system.

and software manufacturer. SCELBI was founded in 1973 by Nat Wadsworth and Bob Findley.

Its first product used the Intel 8008 and was called the CELBI-8H. This machine had a whopping 1K of RAM, and was available as a kit or fully assembled. The kit consisted of circuit boards, a power supply, cabinet, and nuts and bolts. In March 1974, the company started running ads for its $565 kit in *QST*, *Radio-Electronics*, and *Byte* magazines. I think it is worth displaying a picture of the system to see what an early "personal computer" looked like.

Figure 129—SCELBI-8

In 1974, SCELBI announced the SCELBI-8B (with 16K of memory, which was the maximum addressing of the Intel 8008. There was no operating system included, but it could be programmed using the standard Assembler language.

Software programming was an issue that SCELBI saw as limiting sales, so Wadsworth wrote a book called *Machine Language Programming for the 8008 and Similar Microcomputers*, in the hopes that it would help spur sales. The book was well received, and actually might have sold more copies than the SCELBI 8. The company did realize that book sales brought in more profit, so it switched paths and became a software publisher and created a language developer course called SCELBAL, meaning a BASIC language specific for the SCELBI machine to compete against the Altair BASIC.

Scion

In 1978, Scion started life as Micro Diversions — which was located in Tysons Corner, Virginia. Eventually ending up in Reston, Virginia, this company built a video board that fit in an S-100 bus backplane.

Software, however, was just as important to this company as it was developing the video board hardware. (The company also marketed its boards to fit in Multibus, NuBus, and PCI bus.) It also developed a product called Screen Splitter that could "split" the screen (visually) into two separate areas. Another product was called Frame Grabber, which could freeze any area of a screen and digitize it. (While this functionality sounds common today, this was leading technology during this timeframe.)

Scion continues to invent, producing a popular video card called the MicroAngelo, the Mirage 1 graphics terminal, and other related video-handling products.

Sharp

In 1912, Tokuji Hayakawa founded a metal workshop in Tokyo, Japan. He dabbled with making mechanical pencils, and in 1915 produced a mechanical pencil marketed as the "Ever-Sharp." Sharp was a catchy name, and it stuck as the new name for the company.

Relocating to Osaka in 1923 because of a large earthquake in Tokyo, Sharp was now making the first generation of Japanese radio sets. Other electronic component work followed, and in 1953 Sharp started producing television sets. In 1964, Sharp developed a transistor-based calculator.

Sharp had no experience in making computing devices at the time, so the world of using transistors was new to the company. Its first calculator product was priced at more than $1,000. More calculator products followed, with prices continuing to fall to around $300. In 1973, Sharp produced the first calculator with an LCD.

Sharp was a company driven by competition, and this spilled over internally. In the mid-1970s, Sharp had created multiple divisions to allow it to focus on a specific market segment. Two of these, the Computer division and the Television division would soon be at odds with each other over engineering funding and other budgets. The Computer division was producing its own product with a microprocessor-based design. Around this same time, the Television division released a new computer-based series called the X1.

Most home computers had a BASIC language stored in ROM. However, on the X1, its BASIC (called the HU-BASIC) had to be loaded into memory from cassette tape. Sharp did this intentionally to free up as much RAM as possible when not using the compiler. The Japanese even coined a word to describe this design — they called them "clean computers." The cabinet shape of X1 was also much more stylish than others at that time, and it was available in a range of cabinet colors.

The display monitor for the X1 had a television tuner, and a computer screen could be super-imposed on a TV. All the TV functions (channel, volume, etc.) could be controlled from a computer program. (Think of this computer as a very big and expensive remote control!) The character font was completely programmable with 4-bit color—sounds a lot like a personal computer by most definitions...except it was focused on gaming.

In 1978, Sharp produced a home computer kit, the MZ-40K, which was based on Fujitsu's 4-bit MB8843 processor and provided a simple hexadecimal keypad for input. (Although commonly believed to stand for "Microcomputer Z80," the term MZ actually had its roots in the MZ-40K.) This was soon followed by the MZ-80K, K2, C, and K2E, all of which were based on the 8-bit LH0080A Sharp CPU (which was compatible to the Zilog), and it included an alphanumeric keyboard.

Meanwhile, the Computer division was ready to bring its personal (non-kit) PC to the market, and in 1979 announced its MZ product line. The MZ computers included the PC, monitor, keyboard, and tape-based recorder in a single unit (similar to Commodore's PET series). It also was notable for not including a programming language or operating system in ROM.

In an era when floppy disk drives were too expensive for most home users, the MZ's built-in tape drive was a money saver for Sharp's customers. The downside of this was that Sharp was slow to adopt floppy-drive technology when the market moved to it. The MZ was based on the Zilog Z80, and was sold into Europe starting in 1979 for £500. The Z80K product had 48K of RAM, 32K of which was available for user programs. It could run the BASIC, Pascal, and FORTRAN compilers (each had to be loaded into memory before any programming could actually begin). It also could be programmed directly in Assembly code or machine code. The machine came with a built-in monochrome display, a cassette tape drive, and an oddly configured keyboard unlike the accepted QWERTY layout most were using. The display, keyboard, and cassette drive lifted easily on hinges to expose the motherboard and circuitry underneath—a very thoughtful, user-friendly design. High-resolution graphics were limited to preset shapes and icons. While the MZ was a well-designed PC, because it did not come with the standard QWERTY keyboard, this posed a marketing problem for Sharp. More models followed the basic MZ, and it continued to sell throughout the '80s and '90s, although with little success outside of Japan.

Sharp is no longer in the computer business, having divested itself of this division in 1987. Also, it ceased manufacturing its gaming XI systems in the early 1980s. Today, Sharp is alive and well selling consumer products, such as TVs and other electronics, and employs over 50,000 people.

Shepardson Microsystems, Inc.

Just as Bill Gates and his company were off developing their own version of BASIC and other software that ran on what was becoming the "IBM" standard for PCs, Apple needed its own version of BASIC that ran under its operating system. Enter into the picture a small and almost forgotten company that was critical to Apple's early success—Shepardson Microsystems. Its focus and forté was producing operating systems and programming languages for the Atari 8-bit and Apple II computer families.

In 1978, Shepardson Microsystems signed a contract with Apple to develop its first disk-based operating system (known simply as DOS, but different in many ways from Microsoft's DOS). Shepardson Microsystems supplied a file management system, Applesoft BASIC, and other utilities for file management (e.g., copying, deleting, etc.) Similarly, Shepardson Microsystems ended up writing Atari's BASIC compiler along with Atari's DOS.

By the time 1980 rolled around, Shepardson Microsystems realized it had made strategically bad business decisions. In developing software for both Atari and Apple, it had signed contracts giving Shepardson Microsystems no royalty income for its endeavors, which by all accounts, made both Atari and Apple millions of dollars. In 1981, Shepardson Microsystems went out of business.

Shepardson Microsystems was founded in Saratoga Springs, New York, by Robert Shepardson.

Shugart Corporation

IBM had perfected the floppy disk, and the disk drive (hardware) that could read and write data to/from it. This technology was slowly transforming how people could take data from one machine to another. It sounds simple now, but before this, nothing existed to do this simple task.

Alan Shugart saw the demand for floppy disk drives, and after overseeing this development left IBM in 1975 to start his own company in Sunnyvale, California, making a smaller version of the disk drives (from 11" to 5") called the mini-floppy disk drive. Shugart devices held a high reputation for quality, and quickly became the defacto standard for small microprocessor- based computers. Xerox saw this as a potentially lucrative market, and in December 1977 bought the company. Xerox rode high on Shugart revenues for a while, but didn't foresee competition in this area.

After continuing to lose millions of dollars trying to sustain its market share, Xerox closed Shugart operations on January 17, 1985.

Figure 130 – Shugart disk drive with floppy disk

Siemens AG

On October 1, 1847, an ex-engineering officer by the name of Werner Siemens was working on early telegraph technology in Germany. Branching out from Germany to the UK, officially Siemens Brothers and Company Ltd was formed. Fast-forward through decades of incandescent lights, telephones, and other commercial product developments, and in the 1900s, Siemens was now a big company.

More decades followed, intermixed with two world wars, and Siemens survived with its inventions of commercial products. In the late 1960s, Siemens saw the potential market for computers, but apparently was not geared up for either the marketing or engineering in this area. To quickly get a toe-hold (and to test out the market), it sold the Intellec 800 (from Intel) as the SME-800.

In 1974, the incestuous relationship of computer makers in Europe went into high gear. Siemens acquired Telefunken Computer GmbH and Nixdorf Computer. Siemens formed a separate company called Computergesellschaft Konstanz GmbH to sell and service these new computers. At the time Computergesellschaft was formed, it had around $163.4 million worth of computers installed or on order. Around 1980 — the actual date is murky due to different information in publications — Siemens and its newly formed company decided to rid itself of its computer manufacturing and sold Computergesellschaft to Unidata.

Siemens flourished throughout the '80s and continues in today's market with products such as power generators, power transmission and distribution, medical technology, semiconductors, and other technology.

Singer (Singer M&M)

This company had a very early start in a life that eventually saw itself in the computer market. I. M. Singer

& Co. was formed in 1851 by Isaac Merritt Singer, with its headquarters in New York City, New York. In 1885, it introduced the world's first "vibrating shuttle" sewing machine. (There were other sewing machines on the market, but none of this design.).

Singer took a lead in the consumer sewing machine market, and never looked back as improvements and enhancements continued for the next ten decades. Along the way, though, Singer saw a need to use electricity to power its machines, and then this led to the company dabbling more and more in electrical components. WWII (with government contracts) drew Singer more into the world of electronics, and Singer ended up being one of the key contributors to the famous Norton Bomb Sight used by American bombers.

In 1966, Singer bought Packard Bell Electronics, and then the General Precision Equipment Corporation in 1968. Singer's involvement with electronics took such a large turn that a separate division (called the Business Machine division) was created for focusing just on this work. Singer produced flight simulators, GPS devices, and other products for aircraft. Then it was bitten by the computer bug, but lacked the engineering to make serious inroads into this about-to-be burgeoning market. To get its foot in the computer door, in 1970, the Business Machine division purchased Friden (makers of the System 10). [See Friden.] Next, this division also acquired the Cogar Corporation (a manufacturer of desktop intelligent terminals). [See Cogar.]

In 1970, Singer had developed its 4300 series of small, desk-top models (terminal with keyboard, disc storage, tape storage, and central control unit). For several years in the 1970s, Singer set up a national sales force for automating photo-typesetting machines (actually made by Graphic Systems, Inc.) In 1973, Singer announced the next generation of its computers—the Series 110 computer system, which was a low-end, entry system of its System 10. The Series 110 consisted of the models 110-1, 110-3,

110-4, and 110-5, and was priced from $25,000 to $67,000. Each 110 offered what Singer called its Model 24 CPU, with 20K of core memory and one I/O channel (which was double the I/O speed on the System 10). The 110 Series could transmit and receive punched card and print data that conformed to the IBM 2780 and 3780 protocols.

Figure 131—Singer 4300 series models

The 110-1 came with an 8K disk, a keyboard, and a 25-character-per-second printer. The 110-3 had a 1,920-character display, and a 165-character per second printer. The 110-1 and 110-3 could be linked to either the 110-4 or 110-5. Once networked to other systems, it could process up to three jobs simultaneously and thus (according to the sales brochure) "accommodate high-volume user applications." The 110-4 had 30K of core storage, two I/O channels, an 8K disk, CRT terminal, and a 100-line per minute printer. The 110-5 included two CRTs (expandable to three), a 100- or 200-line per minute printer, and two disk drives that could store 20MB. The terminals could be located up to 2,000 feet from the central processor.

In 1974, Singer announced magnetic 9-track tape support. Also available was an operator's console, paper-tape punch, card reader, and card punch. Realizing that software helped spur hardware sales, Singer also supplied a software package called SPA, which allowed for order entry, invoicing, accounts receivable/payable, general ledger, payroll, inventory control, and sales analysis. This package sold for $6,000 and was offered as customized by Singer for each of its customers.

Lack of expandability and "behind the times" thinking limited Singer's market share. Sales were disappointing, and in 1978, Wang Laboratories purchased the Business Machines division.

The following years were filled with turmoil at Singer. In 1987, Paul Bilzerian bought a majority of stock in the company with plans of making the company more profitable and then selling his stock at a healthy profit. Unfortunately for Bilzerian, the plan didn't work out. Parts of the company were sold off to get cash (namely the Electronic Systems division to GEC-Marconi in 1990). The Sewing Machine division was sold in 1989 to Semi-Tech Microelectronics. Singer is now owned by Kohlberg & Company and, yes, over 150 years later it is still making sewing machines.

Software Arts

Software Arts was founded in 1979 by Dan Bricklin and Bob Frankston; these two men developed a software program called VisiCalc. This software provided a spreadsheet that could sum up values in "cells" it displayed, and kept track of the values for easy summing.

Enter Dan Fylstra and Peter R. Jennings whose company, Personal Software, sold software products such as

Microchess and other games. Bricklin and Frankston got VisiCalc to run on the Apple II, and Personal Software was the reseller of this (paying Software Arts a healthy royalty on each sale).

As mentioned in the section on Apple, VisiCalc was like putting jumper-cables on a dead battery. Not to imply the Apple II was a dead battery, but all of sudden the Apple II was given life in a real business setting—and personal computers now had their first "killer app." Figuratively speaking, almost overnight VisiCalc changed the landscape of how personal computers were perceived.

Money was rolling in from royalties and licenses, but competition was now on the market (primarily from Lotus Corporation's Lotus 1-2-3). Sales dwindled to the point that it had an offer from Lotus for its software; it accepted the deal in 1984, and in a brilliant stroke of capitalism at its best, Lotus immediately ceased all further sales of VisiCalc.

Southwest Technical Products Corporation

This company (also known to some as SWTPC) had its original roots with the name DEMCO (short for "Daniel E. Meyer Company"). It was incorporated in 1967 as Southwest Technical Products Corporation of San Antonio, Texas. Southwest Technical Products came into the computer industry on the wave of producing computer kits and, eventually, produced complete computer systems.

In the 1960s, many hobbyist electronics magazines were publishing articles on how one could build his or her own computer from parts—all without a microprocessor, of course. As a publisher who tried things first-hand, Meyer's experience enabled him to show step-by-step instructions on how to do things. Eventually, he started selling kits with all of the parts necessary to build something that resembled a computer. Some kits, however, had intended uses with hi-fi amplifiers and test equipment. So, in this case, a kit purchaser had little practical application for the built kit—it couldn't be programmed easily, it couldn't store data, and in general, it was nothing but blinking lights.

In 1972, Southwest Technical Products had a large enough collection of various kits to justify printing a 32-page catalogue. In January 1975, it finally had figured out how to package a computer terminal kit Moore called the "TV Typewriter," and was sold formally as the CT-1024, which was labelled as a "dumb" terminal (it couldn't do transmit data unless attached to a computer system).

Figure 132—Southwest Technical Products CT-1024
(with optional monitor)

By November of that year, it was delivering complete computer kits based on Motorola's 6800 microprocessor. Southwest Technical Products became one of the first suppliers of microcomputers to the general public, and especially microcomputers using the Motorola 6800 and Motorola 6809 processors. Later the company built more intelligent terminals (e.g., the CT-6144 Graphics Terminal) that had excellent color graphics. Later on, it created a very inventive Data Systems 6845 Video Display Board, which allowed a keyboard to be connected to the processor bus, thereby allowing very fast data input.

Southwest Technical Products sold its SS-50 backplane bus design to other small computer and electronic makers. It also designed one of the first affordable printers for PCs.

Granted, it was a very simplistic printer by today's standards, but it worked quite well.

Southwest Technical Products needed software to entice its customers, and it contracted with Technical Systems Consultants for this. The software produced and marketed included operating systems (FLEX, mini-FLEX, FLEX09, and UniFLEX) and various languages (several BASIC variants, FORTRAN, Pascal, C, assemblers, etc.) and various applications. It also supported Introl's C compiler, Omegasoft's, Pascal compiler, and other accounting spreadsheet packages.

The company was ahead of its time when it came to software, in that it was a proponent of software that could be developed by a community and shared among many for free. (Although when it came to making its own software available, Southwest Technical Products charged for the source code.)

Many of the early computer kit-making companies were out of business by the late 1970s, as IBM and Apple had perfected a computer that did a lot of work, and it didn't have to be put together. Still, Southwest Technical Products hung on, although by the early 1980s, it saw that the kit market was over and done with. It did see a market, though, in customized computers to be used as point-of-sale (POS) computer systems like Singer had produced. Imagine Target Stores or other retailers' check-out lanes that now have excellent scanning devices, machines to give you exact change, etc. In the beginning, even to do the basics of this was difficult to accomplish, and Southwest Technical Products was trying to make a name for itself for this work. In 1990, the company finally closed operations, only to morph into a company called Point Systems — which went belly-up by 1993.

One of this company's lasting legacies was that it was a proponent of open-source[101] programs.

Soviet Union

This section is included as a catch-all for Soviet computers, because these machines were important not only to Russia, but throughout the USSR as well. None of the computer systems (nor calculators) ever achieved "commercial" success outside of the USSR for the following reasons:

- The keyboards were in Russian, and were not laid out in the traditional keyboard patterns used in the U.S. and in Europe.
- The packaging was, well, not attractive; they were made to be functional, not pretty.
- There was a lack of marketing (who needs marketing when there is no competition?).
- Few in the world outside of Soviet bloc countries cared for computers that were outdated clones of others.
- More importantly, commercial success in "Western" terms did not fit within the Soviet model (although some of the Soviet computers were a commercial success from the perspective that they were exported/traded to China, Cuba, and other trading partners — and, yes, even a very few were actually sold to "western" countries in Europe).

To say that the Soviet Union started late in the computer business is an understatement, but as shown in the following, they (just like most other countries) have had a desire for calculators for a long time.

---

[101] Open-source means that software is made available to anyone for free for others to modify and use as they wish. The antithesis of open-source are the Apple and Microsoft operating systems where neither company wants anyone outside of their companies modifying their code.

Figure 133—1890 Russian calculator

After WWII, Russia knew that computers were needed for faster mathematic calculations, and this, of course, fit into military usage. But now Russia had positioned itself with an "us vs. them" (or "them vs. us" depending upon one's point of reference) mentality in regards to communism being the best political and economic model for a country. What this did in relation to computer development was that non-Soviet countries closed their doors to exporting to them, and in so doing left Soviet computer scientists to figure out things on their own—which, it turns out, they did quite well.

Although Russia (and the Soviet Union in general) started late in the computer arena after WWII, they did catch up—although it took them about twenty years. As Russian scientists started poking around at computer technology, their inherent secrecy with their work brought a great disconnection among other computer scientists both outside of the Soviet Union and within.

Enter Esaev Vladimir Petrovich, who in 1954 grasped the importance of computers for military usages. In 1954, he founded the Central Scientific Research Institute 27, which was the very first computer center in Russia. The outcome for this was the Strela computer (there were eight produced)—but in all definitions it was simply a big, electronic calculator and was used strictly for military usages. The key point was that now Russia had a true computer focus. Well, sort of.

It turns out that in addition to the focus on the Strela computer system, other parts of the USSR (namely the military) were developing the 5E89, 5E26, 5E51, 5E65, R567, 5E92b, 5E92, Minsk-1, Minsk-2, Minsk-22, Minsk-23, and Minsk-32. As one will soon grasp from reading this section, the USSR was (and is) a huge amalgamation of many entities—and it was hard to coordinate them for computer development.

Still, the USSR (meaning a bloc of Soviet countries) now had the momentum to develop better computers, and had brilliant computer-oriented scientists ready to lead this charge. Anatoliy Ivanovich Kitov[102] was one of these men, and without his leadership and direction, launching and control of intercontinental ballistic rockers would not have been possible. Computers were now dominating all aspects of military strategic planning.

You can research the specifications of early Soviet computer history by searching on the following Soviet computers through the internet : System A, BESM-2, BESM-4, BESM-6, URAL 11, URAL 14, URAL 16, MIR1, MIR3 Iskra 226, Rasdah-2, Nairi, Dnepr, M-4, M4M, M4-2M, and M4-3M. Yes, the Soviet computer scientists were busy. But why so many models?

Just as computer tinkerers in Japan, France, the United Kingdom, and the U.S. wanted to build something in the way of computers, the same was true in the Soviet Union. However, the powers that be in the Soviet Union didn't really care for "business" processing of data—after all, Soviet leaders controlled all business (or at least they liked to believe they did). What occurred was that the military

---

[102] Kitov was the first Russian to write and defend his dissertation on computer programming in the USSR. The title of his work was, "Programming in the problems of long range missiles exterior ballistics."

had first options for computer designers. Non-military computer designers saw a savvy way around this small conundrum by convincing the powers in charge of budgets to allow computers to be built for "measuring the economy." This was a stroke of genius, as the Soviet powers always loved to tout their economy, and now computers could be built to reinforce their numbers — except many of the agencies were skeptical of other agencies. So, instead of having a wonderful headstart on developing the internet as we know and love it today, and a comprehensive computer focus, Russia (not so much its allies) ended up with many small, proprietary computer networks. These networks linked a small number of computers together — which could not communicate with their other networks. If they had only worked together better, they might have led the world in "internet" technology.

As mentioned throughout this section, the Soviet military was dominating computer development, and clandestine "borrowing" (you can come up with your own word or phrase for this) of computer ideas from others outside the Soviet Union was an established way of doing business. Yet, a computer focus was, indeed, slowly evolving, and the fun really began for Soviet computers in the 1960s and early 1970s. Remember that the Soviet Union was the first country to launch an astronaut, Yuri Gagarin, into "space" (above the Earth's atmosphere) on April 12, 1961. This would not have been possible without the use of computers both on the ground and in the control module. As anyone should be able to understand, the Soviet Union had quickly caught up to the world in specific areas of computer development.

There is an old adage in the business world about how the Australian and Tasmanian platypus is really an animal built by committee — the same could be said for early Soviet computers. Russia and its bloc of allies, which included Cuba, Romania, Estonia, Hungary, Czechoslovakia, and others, all contributed to the actual design, the building of hardware, and the operating systems. And sometimes the USSR was its own worst enemy by having so many departments/ministries/organizations all wanting to control computer development. Here is a short list of such agencies:

- Radiotechnical Institute
- State Planning Committee
- Military Industrial Committee of the USSR Council of Ministers
- Sate Committee on Science and Technologies
- Ministry of Radio Industry
- Ministry of Defense
- Special Design Bureau
- State Committee on Science and Technologies
- Military and Industry Complex
- Department of Special Development
- Scientific Research Institute of Computational Complexes

There are more agencies that could be listed, but hopefully this provides a picture of what it was like inside the Soviet Union to not only get your story heard about some computer you were working on, but also how to compete with others for something as simple as a memory chip, processor chip, or magnetic disk. As an example of what was happening inside the Soviet Union, in 1969, the Ural-16 was developed. This computer had the following characteristics:

- 48-bit addressing
- Fixed-point calculations
- Floating point to seven places
- 300-instruction set
- 14 index registers
- 512 basic registers
- 64 levels of interrupts

- Core memory from 124K to 512K
- Magnetic drum storage of 500K
- Magnetic tape support
- Communication port
- Paper tape reader
- Paper card reader
- 400 LPM printer

Nice machine—and the Soviets produced exactly...one. With so many departments wanting to steer computer development with their own design, the Soviet computer program started to look like a platypus.

It is important to realize that the Soviet Union was very competitive with the U.S. in terms of ICs (see Texas Instruments) used in their space program. By the mid-1970s, Russia had produced its own microprocessors: namely then K532, K581, and K587. The early ones were 8-bit, then 16-bit, and finally 32-bit. Russia was catching on and catching up. Russia's early use of these microprocessors was in calculators, but later they were in small computer systems (meaning they came with keyboards, displays, and storage devices).

In 1970, the M-10 computer was developed (the team led by Mikhail Kartsev) for a missile attack early warning system. His orders were clear (and I'm sure followed by "or else"): the computer had to perform at least five million operations per second (5 MIPS), and support at least 5MB of RAM. The M-10 accomplished what it set out to do, and in 1979 the M-10-M came out with improved addressability and faster processing. Using the M-10-M as a basis for more computers, in the early 1980s the M-13 came out that could support up 34MB of RAM, and could run at 50 MIPS.

In the mid-1970s, a group led by A.M. Larionov proposed that more general-purpose computers (non-military) be developed. Romania and Cuba took the challenge, and the first to come out of this project was the forgettable (think of them as prototypes) ES Computer-1 series.[103] In 1974, the ES line, though, got more serious, and was code-named the ES Computer-2 series (also known as theRyad 2). The following lists what the ES line consisted of each year:

- 1974 – ES-1032, 32-bit, 128K - 1024K RAM, three I/O channels (core memory)
- 1975 – ES-1022, 16-bit, 128K - 256K RAM, two I/O channels (core memory)
- 1976 – ES-1033, 32-bit, 256K - 512K RAM, three I/O channels (core memory)
- 1977 – ES-1035, 32-bit, 256K - 1MB RAM, two I/O channels (semi-conductor memory)
- 1977 – ES-1060, 64-bit, 1MB - 8MB RAM, six I/O channels (semi-conductor memory)
- 1978 – ES-1052, 64-bit, 1024K RAM, four I/O channels (core memory)
- 1978 – ES-1025, 16-bit, 256K RAM, zero to four I/O channels (core memory)
- 1978 – ES-1045, 32-bit, 1MB - 4MB RAM, five I/O channels (semi-conductor memory)
- 1978 – ES-1055, 32-bit, 1MB - 2MB RAM, five I/O channels (semi-conductor memory)

(To show the Soviets' preoccupation with planning for war, all of the ES computers had to be built to withstand a blast load of no less than fifteen g-forces. Additionally, to show how brutal a Russian winter could be, many of these systems were designed to operate down to -40C.) All of these systems ran DOS as the operating system, which was a custom operating system developed for these systems. An operating system (OS) could run multiple tasks at the same time, whereas DOS could only run one task at any given time. From 1973 onward, all ES

---

[103] ES translates from Russian to mean "unified system."

computers could run FORTRAN 4, COBOL, PL-1, and RPG compilers.

Another preoccupation of Soviet thinking manifested itself in the examination of the ES-1032. The development of this machine was in Poland and led by Jacek Karpiński. The ES-1032 was a fine, small computer, but it had one problem. Karpiński apparently didn't like the quality of Soviet-made chips (maybe he just couldn't get any parts, or maybe he just didn't get the memo). Whatever his reasons, he got his hands on some Texas Instrument SN-74 chips — and this was a no-no to Soviet regulators (in other words, "Why didn't you use Soviet parts?"). So, while the ES-1032 was an excellent small computer from many perspectives, the people in charge were upset with its foreign chip usage.

Enter Hungary with its ES-1010 and Czechoslovakia with its ES-1020A, and now these three computers (plus the military with their own development) were all vying for attention and money for continued development. The platypus was still alive, but reasonable minds won out, and Karpiński and his ES-1032 became a standard going forward.

Figure 134—Soviet MIR series (left) and Soviet ES-1032 (right)

IBM's influence enters the picture. Some Soviet computer scientists were allowed to travel to the West (meaning outside of the USSR), and in so doing saw the benefits of having a basic architecture that many could build applications and peripherals around—namely the IBM 360 (and the about-to-be-released IBM 370). Soviet computer scientists fought hard over this problem: should they go down a proprietary road and thus have to develop a lot of products and applications from scratch, or could they adapt their computers somehow to the IBM "standard" and therefore use a lot of the applications already developed in the West? It was a hard question to answer, and it took a few years and arm twisting to arrive at an answer—but finally it was decided that it made sense to be able to either play nice with IBM systems, and/or be able to somehow run the IBM applications on their own machines.

To show the incompatibility issues facing Soviet computer scientists, take for example the interchange of data between an IBM 360 or IBM 370 to/from a Soviet computer. IBM defined a byte as containing eight bits. However, the advanced Soviet BESM-6 used a 6-bit byte scheme and computers of the MINSK line (i.e., the MINSK-32) used a 7-bit byte. This compatibility of a byte size was eventually worked out by designing different hardware components on the Soviet end to do a translation from "west technology" to "east technology".

Computing in the Soviet Union was getting more organized, with countries producing the following:

- Hungary – the ES-1010, ES-1012, and ES-1015 for remote IBM remote processing
- German Democratic Republic – the ES-1045, ES-1055, and the ES-5017 tape drive
- Poland – the ES-7033 printers
- Czechoslovakia – scanning and console terminals
- Russia – card readers/punches, and some ES models

The 1976 Elektronika-60 computer line of systems (which consisted of the 60M and 60T) could execute 250K to 300K instructions per second. It came with 4K x 16-bit RAM, but could be expanded to 32K x 16-bit RAM. This machine was built to compete against DEC's PDP-11. It also gave the world the first Tetris game! The Elektronika-60-1 and the Elektronika-80 small computer systems followed, eventually evolving into the Electronika-85 personal computer (Soviet analogy of DEC's 350 PRO).

These computers used a proprietary operating system called DOS 3.1 or OS 6.1, both developed by Czechoslovakia and Hungary. OS 6.1 could support a whopping 100GB of virtual memory. In 1979, Russia was developing its own computers focusing on telecommunications only.

In 1975, the Elektronika D3-28 came out. In approximately 1976 (and manufactured through 1977), the C50 computer superseded the D23-28. This was a true desktop, stand-alone computer system, and was meant to be either a very expensive (in terms of size and function) calculator, or a personal computer. Its design was based upon the Wang 700 programmable calculator and came with a keyboard (including programmable function keys), a two-line display, and magnetic tape drive that used standard cassette tapes. It also had an interface that allowed a printer to be connected to it. Standard was 16K of RAM, but it was expandable to 128K RAM. Yes, it even had its own proprietary mouse.

In 1979, the Elektronika T3-29 was introduced, and was put together in a self-contained package of all components. It had a full monitor that could display graphics in addition to characters, a keyboard, and dual cassette tapes for storage and retrieval. It used the Russian 589 microprocessor running at 6 MHz, and could support up to 256K of RAM. The T3-29M computer was similarly packaged.

The world was about to change in 1979 when Russia invaded Afghanistan. Because of this, the U.S. (and allies) insisted that all business discussions and computer assistance going on between IBM and Soviet computer scientists cease immediately. Computer parts and assembled computers being exported to Russia came to a standstill. The Soviet Union, by now, though, had a firm grasp on computer technology, and could produce what they needed from a military perspective. As the Russian war wound down, computer business resumed to them. As the Soviet Union became more open and moved into international banking and business, it turned to outside computer makers to supply those needs.

Slightly behind the curve in microprocessor usage and design, in 1980, the U880 8-bit microprocessor was introduced by the German Democratic Republic. This was an almost exact clone of the Zilog 8-bit microprocessor, and adhering to the rigid design criteria set by the computer ministries, it had to be built to withstand extreme temperatures (apparently what is said about Siberian winters is true). The ball was now rolling fast, and other clones of microprocessors followed. The platypus was dead, as computer standards drove the Soviet computer designs.

As you can see, the Soviet Union was very active in computer development—it's just that most outside (and even inside) the Soviet Union didn't know it. Almost all computer work was driven by military needs, and ones not specifically for military use were used "for the people" in some way—but definitely not in a commercial sense. Obviously, the Soviet Union went on to develop more powerful systems after the 1970s, and at last check, the country was still in business and will be for a long time.

Sparck Jones, Karen

This entry is unique from all of the other entries in this book. The reason is that Sparck Jones never produced a hardware or software product; rather she wrote a book that was to have a profound influence on how later generations of computers would search for information.

When most scientists were trying to make people use code to talk to computers, Karen Sparck Jones taught computers to understand human language instead. Let that sink in for a moment. As you have read throughout this book, computers store, read, and transmit data in 1's and 0's—the basic building blocks of all data. Sparck Jones took this to another level in that she wanted computers to somehow understand actual words.

A little background on her early life: Karen Ida Boalth Sparck Jones was born on Aug. 26, 1935, in the textile manufacturing town of Huddersfield, England. Her parents were Alfred Owen Jones and Ida Sparck. Alfred was a chemistry lecturer, and Ida worked for the Norwegian government in London during World War II. While studying at Cambridge, Sparck Jones had the good fortune to meet the head of the Language Research Unit, Margaret Masterman, who succeeded in getting Sparck Jones interested in the world of linguistics.

By the early 1950s, computers had intrigued Sparck Jones, and she closely examined how they worked—namely, how they interpreted commands and stored data. In 1958, she married Roger Needham, a fellow computer scientist, and kept her maiden name—a very unusual occurrence for women at that time. "It maintains a permanent existence of your own," she later said.

Not only was Sparck Jones a self-taught programmer, but she also was an advocate for women to excel in the sciences. Additionally, Sparck Jones saw in the future computers perhaps having too much data that might shape peoples' lives—and she warned anyone who would listen about the social implications of such data carelessly used.

In 1964, Sparck Jones published "Synonymy and Semantic Classification." In this paper, she laid the foundation for how natural language could be processed by computers.

Many academic computer scientists in the 1970s were starting to grasp what the microprocessor was capable of doing, but Sparck Jones' seminal 1972 paper in the Journal of Documentation stood out.

The Intel microprocessor had been on the market for only two years. During that time, she started to explain the significance of how, in the hands of creative people, a powerful and interesting little computer chip could be programmed to do extraordinary things of which big computers (and big computer companies) had not even conceived. In her article she laid the groundwork for the modern companies such as Google, Yahoo, and others that provide internet search engines. (To be clear, she saw computer-to-computer communications as important, but to her it was irrelevant—it was all about the data the computers held and how it could be accessed with words such as "how does the atom work?") In her article she took the unusual approach of combining statistics with linguistics to establish formulas that embodied principles for how computers could interpret relationships between words.

"Anything that does index-term weighting using any kind of statistical information will be using a weighting function that I published in 1972," she said in a 2007 interview with the British Computer Society. Later, for an oral history interview for the History Center of the Institute of Electrical and Electronics Engineers, she said, "All words in a natural language are ambiguous; they have multiple senses. How do you find out which sense they've got in any particular use?"

Sparck Jones wasn't done yet. She continued working on early speech recognition computer systems in the 1980s. In

1982, the British government asked Sparck Jones to work on the Alvey Program (a project to encourage more computer science research across the country). In 1993, she co-authored (with Julia R. Galliers), *Evaluating Natural Language Processing Systems*.

She was just getting warmed up. Sparck Jones became president of the Association for Computational Linguistics in 1994 and a full-time professor at Cambridge in 1999.

On April 4, 2007, Sparck Jones died of cancer, at the relatively young age of 71. Researchers today are still citing her formulas. Her ideas continue to be put into practice as artificial intelligence work is examined more and more.

Figure 135- Karen Sparck Jones

Martha Palmer, a professor in the Linguistics and Computer Science departments at the University of Colorado, said, "It points to how far ahead of her time she was, how consequential her work was, how little it was valued for the first 20 years."

Sparck Jones impacted generations of researchers. Decades before Silicon Valley was coming to the realization that computers could sneak into the private lives of the masses, Sparck Jones cautioned engineers to think of their work's impact on society. "There is an interaction between the context and the programming task itself," she said. "You don't need a fundamental philosophical discussion every time you put finger to keyboard, but as computing is spreading so far into people's lives, you need to think about these things."

She was a woman who spoke up and spoke her mind, and had (and continues to have) an immense impact on how computers retrieve data. She got little credit when she was alive and trying to get companies to use her ideas. Hopefully, those reading this section will remember her for the impact she started to have on the 1970s computer companies.

The next time you ask Google or Apple's SIRI a question and it spits out an answer for you, think back to this amazing woman who had planted this seed some forty years earlier.

Sperry/Rand/Sperry Rand/UNIVAC

While this company is fairly easy to describe, it is hard to call the company by a single name. The reason is because since its beginnings in 1910, it has been known by a number of names, including these three—Sperry, UNIVAC, and Unisys—each of which have name recognition even now.

To start somewhere, though, is to start with Elmer Sperry. In 1910, Elmer (who was both an inventor and businessman) founded the Sperry Gyroscope Company, which made gyro-compasses and other direction-finding devices.

Shift to the early 1920s where the Rand-Kardex Corporation owned the Rand-Kardex office machine business. James H. Rand, Jr. built a $10-million business based on his father's patented recordkeeping system. In 1927, Rand-Kardex merged with five different companies: Remington Typewriter, Dalton Adding Machine Company, Powers Accounting Machine Corporation, and the Safe Cabinet Company. The new combined company was Remington Rand.

Taking another step sideways, Remington had not only made typewriters since 1873, but also was involved in the production of rifles. If you think the family tree has been complicated so far, it is about to get more so. The weapons and typewriter business was good enough to provide Remington with enough funds to buy out the following competition:

- Standard Typewriter Company
- Yost Writing Machine Company
- Monarch Typewriter Company
- Densmore Typewriter Company
- Smith Premier Typewriter Company

(Wouldn't it have been interesting if they would have merged technologies and developed a typewriter that could have fired fifty rounds of ammo a minute?)

The company plot thickens. In 1943, James Rand, chairman and president of Remington Rand, was approached by Loring P. Crosman, who had a plan to design and build an electronic computer for the U.S. government (which was just beginning to understand what a computer could provide it—especially after watching the wizards in England crack Germany's Enigma Machine). Remington Rand was known in the business world for its 90-column punch-card tabulating equipment, so the merger of this equipment with some sort of computer only made sense to Crosman. Rand liked the idea of complementing technologies, and therefore began construction of a new laboratory in Norwalk, Connecticut. By the end of 1948, Crosman had shown that his computer design (to be called the Model 409) was sound and ready for production. The Model 409 was such an immediate success that designs for enhanced versions began.

In 1950, awash with money and needing a place to invest it, Remington Rand purchased the Eckert-Mauchly Computer Company. (Coincidently, its ENIAC computer, built in 1946, was designed and built by J. Presper Eckert and John Mauchly.) This newly acquired company became the UNIVAC[104] division, where both of these aforementioned men subsequently lent their skills to build the first commercially available computer (at least in the U.S.) called the UNIVAC I in 1951. A total of forty-six of them were eventually sold between 1951 and 1958. In 1953, the next model (the UNIVAC 120) was delivered. Approximately 1,000 of these computers were sold before the UNIVAC 1004 came out in 1955. Just so you are keeping up, now we have Remington Rand (made up of several companies), with a division called UNIVAC.

In 1952, Remington Rand bought yet another company — Engineering Research Associates (ERA). ERA was a leader in designing and manufacturing electronic communications and cryptographic equipment.

When Sperry (the gyro-compass company) joined Remington Rand in 1955, the name of this whole collection of companies was changed to Sperry Rand. Over the years, Sperry Rand became an old-fashioned conglomerate of disharmonious divisions (computers, typewriters, office furniture, hay balers, manure spreaders, gyroscopes, avionics, radar, electric razors, etc.). The company dropped the Rand from its title and reverted to Sperry Corporation, and it made a variety of computer equipment, including the Sperry Personal Computer. Then, to assist with "corporate identity," the name was again changed to Sperry UNIVAC.

Jumping backwards, and aside from all the name changes and acquisitions, during the late 1950s and 1960s, UNIVAC (still a division of Sperry) produced a series of mainframe computers meant to compete head-on with IBM's wonderfully marketed system, the IBM 360. With significant success (albeit by having to win a few lawsuits against IBM), UNIVAC grew its customer base. In doing

---

[104] UNIVAC was an acronym for UNIVersal Automatic Computer.

so, it continued to make improvements with the hardware, operating systems, and compiler languages. Its 1100 Series was quite popular during the '60s, and this carried over into the '70s with its 1108 and 1108 continuing to be marketed.

In the 1960s, UNIVAC was one of the eight major American computer companies in an industry then referred to as "IBM and the Seven Dwarfs," a play on Snow White and the Seven Dwarfs, with IBM (by far the largest computer company) being cast as Snow White, and the seven companies—Burroughs, UNIVAC, NCR, CDC, GE, RCA and Honeywell—as the dwarfs. In the 1970s, after GE sold its computer business to Honeywell and RCA sold its computer line to UNIVAC, the analogy to the seven dwarfs became less apt, and the remaining smaller firms became known as the BUNCH (Burroughs, UNIVAC, NCR, Control Data Corporation, and Honeywell).

On to the 1970s, when in 1972, the UNIVAC 1110 was introduced. This machine could allow multiple programs to execute simultaneously; it allowed sixteen access paths to memory for these programs. The intent for these multiple parts of a processor was to enable multiple events (instructions) to be processed at the same time, thus eliminating bottlenecks for contention of these processor parts.

Operating system designers were getting smarter. The 1110 also had extended memory cabinets, which allowed more memory to be added.[105] The 1120 (the next generation of the UNIVAC 1110) introduced an extension to the basic instruction set that most computers used, and this new feature allowed more custom operations done by it than other makers of computers. The UNIVAC 1110 had four base and limit registers, so a program could access

---

[105] Keep in mind that memory was not a single chip as we think of today in our laptops. In the 1970s, memory was physically large—sometimes a foot square, and some only supplied 16K of data storage.

four 64K banks of memory. The company sold a total of 290 processors in the UNIVAC 1110 series.

The UNIVAC 1100 series ran a custom operating system(s) designed by UNIVAC engineers. It ran either EXEC II or EXEC 8. EXEC 8 enabled simultaneous handling of real-time applications, timesharing, and background batch work.

UNIVAC also produced a product called Transaction Interface Package (TIP), which allowed for a transaction processing environment (lots of small transactions such as millions of credit card charges all flowing into the system at once). It offered FORTRAN and COBOL compilers, which meant that users could write programs more easily than in the harder Assembly language that some computer makers required. On later systems, EXEC 8 was renamed either OS 1100 or OS 2200, with modern descendants maintaining backwards compatibility. UNIVAC even developed an operating system called RTOS, which allowed programmers to write applications that performed with even faster execution times. (RTOS, though, was usually limited to scientific work only, so only a few of the 1100 Series ended up with this operating system configured on them.)

In 1974, Sperry announced a small minicomputer called the AN/UYK-15 (V). This was not an easy commercial name to roll off a tongue, although I'm sure it perfectly described some specification the government had, as that is exactly for whom it was built. It had a 16-bit processor, allowed for expandability with added peripherals (e.g., printers, magnetic storage, etc.), had extra fans for cooling, fit in a 19-inch rack, met military requirements that withstood being dropped, and came in a case that could be locked. This product was used for signal processing, radar processing, air traffic control, navigation, telemetry, ship instrumentation, range tracking, and data management.

The AN/UYK-15 (V) had the following technical specifications:

- 8-bit byte, 16-bit, and 32-bit operands
- One to four sets of 16-bit general registers
- Program status register
- 4-level interrupt processing by hardware
- Both 16-bit and 32-bit instruction length
- Memory of 8K to 65K
- One to four I/O channels
- I/O channel priority interrupts
- 115V power supply
- Weighed 170 pounds
- FORTRAN IV compiler
- Various tools such as text editors, debuggers, and other utilities

The company introduced a new series of machines in 1975, with semiconductor memory replacing the bulky core memory. An upgraded UNIVAC 1106 was called the UNIVAC 1100/10. In this new naming convention, the final digit represented the number of CPUs in the system; for example, a two-processor 1100/10 system was designated an 1100/12. An upgraded 1108 was called the UNIVAC 1100/20. An upgraded 1110 was released as the UNIVAC 1100/40. The UNIVAC 1100/60 was introduced in 1979.

The 1980s brought more products of the UNIVAC 1100 line, and in 1982 the 1100-90 liquid-cooled model was announced. In 1986, Sperry Corporation merged with Burroughs Corporation to become Unisys. Many people in the computer industry today will recognize the name Unisys, which is an acronym for UNIted SYStems. Today, Unisys is primarily a consulting company, but it also still sells small computer systems, which are configured with commercially available processors and storage devices.

Sphere Corporation

Based in Bountiful, Utah, in 1975 this company produced several products—mostly surrounding its Sphere 1 system. The Sphere 1 was a self-contained, nicely packaged machine (where the monitor was integrated into the cabinet that also housed the keyboard)[106]. The Sphere 1 used a Motorola 6800 microprocessor, had an onboard ROM, a monitor (limited to 16 lines by 32 characters wide—ASCII only), 4K to 32K RAM, a keyboard with a numeric keypad, serial I/O that could connect up to four floppy disk drives, and operating system written in BASIC. A single kit version sold for $860, or an assembled one for $1,400. A clustered version was offered for $11,300. A clustered version could have up to eight Sphere 1's connected together.

Figure 136—Sphere 1

Additionally, Sphere sold a bare-bones computer board ($350 for a box of parts, or $520 assembled), and a computer board with an added 1K PROM that came loaded with nice tools such as debugging, editing, etc. ($522 unassembled, or $622 assembled).

---

[106] As mentioned throughout this book, ideas were plentiful and some people (companies) borrowed freely others' ideas. The Sphere 1, along with such nicely packaged products like the Sycor models, made buying a fully integrated system easy for the user. Two years later the Apple II was introduced, emulating this pre-packaged design.

A Sphere 2 was a Sphere 1 with a serial communications, audio cassette, or modem interface. A Sphere 3 was a Sphere 2 with more memory (20K RAM), and a more robust BASIC compiler. A Sphere 4 was a Sphere 3 with an added dual floppy disk, a disk-based operating system, and a 65-lines-per-minute line printer.

Speaking of keypads, Sphere did something unique — it wired two keyboard keys in a series, and when both were pressed at the same time, the system would reboot. Maybe this was done because the reset or on/off button were too far away for the user to reach, or perhaps it was just an inventive programmer and hardware designer. The next time you hit CTL-ALT-DEL to reset your computer, think of Sphere.

The Spheres (1-4) were last sold in 1977 after failing to gain much attraction in a growing field of "personal" computers.

Spiras Systems, Inc.

Spiras, based in Waltham, Massachusetts, was an affiliate of USM Corporation. In 1970, the company sold the Spiras-65 computer.

While no one accused the company of copying the Digital PDP-8 rack-mounted design, one could tell that the product had a serious influence on the Spiras-65 design. It had a panel of only a few switches, a numeric keypad, and a few buttons. Primarily the Sprias-65 was a real-time processor (meaning it monitored "events", and if something abnormal happened, it triggered an interrupt that the Spiras-65 would notice and take some programmatic action). They also marketed it as a "general" computer, but in actuality it was more suited for real-time event monitoring. It could be mounted in a rack or as a desktop (as shown below on left). It weighed 100 pounds, making a very hard to move around piece of furniture.

Spiras also made the Spiras IRASCOPE (shown on the right). This product served as a data entry or monitoring peripheral to the Spiras-65.

Figure 137—Spiras-65 and Spiras IRASCOPE

The Spiras-65 had 4K to 56K of 16-bit memory, hardware arithmetic with double precision and floating point, direct memory controllers, hardware priority interrupts, a 200+ instruction set, and a three-week training course. The cost started at $14,400, but with a paper-tape reader and more memory the cost was over $20,000. The Spiras IRASCOPE sold for $6,000.

It used the IDEAL instruction set, which allowed for custom instructions to be added for specialized work. It came with a FORTRAN compiler.

Standard Computer Corporation

This Santa Ana, California, company was formed either in 1968 or 1969. In 1969, Standard Computer developed a computer system called the MLP-9000. While only one was ever produced, it was the genesis of more ideas within the company.

In 1970, Standard Computer produced the IC-7000. This product was marketed as a timesharing system with a microprocessor that could have up to 256K, 36-bit words. The problem was that this company had its feet firmly planted in 1960's technology and thinking.

First, it included a paper-tape reader/punch; second, it bought its keyboard/printer assembly from Teletype. So, it now had a noisy, clunky machine, and the trend was toward a visual CRT, magnetic storage, and a quiet keyboard.

Figure 138—Standard Computer IC-7000

The gold of this system was what was under the cover. What set this system apart from others at the time was that it came with a very sophisticated file system (software), which allowed for very creative random retrievals of data. In today's SQL world, queries like "Select x, y, and z," or "Select all but not j" are fairly normal, but in 1970, Standard Computer was a file/query system ahead of its competition by five years. The file system came with three levels of security, which also made it attractive to many users (including governments). This is another example where a company was sitting on a wealth of technology (this time with software) and didn't know how to exploit it.

Sugarman Laboratories, Inc.

Based in Plainview, New York, in the mid-1970s, this company produced the Series 4000 CRT Data Terminals. What set this product apart from other CRT microprocessor-based terminals is that it offered local storage, unique software, and special keys on the keyboard to flip from page to page, scroll, text edit, page justify, and other word-processing features ahead of other products on the market. Other computers such as Wang were taking note and would build companies worth millions of dollars on these ideas.

Sweda International, Inc.

This company was a division of Litton. (In some ads one could see the name spelled Litton-Sweda, or Sweda Litton.) It was based in Pine Brook, New Jersey, and created several computer-related products.

In the early 1970s, it marketed a stand-alone (add-on) floppy drive, which was manufactured in Japan. This was an excellent idea at the time as both hobbyists and business people wanted extra storage for data or programs. By the time the mid-1970s rolled around, the company had branched out into offering a point-of-sale (POS) system called the Series 600. (This system was used for retail counter sales.)

Two models rolled out in 1976: the 600/60 and 600/80 (both 32-bit processors). These were aimed at the retailer who basically wanted a stand-alone system to collect data and then be able to query it. A minicomputer wouldn't be complete without storage and terminals, and Sweda offered its Series 600 terminal for data entry/querying. (For some reason known only to the engineers who designed this system, it came with a minimum of nine terminals — but one could add seven more.)

Both the 600/60 and 600/80 had a communications controller, which allowed connectivity to an IBM 360 or 370. Transmission speeds were available in 2,400 or 9,600 baud. The Series 600/80 had more disk storage than the 600/60.

A typical eight-lane POS 600/60 system cost $33,000, which was very reasonably priced compared to other small minicomputers on the market at the time. Sweda even offered an optical scanner that read UPC symbols, and the scanned information could then be stored in a local database. What made its scanner unique at the time was that it was an "omnidirectional" scanner. What this meant is that unlike some scanners that forced a bar code to be flat when it passed over the scanner, Sweda's also could read the bar code if it was located on the side of a package.

Sycor, Inc.

Sycor was founded in 1966 by an ex-HP manager, Samuel N. Irwin. Its headquarters was in Ann Arbor, Michigan, and at one time employed over 2,000 people—making it the largest private company in the city. Irwin was an engineer by training, but in talking with ex-employees, they describe him as having that "entrepreneurial spirit"; in other words, he knew exactly where he wanted to go with his ideas. While California had Stanford and the northeast U.S. had MIT for breeding grounds of computer scientists, Michigan had Ann Arbor. Irwin, a graduate of the University of Michigan, decided to base his company in Ann Arbor because he was confident in the quality of computer people he could attract to his new company. His intuition was accurate, as Irwin ended up hiring some excellent engineers from nearby universities—Eastern Michigan University (five miles away) and the University of Michigan (a mere two miles away). The engineers took Irwin's idea for an intelligent workstation and starting designing one; the result was the Sycor 240 delivered to the market in 1974.

Some could argue (quite successfully) that Sycor made one of the first commercial PCs. Although it was nothing like today's PCs (mainly in size and portability), it had all the features of a current-day PC. It was self-contained in a cabinet, could be programmed via a language called Terminal Application Language (TAL), had a built-in keyboard and monitor, it could store data (although it was limited to the technology of the time, which meant either a floppy disk or a cassette tape), and it had serial ports for connecting a printer or communications line. The 240 could be classified as a "smart" terminal because it could be programmed essentially like today's PCs.

A stand-alone terminal product, the Model 250 followed the 240. The 250 didn't have cassette drives or local storage (other than limited memory), rather it was designed to be compatible with IBM's 3270 terminal (with an added feature, though). The 250 could be programmed with Sycor's invented Field Instruction Language (FIL). The selling points of the 250 were: 1) It cost less than an IBM 3270 terminal, and 2) since it could be programmed, it could eliminate data entry errors. A printer, badge reader, and light pen were optional peripherals that could be purchased.

In 1975, the Sycor 440 was announced; this was followed by the Sycor 445 in 1976. Both of these products were a clustered system, where Sycor terminals could be connected to a central processor and data could be shared with the terminal users. The 440 supported four "dumb" terminals made specifically for this system; it had a communications port to connect to a host system (e.g., IBM, using the IBM 2780 or IBM 3780 protocol), a cassette storage system, and a 5MB magnetic disk (optional 10MB available). It could be programmed in Sycor's TAL II language. One of its key features was that it allowed multiple, different jobs (applications) to run at the same time.

Figure 139—Sycor 440 Cluster, Sycor 290 Cluster, Sycor 350 PC

The Sycor 445 was similar in concept to the 440, except that it had a faster processor (the Intel 8080), and it could support sixteen "dumb" terminals. It could be configured with up to 256K of RAM memory, and had a 10MB disk in a single 14-inch platter. The CPU was actually made up of three separate circuit boards. Each board was approximately 8 inches square. Two of the boards held the Intel 8080 processor (supporting chips for things such as prefetching and clocking), and the third board held memory chips (which could hold one to four rows of 64K each[107]). There were approximately sixteen extra card slots making up the backplane, with each slot being custom-wired to do a certain function.

The Intel 8080 could address just 64K of memory, so Sycor's engineers custom-built a memory manager capable of addressing up to 512K of memory. (What this meant was that larger and more programs could be run at once.) This feat by itself positioned Sycor well ahead of its competitors. The hardware used around the 8-bit microprocessor always did the memory fetches two bytes at a time, and kept the additional byte in cache just in case it might be needed. The O/S pre-fetched up to 16 bytes (or eight 16-bit words) of program, since it was more efficient to have the instructions in the CPU itself rather than have

---

[107] When the Intel 80386 came out years later, computer designers were impressed with the pre-fetching it did; Intel never admitted to actually designing this, but rather was vague about how it gathered ideas on how to do it. In reality, the software engineers working on the 445 had beaten the industry in their design to make a CPU run faster.

to wait to fetch them from memory or disk when needed.[108]

The 445 didn't have any BIOS like we think of today when we turn on a computer. The 445 had to be initialized by a disk containing the operating environment each time it was powered on. The 445 could be programmed with COBOL (from the Ryan McFarland Company) or Sycor's proprietary TAL. The 445 had its own custom and proprietary operating system. While the Sycor 445 was a nice product in terms of price and features, it needed faster technology in the form of a central processor to make it a better performing machine. As with many technology companies at the time, ideas at companies such as Sycor were outpacing CPU manufacturers' technology.

Sycor carved out a niche for making robust and extremely easy-to-use systems (both with its PC and its clustered servers). Datapoint sued Sycor for patent infringement in 1977 and, in the end, the court ruled against Datapoint making it immediately liable for $7.5 million and other payments. Over the next ten years those fines would amount to close to $30 million.

In 1978, Sycor was bought by Northern Telecom, Inc. and ceased to exist under the Sycor name.

Sylvania

This company's involvement with computers started with Ultronic Systems. Ultronic was formed in 1960 to produce a stock-quoting machine and to sell services to financial institutions. In 1961, its product, the STOCKMASTER, was

---

[108] An operating system brings in an instruction from a program that someone has written, and then it executes it. The operating system's writers reasoned quite logically that the CPU could be made to get instructions faster if the CPU had ready access to the next instruction(s)—therefore, terms like "pre-fetching" and "pipe-lining" came into being to make a program execute faster.

ready to be installed in brokerage houses, and by 1967, the company had produced 10,000 of these products. During the next few years, products with the catchy names of LECTRASCAN and MARKETMASTER followed the successful STOCKMASTER.

In 1967, Sylvania purchased Ultronic. Later that year, this Moorestown, New Jersey, company offered a low-cost, stand-alone display that could connect to an IBM host or other servers using the IBM 3270 protocol. What it considered "low-cost," though, was expensive for most. Its product, the Videomaster 7000 terminal, sold for a healthy $5,000. The terminal could display up to 960 characters, and came with a full alphanumeric keyboard; the cursor could be positioned with arrow keys. The display itself only had a footprint of 12 in. x 12 in.

Figure 140—Sylvania Ultronic Videomaster 7000

In 1974, Sylvania applied for a patent for a small minicomputer that could connect four terminals and four printers. It is unknown what marketing name was given to this system.

Sylvania held on to the Ultronic products until the early 1980s when Sylvania finally decided to close the Ultronic business as competition was too fierce with the personal computers in the market.

Sysmo Company

This France-based company was but a footnote in the world of computers in the '70s, except that in 1975 it introduced to Europe a wonderfully packaged true personal computer (although pricey, selling at over $9,000). This start-up company was located in Paris, and founded and funded by Michel Carlier. Carlier was an engineer who also had invested in Micro Computer Machines, a Canadian company.

Micro Computer Machines allowed Sysmo to market its MCM/700 computer (under the name Sysmo). Not only was it nicely packaged, but it also had many extra features that could have positioned it for growth in the business world (except for the myopia of Canadian investors). In France, the machine was sold to manage applications while it was programmed with a complex scientific language (APL), which made it much better adapted to scientific and technical fields (e.g., architect design). In a business domain, the extreme slowness of the external memory (cassettes) was prohibitive. For example, it took fifteen minutes to print a pay slip — much more time than a bookkeeper would take doing it manually.

Sysmo filed for bankruptcy in 1978 since sales never took off; at the same time, Micro Computer Machines was on the ropes financially back in Canada (so no additional machines were being shipped to Sysmo). The stock of Micro Computer Machines/Sysmo machines was bought by the French company Generale d'Electricite (later Alcatel) for its own use, and seemed delighted with the machine's mathematical power. Basically, one could feed it a mathematical problem and let it churn on it for a few minutes or hours — time was not important in most of the mathematic work being done, and the engineers were very pleased with the results.

Systems Engineering Laboratories (SEL)

Located in sunny Fort Lauderdale, Florida, this company was founded around 1960. Engineering products were its primary focus (hence the use of that term in the company name), and it went on to produce several well-received products for that area of work.

The company's first product was the Systems Engineering Laboratories (SEL) 820. (This product was custom-built for one customer, so it never became commercially available.) Other products such as the 810A, 840A, 8500, and 8600 followed. The 840A used core memory and had wire-wrapped circuit boards. The 840A offered 24K of RAM, and all four systems used a 16-bit processor. All of these systems included (or had as options) a 24-bit magnetic disk, 9-track magnetic tape, card reader/punch, 300-line-per-minute printer, and other communication interface controllers.

In 1970, the Systems 86 was produced to compete head-on with scientific work that Xerox and IBM offered with their systems. In a 1970 ad, SEL challenged both of these companies to run the same FORTRAN IV program and see which machine performed better. (I couldn't find any results, but one can assume that SEL was confident in the outcome.)

The Systems 86 also offered Assembler, BASIC, and FORTRAN IV compilers. Its system came with a math library of functions, and special hardware diagnostic tools.

In 1975, the Model 32/55 came out. It was a 32-bit minicomputer, and offered a bus speed of 26.6MB per second. The Model 32/75s and Model 32/27 came out as improvements were made in how the backplanes were simplified for manufacturing. Semiconductor memory replaced the core memory from the 32/75 model. All Model 32 systems offered 24-bit instructions and 16MB addressing.

In 1981, SEL was sold to Gould Electronics. In 1989, Gould sold its stake in the engineering products to Encore Computer Corporation, where finally the products were sold off to other companies.

TAB Products Company

This company was founded in Palo Alto, California, by two former IBM salesmen, with an intent to supplement the punched card with computer-related punched-card boxes and containers.

No matter how good companies got at storing punched cards and creating color-coded ways to find these cards, there was only so much money to be made from this line of work. TAB entered the computer product market in hopes of creating substantial revenue because it saw a need in this business area and no one else was doing it. By the time 1975 rolled around, though, punch-card processing was pretty much a dead technology — unfortunately, no one told this company. (Being based in Palo Alto, one would have thought it would have had its ear closer to the ground for new technology and ideas.)

The company's one computer-related product was called the Tab 501 Data Entry Microprocessor. Basically, this product was firmly planted in both the new and old world.

The 501 offered an intelligent keyboard for editing data and error correction as data was keyed in; it offered twenty-eight levels of programming. Instead of a display though (a CRT or some sort of monitor) so the user could see what was being typed, the data was punched directly onto a card, which then went into a hopper.

Figure 141—Tab 501

Tally Corporation

Tally was located in Kent, Washington, and was founded in 1949 by Philip Renshaw. Tally's initial products were a line of paper-tape readers. While these products were a success (and satisfied a need at the time in the market) in the 1950s and 1960s, technology was changing and paper tapes were not the accepted storage media going into the 1970s.

Branching out in 1970, Tally developed a successful line of dot-matrix printers. Also at this time, it produced the Tally 1021 Batch Terminal. It was a stand-alone terminal (not attached to a local minicomputer), and could transmit/receive at 1,200 baud. As options, it had interfaces to a paper-tape reader (no surprise, since it made these), a card reader (yet another dying technology), and magnetic tape recorder/reader. This terminal worked in two ways: 1) The operator could connect to a computer server and key in information directly on the server, or 2) data could be keyed and stored on some storage media where it could be batched later to a computer server.

In a 1970 ad, the company extolled the wonderful features of its product, and ended its ad with, "As a matter of fact, all you add is the girl." Yes, it was a wonderful, but embarrassing, time for advertising.

Figure 142—Tally 1021 Batch Terminal

With its excellent dot-matrix printer technology, Tally held on through 1979, as this was when it merged with Mannesmann Präzisiontechnik to form Mannesmann Tally (which was part of the Mannesmann Kienzle computer group in Germany). Mannesmann Tally (the merged company's name) offered printing solutions in all major technologies into all key markets, along with service and support.

In 1996, some managers bought out the printer products, and Tally was back in business — although this time its office was far from Washington; now it was located in Elchingen, Germany. Dot-matrix and inkjet printers were now produced and sold, and in 2003, the "new" TallyGenicom AG was formed out of a merger with the Genicom company. In 2009, TallyGenicom AG was acquired by Printronix, with TallyGenicom AG retaining the intellectual property and worldwide distribution rights for the TallyGenicom AG serial matrix, inkjet, and thermal technologies. Finally, DASCOM bought the rights in 2009, and DASCOM now markets the full range of the TallyGenicom AG serial, passbook, and mobile printers under the Tally brand name. Not bad for a small company with its roots in a little town in Washington.

Tandem Computers, Incorporated

On a sales trip to Singapore in the early 1970s, a group of HP salesmen heard tales of woe from their customers regarding how bad things happened to their respective businesses when their computers malfunctioned (a nice way of saying their computer "crashed"). Computers failing for whatever reasons were not uncommon in 1970's or even today – things happen. Components fail, software bugs happen, etc. HP's businesses' answers, of course, would be to either purchase two systems and keep one on standby if needed, and/or try to repair the broken system as fast as possible so the users could get back to work. Of course, this was not the first time the salesmen had heard of this problem, but what to do? With the exception of a very few computer makers, the whole idea of making a computer less error-prone was not needed as users were more or less accepting of the fact that computers failed (sort of like it is today when your PC crashes—there is a gnashing of teeth, but no one does anything to make it better). But, one of the salesmen questioned why a computer couldn't be built that could keep working if component failed. James Treybig, a graduate of Rice University in Houston, Texas, was a combination of engineer (who knew just enough about computers to understand them) and business man—a rare breed in those days, and even today.

Treybig left his job at HP soon after his return from Asia and went to work for the business consulting/investing company Kleiner and Perkins. After presenting a business plan to the company with a request for capital, Tandem Computers was officially formed in 1974. The name chosen because it meant "two".

To show the dynamics of the Silicon Valley, Tandem's original building in Cupertino, California, previously housed Four Phase Systems. After about a year of development in their new building, Tandem leased the back part of it to a small startup company called Apple.

Essentially, Tandem was based right at the heart of where other computer companies were trying to make a name for themselves. With a wonderful pool of creative engineers (many from nearby HP) dying to sink their teeth into ideas like developing a computer system that couldn't fail, work started in earnest to design and build this system.

The first core group was made up of Mike Green, Jim Katzman, Dennis McEvoy, Joel Bartlett, Dave Mackie, and Jack Loustaunou. Tandem's business plan called for systems that, in addition to not failing if any single[109] component failed, would process business transactions in real-time and promise that no transaction would be lost once it entered the system. An important part of its business plan also pointed out that this system had to be competitive from a pricing perspective; it anticipated a slightly higher cost of its system, but only marginally. Basically they were offering a lot more realibility at only a little more cost

As with other companies with a clean slate, the software and hardware engineers took this as a challenge to design an operating system and hardware components that could not only detect failures, but keep on running with no interruption to the users — and could even be repaired online (again, with no interruption to the users). The result was the first product called the Tandem/16 (or T/16, and was later renamed the NonStop I when the NonStop II came out). The smallest configuration came with two separate CPUs (of course) on two separate circuit boards (of course), in two separate cabinets with each having their own power supply (of course). Each CPU ran its own set of applications/programs and maintained its own

---

[109] The design was so solid that it turned out the system could actually withstand multiple failures of components, yet still keep running.

memory, which was not shared with any other processor; if any data or information was to be shared between applications running in different CPUs, it was sent (and received) over a proprietary bus connecting the CPUs. The idea behind this design was that if a CPU failed for any reason, the other CPUs would detect the failure and pick up the workload without any interruption to the users. The computer world was about to be introduced to a concept in reliability that no one had ever seen before.

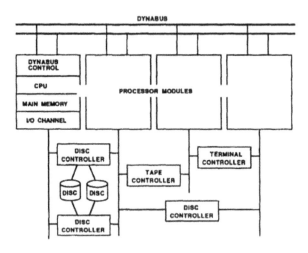

Figure 143—Original fault-tolerant design diagram

As one can see, every device had two access points. Even a disk drive's data could be mirrored on another disk while processing was occurring. All CPUs could communicate to all peripherals, such as disk drives, tape drives, and communication lines no matter what CPU controlled them, and pick up ownership of any device depending upon how the system was configured when it was started.[110] To have any CPU know what the other one was doing, and to be able share components across all of the

---

[110] At any given time, a peripheral could only be owned by one CPU, and all messages to and from it had to go through that CPU; if that CPU died (crashed), the other CPUs would detect this, and automatically reroute input/output messages to that peripheral through another CPU. Basically, Tandem had figured out a way to marry software and hardware fault-tolerance to a whole new level.

CPUs, required a new operating system to be built. Enter people like Bartlett who must have been yearning for such a project since leaving his old company. With input from others (and using his experience with his old company's HP 3000 as a loose guideline), Bartlett was the coordinator of a team to build a completely new operating system[111] almost from scratch. Within a year, the operating system had been written and tested. While using basic computer architectures that he knew should work with his design, he and his team enhanced the way it would have to work to provide complete fault tolerance. Remember, the engineers[112] at Tandem had a clean slate, and they made the most of being allowed to come up with very creative ideas. When it was all done, it was a stroke of genius. The operating system was called Guardian.

A new term called "fault tolerance" was in the press. This term described perfectly what Tandem's computer could provide to businesses' processing of transactions. In 1976, Citibank bought the world's first completely fault-tolerant computer. Tandem's sales soared as businesses realized the strength of being able to offer to their customers a system that never failed. For instance, this spawned successes for banks who could now offer automated teller machines (ATMs), airline reservations became more stable, and in general any business that wanted a leg up on its competition saw Tandem as being the company to get them there.

Tandem, though, was more than a computer company not only to those in the computer industry, but also to its employees and customers. Tandem had a unique culture

---

[111] First called the Tandem Transactional Operating system, and later renamed Guardian.

[112] Jim Treybig came from HP, and he knew where he could find excellent engineers to design and work on his new idea for a computer. To say he raided HP for his engineers might be slightly an overstatement, but somehow HP ended up losing a lot of high-caliber engineers to Tandem. HP was so irritated at this that they posted pictures of Treybig at all HP guard stations with instructions to escort him off of the property if he showed up.

that not only attracted the best and brightest, but also fostered a sense of true entrepreneurial thinking within the company itself. Keep in mind that Tandem, based in Cupertino (which also was home to Apple, Four-Phase Systems, and other startup companies), found itself competing for the high-quality people that these other companies also wanted. Tandem, to attract the caliber of people it was after, offered incentives such as paid sabbaticals, catalogs of gifts from which an employee could choose, stock ownership plans, weekly beer-busts on Friday afternoons, and in general, a very casual work environment. Tandem was a creative and fun place to work — setting the stage for the work environments seen later with Intel, Apple, Google, and others.

To revisit the Guardian operating system once more, some interesting features were created almost by accident as the fault-tolerance was put in place. Because of the way the operating system was designed, the engineers had put in place a system that could grow in size beyond anyone's dreams. After all, if two processors can exchange information on an on-going basis without disrupting the applications, why couldn't 16, or 64, or 256, or more processors act the same way? They quickly figured out that 4,096 processors could be configured, and with that, a vast array of peripherals and controller — again, all being shared within the fault-tolerant environment. In other words, the basic two-CPU Tandem system that was initially envisioned could easily grow to be the largest computer system in the world just by adding processors and other peripherals to it — all in a near-linear performance graph.

Figure 144—Tandem NonStop 1

Today the term "24x7" is used without much need for explanation—24 hours a day, 7 days a week. In the late 1970s, though, the world hadn't given much thought to this phrase until Tandem used it in its advertisements. Tandem had tremendous success with its ads, as it described perfectly that Tandem understood the need for companies to keep running constantly and consistently with no downtime.[113] Tandem rode the success of the NonStop I for five years. Newer and faster CPU chips (plus demands from customers for bigger and more powerful systems) drove Tandem to follow the success of the NonStop I with other systems (still using the Guardian operating system at its core), such as NonStop II, TXP, VLX, CYCLONE, CLX, K-series, and S-series.

Tandem did try its hand in the small PC market in the mid-1980s with the introduction of the IBM compatible Dynamite PC. It was, by all accounts, a "me-too, and lacked features" machine that attracted few buyers. Not learning its lessons from veering from what it did best, Tandem developed a new computer based upon the UNIX operating system in addition to the NonStop operating system. Neither the PC nor the UNIX-based operating

---

[113] Around 2005, at least two customers celebrated over 30 years without any unscheduled downtime using Tandem machines—in other words, although a component might have failed in this span of time, their Tandem systems never failed to keep running. So the next time you use the term "24x7" or hear someone use it, tip your hat to Tandem for adding this phrase to our vocabulary.

system ever sold more than a few units each. Tandem realized the error of its ways, and within two years had folded both projects (which were being developed at Tandem facilities in Austin, Texas).

In addition to hardware components that could communicate to a CPU and update its status, Tandem developed 1) a very successful database product called NonStop SQL, and 2) a product called Pathway that successfully competed against IBM's CICS for transaction processing.

By the mid-1990s, with competition coming from less expensive small servers and in general hardware being more reliable and cheaper, Tandem's sales were declining from a high of $2 billion in 1994. Additionally, Tandem's operating costs from years of careless spending caught up with it. Tandem was still a major player in the computer industry with a large and loyal customer base, though, and Compaq was a cash-rich company that wanted to expand its business. In 1997, Compaq bought Tandem Computers, and the name Tandem Computers faded away.

In 2002, Compaq was in turn swallowed up by HP, thereby taking Tandem full-circle from whence it came almost thirty years earlier. Today, NonStop computers (still known by that name affectionately by a few within HP and with its loyal customers) still enjoy success by offering fault-tolerant processing of transactions for leading companies around the world.

Tandy Corporation

Of all the strange starts into the world of electronics, Tandy ranks as one of the oddest. In 1919, two friends (Norton Hinckley and Dave L. Tandy) went into business selling leather supplies to shoe makers and shoe repair businesses throughout Texas, by driving from city to city.

Eight years later, they either had had enough of life on the road or their families were demanding more time together (or both), and they opened their first retail store in Beaumont, Texas. In 1932, Dave Tandy moved the store to Houston, Texas, as this was a much larger city with more potential for revenue.

Tandy's son Charles entered the family business around 1922. Charles took time away from the company when he joined the military during WWII—leaving the Navy as a lieutenant commander in 1948, and returning to the family business. But now he had ideas on expanding the business into the area of leathercrafts (which every Cub Scout remembers with fond memories as he punched and decorated a hard scrap of leather into a beautiful necklace for his mother). The business agreed to fund this new idea and made Charles the manager of this new division. With a small amount of funding from the parent company, Charles opened the first of two retail stores in 1950 that specialized exclusively in leathercraft. In 1950, the original partners went their separate ways, with Hinckley focusing on the shoe business, and the Tandy men pursuing strictly leathercrafts as a business. Tandy Leathercrafts was born.

Now, the story gets more interesting. As they opened new stores every few months, they knew their idea for craft stores was catching on. Charles had hit upon a market that had low overhead and reasonable profit. In 1955, Tandy Leathercrafts was purchased by the American Hide and Leather Company of Boston (becoming General American Industries in 1956). In an interesting series of events, Charles (using the business name Tandy Group) started buying up shares of his parent company, ending up with 500,000 shares. When a board of directors meeting was held in 1960, the Tandy Group had enough shares to assume control of General American Industries.

The plot thickens. Sales continued to grow, and in 1961, General American Industries was changed to Tandy Corporation, and the corporate headquarters was moved to Fort Worth, Texas. Charles was all about making his company the largest "crafts" reseller in the U.S. In addition to the 125 Tandy Leather stores operating in 105 cities in the U.S. and Canada, Tandy acquired other "crafts" companies. Now comes the interesting part with a link from leather to computers — this was done by consolidating myriad do-it-yourself kits (including small electronic components, namely vacuum tubes and testers for the TV explosion that was going on). In 1963, Tandy acquired a Boston company named Radio Shack, which sold radio equipment to ham operators and electronics buffs.

Radio Shack stores opened by the dozens throughout the U.S. and Canada, and profits soared from a seeming monopoly of selling crafts and electronic components. Tandy had enough entrepreneurial spirit left inside this now huge company to see the potential of money to be made in the up-and-coming personal computer market. Thus, in 1978, Tandy announced the fully assembled TRS80 computer for the unheard-of price of only $399. Tandy had projected sales of 3,000 for the first year, but it actually sold 10,000 units — showing the pent-up demand for people wanting their own personal computer (including keyboard and monitor) instead of the kits and systems that one had to buy, along with other components to make it all work. Apple had figured this out for its product using its proprietary operating system, and Tandy was now doing this for the Microsoft operating system world. The world also was about to change dramatically for the better for Microsoft.

Tandy's first PC only had a black-and-white monitor, but in 1980, a color option was added. IBM was setting the standards (such as they were in the early days of PCs) because of the sheer volume of PCs the company could produce, and if a PC maker wanted to be considered in business, then its machine had to be IBM-compatible (meaning that it ran applications that ran on the IBM PC and under the Microsoft operating system). While the TRS-80 did not fully adhere to IBM compatibility, Tandy's later versions (Tandy 1000 and Tandy 2000) did, and were marketed at less cost and with more features (namely with sound and graphics) than the IBM PC.

Figure 145—Tandy TRS80

The TRS-80, though, had quality issues, and it brought to mind for many the old adage, "You get what you pay for." Bad press was getting out about the TRS-80, and potential new buyers were asking themselves, "Should I pay a little more for a higher quality PC?" While sales started to falter, Tandy considered the TRS-80 a success from a pure total sales perspective, and it thus expanded its overall computer line with bigger monitors, faster CPUs, more memory, a notebook computer, and even a multi-user system.

In 1979, the original TRS-80 was fitted with a faster processor, better keyboard, an external cassette drive (with two game cartridges), and a 12-inch color monitor; it sold for $599. That same year it announced the Level-II TRS-80. This PC had everything the TRS-80 had, plus it had a numeric keypad, 16K of RAM, and 12K Level-II BASIC in ROM. All TRS-80 machines now could have (as an option) up to 48K of RAM. The latest model had interfaces built in for printers, one to four mini-disks (floppies), a telephone acoustic coupler, voice synthesizer, and dual cassette recorders. Also at this time, Tandy was realizing that software was helping to sell the hardware, so it was offering games and a general ledger application (with the promise of more games and applications being offered monthly).

Within the first few years of the TRS-80, over 55,000 consumers bought them to use in their home or office. Eventually, more than 250,000 of them were sold. In 1981, the TRS-80 was discontinued to make way for upgraded and more popular brands and models. All of this computer design work and manufacturing would prove to be a money drain on Tandy.

The Tandy Corporation by the mid-1980s was a large international company with subsidiaries doing business in many countries. Unfortunately, slowly (and too late) Tandy saw the foolishness of owning and operating stores that were attracting fewer and fewer walk-in customers wanting "crafts." Tandy tried to focus its energy and money on computers by opening up a chain of stores in the U.S. (called Circuit City); these also proved to be very unprofitable.

At the time of this writing, Tandy is now paying the price for not paying attention to competition (including the internet) and its undying devotion to its line of computers. Tandy found itself not understanding if it was a retail "crafts" store or a computer manufacturing company — and too much infighting for funding took its toll on both lines of business. Tandy has been out of the computer business for over a decade, and closed all of its retail stores. Its stock reached an all-time low of less than $1 in 2013, and in February 2015, it declared bankruptcy. In most companies, this would be the end of its story, but not in this case. Just as the phoenix rose from the ashes,

Standard General (a hedge fund company) stepped in and supplied needed capital to keep the name Radio Shack (along with approximately 2,000 craft-selling stores) alive long enough to sell its resources and real-estate.

Tektronix, Inc.

This Beaverton, Oregon, company marketed the Tektronix T4002 graphic computer terminal in the early 1970s. It was a one-piece, bulky cabinet (by most standards, even then) measuring 24 in. x 30 in. x 24 in. It came with a standard keyboard, separate numeric keypad, function control buttons, and a lock and key that secured the terminal from unauthorized use.

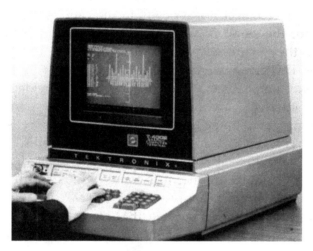

Figure 146—Tektronix T4002

A user could key in a line of data, have it buffered, and then transmitted with one button. This buffering sped up processing tremendously for data entry. It required an external modem for connecting to a host system. A claim to fame for this system was the way the CRT worked very uniquely. Unlike other monitors that had to be refreshed on a continuing basis, Tektronix promised none of that because its terminal had zero flickering, zero drifting, and was able to display 39 lines x 85 characters wide. The T4002 sold for $8,800.

Telefile Computer Products

This Irvine, California, company saw the growth in the minicomputer market, and chose its niche carefully on how to fit in it. Minicomputers were getting larger in processing power and disk storage needs, and those companies making them were all struggling with how to attach all of those disks to the actual CPU. Welcome to the world of "controllers."

Let's say you wanted to attach eight disc drives to a computer. Each of those drives requires some sort of interface to connect it physically to the cabinet. But discs were not the small floppies or cassettes of earlier years; rather, they were of significant size—e.g., 100MB or greater. Discs now were big and couldn't fit easily into a minicomputer cabinet. What a controller provides is a single interface on one end that connects to the minicomputer cabinet, and on the other end it has some number of devices to which it communicates. With Telefile's product, it could connect up to eight discs. It offered the DC-16 product that communicated with most 16-bit minicomputers, and the DC-18, DC-32, DC-36, and DC-10 products that connected IBM-compatible drives to DEC, Sigma, and UNIVAC computers.

Telefunken

In 1903, two competing telegraph companies (one in the UK and one in Germany) found themselves arguing over patent rights. Instead of digging trenches and lobbing bombs on each other (which would come about a mere eleven years hence), they worked it out. On the Germany side, the Gesellschaft für drahtlose Telegraphie System

Telefunken ("The Company for Wireless Telegraphy Ltd.") company was formed — with the name "Telefunken" meaning the company's actual telegraph address.

Telefunken eventually moved into radio and other electronic development areas for both consumer and military products. Jumping ahead through two world wars, it is time for another incest alert. Siemens owned many shares of Telefunken, and when it transferred its shares to AEG, this latter company became the owner of Telefunken (although the name Telefunken would remain until 1967, when it would officially be called AEG-Telefunken).

In the 1960s, Telefunken did some remarkable things — one being to develop the PAL[114] standard for color televisions. It also started to dabble in the world of computers, namely to combat the dominance of IBM. In 1963, it developed the TR 4, and this computer was sold through the mid-1980s at several universities in Germany. (Although by the time even the mid-1970s rolled around, this was a system with antiquated technology — namely paper tape.) Its engineering folks were bright and creative and developed their own "point-and-click" contraption called the Rollkugel (German for "rolling ball"); little did they know that years later, Apple (after seeing Xerox's version of a mouse) would use this idea to completely change how we communicate with a computer today.

---

[114] PAL means Phase Alternating Line. It is a standard for analog TVs to display color that was adapted in many parts of the world.

Figure 147—Telefunken TF 4

AEG-Telefunken had an agreement with Nixdorf Computer AG to work on a more competitive IBM product. AEG thus formed the Telefunken Computer GmbH (TC) division. The aim of this cooperation between the two companies was to develop an IBM-compatible system to attract IBM customers. The outcome was a product called the Telefunken TR 440. Development issues ensued, however, and in 1973, the German government (with country pride at stake) took over this division of AEG Telefunken.

In 1974, the development and manufacture of the TR 4, TR440, and any other computer work was separated into the Konstanz Computer Company (CGK). Nixdorf and Telefunken were both hungry to make a product to compete with IBM, so a strange pact (at least to this author) was reached between the parent company Telefunken and AEG-Telefunken. The agreement said that these two entities would share operating losses through 1973 (which amounted to $32.7 million), after which Nixdorf would take over supporting any losses. When AEG-Telefunken was bought by Daimler in 1985, Telefunken was dropped from the company name.

Teletype Corporation

American Telephone and Telegraph (AT&T) Company's Western Electric formed this company in 1930 after acquiring and keeping the name of the Teletype Corporation. AT&T was big (in terms of revenue) even then, and the federal government did not want it to stifle any competition from companies it acquired. Therefore, Teletype had its own R&D and sales force (which sold, coincidently, primarily to the federal government).

Teletype focused on printers at first, and then eventually added rudimentary keyboards to the products. It produced the Model 15 (of which over 200,000 were built for the military in WWII), Model 28 KSR, Model 32 ASR, Model 19, Model 20, Model 26, Model 28, Model 33 ASR, Model 35, Model 37, Model 37 KSR, Model 38, Dataspeed 40, Model 42, and Model 43, as well as the 4100 paper-tape models (4110 reader, 4120 punch, 4130 asynchronous reader, Inktronic, and the 4140 asynchronous punch). Each of these models improved on the previous model, so by the time 1970 rolled around, Teletype had very robust (but simple) machines for data entry. These devices acted as a console for several different computer makers, and as a time-share terminal for many computer labs in universities. One of the main reasons it was so successful was that it was dependable. Yes, it was slow with its printing like an electric typewriter (the early models had a wheel with all of the characters on it, and this wheel was constantly spinning and stopping to lay out a character on its 400-foot roll of paper).

The later models were trying to keep up with the microprocessor-based terminals on the market, and thus, all of the later models were programmable in BASIC. This meant that they could be custom-programmed to do certain editing and formatting functions instead of just keying and storing whatever was typed.

In 1970, this Skokie, Illinois, company was still trying to survive in a world that was passing it by. It had developed an absolute workhorse in its terminal that was created in the earlier years, but times were changing. Still, it was basic input and printing—hardly anything to get excited about, contrary to the guys in the following ad led its potential customers to believe.

Figure 148—Teletype Inktronic®

Teletype did alter its print-head technology by using inkjet technology—it claimed it could print out 1,200 words per minute (beating HP's "inkjet" technology by many years.) But using any paper to print what was being typed was "old school," as more intelligent terminals with CRT displays were becoming the norm. Still, with a Teletype machine one got both a data entry terminal and a printer all in one—something the "intelligent" terminal makers could not do without the user having to buy a separate printer to attach to the terminal.

The Teletype Corporation continued in operation until January 8, 1982, when Teletype Corporation became

AT&T Teletype. This latter company held on until 1990, but technology had passed it by. Of the three Teletype manufacturing buildings in Skokie, two have been demolished and one is used by a shopping center—where few (if any) people tread never knowing the remnants of the once great company had resided there.

Tempo Computers, Inc.

Tempo, based in Anaheim, California, created a communications concentrator-only minicomputer. A dilemma companies were starting to see was that more and more communication lines were needed to connect "smart" terminal control stations (minicomputers capable of having multiple terminals attached to them).

In 1970, the Tempo 1 was a minicomputer that was built primarily to connect communication lines from Point A to Point B. (These types of machines later became known as communication concentrators.) It had the capabilities of connecting up to 480 data lines, which was very impressive. Secondarily, this system also was designed to be a timesharing system (although with core memory, it was not capable of being fast enough to do much timeshare work).

Figure 149—Tempo 1

The Tempo 1 offered up to twenty-five hardware registers, memory access of 325 nanoseconds, and priority interrupt system that could interrupt the CPU within 2.3 microseconds. For the base price of $15,600, the user got 4K of core memory, a basic set of 100 instructions, FORTAN IV compiler, and the Teletype 33 ASR for input and output.

Texas Instruments (TI)

Texas Instruments was founded in 1951, with its roots fully entrenched in the world of electronic instrumentation. TI, as you will read here and in other books, is a company of many "firsts." TI had a huge impact on the computer industry by employing Jack Kilby as one of its engineers. Kilby was given credit for inventing (actually, "perfecting" might be a better descriptive word here, as others around this same time were working on what Kilby was doing) a little thing called the integrated circuit (IC). The IC (whomever one wants to give credit for inventing it) changed the world. An IC reduces circuitry size, dramatically decreases energy usage, and exponentially increases speed.

While the military was keenly interested in the IC, Texas Instruments was busy trying to figure out a commercial use for this technology. Enter the world of TVs and transistor radios (the world's first in 1954), and don't forget the omnipresent calculator market, of which TI marketed the first "hand-held" version in 1967.

TI kept tinkering with miniaturization, and in 1971 came out with its own (and only one on the market) single-chip microcomputer. Let this sink in for moment. Intel and Motorola were working together to develop their own microcomputer, but these invariably involved many chips — and TI integrated all of the necessary components into one chip. It was so far ahead of the competition that it was assigned (on September 4, 1973) the first patent recognizing this feat of engineering.[115] Now that TI had the "microprocessor chip," what to do with it? They could make faster and smaller calculators (which it did), but you have to give it to TI's thinkers when they started playing around with computer voice generation (and recognition).

In the early 1970s, TI introduced a small and rugged, portable, "dumb" terminal called the Silent 700, meaning it could communicate with a host computer by using a simple protocol. It consisted of a keyboard and a built-in printer, so one could see what was typed and sent from the host computer, all packaged neatly in a plastic case. It was very similar to the Teletype machine that had been on the market for a decade, except that this machine was very quiet — hence the name "silent" given to it.

In 1974, the "intelligent" version of the Silent 700 came out. It was a programmable workstation that included two cassette drives from which to load custom programs and store data (and looked very similar to the Sycor 240). This new Silent 700 had 10K of RAM, and could be programmed using the Texas Instruments Cassette

---

[115] Gilbert Hyatt, formerly of the Micro Computer Company, in August 1990, disputed TI's claim and was thus awarded a patent superseding TI's. This was overturned on June 19, 1996, in favor of TI.

Operating System (TICOL). Similar to other successful desktop cassette systems now coming in the market, data could be batched onto a cassette and transmitted later, or connected to a host for immediate insertion of data to the host system.

Cassettes were clumsy to work with from a technology perspective; namely, how does one find a record stored somewhere on the cassette? Through some inventive programming with TICOL, the TI engineers figured out a way to search for data in a fairly fast manner, thereby reducing time to find and edit a record on the cassette. This new model of the Silent 700 could transmit data up to 1,400 bits per second. It sold for $4,925, and could be leased for $175 to $205 (depending upon length of the lease contract).

Figure 150—TI Silent 700 programmable model

TI, as a manufacturing company, had needs similar to other manufacturers—namely to automate some of its processes. Seeing a niche to be filled for more plant automation, TI developed its 900 series of computers. The Model 960B could be purchased with 8K, 16K, or 24K 16-bit words of RAM—all on a single board. Up to 65K could be configured, but this required multiple boards. The 960B was targeted for industrial automation, process control, scientific work, and data communications. Taking a page out of DEC's design book, the 960B was approximately 18 in. x 12 in. x 24 in. Its face consisted of a series of switches and lights, and it could slide into a custom rack that TI could provide. It set aside special registers to manage communication lines, of which 128 were standard and a maximum of 8,192. The price of an 8K system was $4,350; 16K was $5,850; and 24K was $7,350. Extra memory was available as follows: 8K words for $2,000; 16K words for $3,500; and 24K words for $5,000. (Today, 8GB of memory costs around $80.)

Now that its computer-making juices were flowing, TI introduced the DS330 system. Basically, this system was a disk storage system. It could be configured from one to four drives being controlled by one controller board. (Having one controller per disk provided faster throughput, but was more expensive to configure.) Each disk held 100MB. Up to eight TI Model 923 CRTs (with a programmable keyboard) could be configured to provide access to the DS330 data (or act as a cluster of terminals that could connect to another host system such as IBM).

In 1978, TI introduced the first single-chip Linear Predictive Coding (LPC) speech synthesizer (meaning an artificial production of human speech). The LPC was bundled with TI's specialized microprocessor called the Digital Signal Processor (DSP). This microprocessor (unlike commercial ones from Intel and others) focused on filtering, measuring, and compressing analog signals. Of course, the military could always be counted on to buy into technology like this, but how could TI make commercial money on it? Of all the markets TI could have broken into, it chose the kiddy market; TI's Speak & Spell™ introduced thousands of small tots hearing a word pronounced after typing it in—and in so doing made a bundle of money for TI.

Figure 151 – Texas Instruments Speak and Spell

Also in 1978, TI looked at the commercial market that Apple, IBM, Radio Shack, Atari, Commodore, and others were starting to claim, and decided that it had the wherewithal to compete commercially. TI entered the home computer market in 1979 with the Texas Instruments 99/4, which sold for $1,150. This model showed both technical engineering brilliance and marketing stupidity. For instance, as good as the computer was designed, it lacked any lowercase characters on the keyboard, but TI made sure that calculator keys were embedded in the keyboard as it knew that everyone really loved TI calculators! A 5¼-in. floppy disk drive, thermal printer, speech synthesizer, two serial ports, and/or a PASCAL compiler could be added. As an interesting addition, one also could add what TI called a Peripheral Expansion Box (PEB), in which eight more expansion cards (mostly for device interfaces) could be added.

In 1981, this model was superseded by the TI 99/4A (priced at around $500), and in 1983, a price war left many (including TI) reeling from high development costs and low prices. TI went on to make faster models and some excellent operating systems, but it was not quite compatible enough with the IBM model, with which the world was so enamored—and, therefore, TI saw its computer customer base dwindle even more. Still, TI stayed in the microcomputer market by making IBM-compatible laptops. But by 1997, the company saw that the margins were too thin to stay in this business, so it sold its product line to Acer.

TI's contribution to microcomputers could be argued as minimal at most, but its contribution to the components that went into them was significant. TI continues to be a world-renowned technology company for its IC chip manufacturing (always smaller and smaller), and for creating many products for military use.

Titus, Jon

In 1973, there was an intriguing start to what was to become an even more intriguing product. It started with a Virginia Tech grad student named Jon Titus who wanted to build a home computer (a "personal computer"). From this desire and a bunch of circuit boards, the Mark-8 computer (using the word "computer" very loosely) was born.

At that time, *Radio-Electronics* magazine was vying for readership, and somehow Titus and this publishing company got linked up. The magazine, hungry for new stories about people using the microprocessor, ran a cover story about the Mark-8 in its July 1974 issue.

Figure 152—Radio Electronics advertising the Mark-8

It would be a mistake not to stress enough how this article changed the world. People could read how they could build their own computer. Granted, when and if someone did buy the parts and build it, it was nothing fancy, was hard to program, and could produce very little in the way of any output. (Apple would try this exact model two years later with their Apple I.) But most builders new and understood that; what they had, though, was their very own computer! The article said that for $5 one could get a detailed instructional booklet (no hardware or software) on how to build your own computer. In parallel to this, Titus designed the boards he had told his booklet buyers how to build, so he knew what he was talking about. Building boards was time-consuming, and Titus saw a demand coming that he couldn't keep up with, so he contracted with a company called Techniques that was located in New Jersey for the actual manufacturing. Techniques took Titus' plans, and for about $50, Techniques would supply a buyer with the boards on which to solder the components (which the buyer had to procure from whatever sources he or she could find). Basically, anyone with a little bit of patience and knowledge of both electronics and soldering could build a computer for around $350.

Sales were modest, totaling about 400 board sets and 7,500 booklets. But while the idea of owning one's own honest-to-goodness computer was enticing, few (if any) had any idea of what to do with it once it was built. "Computers had their place doing rapid and complex calculations," says Titus, "but I don't think anybody at that time had any idea that information technology would be as pervasive as it is now." (From an interview in the 1980s.) For instance, even Titus made limited use of his Mark-8, as witnessed by him using his royalties and the payment for the magazine article to buy an IBM Selectric correcting typewriter to keep up with the correspondence. (Word processing software on a personal computer was years away.)

The Mark-8 (also mentioned in some articles as Mark 8) was basically a kit made up of six two-sided boards that were: a CPU, memory address/manual control, input multiplexer, memory, output, and readout. The CPU chip was an Intel 8008, with a 48-instruction set. It also came supplied with cables. People were very creative in their packaging of the boards, as there was no standard on what a box holding them should look like. Here are some examples of what the first Mark 8 computers looked like.

Figure 153—Mark-8 assembled from kit parts and boards, and two versions of how they could be packaged

The reality was that the Mark-8 was a hobbyist's nightmare — it was complicated even for people who liked to tinker, and the newness of the microprocessor in general was something that people were still struggling to understand. Titus wanted to keep improving his circuit boards, thus he was continuing to modify his original board designs. The bad news was that there was a communication breakdown between Titus and his manufacturing partner, Techniques. Techniques was either not keeping up with the changes or simply ignoring them. Some of the ordered boards lacked holes where Titus said they would be, which meant that the buyer had to solder on both sides of each board. If that wasn't hard enough, it was reported that some circuit boards had other manufacturing errors on them and needed modifications in order to work. On top of that, the assembly instructions were hard to decipher, so the bottom line was that putting together a working computer was quite a challenge.

Marketing and project control was not Titus' forte. As if the construction of the machine wasn't hard enough (with some users throwing in the towel and never finishing the machine), some orders simply never got filled by Titus. Within about six months after the announcement of the Mark-8 being available, MITS came out with its 8080 based Altair 8800 computer, which was available both as a kit or completely assembled. To make things worse for Titus, the Altair had a faster processor and was selling for the same price as the Mark-8. This obviously was not good news for Titus, but he wanted to make a go out of his fledgling company.

While the Mark-8 was designed for hobbyists, Titus did come out with another model that was aimed at universities (to be used as a teaching machine similar to the Kenback computer) and companies for process control work. This latter model was called the Mark-80 and was based on the Intel 8080 processor. The Mark-80 had a CPU card, a memory card (3K of read/write memory and 1K of EPROM), a front-panel card (with LED lights and switches), and a serial I/O board.

Unfortunately, Titus was seeing his dream die from lack of sales, but he did accomplish something important with his products—namely, it inspired many hobbyists who turned their ideas into companies and/or simply started figuring out what this microprocessor craze was all about. Bill Gates was one of those readers—and maybe Steve Jobs and Michael Dell were reading it also. Another inspired person named Robert Suding of the fledgling Digital Group Company.

Today, the Smithsonian Institution honors Jon Titus and his Mark-8 by showing it as one of the first "personal" computers ever offered. Titus still hears regularly from hobbyists who want to recreate or tinker with the original design. Devotees remember the Mark-8 with affection as a hardworking machine that proved home computers for the masses were possible.

Toshiba

Toshiba Corporation was founded in 1938 as Tokyo Shibaura Electric K.K. in Tokyo, Japan. The simplified name, Toshiba Corporation, did not come about until 1978. As was the case with many growing companies, Toshiba found itself with many product lines and divisions, and its personal computer division was about to provide a strategic importance to Toshiba.

As was also typical of many companies, Toshiba grew because of both internal growth and acquisitions. Toshiba was (and is today) a very innovative company in that it holds a number of "firsts" in Japan: radar (1912), the TAC digital computer (1954), transistor television and microwave oven (1959), color video phone (1971), Japanese word processor (1978), MRI system (1982), laptop personal computer (1986), NAND EEPROM (1991), DVD (1995), the Libretto notebook personal computer (1996), Japanese keyboard, and HD DVD (2005).

Toshiba continued with research and development of computers even after it withdrew from a joint project with the University of Tokyo in 1956. The TOSBAC-3400 in 1964 was the first Toshiba computer to come complete with an operating system. This brings up the history of the Toshiba operating systems, which happened in stages. First, Toshiba developed its own operating systems for its own computer products, then in joint development with universities, and lastly, by licensing operating systems from U.S. computer companies. By 1970, Toshiba had developed and marketed several lines of small computers to compete with IBM's smaller configurations, and to do strictly scientific work.

In mid-1970, the 16-bit TOSBAC-40A was released. In December of the same year, the TOSBAC-40B came out; this model increased the number of base instruction sets, and offered more I/O channels. In 1973, the TOSBAC-40C came out and offered a machine cycle speed of 200ns. Within two years, the TOSBAC-40D and TOSBAC-40L (with the latter finally being able to condense the processor to one board). All of these aforementioned TOSBAC models (40A-40L) were 16-bit-based.

In 1974, Toshiba turned to its own engineers and developed the ACOS-6 operating system for its ACOS 77 computer line, which was the last of Toshiba's mainframe endeavors. ACOS-6 was developed based upon enhancements to its GCOS-3 operating system, whose license it had obtained from Honeywell in the 1960s. The new ACOS-6 added a number of new functions, such as a virtual memory system, faster memory access control with a domain protection (meaning applications running in one part of the computer could not access or corrupt memory being used by another applications), and a shared library function.

In 1978, Toshiba released its first 32-bit computer, called the TOSBAC-7/70. While an excellent minicomputer in many regards (namely speed and memory addressing sizes), it never caught on to a large enough market to sustain it.

Being able to input data using an English style of keyboard was difficult at best for many Japanese. And with IBM (and IBM-compatible machines) controlling the market, the Japanese seemed to be stuck. With a stroke of brilliance, the Toshiba engineers figured out a way to represent a reasonable Japanese character set and how to convert this information into data that could be stored as regular English characters. **Though this might seem like a small and perhaps obscure note in history to many, this one engineering feat propelled the Japanese computers to a level of acceptance they had not achieved to-date.** The outcome of this work was the Toshiba JW-10 (announced in 1978, and first sold in 1979). This system functioned as a data-entry system with its own monitor, printer, special keyboard, telecommunications port, and local magnetic storage. The first picture below shows the overall system, and the second picture is a close-up of the keyboard — which shows its complexity.

Figure 154—Toshiba JW-10 (with permission from Information Processing Society of Japan)

Figure 155—Toshiba JW-10 Japanese-style keyboard

Later the same year, Toshiba transferred its computer business to the former NEC—now Toshiba Information Systems, Inc. (which was a joint venture between Toshiba and NEC).

As one can see from above, Toshiba was very inventive and ambitious to conquer the computer market in Japan. Today, Toshiba continues to make laptops, along with many other consumer and commercial business products. It continues to be a multinational conglomerate Japanese corporation still headquartered in the same city where it started.

Tracor Data Systems, Inc.

This company started life in 1955 as Associated Consultants and Engineers, founded by Richard N. Lane, Frank W. McBee, Dr. Chester McKinney, and Jess Stanbrough, with Lane being named as president. The company's early success had them focusing on contracts with the U.S. Navy and Union Carbide, providing them custom instruments and other electronic components. In 1960, the company was renamed Texas Research Associates, and in 1962, a merger with Textran Corporation caused it to rethink its company name once again—and thus Tracor was finally born. It was incorporated on December 11, 1969.

Tracor made (or acquired) several products—from a minicomputer to two products for remote data entry and storage. Three acquisitions were Bright Industries, Inc., Peripherals General, Inc., and Remcom Manufacturing Company.

Another Tracor product was the TDS-1601 character printer. This product was marketed as a replacement for the Teletype Model 33 and Model 35 products. The TDS-1601 had a keyboard, used a roll of paper, had an acoustic coupler built in, and was enclosed in a nice little case.

Figure 156—Tracor TDS-1601

The company also produced the TDS-1702 synchronous recorder. It was a magnetic tape machine that had a read/write synchronous speed from 4 inches to 37.5 inches per second, could support 7- or 9-track tapes, and offered formatting of either 556 or 800 bits per inch.

It also sold the TDS-1255 minicomputer, which consisted of a card reader, a magnetic hard drive, a line printer, the TDS-1601 console, and a central processor cabinet.

In 1971, though, something interestingly happened at Tracor—it dropped its whole line of hardware products, and continued under the name Tracor Computer

Corporation (as a "services" company). In its divestiture of the hardware products, Tracor promised to seek a company to continue support for the Tracor products. At the time of that announcement, Tracor had $17.5 million in reserves.

In 1976, Tracor became the first Austin, Texas, -based computer company listed on the New York Stock Exchange. Also that year, feeling the pull of the minicomputer market and potential money to be made from it, the company felt the need to return to the hardware business one more time (not to make a minicomputer, but rather products to use with them). The outcome was the Tracor Analytical Processor (TAP). This product could interface to many devices at once (minicomputers and peripherals) and could visually show what information was actually being sent to/from them. This was a very helpful invention for debugging a communications problem between two devices. The TAP had interfaces for a Teletype, paper punch/reader, and a cassette drive, so it could log data as it was being sent through the TAP.

In 1981, Tracor branched out and created Rokar International in Jerusalem, Israel. This company focused on the development of electronic components for military and some commercial use. In 1986, Tracor was acquired by Westmark Systems, but in 1989, Westmark filed for bankruptcy protection. In 1991, Tracor was sold.

Back in life with control of its own destiny once again in 1993, Tracor acquired the Vitro Corporation. In 1994, Tracor purchased GDE Systems Inc. from the Carlyle Group (GDE was formerly General Dynamics Electronics). Giddy from the money rolling from the money these companies were making, in 1996, AEL Industries (an electronic warfare systems and components manufacturer) was acquired.

In 1998, after a long and profitable run, Tracor was acquired by Marconi Electronic Systems (a subsidiary of

General Electric Company). In 1999, Marconi Electronic Systems was acquired by British Aerospace to form BAE Systems, which then became BAE Systems Integrated Defense Solutions (using key Tracor technology).

Forty-seven years after its inception as a small electronics company in Austin with a focus on military components, one could say the company has done rather well.

Triumph-Adler

This company had its roots starting in 1896 by Siegfried Bettmann as the German Triumph Motor Works company in Nuremberg, Germany (a subsidiary of the Triumph Cycle Company, Coventry, in the UK). Up until the 1950s, Triumph built, at one time or another, typewriters, bicycles, motorcycles, automobiles, and trolley wheels.

In 1957, Triumph bought shares in a small company called Adler. Together, they produced office machinery (mainly adding machines and calculators). In 1970, Triumph-Adler was making (or reselling) digital calculators with product names such as the Triumph-Adler1200, Triumph-Adler1210, Triumph-Adler1204, Triumph-Adler 10, and Triumph-Adler1214.

In 1973, Triumph-Adler decided to go bigger by jumping into the computer craze and produced a small desktop type of computer made specifically for banks and larger companies that could afford this type of automation. Its machine was called the Datentechnik (aka Triumph-Adler1000), which superseded earlier attempts at the same business, but those products never sold (mainly because they were as large as a desk). Triumph-Adler would provide custom software to each customer, thereby making the systems very attractive to the customer (although providing a nightmare for support for Triumph-Adler). The specifications for the Triumph-Adler1000 were as follows:

- 4K of RAM (1K for the operating system, 3K free)
- CPU from 112 standard TTL-building blocks
- Three tape drives (cassettes)

Figure 157—Triumph-Adler 1000

In 1979, Volkswagen acquired a majority of stock in Triumph-Adler. A year later, Triumph-Adler acquired a majority stake in Pertec Computer Corporation, which had developed what it had dubbed as the first personal computer (in reality, this was a stretch as several other companies were already making this claim by now — some by as much as five years earlier). Through more acquisitions and partnerships, Triumph-Adler today (sans its computer products) is thriving as a maker and distributor for copiers and calculators, and is officially known as Triumph-Adler GmbH.

Unidata

Unidata had a short life even by many small computer startup standards in the '70s. Located in Munich, Germany, Unidata was started in 1972 with the principle that Europe (but with an emphasis on Germany) should be stronger to compete with the computer giants such as the United States' IBM. Country pride as at stake to make something to compete in the large computer market.

Unidata was not really a computer company per se, but rather a pooling of computer development with resources from CII (which was funded in a large part by the French government), Philips, and Siemens.

Philips was brought to the computer party because of its development and production of semi-conductors. Siemens brought peripheral technology such as magnetic storage devices (e.g., tape drives and disk drives) and also its laser printer. CII was brought in to tie it all together, since, after all, it had been developing a line of computers (with the assistance of Bull and Honeywell).

It was a complicated working arrangement. Philips was assigned the role of developing a "small" computer system; Siemens was assigned to develop a "medium" size computer system; and CII was left to design the "large" computer system — all designed with the aim of competing head-on with specific models of IBM. Code names were used internally for these development efforts, with X0 referring to the Philips' work; X1, X2, and X3 assigned to Siemens; and X4 and X5 assigned to CII.

Each company drew on the expertise already within their respective companies, and within two years Unidata was ready to release its first products: Philips announced on January 15, 1974, the model Philips 7720; Siemens announced on September 16, 1974, the model Siemens:7730; and also on September 16, 1974, CII announced the model CII 7740.

Epitaph: The 7720 and 7730 never gained any market share, and many factors probably contributed to this — namely a lack of marketing. (Plus, both Philips and Siemens had competing products in this space, so why produce a product to compete against oneself?) CII, though, (and with French pride at stake), refused to let the 7740 die. After disappointing acceptance by businesses, CII enhanced the 7740 and came out with the 7755, 7750,

7748, and 7760—all failing to attract enough sales to support the time and money the French government and CII were devoting to this.

It was, if one looks upon this endeavor objectively, a somewhat noble idea of reclaiming the European computer market by European companies. It never overcame the realization that governments should probably keep their hands out of free enterprise and let companies compete on their own merit. German and French politics (notwithstanding the aforementioned companies exhibiting the squabbling over who builds and markets what) finally proved too much for Unidata to overcome. On December 19, 1975, Unidata was dissolved (with Siemens acquiring any Unidata business after Philips pulled out of the consortium on September 3, 1975).

UNIVAC

Refer to the Sperry Corporation section for more information.

Varian Data Machines (aka Varian Data Systems)

Varian Associates was started in 1948 in San Carlos, California, and was the early leader in vacuum-tube enhancements, linear accelerators, and other new technology for the atomic age. Varian Associates formed Varian Data Systems in 1966. Realizing that Palo Alto was the hub of new technologies, it moved its headquarters to be closer to the computer development action. Varian Data Systems' first system was the 620-series (I, F, and L models), but this was limited in expandability and processing speed.

The Varian 620/f offered a 750-nanosecond instruction execution time, and came with Varian's proprietary VORTEX operating system. It was marketed primarily against Xerox's Sigma 3 and DEC's PDP-8, as it was a rack-mounted machine that looked very similar in shape and size to those competitors' products. The 620/F, though, sold for $48,000, which was about half of the price of the competitors' products. Still, Varian knew it needed to play catch-up quickly if it wanted to remain in the market; the Varian 73 was Varian's attempt to do that.

Figure 158—Varian 620/f

The Varian 73 had 64-bit control words and sixteen registers. Because of its large instruction size, it was a faster machine than its competition. It was available with either semiconductor or core memory.[116] Varian claimed a 165-nanosecond microinstruction execution. This machine offered direct memory access for its I/O devices, and Varian claimed it could transfer data up to 3.03 million words per second.

It offered two operating systems for the Varian 73: Varian Omnitask Real-Time Executive (VORTEX; proprietary and multi-tasking), and Master Operating System (MOS; proprietary and limited to batch processing). Varian offered its own DAS assembler language, as well as FORTRAN IV, BASIC, and RPG IV languages.

---

[116] Core memory was an older technology that every company was phasing out. The only reason any company would buy a system with core memory was that it was cheaper than semiconductor memory.

Additionally, it offered many utilities and a batch scheduler called the Basic Executive Scheduler and Timekeeper (BEST). The processor and ROM was on one board (15 in. x 19 in.), and extra boards had to be added to add more memory. The front panel had a series of lights and push buttons mainly used for monitoring running applications and debugging.

Taking a page from Tandem Computers' fault-tolerant design, Varian designed its memory cards to be dual-ported. This meant that if one access path failed for whatever reason, a backup path should provide access to the memory data.

The Varian 73 allowed for hardware interrupts up to sixty-four levels (at an increased price to the buyer). While this was a nice feature for process control applications, it generally wasn't needed for "normal" business processing. In other words, the Varian 73 was starting to confuse its market. As for peripherals, the Varian 73 could accommodate fixed head discs, drum memories, magnetic tapes, teletypes, paper tapes, card readers, card punches, line printers, digital plotters, analog inputs and outputs, CRT displays, modems, and other communication controllers. Lastly (and again taking notice of Tandem Computer's fault tolerance), Varian added a restart option with battery supplies that could retain data in memory.

The Varian 73 was well designed from several perspectives. First, it was faster and more flexible (with lots of software for lots of peripherals) than many of its competitors. Unfortunately, it could not expand easily to grow beyond a department's use, and it was having an identity crisis—was it a business machine or process control machine? Varian's sales were disappointing, and maintaining sales and support across the U.S. and in Australia, Canada, South America, Europe, and Africa was expensive. The last sales found for Varian Data Machines were in 1977. In 1999, Varian Associates split into three divisions: Varian Inc., Varian Semiconductor, and Varian Medical Systems.

Video Systems Corporation

Based in Pennsauken, New Jersey, and with sales offices scattered across the U.S., Video Systems produced the VST-1200 (1000) CRT Data Terminal and the VST/2000.

These were self-contained systems that included a monitor, keyboard, and numeric keypad. The specifications were as follows:

- 12-inch display
- Capable of displaying 1,296 characters (72 characters wide by 18 lines)
- 60Hz refresh rate
- Parity checking/generation (even, odd, or none)
- Built-in modem giving 110, 150, 300, 600, or 1,200 baud speed; an optional 2,400 baud modem was available
- Printer interface
- Communications interface with TTY or RS232
- 120 watts
- Weighed 53 pounds
- Measured 18 in. x 18 in. x 18 in.

Figure 159—VST/2000

473

The VST/2000 was capable of displaying 2,596 total characters, with 72 characters per line. The selling price was $1,795 for the VST/1200 (slightly lower if bought in quantities of five or more), and the VST/2000 sold for over $2,000.

Videotron Ltd.

In 1974, this company produced a graphic display system, which was a radical change from the then-standard character-only displays. However, other small companies were coming out with competing graphic terminals at this same time.

Videotron's product consisted of a 16-bit CPU with 32K of memory. Because of its capability of displaying graphics in addition to characters, it was marketed as a system to be used for things such as intricate circuit designs. It had a built-in communications card that transmitted at 2,400 bits per second, and a light pen that interacted with the displayed information. This company was based in Budapest, Hungary.

VisiCalc

Two guys, Dan Bricklin and Bob Frankston, working together in the Boston, Massachusetts, area in 1979 perfected (and sold) what was to be known in the industry as a spreadsheet for accounting calculations. Another term the world would one day adapt for this was that of "killer app," meaning that it was an application that killed the competition.[117] I am including this software to explain that no matter how creative the engineers were in creating fancy hardware, unless someone could make a good

---

[117] IBM had this with a software package called CICS; it ran on the IBM platform only (or IBM-compatible platforms), and it allowed users to display data and have it processed by following CICS programming rules. IBM realized this was their "killer app," and it drove (and still drives) significant IBM sales.

business case for using a computer, then the whole PC craze might have ended with a bunch of hobbyists playing with them in their garages and basements.

While the Apple II was a nicely packaged personal computer, VisiCalc added to its acceptance by showing the world how exciting point-and-click applications could be when used in a true business setting. Without exaggeration, it can be said that VisiCalc helped make Apple a success in its early days. As the 1980s rolled around, VisiCalc could be purchased for other PCs, and thus spurred yet more PC growth. While the owners of VisiCalc were selling their software from $100 - $250 (depending upon platform and options), competition came from a little company called Lotus Development, which introduced its Lotus-1-2-3 spreadsheet product. Sales dropped for VisiCalc, and in 1985, it sold its product rights to Lotus Development—which quickly dropped VisiCalc from its portfolio.

Wang

Wang was founded in 1951 by An Wang. Computer memory storage was an issue that IBM and others were constantly trying to tweak to make it faster and more plentiful—and one of Wang's early inventions was a modified type of magnetic storage logic circuit.

As was noted with other companies documented in this book, several companies had their start in the calculator business—and likewise Wang saw this as an inroad into the business he envisioned. Wang's first product was a calculator based upon the electronics available at the time (which means big and slow). Wang, though, had an idea of attaching calculators, typewriters, and Teletype terminals to a small, department-sized computer.

From its headquarters location in Lowell, Massachusetts, in 1971, Wang announced its first try at automating document entry and retrieval with the Wang 1200 (although it was not commercially available until 1972). The design was odd, but it worked; it used IBM Selectric typewriters for keying and printing, and dual cassette decks for storage. For those used to keyboards on laptops today, picture this: The operator of a Wang 1200 typed text with an electric typewriter. When the Return key was pressed, the data from that line was written to a cassette tape. One cassette held roughly twenty pages of text, and the information could be retrieved by printing the contents on continuous-form paper in the 1200 typewriter's shared printer. The stored text also could be edited with basic editing functions including Insert, Delete, Skip (character, line), and so on. Slow, tedious, and prone to problems (e.g., cassettes were prone to have bad magnetics and therefore wouldn't record at certain times — and although a skip here and there for music was fine, every bit on the tape was important to a computer), it did allow documents to be typed in and shared within a small group fairly consistently.

Companies saw a potential savings in labor (and therefore reduced costs). This simple little product revolutionized the way documents could be automated and shared, and got the juices flowing for a more sophisticated operating system eventually developed and marketed as the Wang Office Information System (OIS).

The Wang OIS was an operating system unto itself. It had an interesting feature called the "Glossary" function. A Glossary was a word processing document that was "attached" to a workstation; different workstations in the cluster could have different glossaries attached to them. This Glossary contained shortcuts (now called macros in software such as Word) to frequently typed phrases. For example, an operator could add the phrase "My amazing boss…" into a Glossary document, and then have the whole phrase put into a word processing document simply by pressing (for example) the GL key and the letter

"M," thus saving time when typing a document. Very inventive.

Wang also developed another operating system called Alliance. This was built with word processing still at its core. The system was Tempest certified,[118] and the U.S. government deployed it in most of its embassies around the world. A really creative feature of the Alliance O/S is that it ran another Wang product called Visual Memory Database (VMD). VMD could index every word contained in every document stored either on the workstation or central computer. What this meant was that if a manager wanted to know how many documents contained the word "butt-head," all he or she had to do was search for it, and a list of those documents (along with an exact line number where it was found) was presented.

In 1973, Wang made a huge leap forward with its "made for a single user" Wang 2200 product. Like other products starting to appear on the market, the 2200 was a self-contained workstation, meaning that it had its own cabinet containing its small display monitor (using a CRT type of technology), cassette tape storage unit, a keyboard, and it could run BASIC. Approximately 65,000 of these units were eventually shipped.

In late 1974, an improved Wang 2200 VP model came out; this product had a faster CPU chip, and performance was said to be more than ten times that of the 2200. This product was followed by the yet faster performing Wang 3000 series.

---

[118] Tempest-certified defines how other computers can be spied upon, and how to protect one's own computer from being spied upon. Requirements include lead shielding, placement of machines away from others, filters on air ducts, wiring, and piping standards in the building itself, etc. In other words, "shhhhhh."

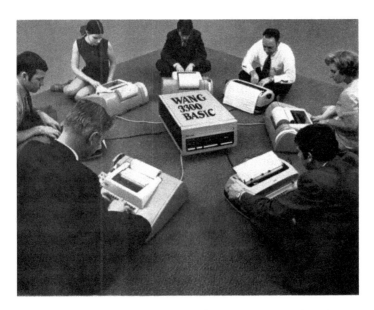

Figure 160—Wang 3300 (maybe if Wang had included chairs, it would have sold more systems?)

During the 1970s, approximately 2,000 Wang 2200T computers were shipped to the USSR. During to the Russian/Afghan war in the 1980s, the U.S. and the Coordinating Committee for Multilateral Export Controls (COCOM) imposed export restrictions on most computers (including Wang) to the Soviet Union. Rumor has it that in 1981, Russian engineers at Minpribor's Schetmash factory in Kursk reverse-engineered the Wang 2200T and created a computer it named the Iskra 226. (In actuality, Russia started development for the Iskra-226 in 1978, two years before its Afghan war.)

Enter into the picture two interesting Wang employees: Harold Koplow and David Moros. A 2002 *Boston Globe* article referred to Koplow as a "wisecracking rebel" who "was waiting for dismissal when, in 1975, he developed the product that made computers popularly accessible." In Koplow's words, "Dr. Wang kicked me out of marketing. I, along with Dave Moros was [were] relegated to Long Range Planning—'LRPed.' This...was tantamount to being fired."

With no resources and few guidelines (which is like offering drugs to junkies for these guys), Koplow and Moros were told to design a better word processing machine. The first thing they did was to write a "user's manual," not having the product behind it. In other words, they wrote a document describing how a word-processing system should work. They convinced Dr. Wang to turn it into a real project, and in June 1976, the Wang 1200 WPS (meaning Word Processing System) was introduced. Today, we might think of this design as silly, as in "why not just give everyone their own software, let them create a document, and then send it off to a distribution list?" In the 1970s, though, the concept of everyone having their own software on a sort of "personal" workstation was an idea that was years down the road in the future. Here is how the Wang 1200 WPS worked:

- Each workstation contained its own Intel 8080 microprocessor (later versions used a Z80).
- Each workstation had 64K of RAM.
- There was no local disk storage; rather disk storage was centralized on the "master" CPU that controlled the others; anyone on the Wang proprietary network could share the documents with others.
- All of the workstations were connected via high-speed dual coaxial cable (called the "928 Link"); Wang figured out how to network multiple Wang 1200 masters together, thereby allowing file sharing among hundreds of users.
- The systems were fairly easy to manage, so any small office could set up this computer network in an era where specialized "computer operators" usually had to be hired.

All software for the systems was developed by Wang Laboratories, and the operating system, file formats, and electronic interface specification were closely held proprietary secrets. (Taking a page from Wang's playbook, Apple in the early days also did not want third parties developing applications or connecting with its systems.)

By the late 1970s, Wang engineers had improved their networking capabilities to connect up to 240 Wang machines. But just because it was possible to do this didn't mean it was practical. What Wang was finding out (and most others struggled with then and still today) was that when one system in the network acted as a control point, this became not only a bottleneck for performance, but a potential for a failure point — thereby shutting down the whole network-sharing scheme if something happened to the network control point.

The first Wang Virtual System (VS) was introduced in 1977, and with it a series of powerful computers that could support from a few to hundreds of users. VS systems included the VS5E, VS15, VS45, VS65, VS85, VS90, VS100, VS6230, and VS8460 systems. The VS was aimed directly at the business data processing market in general, and IBM in particular. While BASIC, Forth, RPG II, PL/1, and FORTRAN programming languages were available, the VS systems were typically programmed in COBOL. Wang saw his VS systems as competing head-on with the IBM mainframe in terms of performance.

Wang continued to flourish into the 1980s by developing the Wang OFFICE family of applications (continuing Wang's love with word processing). Whether one called Wang's final evolution of products minicomputers or mainframe, the fact is indisputable that it had developed a small networked system that could process (create, store, edit, share) documents at a high rate of speed.

Dr. Wang felt a personal sense of rivalry with IBM from an earlier time (the mid-1950s to be exact) with a battle brewing between the two over patents for magnetic core memory. Therefore, his drive from developing small word-processing products to competing with IBM mainframe-like products was something of which he was very proud.

Wang continued to make small inroads into IBM's and DEC's markets in the 1980s, but Wang's salesforce seemed to misunderstand the true capabilities of the VS systems. (Wang salespeople still thought of their systems as a word processor, sort of like the world thinks of HP as "the printer company," even though both Wang and HP had much more to offer).

The littoral mark of the VS series was about 30,000 systems operating worldwide at one time in the mid-to-late 1980s, which is a very impressive installed base of customers. The 1980s saw Wang incompatibility issues with the new "standard" IBM PC, distracting lawsuits, and quality control problems. A common view within the computer community was that Wang Labs failed because it specialized in computers designed specifically for word processing — but this perception is wrong.

Probably closer to the truth of Wang's failure (the company's, not An Wang's) was the insistence that An's son, Fred Wang, succeed him. Fred was first made head of research and development, then president of the company. Key R&D and business personnel protested Fred's promotions, and many left the company. Amid declining revenues, John F. Cunningham, resigned as president and chief operating officer of Wang Labs over a protest and disagreement with Fred Wang on how to turn the company around.

In 1994, Wang declared bankruptcy. The complex of three Wang towers in Lowell, which at one time housed 4,500 workers in over a million square feet of office space, was foreclosed and sold at auction in 1994. Wang emerged from bankruptcy in the mid-1990s somehow with $200 million in cash. In the late 1990s, Wang bought the Olsy division from Olivetti and the company's new official name was changed to Wang Global. Wang now wanted to be known as a "network service" provider instead of a computer manufacturer. In 1999, Wang Global, with $3.5 billion in annual revenues, was acquired by Getronics (a Netherlands company, which was actually a smaller company with "only" $1.5 billion in revenue).

In 1997, Wang reported having about 200 Model 2200 systems still under maintenance around the world. On July 21, 2008, Wang's VS customers were notified that they would no longer receive support from the company holding patents to the Wang products.

Xerox Incorporated

To write about Xerox (and specifically XDS and PARC) at this point in this book, I could have almost used the old cliché, "saving the best for last" without exaggeration or hyperbole. To start at the beginning, Xerox was founded in 1906 in Rochester, New York, as the Haloid Photographic Company. The word Xerox, which the world has come to equate with copiers, was a mixture of Greek words meaning "dry writing."

Skipping ahead six decades (since the '70s is the focus of this book), Xerox found itself at the top of the heap of copier companies, and still with its headquarters in Rochester, New York (which will turn out to be both good and bad, as hopefully you will understand shortly). Today, phrases such as "I need to Xerox this" are still heard around most of the industrialized world. Although there were constant improvements to photocopying over the years, the '60s became a time when Xerox wanted more business and revenues, so they went on an acquisition binge. Most notable were the 1969 acquisition of Scientific Data Systems (and its Sigma line of computers),[119] and a year later the founding of the Palo

---

[119] Xerox paid $918 million for SDS; in 1975, after realizing that the time-share market was dead and no one (not even the PARC engineers) wanted these systems, Xerox took an $84.4 million write-off for SDS computers. Begrudgingly, Xerox allowed the PARC folks to start development on their own larger computer, calling it the MAXC.

Alto Research Center (PARC) to focus on computer technology. (The name Palo Alto Playground Center would have been just as appropriate because to the engineers there, it was a place to come up with ideas and have fun — welcome to the Silicon Valley.)

Parent: "Eat your vegetables."

Child: "No, I don't want to."

In a nutshell you now understand the relationship between Xerox headquarters, and its upstart PARC located within a stone's throw from Stanford University, and about ten miles north of the rest of Silicon Valley. In 1969, Xerox's chief scientist, Jack Goldman, approached George Pake, (a physicist specializing in nuclear magnetic resonance, and provost of Washington University in St. Louis) about starting a second research center for Xerox. Pake selected Palo Alto, California, because of the engineering pool and climate of inventive ideas. While the 2,351-mile buffer between PARC and Xerox headquarters in Rochester afforded scientists at the new lab greater freedom to undertake their work, the distance would eventually serve as an impediment in persuading management of the promise of some of their greatest achievements.

Much of PARC's early success in the computer field was under the leadership of its computer science laboratory manager Bob Taylor, who guided the lab as associate manager from 1970 to 1977 and as manager from 1977 to 1983. PARC (formerly known at one time as Xerox PARC) was primarily and foremost a research and development division with Xerox. PARC would go on to important developments such as laser printing, Ethernet communications protocol, packaging of what would be known as the personal computer, graphical user interface (GUI), what would eventually be considered as "desktop" point/click, object-oriented programming, amorphous silicon (a-Si) applications, and advancing very-large-scale-integration (VLSI) for semiconductors. These were busy folks.

In March 1973, the PARC folks released (internally) a computer called the Alto. This machine was unlike many computers in that the microcode (the instructions that run the machine itself) was not hidden from the programmer. Programmers loved this opportunity to play with the operating system language, and by doing this a few were able to speed up performance of the machine. (This was similar to how the Linux operating system was developed and supported by a world community.) The Alto had the following characteristics:

- A bit-slice arithmetic logic unit (ALU) based on Texas Instruments' 74181 chip
- 128K – 512K bytes of ROM
- Magnetic disk with removable platters of 2.5MB
- Base machine and one disk were housed in a cabinet about the size of a small refrigerator; one additional disk could be added in daisy-chain fashion
- CPU interacted directly with hardware interfaces (memory and peripherals)
- Microcode supported up to sixteen cooperative tasks, each with fixed priority
- Ethernet was supported
- Only common output device was a bi-level (black and white) CRT display with a tilt-and-swivel base, mounted in "portrait" orientation rather than the more common "landscape" orientation
- A custom, detachable keyboard
- A three-button mouse (internal users loved this as they could point and click at something on the screen—something that no one had thought of before)
- An optional five-key chord keyset

On their first pointing device, the buttons were three narrow bars, arranged top to bottom rather than side to side. These buttons were named after colors used in the documentation. The motion was first sensed by two wheels perpendicular to each other. Later, these wheels were replaced with a ball-type pointing device (development credit given to Bill English).

The keyboard was a most interesting design in how it sent characters to the computer itself; each key was represented as a separate bit in a set of memory locations. This enabled the computer, for instance, to read multiple key presses simultaneously. This feature was used to alter where from the Alto would boot. The keyboard value could then be used as a sector address on the disk from which to boot the computer. (In other words, by creatively holding down certain keyboard characters, different microcode and operating systems could be loaded. A term I found amusing was supposedly used inside of the PARC facility — it was called the "nose boot," where many combinations of keyboard characters required many fingers, so operators had to get creative on how to push multiple buttons at the same time.)

Several other I/O devices were developed for the Alto, including a TV camera, the Hy-Type daisywheel printer, and a parallel port (which was used to speed up printing). In other words, the guys and gals at PARC were having fun creating computer enhancements to the boring "me-too" things that everyone seemed to be doing.

Putting the hardware aside, the Alto also had some leading software ideas. One was a tool that enabled the system to keep track of files on a disk and then easily retrieve them. Today, we take this for granted on all computers, but in the 1970s, to make something so easy to use was way ahead of its time.

The Alto had its own programming language called BCPL, which was later replaced by the Mesa language.

By all definitions, the Alto was a personal computer. It might not technically be the "first" PC, but this one was rich in features that no one had — even Apple. By 1977, Xerox had 400 Altos installed internally (both at PARC and at Xerox headquarters) in an effort to show Xerox management the potential market and revenues the Alto could produce. For instance, email (which we all take for granted today) was in its infancy in the mid-1970s, but the PARC folks had perfected this and was using it daily to connect users. The Alto was a nice, robust, personal computer that by all rights (with a little repackaging perhaps and some marketing) could have taken the "personal computer" market by storm. Instead, Xerox's response was "ho hum," it can't even make copies!

In 1978, Xerox donated fifty Altos to several universities to help spur innovation about the next generation of computer scientists.

Figure 161 — Xerox Alto

It has been said that "distance makes the heart grow fonder," but not in this case. Xerox (the parent company located on the East Coast) was slow to realize the value of the technology that had been developed at PARC — after all, Xerox was <u>the</u> copier company in the world, and the

West Coast folks at PARC thought of themselves as anything but a copier company. Continuing to live in their own creative world, after the Alto system, PARC would go on to develop a succession of more powerful workstations informally termed "the D-machines" with creative names such as Dandelion, Dolphin, Dorado, and the Dandel-Iris.

When Xerox finally entered the PC market with the Xerox 820, it rejected the Alto design and opted instead for a very conventional model, a CP/M-based machine with the then-standard 80- by 24-character-only monitor and no mouse. With the help of PARC researchers, Xerox eventually developed the Xerox Star and the Xerox Star 6085. After watching Apple's Macintosh success, Xerox probably realized its mistake in not marketing the Alto and instead of developing a "me-too" IBM clone—but it was too late. The Star series PCs were expensive and never caught much of a market share. Within a short time, Xerox pulled the plug on the Star PC, and it would not enter the PC market again.

A number of PARC engineers left to join Apple Computer when they saw the fun the Apple folks were having with the mouse and icons—and because of Xerox's lack of recognition as to what the PARC folks had developed.

Another product to come out of PARC was the Xerox NoteTaker, developed in 1976. It never entered production or was sold to consumers, but it was truly a "portable" PC (weighing in at a respectable 22 pounds, which was considered lightweight in those days), and would eventually be copied by such companies as Osborne Computer Corporation and Compaq.[120] The NoteTaker was developed by a team that included Adele Goldberg, Douglas Fairbairn, and Larry Tesler. This computer was actually a very sophisticated machine that had a built-in

---

[120] Earlier in this book, I suggested reading about G.M. Research and about James Murez—as he legitimately held the first patent for a portable PC.

monochrome display monitor, a floppy disk drive, and a mouse. It had 128K of RAM and used a 1 MHz CPU. It used a version of the Smalltalk operating system that was written for the Xerox Alto. The NoteTaker fit into a case similar in form to that of a portable sewing machine; the keyboard folded out from the bottom to reveal the monitor and floppy drive.

PARC[121] is alive and well today, still existing as a company within Xerox. The following is a summary of Xerox's major accomplishments during the 1970s:

- 1971 – Laser printing
- 1972 – Object-oriented programming (spurring development of such languages as C, C++, and Java)
- 1973 – Ethernet connectivity for computers
- 1974 – Solid-state lasers
- 1975 – Graphical user interface (GUI)
- 1977 – Very large scale integration (VLSI) electronic circuits
- 1978 – WORM technology (a way for programs to replicate themselves on the computers; nothing nefarious was in mind when this was done to help math computations spread over different computers
- 1979 – Linguistic technology software

In summarizing key dates for Xerox, July 1975 must be mentioned. While one can argue that competition was tough in the minicomputer and mainframe computer areas, Xerox's management wanted to focus on other

---

[121] There are three other names, along with their ideas, of note that came from PARC. The first two, Chuck Geschke and John Warnock went on to form Adobe. (Every time you create a PDF document, think of Xerox.) Another person to make an impact on technology was Charles Simonyi. Charles developed a word-processing application, naming it BRAVO. Charles would end up leaving PARC and going to work for a fledgling company called Microsoft, where BRAVO's ideas and functionality would serve as the basis for the successful Microsoft Word product. To say that PARC was full of creative people would almost be an understatement.

business areas. Therefore, it was at this time that Xerox decided to withdraw from the minicomputer and mainframe markets.

During the 1970s, the XDS division was controlling the large timesharing Sigma product line that had accompanied the SDS acquisition. This product group was very successful for Xerox for a while as it placed the company squarely in competition with IBM's mainframe.

The primary operating system for the Sigma 900 series was called Monarch. The Sigma 32-bit series was used for real-time and batch monitoring (RBM), and batch and timesharing monitoring (BTM). In 1971, a more sophisticated timesharing system called UTS/XOS was released, which was developed into CP-V. The RBM operating system was replaced by CP-R, a real-time and timesharing system.

Although the Sigma product line was excellent in many aspects, sales could not sustain its manufacturing and support costs. The minicomputer market had cut into the need for a large mainframe, and Xerox had no answer for this. Eventually, Xerox came out with its own Sigma version, calling its new products the Sigma 550 and Sigma 560 models, but it was too late for the customers to take notice. In 1975, most Sigma rights were sold to Honeywell, which went on to produce this product line for a few more years, and supported it through the mid-1980s. Also around 1975, Xerox shut down the XDS division after losing (by some estimates) hundreds of millions dollars.

In 1979, several ex-SDS/XDS engineers started another company in an attempt to restart the Sigma line with a new brand and new features. They called this new system the SDS-420. They had mediocre success, but never enough sales to keep the company solvent, and in 1984 went out of business.

Ximedia

In 1978, this San Francisco, California, company offered the Fox-1100 programmable terminal. What was curious about the marketing for this terminal was that it took a terminal from Perkin-Elmer (which it fully disclosed in its ads) and made enhancements to it. The advertised Fox-1100 had the following features:

- 80-character wide x 24-line display
- Resettable tab stops (similar to what an old typewriter did fifty years earlier)
- Full keyboard (upper and lower case) with a numeric keypad
- Display had a hood to cut down on glare
- Direct cursor control
- Fully assembled and tested (It is hard to fathom that these words were needed in an ad, but in 1978, kits were still being sold.)

The Fox-1100 sold for $1,295. In the category of "What was its marketing department thinking?" if anyone wanted a full product description, he or she had to send $1 to the company.

Zilog

Zilog was incorporated in Los Altos, California, in 1974, and founded by Federico Faggin and Ralph Ungermann (who went on to found his own company, Ungermann Bass). Faggin, along with other bright Intel engineers, left Intel with ideas on how to compete against his old company, which pretty much owned the lion's share of the microprocessor business. (Note to big companies with smart engineers: keep them happy or they will leave and compete against you!) Zilog quickly settled on competing with the Intel 8080 microprocessor. Exxon was a key financial backer of Zilog in its early days, and eventually acquired the company (only to be repurchased by the Zilog management at a later date).

The Zilog Z80 was an 8-bit microprocessor and sold starting in July 1976. It was aimed at competing head-on against the Intel 8080A microprocessors. By licensing its design to other vendors (and by supplying wonderful development products so its customers could load its operating system and other software), the Z80's acceptance as a solid microprocessor gained traction. The Z80 offered more instructions for the O/S including bit manipulation, block moves, block I/O's, byte searching, more registers, more interrupt registers, and less power usage as it was built with fewer component chips.

The Z80 competed well against the Intel 8080A, and throughout the '70s and '80s it enjoyed a reputation as a solid performer. After Zilog went public in 1991, and had years of more success, Texas Pacific Group acquired it in 1998. Timing was not the best as this new company wanted to change directions in the microprocessor development area, and demand started to wane for its products. After refocusing on its key strengths, by 2007 the company was again making a profit. Relying on the 8-bit word, though, turned out to be its downfall—as sales plummeted with companies moving to faster and high-addressing microprocessors. In January 2008, Zilog turned down a buy-out offer by Universal Electronics, Inc.

Slowly, parts of the company were sold off along with certain patents. In December 2009, the IXYS Corporation bought the company for a little over $62M in cash. Since early 2010, IXYS has focused on development in the industrial and consumer markets. Keeping the Zilog name (and as a division within IXYS), more microcontrollers and software would come out later, showing the strength of the Zilog development engineers.

Zuse KG

It is only fitting that this chapter concludes with this company. This book's introduction and description of early computers discussed Konrad Zuse. He had single-handedly built an electromechanical computer in 1939, which he aptly called the Z1. (There is a picture of the Z1 earlier this book.)

The Z1 was built using very precisely engineered hardware to generate an electronic signal, which would then trigger a mechanical "gate" to open or close. The whole idea was that by inputting a set of commands on one end, an answer would eventually come out the other end. It did have rudimentary memory to retain data it was working on, but this memory itself was electromechanical in nature. What this meant was that once the machine was turned off or a calculation was over, the "memory" disappeared (or should have, but as with anything mechanical, gates could be left closed or open by mistake).

Building upon the Z1, and learning and improving on its design, the Z2, Z3, and Z4 came along over a span of a few years, driven by the German army's need for better calculations for their weapon trajectories and precise manufacturing. Zuse had designed his machines to be programmed with instructions that made sense to him, but were hard to understand for the novice user. These instructions were called "machine instructions." If Zuse wanted his machines to be more useful for others to use, he would have to write all of the programs for them, teach others his complicated machine language, or develop something easier. He chose to develop a language called Plankalkül (meaning "plan calculus").

Before Plankalkül, if a programmer wanted to add two numbers together, then machine instructions such as LAST A TO REG C, FÜGEN B TO REG C, LEGEN REG C had to be input to the computer. With Plankalkül, a programmer could simply code ADD A TO B. Plankalkül can be rightfully considered the first high-level programmer language developed. Almost every programming language developed to date has used Zuse's idea.

In 1949, Konrad formed the Zuse KG company to continue his work and hopefully to find a market for the new and improved machines (e.g., Z5, Z11, Z23, and Z25). Unfortunately for Zuse, more powerful computers were coming out of the United States and taking over the European computer market. Zuse could not compete, and in 1971 his assets were bought by Siemens AG and Zuse dropped out the market. Because his ideas and company survived for over five decades, he barely squeaked by to be included in this section of 1970s companies.

Did he contribute anything relevant with the microprocessor? Of course not. But, his idea for a high-level programming language spurred on Microsoft and other companies whether they were aware of Zuse or not.[122] Konrad Zuse died in 1995 at the age of 85.

---

[122] Zuse's machines were "finite" in their retention of information—either the data/switch was set to a "state" (closed or open), or it wasn't. He went on to write many articles on how finite-state machines could work, but this only seemed to spur more imagination in him. He surmised that when something is in a "state," there were electrons causing that to occur. In other words, finite objects were caused by an infinite number of variables causing that to happen. Taking this one more step, Zuse envisioned the whole universe being built that way—he was nothing if not creative.

Chapter 4
The foundation they built

Mice

Before I summarize the wonderful ideas from the listed companies, I want to discuss the ubiquitous mouse a little more. I could have included the following in a footnote, but I wanted to ensure that it was understood that neither Apple nor Xerox invented the mouse. Yes, Jobs had seen a small rectangular box at Xerox that could be tethered to a computer, and then could be used as a cursor to point to something.

While no proof exists that Xerox stole this mouse idea from another source (after all, it was the 1970s and many people "borrowed" ideas from others freely), the fact is that others more than thirty years earlier had already developed something similar to a trackball/mouse. The award for a working mouse should go to Professor Ralph Benjamin, working for the Royal Navy Scientific Service in the mid-1940s. He wanted something to track missile trajectories, and necessity being the mother of invention, he developed a tracking ball that allowed him to plot such trajectories easily. In 1952, Ferranti-Canada came out with a tracking device made from a five-pin bowling ball (smaller than the traditional ten-pin bowling ball used today in the U.S.). The engineers — Tom Cranston, Fred Longstaff, and Kenyon Taylor — worked together to develop their own version of a "mouse;" of course, calling it a "mouse" never crossed their minds, rather it was a "tracking rolling thing".

Additionally, Telefunken and the Soviet computer scientists had their own "mouse" versions.

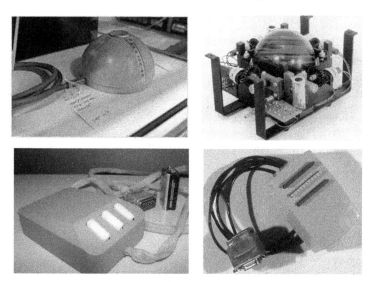

Figure 162—Old versions of the mouse
Top: Telefunken's, Ferranti Canada's
Bottom: Soviets', Xerox's

A NASA engineer named Douglas Englebart (the idea guy), along with Bill English (the engineer who could actually build the thing, together (in 1964) came up with their functioning "mouse." It had one button and was made out of wood, was shown in a demo to many others, and worked similar to a modern mouse. Even the Soviet Union had developed a rudimentary version of a mouse sometime in the 1960s. Not to stop there, in 1968, engineers at Telefunken had developed one. Lastly, Computer Display Systems had developed a trackball/pointing mechanism in 1971.

Whatever the roots of the "roller-ball cursor-pointing thing," Steve Jobs the consummate idea guy) was confident that Wozniak (the software tinkerer) could figure out how to control the device to display something on the screen. But how does one physically build a mouse? One could have borrowed/stolen one from Xerox, but Jobs wanted his own. Jobs contracted a company called Hovey-Kelley Design and told them to build it. The president, Dean Hovey, heard Jobs' explanation for a device that had to move in all directions—up and down and left and right. It also had to be small and be able to be used on a table. Hovey had a vague idea of what Jobs wanted (although maybe Hovey had even seen one in action from any of the above companies listed)—whatever his knowledge of a "pointing device," away he went to build this "thing." His first stop was at a Walgreens pharmacy. He bought some roll-on deodorants because he had an idea of how a ball might work on this mouse to allow movement—he wasn't quite sure how, but the ball was small and would allow the movement he was after. He also bought a small butter dish to act as a rectangular top, and from these items he built his first mouse prototype.

Something as simple as a mouse was about to become so common that we, today, cannot think of a PC or laptop without one. The 1970s was a time when ideas were borrowed freely—and improved upon—which is, after all, what this book is about.

Software

VisiCalc was mentioned earlier as being a catalyst that helped propel Apple (and other PC makers) into the workplace. Additionally, though, processing documents (also known as "word processing" in a format that could be easily shipped around from user to user) was also important to the PC and Apple world—it made personal computers more practical for the typical business.

Although Wang was way ahead of the industry in how it processed documents, it remained proprietary in nature. What this did was open the door to enterprising idea people to develop something more "commercial";

something that could be sold to run on various kinds of computers, not just Wang, for instance. Out of these ideas came products like WordPerfect, Microsoft Word, , and WordStar , to name a few.

This is competition at its best. WordPerfect came about from a project for Brigham Young University in Salt Lake City, Utah. Two men at the university, Bruce Bastian and Dr. Alan Ashton wrote software to process documents for a Data General minicomputer. The smart thing they (Bruce and Alan) did was keep the rights to their work, and in 1980 had formed Satellite Software International. The interesting phenomenon this started was to spur Microsoft to work on improvements to the Microsoft Word product. Then when WordPerfect came out with enhancements to compete, Microsoft responded with its own enhancements to Word—and the winner from this was the ordinary computer user who now had an excellent choice of document processing packages to use. Software began driving PC sales at a rapid rate starting in the early 1980s.

Chinese Information Processing Systems (CIPS)

The Soviet Union seeded the People's Republic of China (PRC) with computer technology starting the mid-1950s. While I'm sure the PRC was grateful, the same issues going on with the Soviet Union manifested themselves within the PRC. While a long chapter could be written about how computers evolved within the PRC, the key point was that the PRC wanted to make the computers more useful in general.

Having a keyboard in Russian or English was not helpful to most Chinese as they were used to representing characters in Chinese. The Chinese character set consists of about 7,000 characters. Each character consists of a two-dimensional pattern into which a syllable has been incorporated. Computers were being programmed to handle a limited character set (English alphabet, some special characters, and some Russian Cyrillic), so to add 7,000 more was a huge project – and to make a keyboard with 7,000 keys was impractical.

By the early to mid-1980s, the PRC was facing a dilemma—they wanted to use minicomputers more, but wanted to enter, store, manipulate, and print in Chinese. Feeble attempts had been tried, but it wasn't until 1984 when two men from the University of Sydney (Australia), developed a solution. C.Y. Chung and H.R. Hwa, using a VAX 11/780 and the C programming language, came up with a way to process many of the Chinese characters. (Their abstract and details on doing this are complicated, and therefore are not included, but explore this area more if you are interested.)

Their approach was expanded upon by others, and today the PRC is very comfortable with computers using the CIPS approach developed by Chung and Hwa. (These two men are not given the credit they deserve in history, but they changed the way computers were used and accepted using non English character sets.) To summarize, CIPS would not have been possible without the microprocessor, and it shows how people were starting to use software to do some very creative things with the faster and faster improvements in computer technology.

Legacies They Left

If you have made it this far through most of the 1970s companies and their creative ideas, hopefully you will see the impact the microprocessor was having in the world. Some person asked, "How do we store information cheaply?" A person/company replied, "Cassettes!" "No, 8-track cartridges!" "No, floppy disks!" And then someone at some company released a small and inexpensive magnetic drive. This scenario was repeated multiple times a year to solve keyboard issues, monitor issues, and, of course, "communications" between this smart little devices. Every one of these aforementioned companies believed they had a product to make their millions of dollars. Some exceeded that and some only sold one or two systems.

And what was the impact on businesses? Perhaps a better question to ask is, what was the impact on the huge, pre 1970 computer computers who ruled the computer world? It was huge. As the 1980s rolled around, big computer systems were losing their market share. Today, this is the reality of the computer world now:

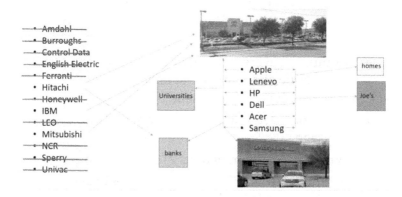

Figure 163—Post-1970 Impact

While the above picture obviously does not represent every business market, its intent is to show the impact of the microprocessor on the business world. Most "big" computer makers on the left could not compete any longer, and they drifted away to a footnote in history. The growth of the microprocessor usage changed the business world. "Joe's" small business, who at one time could only use a calculator to keep track of his business sales, can now have access to a fast computer to handle all of his business functions.

Another way to summarize pre 1970:

- Independent computer manufacturers/designers (e.g., LEO, Ferranti, IBM, Burroughs, etc.) were in business.
- IBM "standards" for mainframe work was what most other vendors had to conform to.
- IBM terminal protocols and remote cluster protocols were so pervasive that almost all terminal makers had to offer these.
- Memory of 16K was considered a lot of memory.
- Punched cards, paper tape, and large magnetic reels of tape were used for both input and output.
- Magnetic disks held approximately 10MB of data.
- Time-sharing was available to small to medium companies because they could not afford to own their own computer.
- Computers were thought of as expensive and had a mystique about them that only computer scientists could comprehend.
- A cursor positioning device ("mouse") was limited in usage.
- With the exception of a very few, screen bit-mapping was unheard of — screen character processing was the standard.

And yet another view of what these 1970's companies did:

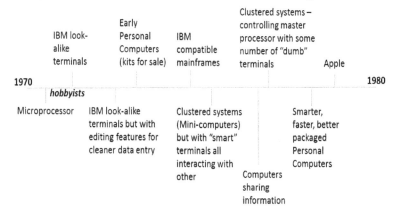

Figure 164—The 1970s Decade

After 1980:

- IBM "standards" continued in the mainframe area.
- It was still the "wild west" when it came to connecting minicomputers and things like printers; every company, it seemed, had developed their own proprietary methods to connect "things"; it would take several years until companies like Belkin figured out they could own a business just by selling products that connected "things" to other "things."
- Large minicomputers were offered that dug into IBM mainframe sales.
- Multi-gigabyte RAM
- Multi-core processor chips
- Hundreds of terabyte databases
- Fault-tolerant operating systems and hardware components used for 24x7 processing
- Internet protocol more easily connected different kinds of computers
- Programming language standards and portability helped spur a new breed of programmers

- Lightweight and powerful laptops were common
- Computer mouse and/or touchpad were common and expected with every PC or laptop
- Bit-mapping on a screen became standard
- Touch-screen displays showed that a finger could act as a computer mouse
- Cell phones connected the world
- Smart cell phones put a computer in your pocket
- Computers were now for the masses

By the time the 1980s rolled around, the "cord had been cut" and untethered small and mid-sized companies from having to buy expensive mainframe computers. In fact, many microprocessors were now packaged together to look like one computer powerful enough to replace the older, larger, more expensive mainframe systems. As stated earlier, IBM was the powerhouse in computer revenues, and because of this it could spend more for R&D, which in turn enabled it to constantly improve on its products. IBM and other large mainframe companies were manufacturing their own processor chips, which made it proprietary to that manufacturer. When Intel developed its commercial microprocessor, it was priced cheap enough for people to develop an alternative to the mainframe—namely the minicomputer—which could take processing off the mainframe and into a business which previously could not afford their own computer. As Intel improved on its microprocessor, it got faster and soon more powerful personal computers were flooding the market—opening up commercial markets that never existed before: email, digital photography, and amazing graphic and automation to name just a few.

At first (1971 to about 1973), there were two schools of thought: either replace IBM or play with IBM. With the exception of a few companies located in France, Germany, Japan, and the UK, most took the latter approach. By the end of the 1970s, that thought was still pervasive, but more and more companies were questioning "Why do we need IBM when we can do just as much, and maybe more for less cost.

Competition was always there with, "I can do this better than you!" to grab more market share. Initially, many of these clustered configurations (minicomputers) could only support four terminals, but it didn't take long for companies to modify their operating systems to keep track of eight, sixteen, thirty-two, and even thousands of terminals. The demand grew for Intel, and Intel responded by making faster and less expensive microprocessors to keep up with the ideas people were having. This, in turn, spurred on innovation by making the operating systems do more, and to do it faster. Here was what was going on the microprocessor world:

- 1970 – First RAM *commercial** chip by Intel – could execute 60,000 instructions per second
- 1971 – Intel 4004 (10.4 microsecond)
- 1971 – Intel 8008
- 1974 – Intel 8080
- 1975 – MOS Technology 6502
- 1976 – Zilog Z80
- 1977 – Motorola 6809
- 1977 – Motorola 6802
- 1978 – Intel 8086
- 1978 – Fujitsu MB8843
- 1979 – Motorola 6800
- 1979 – Intel 8088
- 1979 – Motorola 68000
- 1979 – Zilog Z8001/Z8002
- 2021 – Intel i9, 5.2 GHz*, 20mb memory, 10 cores

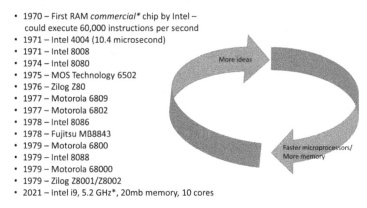

Figure 165: The Circle of Creativity

Businesses were catching on to this new "we don't have to be tied to a mainframe (e.g. IBM)" mentality, but as more of the data and processing was moved away from IBM, some were growing irritated about the built-in limitations manufacturers created with their minicomputer designs. Additionally, computer parts in the mid-1970s were not as reliable as they are today, so computers would stop when a fault was detected. Businesses expected something better, and some computer manufacturers responded to address this problem. [See Tandem Computers.]

By the mid-1970s, companies that were simply trying to market a replacement for an IBM 3270, or create a better card reader or paper-tape reader were behind the times, since companies no longer wanted these products. Instead, they were accepting that magnetic media (whether it be a hard disk, floppy disk, cassettes, or magnetic tape) was a better solution is many ways – they were faster, didn't jam, didn't tear, and required less storage to name just a few benefits.

Personal computer kits were coming into the market, and anyone remotely interested in a computer (whether it be a hobbyist or small business) could shell out $400 and buy one. The "kit" companies responded by pre-assembling them, and then other companies had better ideas for a keyboard, display, and a mouse to help drive their sales. Apple soared to the top not only because it recognized that users wanted these things, but also because it was smart in its packaging and bundling of all the computer pieces a user would need. No longer did a user have to buy some parts here and some parts there to get his/her computer to work. Apple was brilliant in its packaging and marketing.

Other companies were paying attention, and this in turn also drove them to develop better packaging, as well as other features to compete with not only Apple but with each other. Intel was huffing and puffing hard to keep up and develop the features computer makers wanted, and now two other microprocessor companies (Motorola and Zilog) jumped in with their own competing microprocessors.

And then...computers got even smaller, and someone had the bright idea of putting a battery in one and making it light enough to carry. A mere five years earlier, with the exception of maybe two or three engineers, no one could fathom something like this being possible.

As mentioned above, the world also was taking note, and Canada the UK, France, Germany, Italy, and Japan were developing their own computers to compete not only with IBM, but also in the minicomputer and PC space. (And not just in their respective countries, but across the globe.) As shown by the Soviet Union's successful space programs, they (the Soviets) certainly had their own powerful computers, but they were never allowed to compete in the world market.

Before I leave the topic of geographic location, if you were to glance in the Index and look for companies referenced by U.S. state, there are an overwhelming number of them located in California. But Massachusetts, Michigan, Florida, Colorado, Utah, Texas, New Mexico, Illinois, and a smattering of others also are represented. What this says is that ideas easily crossed borders way before cell phones and the internet made it easier to exchange information. Magazines, universities, and conferences helped fan the computer flames that were spreading not only across the United States, but across the world as well. The folks in California just happened to be tightly grouped together, and in that area, the fire burned at a high temperature.

As mentioned above, application software was important to increase computer sales, but operating system software (the core program that controlled everything going on inside of a computer) was even more so important. Operating system software was now key to every computer maker, and their operating system designs were very unique and powerful – much more than IBM had imagined.

Hundreds of questions were posed by software developers every day when they were trying to make something a little bit better in order to make their company's product(s) better – and more competitive. This was a typical day during the 1970s for almost every computer maker.

Pause here and realize that at one time the microprocessor was a blank "sheet" of paper. Intel wasn't sure what to do with it, and at first no one did either. No one knew how to write a multi-tasking operating system with virtual memory and allow peripherals to store data directly into memory. No one knew how to alter an operating system's instruction path with interrupts of various kinds, or figure out how a mouse worked. How could a computer load its own operating system simply by being turned on, and how could digital pixels be displayed instead of characters on a screen? How could a voice or a blink of an eye be recognized? And on and on and on. What was a floppy disk? How can I squeeze more memory into a smaller and smaller space? People were figuring this out.

Who was the first person to develop a PC? Who was the first company to market a PC? Several lay claim to these titles, and it's not important (at least to this author) as to which one is the legitimate holder. So much was happening at almost the same time that to determine a winner might come down to months or days or maybe even hours. Some got patents issued, and some didn't. Bragging rights are important, though, to many, and the readers and actual builders can squabble among themselves. What is important is that every one of these 1970 companies contributed an incredible amount of inventiveness and ideas to spur on the computer industry to become what we know today. Yes, the computer industry would have gotten there somehow on its own, but the acceptance of computers needed a spark — and these people in the 1970s lit that fire.

There is a hypothesis put forth by some paleontologists and historians that significant "things" have happened in humankind's past that can be attributed to "group dynamics." To clarify, let's say that you like to draw, but since you live alone on a mountain top, you don't do a lot of doodling because there is no one around to appreciate it or to challenge you to draw something better than the person next to you. If there is a crowd of people, though, ideas are shared more, and people are urged (either from outside or within) to do better. I believe that this is exactly what happened in the 1970s in the growth of computers. Jack Kilby, John Blankenbaker, Jon Titus, Robert Suding, Mers Kutt, James Murez, James Treybig, Ken Olsen, Steve Wozniak, and others were all sparks and it made them and others better computer designers.

In the 1970s, people (both business people and engineers) had ideas of what they wanted to do with a computer. But, like Di Vinci who needed an engine, microprocessor using companies sometimes failed (probably more than 50 percent) because technology lagged behind for their ideas to work. Take for instance the technology we call a "touch screen." It's a wonderful invention that has opened up markets and functionality that engineers in the 1970s couldn't fathom because the microprocessor was not capable of executing the instructions needed to make it work. (The next time you swipe your finger across a smartphone display, pause and marvel at this technology that allows a program to calculate where the X and Y axis started, and the speed and direction it went next).

In 1972, an HP calculator sold for $100, and in 1975 it was selling for $25. Today, a basic calculator is no more than a few dollars at most. In the 1970s, numerous programming languages were all claiming to be the best and easiest to use. For instance, the COBOL language could be used on different computers, but how it was written, compiled, and executed was proprietary to every computer maker. A small group from Australia wanted to tackle this problem, and the outcome was a language call Pogo. Although this language failed to catch on, it planted the seeds of developing more portable languages and, thus, C, C++, and Java were eventually born.

Today, the world is teeming with ideas about how to use computers—hopefully a majority of them are for the betterment of society. All that most people have to do is just make use of the technology at their fingertips. But there are some people with ideas that...well, the technology hasn't yet been developed. To those folks, remember the time-honored phrase that "necessity is the mother of invention." Someone, somewhere will invent what you need (perhaps it will be you!) and off you will go.

So where did some of these 1970s companies go? Most are gone, but their ideas live on. Even some of the outstanding ones were eventually swallowed up inside of larger companies. Tandem Computers is unique, though, among the 1970's companies as their operating system and architecture was so advanced that it is still be sold 50 years later.

The Diversification outside of building computers was the key, as was noted by many of the Japanese companies still in business after eighty or more years. If you started a company in 1970 with only one computer-related idea, your chance of survival for even more than a year was slim. This was because competition was looming for every company—with someone ready to make an improved version of your product at a lower cost.

Running a computer company is hard. To keep up with both the competition and demands from the users there are not only constant R&D costs, but also manufacturing costs, marketing costs, and support costs. Inexpensive, commercially available computers that are fairly reliable today rule most of the small- to medium-sized business market. There are only a few large computer companies selling to large businesses—and IBM remains one of them even after seventy years.

But still, the 1970 computer companies tried, and they seeded the 1980s with their ideas. Although the IBM PC (and the standard set by that product) was not released until 1981, hopefully after reading this book, you can understand the building blocks that were needed to create such a machine. The evolution and revolution was started by people playing in garages and basements, creating games, and comparing notes on the cool things they just made their computer toy do. The microprocessors in use today are a variation on the original microprocessors developed in the early 1970s. Eventually, these will be replaced by some technological breakthrough and computers will take a leap forward in speed and functionality. Here are some of the functions provided by the microprocessor as you drive down the road:

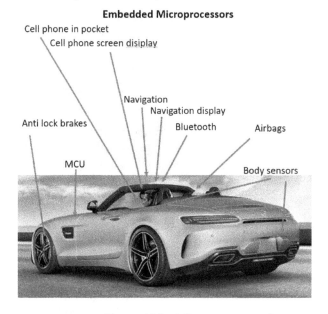

Figure 166—Microprocessors in use

Think about what the microprocessor allows and is giving us. Driverless cars will fundamentally change the world of many businesses, namely automobile insurance companies. With these new ideas for business uses came the need to hold more and more data — and the creation, of course, of technology to accommodate this need. The ability to store data and quickly access it opened up business functions that could only be dreamed about in

1970. Throughout the decades until today, the computer market has evolved greatly — and continues to evolve. The cell phone of today will be replaced eventually with something yet more sophisticated. Artificial Intelligence (AI), robotics, IBM's Watson, and Quantum Computing (while not quite ready for day-to-day businesses) are computer technologies that are amazingly fast. In November 2019, IBM was able to achieve 148.6 petaflops performance. That is 148,600,000,000,000,000 instructions per second. Imagine the possibilities such as presenting a problem to this computer such as "Find a cure for cancer," then let it churn away until it comes up with a few solutions. This is the future.

The computer era of the 1970s changed almost everything we do today, and certainly touches almost everyone on this planet even now, as technology continues to advance with lightning speed.

The computer as we think of it today started with the first electro-mechanical versions started with products like the Z1. Then came the next generation of IBM, English Electric, and others who started to think about how computers could be used in a more traditional business setting. The following generation's use of computers has been about this book — the inventiveness of how to make computers more accessible and easier to use for everyone. The early computer pioneers, especially those in the 1970s, took their blank sheets of paper and started designing computers almost from scratch. As you boot up your laptop or cell phone, save pictures to the "cloud," exchange emails and texts, or browse the internet, remember the technologists from the 1970s who gave life to the microprocessor and made this all possible.

Many companies formed in the 1980s and beyond believe that they invented something that changed the world. I would challenge that. Facebook, for example, is simply software. It could not exist if not for the creative minds that developed the internet and personal computers. Cryptocurrencies are just software; they also could not exist without microprocessors and the Internet. While improvements have been made in certain computer areas, little has been done to invent or innovate anything on the scale of what was accomplished in the 1970s by the companies in this book. With little doubt, almost all who are involved in computers today owe their professions to what occurred in the computer industry in the 1970s.

Glossary

APL – A computer programming language (named after the book A Programming Language) developed in the 1960s by Kenneth E. Iverson.

ASCII – American Standard Code for Information Interchange. Think back to the old days of Morse coding where a "..." or ".-.", or "---"meant something to the person on the other end of the wire. Computers have a need to know what a series of bits mean, and the ASCII set of values was thus developed. It originally was 7-bit character code where every bit represented a unique character. For instance, a "$" was 0100100, an "H" was 1001000, etc.

BAUD – A term usually used to describe the speed of a communication device. Originally it meant the number of "tones" sent between two computers, but with the digital age it adapted the meaning of "bits per second". The higher the baud rate, the faster data could be sent. A modem described as 9600 baud meant that it was capable of transmitting or receiving up to 9,600 bits (or 1,200 bytes) per second. Again, think of a byte as a character—like those that make up the words in this sentence.

CISC – Complex Instruction Set Computing; is a CPU design where single instructions can execute several low-level operations. Picture a spouse saying "Take out the trash," but in reality, the door has to be opened, the trash can picked up, walked to the street, and then you return to napping on the couch.

C/PM – Control Program for Microcomputers; Digital Research, Inc. developed this generic operating system to help jump-start people playing with the early microprocessors; the requirements for its use was that it had to be an 8-bit microprocessor with a maximum of direct addressable memory of 64K bytes.

CMOS – A complementary metal oxide semiconductor (CMOS) is a type of integrated circuit technology. In the "old days" of pre-2000, it was usually associated with a battery-powered chip that is used in laptops and PCs; it holds information such as date/time and system control functions when one turns on the machine. Today, most computers no longer use CMOS chips, but instead depend on other forms of non-volatile memory.

CRT – Cathode ray tube; think of an old TV screen in which a signal (or characters when used in a computer system) was beamed from a point in the back to a focal point on the back of the glass screen.

DMA – Direct memory access; instead of, say, a disk retrieving data and handing it back to an application to store or process, with DMA the disk stores the data directly into memory, and with an interrupt tells the CPU "I've stored the data and done my work—now it's up to you."

DRAM – Dynamic random access memory; similar to RAM chips, but requires constant electrical current through it to hold the data in place; smaller and more compact than RAM, it meant that computers could be smaller. A DRAM chip actually "drained" (or lost and forgot) its contents if it wasn't refreshed with power at some point.

EBCDIC – Extended Binary Coded Data Interchange Code is similar to ASCII in concept, except IBM wanted its set of values to represent values.

Interrupt – A computer rarely, if ever, sets idle—especially if it's working on bunch of programs at the same time; for instance, assume a program is asking you for input from your display; while this is going on it has shuffled things around inside of the CPU so it is now working on something else. Finally, you hit the RETURN key, and this will cause an "interrupt" eventually to make its way to the CPU telling it that you are ready to have your information processed. These types of interrupts literally go on hundreds (if not thousands) of times per second for the fast computers we have today. Another example is if a nuclear plant is about to overheat—an interrupt from a sensor alerts the CPU to take immediate action (to "interrupt" what it was doing), and hopefully that's what it does.

LSI – Large Scale Integrated circuit; a complex integrated circuit containing usually hundreds tiny gadgets known as logic gates and transistors—all placed on a single semiconductor chip.

Magnetic core (or simply core) memory – The best way to describe this is actually as an example; magnetic core was made up very, very, very tiny metal rings, which had two wires running at right angles through them that would send a current from one direction or another through it— thereby changing its polarity from an "on" or "off" state. It was hard to manufacture, prone to failures, slow, and couldn't remember any value if current was turned off to it.

Microsecond - 1 µs cycle (or vice versa)

MOS – Metal oxide semiconductor is a type of transistor used for amplifying or switching electronic signals.

Nixie tube/display – Using what is called a cold cathode display, it is an electronic device for displaying numerals or other information using glow discharge.

ns – A notation for nanosecond.

PROM – Programmable random only memory; meant that the chip was programmable by a computer program; its contents could be altered at any time if the programmer knew how to do this.

RAM – Random access memory; computers (even today's fastest laptops or smart phones) are made up of computer chips that are formatted into byte segments. It is up to the computer running the device to figure out what it wants to do with them. It can load data (or a program) into it and then write data over it if it wants—as noted above, it is up to the computer to figure out what it wants to do with it.

RAM simply is a form of computer memory storage and is usually embedded on integrated circuits inside of any computer. Before this, computer memories were bulky and, therefore expensive, to enclose in computer cabinetry. RAM changed the landscape inside of computers and gave programmers more leeway in writing applications by providing faster execution times and more memory in which to store data needed by a program. Some of the early IBM systems had 16K of RAM, which made programmers write very efficient code as the complete program had to fit in only 16,000 bytes of this RAM. Then, 32K RAM came on the market, only to be followed by 64K, 128K, 256K, and so on, where today it is not uncommon to have a CPU to have 16GB of RAM (that's 16,000,000,000 bytes for memory usage). Yes, programmers can write programs that are unbelievably large, but with this usually comes a lot of functionality that could only be dreamed of in 1971.

RISC – Reduced instruction set computing (see CISC for a comparison). A RISC as a CPU design doesn't mean that there are fewer instructions, but rather says that the instruction length is more well defined (should actually be the same), and the load and store instructions are separated.

ROM – Read only memory; similar to RAM, information can only be read from this memory. If you are a computer manufacturer wanting to keep your operating system from being "hacked," one safe way to do this would be to "burn" your instructions into a ROM chip so that no one would tamper with the contents. The bad side of this is that when a company wanted to do an upgrade ("patch") to its operating system, instead of sending out a new program to upload, the company would have to send out new ROM chips to be plugged into the circuit board.

S-100 Bus – This is a backplane consisting of "sockets" in which a 100-pin circuit board (of a variable number depending upon the size of the backplane used in the computer) can be inserted. The circuit boards could be memory, a CPU, firmware, or whatever could fit and was custom for the builder of the circuit board.

Second (and its parts) – 1/60th of a minute millisecond = 1/1,000th of a second (thousandth) microsecond = 1/1,000,000th of a second (millionth) nanosecond = 1/1,000,000,000th of a second (billionth).

SRAM – Static random access memory chip; didn't have to have power going to it to retain its contents of 0's and 1's.

TTY - A teleprinter (also known as a teletypewriter or Teletype) is an electromechanical typewriter looking and acting machine that was used to send and receive messages using a very simple protocol between the TTY machine and a host system. TTY machines rarely (if ever) had a display screen, but rather a roll of paper for the messages to be displayed.

Bibliography

Alphonso, Caroline, "Canadian hailed as father of PC," *Globe and Mail*, September 20, 2003.

Amdahl, Gene M., and William S. Anderson, "Computer Architecture and Amdahl's Law" and "An Interview with Gene M. Amdahl," individual articles from *IEEE Solid-State Circuits Society News*, 2007.

Andrew, J., from: *Der Computer, mein Lebenswerk* (in English translated from German), Berlin/Heidelberg: Springer-Verlag, 1984.

Arensman, Russ, "Unfinished business: managing one of the biggest spin-offs in corporate history..." *Electronic Business*, October 2002.

Arnold, M. G., and N. Wadsworth, *SCELBAL: A Higher Level Language for 8008/8080 Systems,* Scelbi Computer Consulting (Milford, CT), 1976.

Bagnall, Brian, *On the Edge: The Spectacular Rise and Fall of Commodore*, Variant Press, 2006.

Bajarin, Tim, interview with author regarding Creative Strategies and Homebrew Computer Club, 2016.

Barna, Arpad, and Dan I. Porat, *Introduction to Microcomputers and the Microprocessors*, Wiley, 1976.

Bartlett, Joel, et al., "Fault Tolerance in Tandem Computer Systems," Tandem Technical Report, 1986.

Bell, Gordon C., et al., *Computer Engineering - A Digital Equipment Corporation View of Hardware Systems Design*, Digital Press, 1978.

Bell, Gordon C., "Digital Computing Timeline," http://research.microsoft.com/en-us/um/people/gbell/digital/

timeline/1962-1.htmBerkeley, Edmund, *Giant Brains, or Machines That Think*, John Wiley & Sons, 1949.

Berlin, Leslie, *Troublemakers – Silicon Valley's Coming of Age*, Simon and Schuster, 2017

Best, Richard, et al., *Digital Modules: The Basis for Computers,* Digital Press, 1978.

Bird, John Peter, *Leo First Business Computer*, Hasler Publishing Ltd., 1994.

Bowden, B. V., *Faster Than Thought,* New York, Toronto, London: Pitman Publishing Corporation, 1953.

Brillinger, P. C., and D. D. Cowan, "A complete package for introducing computer science," *SIGCSE Bulletin*, November 1970.

Broad, William J., "Computer 'whispers' worry Washington," *The Globe and Mail*, Toronto, Ontario, April 9, 1983.

"Burroughs Display Systems," http://archive.computerhistory.org/resources/text/Burroughs/Burroughs.Display_Systems, 1965, 102646312.pdf, Defense and Space Group Marketing Division, 1965.

"CDC 6600," *Computer World*, July 30, 1975, page 16.

Ceruzzi, Paul E., *A History of Modern Computing,* Cambridge, MA: MIT Press, 2003.

"China Deal For Burroughs," (*The New York Times*, http://www.nytimes.com/1985/01/03/business/china-deal-for-burroughs.html), retrieved September 1, 2015.

Chung, C.Y., and H. R. Hwa, *Journal of Computer Science and Technology*, Volume 1, Issue 2, June 1986.

Cohen, Bernard, *Howard Aiken, Portrait of a Computer Pioneer*, Cambridge, Massachusetts: The MIT Press, 2000.

Collier, Bruce, *The Little Engine that Could've: The calculating machines of Charles Babbage*, Garland Publishing Inc., 1970.

Commodore Computers, "MOS – The Rise of MOS Technology & the 6502", http://www.commodore.ca/commodore-history/the-rise-of-mos-technology-the-6502/, retrieved May 1, 2016.

Cooke-Yarborough E.H., *Introduction to Transistor Circuits*, Edinburgh, 1957.

———— "Some early transistor applications in the UK," *Engineering and Science Education Journal,* June 1998.

Copeland, Jack, *Colossus, The Secrets of Bletchley Park's Codebreaking Computer*, Oxford: Oxford University Press, 2006.

Couffignal, Louis, *Les machines à calculer; leurs principes, leur évolution*, Paris: Gauthier-Villars, 1933.

Crisp, John, *Introduction to Microprocessors*, Butterworth-Heinemann, 1998.

Dasgupta, Subrata, *It Began with Babbage – The Genesis of Computer Science*, Oxford University Press, 2014.

Davis, Gillian M., *Noise Reduction in Speech Applications*, CRC Press, 2002.

Deagon, Brian, "MAI Phasing Out Production in Shift to VAR," *Electronic News*, 1991.

Derfler, Frank J. Jr., "Moonshine, Dixie and the Atari 800," Kilobaud, https://archive.org/stream/kilobaudmagazine-1980-09/ Kilobaud_Microcomputing_1980_September#page/n97/ mode/2up, 1980.

"Despite High Hopes, Xerox Now Part of DP History," *Computer World*, July 30, 1975.

Ditlea, Steve, *Digital Deli: The Comprehensive, User-Lovable Menu of Computer Lore, Culture, Lifestyles and Fancy*, Workman Publishing, 1984.

Dvorak, John C., "IBM and the Seven Dwarfs — Dwarf One: Burroughs," Dvorak Uncensored, 2006.

Eadie, Donald, *Introduction to the Basic Computer*, Prentice-Hall, 1968.

Earls, Alan R., *Digital Equipment Corporation*, Arcadia Publishing, 2004.

Eck, David J., *The Most Complex Machine: A Survey of Computers and Computing*, A K Peters, Ltd., 2000.

Enslow, Philip H., Jr., *Multiprocessor Organization—A Survey*, Computing Surveys, 1977.

Enticknap, Nicholas, "Computing's Golden Jubilee," Resurrection (The Computer Conservation Society) (20), ISSN 0958-7403, 1988.

Essinger, James, *Jacquard's Web, How a hand loom led to the birth of the information age*, Oxford University Press, 2004.

Essinger, James, *Ada's Algorithm*, Melville House Publishing (originally published by Gibson Square, Ltd, London), 2014.

Faggin, Federico, et al., "The History of the 4004, IEEE Micro," Los Alamitos: IEEE Computer Society, December 1996.

Felt, Dorr E., *Mechanical Arithmetic, or The History of the Counting Machine*, Chicago: Washington Institute, 1916.

Fensom, Jim, Harry Fensom obituary, *The Guardian*, November 7, 2010.

Ferry, Georgina, *A Computer called LEO Lyons Teashops and the World's First Office Computer*, Fourth Estate, 2003.

Freiberger, Paul, and Michael Swaine, *Fire in the Valley: The Making of the Personal Computer,* New York, NY: McGraw-Hill, 2000.

Fulton, Steve, *Atari: The Golden Years - A History, 1978 - 1981*, Gamasutra, 2008.

Garland, Harry, "Design Innovations in Personal Computers," Computer IEEE Computer Society, 1977.

Gernell, Francois, interview, http://www.forumpatriote.org/ viewtopic.php?f=42&t=25701, July 2010.

Girvan, Ray, "The revealed grace of the mechanism: computing after Babbage," *Scientific Computing World*, May/June 2003.

Gladwell, Malcolm, *Outliers The Story of Success,* Little, Brown and Company, 2011.

Gray, Stephen B., "The early days of personal computers," *Creative Computing*, Volume 10 Number 11, 1984.

Greenberg, Mark, and Charles Grant, Kentucky Fried Computers advertisement, *BYTE*, February 1977.

Grimaldi, John, interview with author regarding Dicomed, 2015.

Hagan, Thomas A., et al., *Fall Joint Computer Conference,* 1968, pages 747-749.

Hally, Mike, *Electronic Brains / Stories from the Dawn of the Computer Age*, Granta Books, 2005.

Hargreaves, C.M., *The Philips Stirling Engine*, Elsevier Science, 1991.

Haqq-Misra, Jacob, *Giving Konrad Zuse His Due*, Earth, November/December 2017

Helm, Leslie, "The Merger Wave Bearing Down on Minicomputer Makers," *Business Week*, November 28, 1988.

Henderson, Tom, "Comshare Hopes End of Turmoil Is at Hand," *Detroit News*, September 28, 1997.

Hodges, Judith, and Deborah Melewski, "Comshare Inc.," *Software Magazine*, July 1993, p. 102.

Hughes, Agatha C., *Systems, Experts, and Computers,* MIT Press, 2000.

Hyman, Anthony, *Charles Babbage: Pioneer of the Computer,* Princeton University Press, 1985.

IEEE Xplore Digital Library, "*Evolution of the minifloppy (TM) product family*", retrieved May 1, 2015, https://ieeexplore.ieee.org/document/1059748/

Ifrah, Georges, *The Universal History of Computing: From the Abacus to the Quantum Computer*, New York: John Wiley & Sons, 2001.

Intel's First Microprocessor—the Intel 4004, Intel Corp., 1971.

Isaacson, Walter, *The Innovators*, Simon & Shuster, 2014.

——— *Steve Jobs*, Simon & Schuster, 2011.

——— Leonardo Da Vinci, Simon & Schuster, 2017.

Jefferson, David J., "MAI's Patton Quits as Chief Executive, President Amid Duel for PRIME Computer," *The Wall Street Journal*, June 21, 1989.

Kaye, Glynnis Thompson, *A Revolution in Progress – A History to Date of Intel*, Intel Corporation, 1984.

Kellahin, James R., "The 1440: A calculator with memory, square root and other new features," *Radio-Electronics* (Grensback Publication), July 1973.

Kenney, Charles C., *Riding the Runaway Horse: The Rise and Decline of Wang Laboratories*, Little, Brown and Company, 1992.

Kidder, Tracy, *The Soul of a New Machine,* Little, Brown and Company, Reprint edition July 1997 by Modern Library, 1981.

Kilby, Jack, *The Chip that Jack Built*, Texas Instruments, 2008.

———— Nobel lecture, Stockholm: Nobel Foundation, 2000.

Knight, Robert, "At the Helm of Comshare, Crandall Executes Plan," *Software Magazine*, July 1989, p. 90.

Kontoghiorghes, Ericos, *Handbook of Parallel Computing and Statistics*, CRC Press, 2006.

Los Angeles Times, *"Xerox to Close Its Shugart Disk-Drive Manufacturer,"* retrieved May 1, 2015, http://articles.latimes.com/1985-01-17/business/fi-7894_1_xerox-spokesman

Lavington, S. H., *Moving Targets – Elliott-Automation and the dawn of the computer age in Britain*, 1947-67, Spring 2011.

Lavington, Simon, *A History of Manchester Computers* (2 ed.), Swindon: The British Computer Society, 1998.

Ligonnière, Robert, *Préhistoire et Histoire des ordinateurs (Prehistory and history of computers)*, Paris: Robert Laffont, 1987.

Littman, Jonathan, *Once Upon a Time in ComputerLand: The Amazing, Billion-Dollar Tale of Bill Millard*, Los Angeles: Price Stern Sloan, 1987.

Lundell, E. Drake, Jr., "Tracor Drops Computer Product Business," *Computer Industry*, 1971.

Lundstrom, David, *A Few Good Men from UNIVAC*, Cambridge, Massachusetts: MIT Press, 1987.

Machover, Carl, "Computer graphics terminals: a backward look," Spring Joint Computer Conference, 1972, pages 439-446.

Markoff, John, "Market Place; Digital Finally Follows a Trend," *The New York Times*, July 16, 1990.

Mason, Mark, "Foreign Direct Investment and Japanese Economic Development, 1899–1931," *Business and Economic History*, Second Series, Volume Sixteen, 1987.

McCusker, Tom, "The Datamation 100," *Datamation*, June 15, 1992.

——— "High Stakes Turn This Risk Taker Into a Miracle Maker," *Datamation*, September 15, 1988.

McKay, Sinclair, *The Secret Life of Bletchley Park: The WWII Codebreaking Centre and the Men and Women Who Worked There*, Aurum Press Ltd., 2010.

Michalopoulos, Demetrios, "New Products: Wang's new "deskette" computer brings direct-access processing to small user," *Computer* (IEEE), July 1977.

Milford, Annette, "Computer Power of the Future - The Hobbyists," *Computer Notes* (Altair Users Group, MITS Inc.), April 1976.

Miller, David Donald, "OpenVMS Operating System Concepts," Elsevier, 1997.

Mims, Forrest M., "The Altair story; early days at MITS," *Creative Computing*, November 1984.

——— "The Tenth Anniversary of the Altair 8800," *Computers & Electronics* (Ziff Davis), 1985.

——— *Siliconnections: Coming of Age in the Electronic Era*, New York: McGraw-Hill, 1986.

"Mitsubishi Corp to launch $197 million takeover bid for Yonekyu," *Reuters*, January 18, 2013.

Moseley, Maboth, *Irascible Genius, Charles Babbage, inventor*, London: Hutchinson, 1964.

Müller, Armin, *Kienzle. Ein deutsches Industrieunternehmen im 20. Jahrhundert (Kienzle. A German Industrial Enterprise in the 20th Century)*, Verlag: Stuttgart, 2014.

Murez, James, interview with author regarding GM Research, 2016.

Murray, Charles, and John Wiley, *The Supermen: The Story of Seymour Cray and the Technical Wizards behind the Supercomputer*, New York: John Wiley, 1997.

NEC Corporation, The First 80 Years, NEC Corporation, 1984.

Nicholas, Lynn H., *The Rape of Europa*, Vintage Books, 1995.

NNDB, http://www.nndb.com/people/972/000205357/, retrieved January 28, 2016.

New York Times, obituaries, December 10, 2018

Odagiri, Hiroyuki, *Technology and Industrial Development in Japan*, Oxford University Press, 1996.

Ogdin, Jerry, "Computer Bits," *Popular Electronics* (New York: Ziff-Davis), June 1975.

Ornstein, S. M., et al., "The terminal IMP for the ARPA computer network," Proceedings of the November 16–18, 1971, Fall Joint Computer Conference, 1971.

Oxford English Dictionary (2 edition), Oxford University Press, 1989.

PDP-11/40 Processor Handbook, Digital Equipment Corporation, Maynard, MA, 1972.

Pearson, Jamie P., *Digital At Work - Snapshots of the First 35 Years*, Digital Press, 1992.

Peck, Merton J., and Frederic M. Scherer, *The Weapons Acquisition Process: An Economic Analysis,* Harvard Business School, 1962.

Peek, Jerry, et al., *Learning the UNIX Operating System: A Concise Guide for the New User*, O'Reilly, 2002.

Peterson, Patrick, "Harris considers PB overhaul," Melbourne, Florida: *Florida Today*, 17 October 2010.

Pigott, Peter, *Air Canada: The History,* Dundurn, 2014.

Pournelle, Jerry, "Computers for Humanity," *BYTE*, July 1982.

Price, Robert M., *The Eye for Innovation: Recognizing Possibilities and Managing the Creative Enterprise*, New Haven: Yale University Press, 2005.

Randell, Brian, et al., "Obituary: Allen Coombs," *The Independent*, March 15, 1995.

Randell, Brian, "From Analytical Engine to Electronic Digital Computer: The Contributions of Ludgate, Torres, and Bush," *Retail Automation to 1983*, San Jose: Creative Strategies International, 1982.

"Raytheon announces Justice Department approval of Texas Instruments acquisition," *Business Wire*, July 2, 1997.

Retrieved *"Chronological History of IBM,"* IBM, October 15, 2015

Rifkin, Glenn, and George Harrar, *The Ultimate Entrepreneur - The Story of Ken Olsen and Digital Equipment Corporation*, Contemporary Books, 1998.

Roberts, Ed, "Electronic desk calculator you can build," *Popular Electronics* (Ziff Davis), November 1971.

Roberts, H. Edward, and William Yates, "Altair 8800 mini-computer," *Popular Electronics* (Ziff Davis), January 1975.

Roberts, H. Edward, and Forrest M. Mims, *Electronic Calculators,* Howard W. Sams, 1974.

Roland Corporatoin, https://www.factmag.com/2017/04/02/ikutaro-kakehashi-life/ "The life and times of Ikutaro Kakehashi, the Roland pioneer modern music owes everything to," retrieved 28 Jan 2020

Roland Corporation, WWW.ROLAND.COM, "Roland Corporate Data" http://www.rolandcorporation.com/Retrieved 29 May 2017

Rosenberg, Robert, "Company Fumbles Its Alliance with Giant IBM," *The Boston Globe*, July 28, 1992.

Sachen, Vibhav Kumar, and Neelesh Ranjan Srivastava, *Introduction to Microprocessors*, Acme Learning Private Limited, 2011.

Sale, Tony, http://www.codesandciphers.org.uk/enigmafilm/, "Making the Enigma ciphers for the film *Enigma,*" retrieved November 12, 2014.

Salsberg, Arther, "Jaded Memory," *InfoWorld* (InfoWorld Media Group, Inc.), November 12, 1984.

Schein, Edgar H., et al., *Digital Equipment Corporation Is Dead, Long Live Digital Equipment Corporation - The Lasting Legacy of Digital Equipment Corporation*, San Francisco: Barrett-Koehler, 2003.

Schuyten, Peter J., "Technology: The Computer Entering Home," Business & Finance, *The New York Times*, December 6, 1978.

Scrupski, Stephen, "Coming: cheap, powerful computers,*" Electronic Engineering Measurements Filebook*, McGraw-Hill, 1965.

Shannon, Claude Elwood, *A symbolic analysis of relay and switching circuits*, Massachusetts Institute of Technology, 1940.

Skidmore Sell, Sarah, "Ray Tomlinson, inventor of modern email, dies," (The Associated Press) *The Dallas Morning News*, March 7, 2016.

Smotherman, Mark, *PRISM (Parallel Reduced Instruction Set Machine),* Clemson University School of Computing, 1978.

"Speak & Spell, the First Use of a Digital Signal Processing IC for Speech Generation, 1978". *IEEE Milestones. IEEE.* Retrieved 2015-08-28

Stine, G.H., *The Untold Story of the Computer Revolution*, Arbor House, 1985.

Stokes, Jon, *Inside the Machine: An Illustrated Introduction to Microprocessors and Computer Architecture*, San Francisco: No Starch Press, 2007.

Strunk, Peter, "Die AEG. Aufstieg und Niedergang einer Industrielegende (Rise and Fall of an Industrial Icon)," Nicolai, 1999.

Swade, Doron D., "Redeeming Charles Babbage's Mechanical Computer," *Scientific American*, February 1993, p. 89.

Sweet, Ken, "Texas Instruments to buy National Semiconductor for $6.5 billion," CNN, April 4, 2011.

Taylor, Alexander L., III, *The Wizard Inside the Machine*, Texas Instruments, April 16, 1984 (subscription required).

Tempo 1 System Reference Manual, Tempo Corporation, Inc., 1969.

Terdiman, Daniel, "The untold story behind Apple's $13,000 operating system," CNET, 2013.

Terekhov, Andrey N., Lecture, University of St. Petersburg, 16 January 2014.

Thiele, Erdmann (Hrsg.), "Telefunken nach 100 Jahren - Das Erbe einer deutschen Weltmarke (Telefunken after 100 years - the heritage of a German global brand)," Nicolaische Verlagsbuchhandlung, 2003.

Thornton, J. E., *Design of a Computer: The Control Data 6600*, Scott, Foresman, 1970.

Titus, Jon, interview by Florida Gulf Coast University, http://chc61.fgcu.edu/home.aspx, 2007.

Turing, Alan M. (edited by B. Jack Copeland), *The Essential Turing*, Oxford University Press, 2004.

USA Today, *Black engineer changed video games*, Mike Snider, February 28, 2020

Vardalas, John, "From DATAR to the FP-6000," *IEEE Annals of the History of Computing*, Vol 16 No 2, 1994, pp. 20-30.

Vardalas, John N., *The Computer Revolution in Canada: Building National Technological Competence (History of Computing)*, Massachusetts Institute of Technology, 2001.

Vasilievich, Rogachev Yury, *Computer engineering from M-1 to M-13 (1950-1990)*, Soviet ministry, 1998.

Veit, Stanley, *Stan Veit's history of the personal computer*, WorldComm Press, 1993.

Verma, G., and N. Mielke, "Reliability performance of ETOX based flash memories," IEEE International Reliability Physics Symposium, 1988.

Wadsworth, Nat, *Machine Language Programming for the 8008 and Similar Microcomputer*s, Scelbi Computer Consulting, (Milford, CT), 1973.

Wagner, Robert L., and Evan L. Ragland II, Patent 3669237, "Double Helical Printer," June 1972.

Wang, An, and Eugene Linden, *Lessons: An Autobiography*, Addison-Wesley, 1986.

Wilkinson, Bill, *The Atari BASIC Source Book*, Compute! Books, 1983.

Williams, Kathy, and James Hart, "Comshare, Expanding the Third Dimension," *Management Accounting*, September 1995, p. 59.

Winchester, Simon, *Pacific*, HarperCollins Publishers, 2015.

Winston, Brian, *A History: The Telegraph*, Media Technology and Society, 1998.

Worthy, James C., *William C. Norris: Portrait of a Maverick*, Ballinger Pub Co., 1987.

WWW.Fairchildimaging.com

Young, Jeffrey S., *Forbes Greatest Technology Stories: Inspiring Tales of the Entrepreneurs*, John Wiley & Sons, 1998.

Zuse, Konrad, *The Computer – My Life*, Springler-Verlag, 2010.

Index

531

www.ingramcontent.com/pod-product-compliance
Lightning Source LLC
Chambersburg PA
CBHW071230050326
40690CB00011B/2058